# TEXTBOOK

# Conflict of Laws

CONSULTANT EDITOR: LORD TEMPLEMAN
EDITOR: NIAMH MOLONEY
LLB (Dublin), LLM (Harvard)

OLD BAILEY PRESS

OLD BAILEY PRESS
200 Greyhound Road, London W14 9RY

1st edition 1997
Reprinted 2000

© Old Bailey Press Ltd 1997

Previous editions published under The
HLT Group Ltd.

ISBN 1 85836 225 3

*British Library Cataloguing-in-Publication.*
A CIP Catalogue record for this book is
available from the British Library.

*Acknowledgement*
The publishers and author would
like to thank the Incorporated
Council of Law Reporting for
England and Wales for kind
permission to reproduce extracts
from the Weekly Law Reports, and
Butterworths for their kind
permission to reproduce extracts
from the All England Law Reports.

Printed and bound in Great Britain

# Contents

# Preface

Old Bailey Press textbooks are written specifically for students. Whatever their course they will find our books clear and concise, providing comprehensive and up-to-date coverage. Written by specialists in their field, our textbooks are reviewed and updated on a regular basis. A companion Casebook, Revision WorkBook and Statutes are also published.

In addition to the updating that we undertake, we have included a chapter called 'Recent Cases' which includes the most significant new cases relating to the subject area. In order to assist the student extracts from the judgments and commentary, where appropriate, have been included. In many instances these cases highlight new interpretations of particular facets of existing law.

Knowledge of recent cases is extremely important for those studying for their examinations. It demonstrates not only an active interest in the law as it develops, but also the dynamic nature of the law which is constantly adapting to changing social and economic trends.

This *Conflict of Laws* textbook is designed for use by students who are studying the Conflict of Laws or Private International Law (to give the subject its other common name) in their course.

Coverage of recent developments includes *Airbus Industrie GIE* v *Patel* (1996) The Times 12 August where the Court of Appeal reiterated that it was possible to grant an injunction to restrain foreign proceedings to protect proceedings outside of England, where this was necessary to prevent an injustice, and gave guidance on factors to be considered. The courts' desire to avoid forum shopping was in evidence in *Internationale Nederlanden Aviation Lease BV* v *Civil Aviation Authority* (1996) The Times 15 August, while nevertheless allowing an action in other than the most natural forum because this was the only way in which the plaintiff could fund the action: *Connelly* v *RTZ Corporation plc and Another* (1996) The Times 12 July. In the tort field the European Court has decided that the place where the harmful event occurred for the purposes of article 5(3), Schedule 1 Civil Jurisdiction and Judgments Act 1982 does not cover the place where the victim claimed to have suffered financial loss consequential on initial damage in another Contracting State: *Marinari* v *Lloyds Bank plc (Zubaidi Trading Co, Intervener)* (Case C–364/93) [1996] 2 WLR 159. Two new family law cases deal with the issue of consent in alleged child abduction cases: *Re C (Abduction: Consent)* [1996] 1 FLR 414; *H* v *H* (1996) The Times 14 August.

This edition reflects the author's view of the law as at 31 January 1997.

# Table of Cases

# Table of Statutes

# 1

# Introduction and the General Principles of the Conflict of Laws

1.1 The scope and nature of the subject

1.2 Choice of law rules

1.3 Stages in the choice of law process

1.4 The meaning of 'country' in the conflict of laws

## 1.1 The scope and nature of the subject

It frequently comes as a surprise to both law students and laymen to learn that on occasion an English court will apply to the resolution of the dispute before it, not its own law, but the law of some foreign country. A moment's reflection, however, shows that cases can readily arise before an English court in which the application by the court of its own law (known usually as the law of the forum or lex fori) would be both inappropriate and unjust.

Suppose, for example, that H, a Frenchman who has never lived outside France, dies intestate leaving a large sum of money in a bank account in London. It seems quite inappropriate and unjust that English law rather than French law should determine which of H's relatives will inherit the money. So, should such a case arise before an English court, that court would not apply the lex fori but would apply French law as the law of the cause or lex causae. We shall return to this example.

### The scope of the conflict of laws

It would be easy to multiply examples in which the inclusion of some foreign element or elements in the facts of the case results in the application of the lex fori being inappropriate and unjust. English courts, however, do not simply cease to apply English law in an arbitrary manner or whenever they feel that another legal system would be more appropriate; there are rules of English law which tell the courts when they should apply foreign law and which foreign law to apply. These rules, known as 'Choice of Law rules', form the central topic dealt with in courses on the conflict of laws and a major part of this book will be devoted to those choice of law rules which fall within most conflict of laws courses. However, there are two other areas of law which are so closely linked to choice of law that they are usually considered part of the conflict of laws (and they certainly fall within the typical syllabus).

First, before a court can choose the appropriate law to apply to a particular matter, a dispute over which it has *jurisdiction* must arise before it. In other words logically prior to the question of choice of law is the question of *choice of court*. So we will need to study carefully the jurisdictional rules of the English courts: in what circumstances will they hear a case and in what circumstances will they decline to hear a case?

Over the last decade this topic has come to be dominated by special rules – derived from the Brussels Convention 1968 – which owe their origin to the United Kingdom's membership of the EC. The details are set out in Chapter 4, section 4.3.

Secondly, a plaintiff may bring his action in a foreign court; he may hear with pleasure judgment pronounced in his favour; and then discover to his dismay that the defendant (and all his assets) have absconded to England. Whether such a plaintiff has any remedy will depend upon whether the English courts will enforce the foreign judgment; and a complex body of rules governs the recognition and enforcement of foreign judgments. This body of rules is widely recognised as forming part of the conflict of laws and forms an important part of the typical syllabus. This area of the law too has been greatly affected by the Brussels Convention 1968.

These three subjects – jurisdiction, choice of law, and the recognition and enforcement of foreign judgments – comprise the conflict of laws. One important aspect of the subject, however, is excluded from the Bar finals syllabus. This is the choice of law aspects of family law. Since family law, however, forms an important part of most courses in this subject we will deal with this topic in full in Chapter 9. This is convenient since choice of law in the family is a self-contained subject.

## The nature of the conflict of laws

The conflict of laws is unlike any other subject you have studied. In part this arises from the fact that other legal subjects deal with the application of rules (however subtle and complex) to facts while the conflict of laws deals with the application of rules to the task of selecting a legal system. However, there are at least two further reasons why the conflict of laws is different.

First, the application of foreign law by an English court poses jurisprudential problems. If law is the command of the sovereign, how is it possible that the command of a foreign sovereign should be obeyed by English judges? Great tomes have been written about this and similar questions, and learned jurists have disputed for centuries about the theories that surround this branch of the law. Such theoretical matters, fortunately, do not fall within the ambit of this book. (Those interested may commence by reading P M North's and J J Fawcett's *Cheshire and North's Private International Law*, 12th ed, 1992, Chapter 2 (hereafter referrred to simply as 'Cheshire'), and J H C Morris, *The Conflict of Laws*, 3rd ed, 1984, Chapter 34.) For us the position is much simpler: foreign law is on occasion applied by English judges because *rules of English law direct the judges to apply the foreign law in those circumstances*. And our task is simply to study those rules which direct the application of the foreign law.

This makes clear an important point that should be stressed: the conflict of laws is as much a part of English law as is the law of contract or tort. We are concerned with the rules (of English law) that direct that in certain circumstances foreign law should be applied; we are not concerned with the foreign law as such. Thus, even although the conflict of laws is sometimes called private international law, the subject is quite different from public international law. Public international law deals primarily with the legal relationship between states and establishes a legal order governing states that is distinct from the various national legal systems. Private international law, on the other hand, is concerned primarily with the legal relationship between individuals, and the word 'international' serves only to mark the existence of those foreign or international elements that raise the question of whether the lex fori is the appropriate law to apply or not.

Secondly, the conflict of laws is rather different from other subjects because the application of choice of law rules gives rise to certain unique questions. The reputation that the conflict of laws has for being difficult rests very largely on these questions. They will be explained in detail in due course (see Chapter 2, section 2.5) but for the present it will be sufficient if we name them: renvoi, characterisation, and the incidental question. It is not possible to understand the conflict of laws without mastering them. They cannot be omitted from your studies. The reason for this is that the questions of renvoi, characterisation and the incidental question may arise in practically any context; so whatever area of the subject you are working in, you will have to be alert to these questions arising.

## 1.2  Choice of law rules

The time has come to look a little more closely at choice of law rules. It will be best to begin with an example. It is a well established choice of law rule that 'succession to movables of an intestate is governed by the law of his domicile at the time of his death' (Dicey and Morris, rule 97; *Dicey and Morris's The Conflict of Laws*, 11th ed, 1987, edited by Lawrence Collins and others, is the leading textbook on the English conflict of laws; it is frequently relied upon by the courts and hereafter will be referred to as 'Dicey and Morris').

Before we can analyse this rule two of the words used in it should be explained. First, the word 'movable'. Unlike practically every other legal system the English law of property does not divide property into immovables (such as land) and movables (most other things – cars, books, jewels, etc) but divides property into the more difficult categories of personalty and realty. However, the English conflict of laws adopts, in recognition of the approach of other legal systems, the movables/immovables distinction. Hence the appearance of the word in the rule given above. (This question is discussed in more detail in Chapter 2, section 2.5 and Chapter 7, section 7.1.)

Secondly, the word 'domicile'. In English law everyone is domiciled somewhere. But determining where a person is domiciled is often quite difficult because a complex and sometimes uncertain set of rules must be applied to determine that question. We will discuss these rules in some detail in Chapter 3; for the present, however, it is sufficient if we take 'domicile' to mean simply 'permanent home'. Rule 97, quoted above, is a good example of the use of the concept of domicile; it is used to link a person with a legal system, and that legal system can then be appropriately applied to resolve the dispute before the court. It is because domicile is used so frequently in this and other roles that special rules have grown up around it.

Now on to the choice of law rule itself. It is easily divided into two parts. First there is the 'category' – succession to movables of an intestate – then there is the 'connecting factor' – the law of his domicile at the time of his death (or lex ultimi domicilii). The category determines what kind of case is involved, and the connecting factor acts as a 'signpost' indicating the appropriate legal system that is applicable. Thus in the simple example given above in section 1.1 the question of succession to an intestate's movables (the money in the English bank account) arises. The deceased is obviously domiciled in France; thus, applying the choice of law rule under discussion, we readily reach the sensible conclusion that French law should be used to determine how the money should be distributed.

## 1.3 Stages in the choice of law process

The application of a choice of law rule is in practice far more complicated than the application of rule 97 to our simple problem of the French intestate who died leaving money in an English bank. In fact, Professor Cheshire has put forward a four-stage scheme which may be used to describe the choice of law process (see Cheshire, Chapter 3). Every conflict of laws case must pass through each of these stages, but frequently one or more stages is uncontroversial and so hardly needs to be mentioned. We will find it useful to outline these four stages although we will not follow Professor Cheshire slavishly.

### *Jurisdiction*

In every case (not just conflict of laws cases) the court must have jurisdiction over both the defendant and the cause of action before it can hear the case and resolve the dispute. However, given the foreign elements that arise in conflict of laws cases, jurisdiction is often a crucial part of such cases. And for this reason we consider in detail the jurisdiction of the High Court in Chapter 4.

## Classification or characterisation

In our simple application of rule 97 above we deftly avoided an important problem in the conflict of laws: we took it for granted that a problem over a French intestate's money in an English bank fell within the category of 'succession to the movables of an intestate' and that, therefore, rule 97 was applicable. In fact it is not always self-evident whether a particular matter falls within a particular category or not. For instance, under some legal systems widows are entitled to a certain proportion of their husbands' estates (known in Scots law as the ius relictae). Now if a widow were to make such a claim against her intestate husband's estate, it is not obvious that the case involves 'succession to the movables of an intestate'. It is arguable that the ius relictae is 'a proprietary consequence of the marriage' not a matter of succession at all. Now, subject to some presently irrelevant limitations, the proprietary consequences of marriage are governed by the husband's domicile at the time of the marriage (see Dicey and Morris, rule 115/6 (the rule being stated here is not entirely free from doubt; I am stating it in this form for ease of exposition)). Thus if our intestate was domiciled in Scotland at the time of his marriage, but dies domiciled in France, then if the widow's claim is a matter of intestate succession, French law will govern, while Scots law will govern if it is a matter of matrimonial property.

The process whereby it is determined whether a particular matter falls into one of the potentially applicable categories or not is known as classification or characterisation. We shall consider it in more detail in Chapter 2, section 2.5 For the present it is sufficient to say that it is a rather controversial area of the conflict of laws. There is an array of academic theories suggesting how the problem is to be solved but very little consensus amongst the scholars. And when the problem arises in concrete form in litigation then, very frequently, the judge (as well as counsel arguing the case) fails to recognise it!

## Selection of the lex causae

Once it has been determined that the court has jurisdiction, and the matter has been characterised, then we simply need to apply the relevant choice of law rule. For instance, if we have decided that the dispute over our intestate's bank account is a matter of 'succession to movables' then the relevant rule (rule 97) tells us that the lex causae is the lex ultimi domicilii.

Put more formally, having categorised the matter we then turn to the choice of law rule to discover the connecting factor; and having discovered it, it will, after the application of the appropriate rules or the determination of the relevant facts, point to the lex causae.

### Determination of the connecting factor

The way in which the connecting factor points to the lex causae differs from connecting factor to connecting factor. Some connecting factors are purely factual.

For instance, in many property matters the connecting factor is simply the position (or situs) of the property, so the lex situs is the lex causae (see Chapter 7, sections 7.3 and 7.4). And the position of property is simply a matter of fact.

On the other hand, as we have seen, domicile is a most important connecting factor. But domicile is not a simple matter of fact, it depends upon the application of the rules of the law of domicile (see Chapter 3). The difficulty that arises from the introduction of rules of law into the determination of domicile (as well as other connecting factors) is that different legal systems mean different things by domicile. It is quite possible, for instance, for a person to be domiciled in England according to the rules of French law but to be domiciled in France according to English law. So the question arises: if rules of law have to be used to determine the connecting factor, from which legal system are they to be chosen? Fortunately, English courts have given a consistent answer to this question: the connecting factor is to be determined by the lex fori. Thus in *Re Martin* [1900] P 211 Lindley MR said of a testatrix who was domiciled in England according to French law and domiciled in France according to English law:

> 'The domicile of the testatrix must be determined by the English Court of Probate according to those legal principles applicable to domicile which are recognised in this country and are part of its law.'

(See also *Re Annesley* [1926] Ch 692 at 705.)

There are two exceptions (neither of which need concern us overmuch) to the general principle that the lex fori is used to determine the connecting factor. First, where nationality is used as a connecting factor then obviously only the national state can determine whether a particular person is a national of that state or not. However, nationality is a connecting factor that plays but a slight role in the English conflict of laws (see, for instance, section 1 of the Wills Act 1963 discussed in Chapter 7, section 7.8). Nationality is also used as a connecting factor in the law relating to the recognition of foreign divorces (see s46(1)(b) of the Family Law Act 1986 discussed in Chapter 9, section 9.4 *Part II of the Family Law Act 1986*).

Secondly, s46(5) of the Family Law Act 1986 provides that 'for the purpose of this section, a party to a marriage shall be treated as domiciled in a country if he was domiciled in that country ... according to the law of that country in family matters ...'. Section 46 concerns questions such as the recognition of overseas divorces, annulments and legal separations, ie matters beyond the ambit of this course. This is discussed fully in Chapter 9, section 9.4 *Part II of the Family Law Act 1986*.

## Renvoi

The connecting factor, having been determined in the manner set out above, points clearly towards a particular lex causae. But what is meant by lex causae? Suppose that the connecting factor indicates that the law of X was applicable. X's law, however, has its own choice of law rules, which use different connecting factors from those used by the lex fori and which, if they were applied, would indicate say, that the law of A, not the law of X, should be applied. Since X's conflict rules, as we have seen (see section 1.1 *The nature of the conflict of laws*), form part of the law of X it appears prima facie that X's conflict rules should be applied, ie there should be an onward reference to the law of A. This is the famed, perhaps notorious, problem of renvoi. We will discuss it in detail in Chapter 2.5. For the present it is sufficient to note, first, that determining the connecting factor may still, because of renvoi, leave the lex causae uncertain; and, secondly, that even although many have been tempted to ignore renvoi (and simply to apply the internal law of X if X is indicated by the connecting factor), renvoi provides a convenient device that can be used by the judges to achieve an appropriate result.

## *Application of the lex causae*

Judges do not know the law of foreign countries, and thus even where the lex causae is clear some mechanism has to be provided to inform the court of the actual rules of the foreign law that are applicable. In broad terms, foreign law is treated as a question of fact and has to be proved by expert evidence. We shall deal with this topic in full in Chapter 2, section 2.2.

However, when the content of the foreign law has been determined it may become clear that when applied to the facts of the case it leads to a result that is contrary to public policy. In such circumstances the English court will exclude the application of the foreign law, notwithstanding that it is applicable in terms of the choice of law rules. We shall consider the exclusion of the foreign law in Chapter 2, section 2.3.

## 1.4 The meaning of 'country' in the conflict of laws

It is important to understand that in this book, as in most books on the conflict of laws, the word 'country' is given a legal rather than a political meaning. We do not mean 'the territory subject to the same sovereign power' but we do mean 'the territory subject to the same legal system'. Thus the United Kingdom, although subject to the same sovereign power (the Crown in Parliament), contains three legal systems within it and thus, from the point of view of the conflict of laws, three countries. The three countries are Scotland, England and Wales, and Northern Ireland. There are major and important differences between the law of Scotland and that of England and Wales, but the differences between the law of England and Wales and that of Northern Ireland are slight for the purposes of the conflict of laws.

The important point to note is that conflict of laws problems can arise just as readily between the law of England and that of Scotland as they can arise between, say, the law of England and that of France.

What applies in this regard to the United Kingdom applies to the rest of the world as well. Thus each state of the United States of America has its own legal system and is treated as a separate country from the point of view of the conflict of laws; thus it is not enough to say that the law of the United States applies to a particular matter, it is necessary to specify whether it is the law of California, or New York, or one of the other fifty states that applies. The various states of Australia and the provinces of Canada as well as the component parts of most composite political entities are also different countries.

Finally we may note the following subtle point. Although the United Kingdom consists of three countries, particular statutes may apply to all three countries in the identical manner. For the purposes of that statute, then, the United Kingdom is one country. Other statutes apply to Great Britain, and such statutes reduce the number of countries to two: Great Britain (Scotland, England and Wales) and Northern Ireland.

# 2

# Preliminary Topics

2.1  The proof of foreign law

2.2  The exclusion of foreign law

2.3  The special conceptual problems: renvoi, characterisation and the
incidental question

2.4  Substance and procedure

2.5  Public international law and the conflict of laws

2.6  The time factor

## 2.1  The proof of foreign law

### Foreign law is treated as a question of fact

The opinions of some academic lawyers to the contrary, judges may be taken to
know the law; and they, therefore, do not need special instruction in the law before
they can decide the case before them. (Although they do, of course, listen to
counsels' arguments on the legal points in issue.) Cases involving foreign law,
however, are rather different: it is quite unreasonable to expect a judge to be
sufficient of a legal wizard to be able to master, without special aid, the detailed and
intricate provisions of some foreign legal rule that may be disputed before him in a
conflict of laws case. And even the most able of counsel could easily find himself or
herself at sea in such a case unless there was some mechanism whereby the
necessary expertise could be brought before the court.

The mechanism in English law whereby this necessary expertise is brought before
the court is the principle that foreign law is treated as a question of fact. Foreign
law is, of course, not a question of fact; it is obviously a question of law (albeit
foreign). But if foreign law is treated as a question of fact, then, just like any other
question of fact that may be relevant to a dispute, it follows that it must be pleaded
and proved by the party which seeks to rely upon it. The requirement that the
applicability of the foreign law should be pleaded underlines the extent to which
English law treats foreign law as fact, for the general principle is, of course, that one
should not plead matters of law but only matters of fact.

9

Questions of fact are naturally for the jury (when there is one) to decide. But given how confused judges and counsel can easily become over the intricacies of foreign law, it would be quite impractical to expect the jury to form a considered opinion about the state of foreign law. Thus s69(5) of the Supreme Court Act 1981 (replacing similar legislation in force since 1920) provides that where 'it is necessary to ascertain the law of any other country which is applicable to the facts of the case, any question as to the effect of the evidence given with respect to that law shall, instead of being submitted to the jury, be decided by the judge alone'. This rule applies to criminal trials as well as civil matters (*R v Hammer* [1923] 2 KB 789).

Section 69(5) is statutory recognition of the peculiar status of foreign law as fact, but the judges are equally aware of this. Thus in *Parkasho v Singh* [1968] P 233 Cairns J said that 'foreign law is a question of fact of a peculiar kind' and was thus more ready to interfere with the decision of magistrates on a question of foreign law than would be the case if they had decided an ordinary question of fact.

## *The admissibility of evidence tendered to prove foreign law*

### Admissibility of expert opinion

It is well settled that the evidence required to prove foreign law 'must be that of qualified experts in the foreign law' (per Lord Wright in *Lazard Brothers & Co v Midland Bank* [1933] AC 289), and that such evidence will be admitted as evidence of the foreign law. It is, however, less clear exactly who is a 'qualified expert'. Given the range of legal qualifications recognised in the different countries of the world whose law may have to be proved before a English court, it is probably impossible to lay down rigid rules as to the qualifications required of the necessary expert.

It is clear, however, that a foreign judge or legal practitioner or former legal practitioner is competent (*Baron de Bode's Case* (1845) 8 QB 208). But is a person who has only academic qualifications? Although there are statements in cases such as *Bristow v Sequeville* (1850) 5 Exch 275 distinctly hostile to experts who have merely academic qualifications, the better view appears to be that where the academic has special expertise in a particular area his evidence should be admitted even if he is not qualified to practise in the jurisdiction in question. Thus in *Brailey v Rhodesia Consolidated Ltd* [1910] 2 Ch 95 the evidence of the Reader in Roman-Dutch law to the Council of Legal Education (who was not qualified to practise in Rhodesia) was admitted to prove the law of Rhodesia. In any event the question is now settled as far as civil proceedings are concerned by s4(1) of the Civil Evidence Act 1972 which provides that:

> 'A person who is qualified to do so on account of his knowledge or experience is competent to give expert evidence as to the law of any country or territory outside the United Kingdom, or of any part of the United Kingdom other than England and Wales, irrespective of whether he has acted or is entitled to act as a legal practitioner there.'

It is also clear that the expert need not have either academic or professional qualifications if he has had appropriate practical experience of the law in question. Thus an ex-Governor of Hong Kong has been held competent to give evidence of the marriage laws of the Colony (*Cooper-King* v *Cooper-King* [1900] P 65 (apparently the ex-Governor's fees for such a service were substantial lower than those of the legally qualified experts in the laws of Hong Kong)). And a Persian diplomat was allowed to testify as to the laws of Persia given that there were no professional lawyers in that country and that all diplomats had to be conversant with Persian law (*In the Goods of Dhost Ali Kahn* (1880) 6 PD 6). There are many other similar cases. The common law on this subject (outlined above) has been fortified as far as civil proceedings are concerned by s4(1) of the Civil Evidence Act 1972 (cited above) which makes it clear that the necessary expertise may be derived from either 'knowledge or experience.'

Once it is determined that a particular person is qualified as an expert he then gives evidence in the usual way. Typically the expert will give oral testimony and may be cross-examined on the evidence that he gives. During the course of his testimony he may refer to foreign codes, statutes and other legal materials to refresh his memory. Affidavit evidence of foreign experts has exceptionally been admitted.

## Admissibility of prior decisions of the English courts as to the foreign law

The same questions of foreign law frequently arise before the English courts. Can the court admit as evidence of the foreign law a prior English decision as to that question of foreign law? At common law the answer to this question was a clear no (see *Lazard Brothers & Co* v *Midland Bank* [1933] AC 289). After all the prior decision was simply another court's opinion as to a matter of fact (the state of foreign law), and such opinions are inadmissible in principle (see *Hollington* v *Hewthorn & Co Ltd* [1943] KB 587). The result was that trite questions of foreign law had to be proved over and over again by expert evidence.

This inconvenient state of affairs has now been changed by s4(2)–(5) of the Civil Evidence Act 1972. In broad terms s4(2)(a) provides that where the prior decision is 'reported or recorded in citable form' it shall 'be admissible in evidence for the purpose of proving the law of that [foreign] country'. A decision is 'reported or recorded in citable form if, but only if, it is reported or recorded in writing in a report, transcript or other document which, if that question had been a question as to the law of England and Wales, could be cited as an authority in legal proceedings in England and Wales' (s4(5)).

Although s4(2)–(5) regulates the admissibility of prior decisions in civil proceedings, the prior decision which is admitted to prove the state of foreign law may be either civil or criminal. More precisely, the prior decision may be a decision at first instance in either the High Court or the Crown Court (as well as a number of other less important courts but not including the County Court) as well as appeals from such decisions. Privy Council decisions, provided they derive from an appeal from a court outside the United Kingdom, are also admissible.

A party wishing to rely upon such a prior decision cannot, however, take his opponent by surprise. Thus s4(3) requires that a party wishing to adduce such evidence must give every other party notice, in accordance with the rules of court, of his intention to adduce such evidence. The court has a discretion to waive the requirement of notice.

## Weighing the evidence

Thus far we have dealt with the admissibility of evidence of the foreign law. However, admissibility is not the end of the matter. It is still necessary for the judge to consider all the evidence of the foreign law that has been admitted and where it is in conflict to decide which evidence he rejects and which he accepts before making his finding on the question of foreign law.

Before discussing the common law on this question, it is convenient to deal with s4(2)(b) of the Civil Evidence Act 1972 which regulates the weight to be given to evidence of prior decisions on the question of foreign law admitted in accordance with the provisions just discussed (in section 2.1 Admissibility of prior decisions of the English courts as to foreign law). Section 4(2)(b) provides that where such a prior decision is adduced the foreign law in question 'shall be taken to be in accordance with that ... decision unless the contrary is proved'. This amounts to a presumption that the prior decision is correct on the question of foreign law. The result of this is that a party who disagrees with a finding of foreign law contained in a prior decision must, as soon as he is given notice of another party's intention of adducing that decision in evidence, set about finding contrary evidence of the foreign law in the form of experts' opinions which will be admissible at the trial. Disagreeing with the finding in a prior decision as to foreign law does not mean that the prior discussion is in error. It may be, for instance, that the foreign law has changed since the first court made its decision.

However, it is not uncommon for different English courts to differ on particular points of foreign law. And the proviso to s4(2)(b) is designed to deal with just this eventuality; it provides that where a prior decision 'conflicts with another finding or decision on the same question adduced ... in the same proceedings', s4(2)(b) 'shall not apply', ie the presumption that the prior decision is correct does not apply. Were it not for this proviso, the following bizarre position could arise. Two conflicting decisions on a question of foreign law could be adduced in accordance with the section, and the court would be bound to accept both as the law of the foreign country!

Now back to the common law and the weight to be attached to the admissible evidence of experts. Where the expert evidence is uncontradicted the court will generally accept it (see *Rossano* v *Manufacturers' Life Insurance Co* [1963] 2 QB 352). However, the court is not bound to accept the expert's view, and examples abound of occasions on which the English courts have rejected an expert's view because, for example, it was 'patently absurd ... or inconsistent with the rest of his evidence' (*Tallina Laevauhisus A/S* v *Estonian State Steamship Line* (1947) 80 Ll LR 99 (CA) at 108). In other words the court cannot be prevented from using its common sense in regard to the expert evidence before it. Where the court rejects the evidence of the expert, it must form its own view of the foreign law in the manner described in the next paragraph.

If the court is not bound to accept the uncontradicted evidence of experts in the foreign law then, a fortiori, it is not bound to accept the evidence of experts who contradict each other. Indeed, in this situation the court faces the difficult task of choosing between the experts. In these cases it is the duty of the court to examine all the evidence and form its own view of the foreign law. To this end the court is entitled to look at the foreign statutes, decisions and textbooks that have been referred to by the experts. The 'court will not conduct its own researches into foreign law' (Morris, *The Conflict of Laws*, 3rd ed, 1984, at 39); thus it will not refer to such statutes, decisions and textbooks unless referred to by the expert, and even then the court will refer to these sources only to the extent that they have been referred to by the expert. For instance, an expert may not regard an entire textbook as authoritative but only the part that he cited to the court; thus it would be improper for the court to rely upon a portion of the text that the expert did not draw to the court's attention. Forming an opinion in such case may be very difficult, for the question of foreign law upon which the English judge has to make up his mind may be a question that is entirely novel to the foreign legal system, and there may simply be no settled or authoritative view on the matter. (This was the case in *Re Duke of Wellington* [1947] Ch 506.)

## The burden of proof

In accordance with general principles, the burden of proof of foreign law lies on the party who seeks to rely upon the foreign law by basing his claim upon it or by raising it as a defence. Should that party fail to adduce any evidence of the foreign law, or adduce insufficient evidence of that law to enable the judge to form an opinion of the relevant question, then the court will apply English law. This result is not in accordance with the general principles of evidence (although it is obviously sensible), for where a party relies upon a particular fact for his claim or defence, and then fails to prove that fact, his claim or defence simply fails. With matters of foreign law, however, the claim or defence does not necessarily fail; all that happens is that English law will be applied and under English law either party may succeed. Usually, however, this point will be of little consequence, because the party who sought to rely upon foreign law probably did so because he knew he would fail under English law.

## Dispensing with the proof of foreign law

As we have seen, proving foreign law by the use of expert evidence can be a difficult, expensive and haphazard task; thus it is not surprising that attempts should be made to render this task less onerous in special circumstances. We will consider in this section some of the ways in which this has been done.

1. The Evidence (Colonial Statutes) Act 1907 facilitates the proof of any laws made by the legislature of a 'British possession'. Section 1(1) provides that 'Copies of Acts, ordinances, and statutes passed (whether before or after the passing of this Act) by the Legislature of any British possession, and of orders, regulations, and other instruments issued or made ... under the authority of any such Act, ordinance or statute, if purporting to be printed by the Government printer, shall be received in evidence by all courts of justice in the United Kingdom without any proof being given that the copies were so printed.' This allows the text of such laws to be proved without further evidence, although expert evidence may have to be called to show that the law in question has not been repealed (*Jasiewicz* v *Jasiewicz* [1962] 1 WLR 1426).

   The provisions of this Act are most useful. Since most 'British possessions' share the English common law, when the application of some question of a British possession's law arises before an English court the dispute almost invariably concerns some statutory matter, and the relevant statutes are readily proved through reliance on s1(1).

   Moreover, although 'British possession' is defined (in s1(3)) as 'any part of His Majesty's dominions exclusive of the United Kingdom', s1(1) continues to apply to most Commonwealth countries (and even some countries which have ceased to be members of the Commonwealth but which used to be 'British possessions') notwithstanding that they have become republics and thus ceased to be part of Her Majesty's dominions. The reason for this is that in granting independence to these countries Parliament usually made provision for the continuance in force of existing laws in relation to that country including, of course, s1(1). Thus s1(1) can be relied upon to prove the statute laws of most countries which used to be part of Her Majesty's possessions.

2. The British Law Ascertainment Act 1859. This measure permits 'any court within Her Majesty's dominions to seek the opinion of a superior court elsewhere in Her Majesty's dominions' on a question of law, where the first court considers that it is 'necessary or expedient ... to ascertain the law applicable to the facts of the case as administered in [that] other part of Her Majesty's dominions'. The procedure is simply that the first court (either on its own motion or when requested by counsel) states a case posing the disputed question of law and remits same to the second court. The second court then usually hears counsel on the matters of law in dispute and then delivers its opinion. The second court's opinion is binding upon the first court (s3), but does not bind the House of Lords or the Privy Council (s4).

   Note that the provisions of the British Law Ascertainment Act 1859 constitute an exception to the rule that the applicability of foreign law must be pleaded; for where the court of its own motion states a case for the second court's opinion on the question of foreign law, then the foreign law is not pleaded; yet as we have seen it is applicable and indeed binds the first court.

As before, the provisions of the British Law Ascertainment Act 1859 remain applicable to many Commonwealth and non-Commonwealth countries that are no longer part of Her Majesty's dominions. None the less, this statute is little used chiefly because of the delay and extra expense involved; litigants prefer to have the matter settled once and for all by the first court. (There used to exist a similar measure (the Foreign Law Ascertainment Act 1861) applicable in certain circumstances to countries that had never been part of Her Majesty's dominions, but it was repealed by the Statute Law (Repeals) Act 1973.)

3. The European Communities Act 1972 provides in s3(2) that 'Judicial Notice shall be taken of the Treaties [establishing the EC], of the Official Journal of the Communities and of any decision of, or expression of opinion by, the European Court ...'. Thus where reference is made (under the provisions of s2(1), (4) or in terms of the Treaties) to matters of European law, it is not necessary that those matters should be proved by evidence. However, these questions do not strictly speaking form part of the conflict of laws, and detailed consideration of them is best left to the specialised courses in European Community Law.

4. The court may decide questions of foreign law without proof where the parties agree to request it to do so. Generally, though, the courts are reluctant to adopt this course for they recognise their limitations in this regard. They are, however, more willing to interpret foreign statutes without expert evidence of the foreign law (see *F & K Jabbour* v *Custodian of Israeli Property* [1954] 1 WLR 139 at 147–149 and *Wilson, Smithett & Cope Ltd* v *Terruzzi* [1976] QB 683 at 692). There are also some cases (for example, *Re Cohn* [1945] Ch 5) where the court has determined matters of foreign law apparently in circumstances in which no evidence of that law was given. In these cases there must surely have been a tacit agreement between the parties that the court should determine the matter without proof.

5. The need to prove foreign law can also be avoided where one of the parties admits the applicable foreign law.

6. Finally, the principle that judicial notice will be taken of notorious facts may sometime extend to taking judicial notice of foreign law. Thus in *Saxby* v *Fulton* [1909] 2 KB 208 at 211 judicial notice was taken of the fact that roulette was not unlawful in Monte Carlo.

## The special position of the House of Lords

As we have seen, for the purposes of the conflict of laws Scotland is a foreign country, and so Scots law needs to be proved before English courts, and English law needs to be proved in Scottish courts. The House of Lords, however, is the final court of appeal in civil matters for both England and Scotland. If the normal rule in regard to proof of foreign law were followed in regard to conflicts of English and

Scots law before the House of Lords, then some very odd situations could arise. For instance, the House of Lords might authoritatively lay down a rule of Scots law one day in an appeal from Scotland, and require expert evidence thereof the next day when the same point arose in an English appeal in which Scots law was the lex causae! This state of affairs is avoided by the rule that the House of Lords takes judicial notice of Scots law when hearing an English appeal, and takes judicial notice of English law when hearing a Scottish appeal (see *MacShannon* v *Rockware Glass Ltd* [1978] AC 795 at 815).

## 2.2 The exclusion of foreign law

Once the application of the choice of law rule has selected the appropriate lex causae, and the relevant rules of that lex causae have been proved in the manner described in section 2.1, then in the normal course of events the foreign rules will simply be applied by the court to the facts of the case to resolve the dispute. However, there are occasions on which this will not occur and the court will refuse to apply the rules of foreign law; in this section we will be considering some of those occasions.

The essential reason for this occasional non-application of the otherwise applicable lex causae is that in the particular circumstances the application of the lex causae may lead to a result that is inconsistent with some fundamental principle of the public policy of the lex fori. Two points should be stressed at this point:

First, that the public policy we are here concerned with is not the same public policy that we would be concerned with in a purely domestic case in which no question of applying any law other than the lex fori arises. The mere fact that the application of the foreign law may lead to a result contrary to some mandatory rule of English law or some principle of domestic public policy is not enough to cause the court to refuse to apply the foreign law. Thus, to give an example, it is a mandatory rule of English law that the parties to a marriage should be present at the ceremony; but that does not prevent an English court from recognising a proxy marriage contracted elsewhere (see *Apt* v *Apt* [1948] P 83 and Kahn-Freund, *General Problems of Private International Law*, 1980, at 281–282; see also Cheshire, 128–137). The legal systems of the world are very diverse, and the application of this exclusionary principle should be exercised sparingly and with tolerance.

Secondly, in applying this exclusionary principle the court in most cases is not sitting in judgment on the merits or otherwise of the foreign law, but is simply holding that in the particular case the application of that law leads to a result which is contrary to the distinctive public policy of the lex fori. There may be some foreign laws – for example, laws rendering slavery lawful – that would be repugnant as such, but by and large it is the result of the application and not the law which is excluded. Thus the application of a particular foreign law may be excluded in one case but allowed in another case where its application does not lead to a result repugnant to public policy (see Kahn-Freund, op cit, 282–283).

We will now consider some of the major categories of cases in which this principle has been operative. We should first of all note that in deciding whether a particular rule would fall within one of the categories about to be discussed, the English courts will apply the principles of English law and not those of the foreign legal system. Thus the mere fact that a foreign legal system does not consider one of its laws a penal or a revenue law does not prevent an English court from excluding the application of that law on one of those grounds (see *Huntingdon* v *Atrill* [1893] AC 150 and *Metal Industries (Salvage) Ltd* v *Owners of the SS Harle* 1962 SLT 114).

## Penal laws

It is an unchallenged principle of English law that English courts will not enforce foreign penal laws. In Lord Watson's words in *Huntingdon* v *Atrill* this 'rule has its foundation in the well recognised principle that crimes, including in that term all breaches of public law punished by pecuniary mulct or otherwise, at the instance of the State government, or of someone representing the public, are local in this sense, that they are only recognisable and punishable in the country where they were committed. Accordingly no proceeding, even in the shape of a civil suit, which has as its object the enforcement by the State, whether directly or indirectly, of punishment imposed for such breaches ... ought to be admitted in the courts of any other country.'

The important point that emerges from this is that the penalty exacted must be exacted by the state. Thus stipulations for contractual penalties are not struck down by this rule for they are not 'exigible by the state in the interest of the community [but by] private persons in their own interest' (per Lord Watson in *Huntingdon* v *Atrill*). Moreover, where a statute imposes a penalty that is not 'exigible by the state' that law will be enforced. Thus in *Huntington* v *Atrill* a New York statute which held directors liable to the creditors for all the debts of company upon proof that false reports of the company's financial position had been issued was enforced.

Another example of the operation of the exclusionary principle (in which the law was denied enforcement) is found in *Banco de Vizcaya* v *Don Alfonso de Borbon y Austria* [1935] 1 KB 140. Here a Spanish decree declared the deposed King of Spain to be a traitor and all his property forfeit to the Spanish State.

However, because of the operation of this principle the Banco de Vizcaya (a nominee of the Spanish State) failed to obtain the securities which the King had deposited in a London bank.

The principles just discussed were confirmed in *United States of America* v *Inkley* [1988] 3 WLR 304 (CA). What had happened was that Inkley, a British subject, had been charged with various criminal offences under the laws of the United States. A US district court released him on bail on condition that he entered into an 'appearance bond' for $48,000. He also obtained the leave of the court to return to

England for 30 days. He returned to England but did not, thereafter, return to the US to stand trial. The United States obtained a final judgment in the US civil courts against him for the amount of the 'appearance bond' and now sought to enforce this judgment against the defendant in England. The Court of Appeal, however, refused to allow the judgment to be enforced, holding that 'notwithstanding its civil clothing, the purpose of the action ...was the due execution by the USA of a public law process aimed to ensure the attendance of persons accused of crime before the criminal courts'. In reaching this conclusion the Court of Appeal, quite correctly, followed *Huntington* v *Atrill* in holding that the court asked to enforce the foreign law (of judgment) had the final word in determining whether a particular action involved the execution of a penal law of another state. Naturally, the English courts would have regard to the attitude adopted by the relevant foreign courts in deciding this matter, but whether a particular action was penal was to be determined according to the criteria of English law.

Although it is clear that no foreign penal law will be enforced in an English court, this does not mean that such laws will be denied all effect outside the state which enacted them. Thus if an English choice of law rule directs the application of some foreign legal system then the penal rules of that system, if relevant, will be applied, for example, to render a contract illegal and thus unenforceable in England. *Kahler* v *Midland Bank* [1950] AC 24 (discussed below in Chapter 5, section 5.2 *Illegality*) is an example of such a case. This is usually expressed by saying that while foreign penal laws will not be enforced they will be recognised. What this really means is that in cases such as *Banco de Vizcaya* (an enforcement case) the foreign law claims applicability in its own right in the English courts, while in recognition cases the English choice of law rule has already selected the foreign legal system as the lex causae and is thus more willing to see the foreign law applied.

## Revenue laws

Since *Government of India* v *Taylor* [1955] AC 491 it has been quite clear that English courts will not enforce foreign revenue laws. As Viscount Simonds said: '... tax gathering is not a matter of contract but of authority and administration as between the state and those within its jurisdiction.' It was, therefore, a matter for the state and its citizens, not for the English courts.

Furthermore, the concept of a revenue law is a wide one. Not only are such obvious candidates as income tax, capital gains tax and death duties included, but also municipal rates (*Municipal Council of Sydney* v *Bull* [1909] 1 KB 7) and customs duty (*Attorney-General for Canada* v *Schultze* 1901 9 SLT 4). Difficult questions, which have not yet been resolved in English law, arise in regard to compulsory payments into social security schemes. Although such payments are usually compulsory – and this suggests that they have much in common with a tax – they also are similar to an insurance premium in that the payer is insuring himself against redundancy, illness or whatever. The Scottish courts in *Metal Industries (Salvage)*

*Ltd* v *Owners of the S S Harle* (above) refused a claim by the French government for contributions to the French health insurance scheme which the shipowners (under French law) ought to have paid on behalf of their employees. It is likely that the English courts would decide such a case in the same way.

Indirect enforcement is just as surely hit by this principle as is direct enforcement. Thus in *Rossano* v *Manufacturers' Life Insurance Co* [1963] 2 QB 352 the defendant insurance company sought to avoid having to pay the plaintiff's policies out on the ground that the Egyptian authorities had obtained an order against them requiring them to pay the plaintiff's Egyptian tax bill. This defence failed since it amounted to indirect enforcement of the Egyptian tax laws.

However, difficult questions sometimes arise with indirect enforcement. Take *Peter Buchanan Ltd* v *McVey* (an Irish case approved in *Government of India* v *Taylor* and reported [1955] AC 516n). Here the liquidator of a Scottish company whose only creditor was the United Kingdom revenue authorities sought to recover in the Irish courts a debt (which had nothing to do with tax) owed to the company by McVey. This was refused, Kingmill Moore J holding that the whole object of the action was the collection of revenue and to allow recovery would amount to indirect enforcement of a revenue law. In *Peter Buchanan* this was doubtless so, since if recovery were allowed the UK revenue would be the only beneficiary and there was little doubt that the liquidator and the revenue were working hand in glove.

But what is the position if the revenue was only one of a number of creditors on whose behalf the liquidator was seeking recovery of the debt? The ordinary creditors are surely not to be denied what is their due simply because the company owes money to the revenue as well as to them? The point has never been before an English court, but the Australian courts in a similar case (*Ayres* v *Evans* 56 FLR 235) have readily distinguished *Peter Buchanan* and held that the liquidator was not indirectly enforcing a revenue law even although the revenue might draw some benefit from the liquidator's action.

For many years it was thought that revenue laws would not even be recognised. However, in *Regazzoni* v *K C Sethia Ltd* [1958] AC 301 Viscount Simonds said: 'It does not follow from the fact that the court will not enforce a revenue law at the suit of a foreign state that today it will enforce a contract which requires the doing of an act in a foreign country that violates the revenue law of that country.' And in reliance upon this principle the courts have refused to countenance the evasion of tax in a foreign but friendly state. Thus in *Re Emery's Investment Trusts* [1959] Ch 410 a husband who had acquired certain shares in an American company in his wife's name, in order to avoid the payment of US federal tax, was denied a share in the proceeds after his wife had sold the shares. The husband could not rebut the presumption of advancement simply by showing that his intention was to evade the US tax. Of course, here the husband had to plead and prove his evasion of the US tax laws in order to establish his claim. But do the same principles apply where there is no need to rely on the illegality in order to establish a claim?

This was one of the questions posed in *Euro-Diam Ltd* v *Bathurst* [1987] 2 All ER 113. What had happened here was that the plaintiff, an English company, was a diamond supplier and had sent some diamonds to one of its German customers on a sale or return basis. In order to enable the customer to evade the payment of German customs duty on these diamonds the plaintiff issued an invoice that stated that the value of the diamonds was $131,411 instead of their true value, $223,000. The plaintiff insured the diamonds with an English company in an insurance contract presumably governed by English law. The diamonds were stolen and the plaintiff sued the insurers to recover their true value. The insurers sought to avoid liability on a variety of grounds that amounted in essence to an assertion that the insurance contract was tainted with illegality and, therefore, unenforceable.

The difficulty with this was that the taint of illegality did not come from English law. Not only was the insurance contract lawful by English law but also the premiums were to be paid in England and any claims on the policy were to be made in England. So the taint of illegality could only derive from the German laws in regard to customs duty. Would these be recognised so that Euro-Diam could not recover? Staughton J held not. He did so on a number of grounds that are not presently relevant (see Chapter 5, section 5.2 *Illegality*), but in addition he distinguished *Re Emery's Investment Trusts* by saying 'A plaintiff fails for illegality (under a foreign law) if, in order to establish his claim, he must plead and prove conduct which is illegal by the law of the foreign country and which occurred in the territory of that country.' Thus Euro-Diam could succeed, but the husband in *Re Emery's Investment Trusts* could not.

We shall discuss this case more fully when dealing with illegal contracts. It should be noted though that, notwithstanding the way in which Staughton J distinguishes *Re Emery's Investment Trusts*, the learned judge deals with the case as one concerned with illegality rather than with the recognition of foreign revenue laws.

## Expropriatory or confiscatory laws

During the 20th century many governments of many different political hues have expropriated the property of their citizens, sometimes with compensation, sometimes with inadequate compensation and sometimes with no compensation at all. Naturally, owners of property have adopted many different stratagems to remove their property from the grasp of the expropriating states, and the states concerned have been equally astute in their attempts to lay their hands on the property in question. Where for one reason or another – usually because expropriated property has been brought to England – cases of expropriation by foreign governments come before English courts, complicated questions of the conflict of laws arise. One of the major issues raised in such cases is whether the foreign law that effects the expropriation should be enforced or recognised by the English courts.

This question, however, is so intermingled with the principles of choice of law in cases involving property that it is proposed to postpone discussion of these principles until we have considered in more detail the question of choice of law and property (see Chapter 7, section 7.6).

## Public policy proper

We have thus far discussed particular situations in which for one reason or another the exclusionary rule has come to prominence. In this section we discuss some of the less prominent areas in which English courts will refuse to enforce an otherwise applicable foreign law.

### Contractual cases

Doubtless there are some contracts which, even if governed by a foreign law, an English court would refuse to enforce as being contrary to public policy. The difficulty is that it is almost impossible to extract from the cases the principles applicable, and, in any event, considerations of domestic public policy tend to become irretrievably mixed up with the considerations of public policy from the point of view of the conflict of laws.

Some of the cases may be mentioned. Contracts to trade with the enemy will not be enforced (*Dynamit A/G v Rio Tinto Zinc* [1918] AC 260), and contracts to break the laws of friendly countries will not be enforced (*Foster v Driscoll* [1929] 1 KB 470 and *Regazzoni v K C Sethia*). Where a contract is obtained by coercion, it will not be enforced by an English court (*Kaufman v Gerson* [1904] 1 KB 591). The difficulty with the latter case is that the contract in question was probably not obtained by coercion, and that in any event the foreign legal system almost certainly has its own rules dealing with and defining coercion. Those rules should prima facie apply unless there is something so outrageous and unjust about them so as to offend a fundamental English public policy.

*Lemenda Trading Co Ltd v African Middle East Petroleum Co Ltd* [1988] 2 WLR 735; [1988] 1 All ER 513 dealt with the relationship between the public policy of foreign states and English public policy. In a contract governed by English law the defendants agreed with the plaintiffs that a commission would be payable to the plaintiffs, in consideration for the plaintiffs' assistance in procuring the renewal of the defendants' contract for the supply of oil with the Qatar national oil company. Such an agreement for the use of personal influence in return for money was contrary to English public policy and the public policy of Qatar. The court (per Phillips J) held that a foreign state's public policy would not of itself prevent the enforcement of a contract in England. In this case, however, 'international comity combined with English domestic public policy to militate against enforcement'.

The relationship between duress rendering the contract voidable under the lex causae (which was also the lex fori) but not under the law of the place where the acts were performed was explored in *Dimskal Shipping Co SA v International Transport Workers' Federation* [1991] 4 All ER 871. This is discussed in full in Chapter 5, section 5.2 Essential validity of the contract.

**Questions of status**

English law will not recognise a discriminatory or penal status. Thus slavery or civil death will not be recognised, and neither will discriminatory measures against persons of a particular religion or race. In these cases the English courts refuse 'to engraft on free countries the paralysing restrictions of despotisms' (Cheshire, 133, quoting Wharton *The Conflict of Laws*).

## A problematic category: 'other public laws'.

There is some doubt about whether there is a residuary category of 'other public laws', ie laws which do not fall foul of any of the categories already mentioned which would not be enforced, although the existence of this category had long been advocated by Dicey and Morris (in rule 3). However, only Lord Denning's judgment in *Attorney-General of New Zealand* v *Ortiz* [1982] 3 WLR 570 (CA) had clearly accepted this category. Now in *United States of America* v *Inkley* [1988] 3 WLR 304 (CA) the Court of Appeal approved, albeit obiter, this residuary category. The laws which fall into this category will be those that amount to an exercise of sovereign power within the territory of a sovereign, ie the exercise of powers which only sovereigns can exercise.

This question of 'other public laws' was raised in the *Spycatcher* litigation in Australia. In *HM Attorney-General for the United Kingdom* v *Heinemann Publishers Australia* (1988) 78 ALR 449, the case that established that *Spycatcher* could be published in Australia, the High Court of Australia held that to allow the Attorney-General to succeed would amount to the indirect enforcement of a public law of a foreign state. To most conflicts lawyers this result seems bizarre, for the Attorney-General was relying almost exclusively on Peter Wright's duty of confidentiality to his erstwhile employer, essentially a private law matter. Moreover, the Court did not clearly identify what the public law was that was being indirectly enforced; it was certainly not the Official Secrets Act 1911, for the Attorney-General action did not depend on that Act at all. This case is critically discussed by Collier in [1989] *Cambridge Law Journal* 33.

## The evasion of the law

Unlike most other European legal systems English law does not have a general doctrine of the evasion of the law. But what is the doctrine of the evasion of the law? Where persons, in order to avoid the application of the normally applicable legal system (viz, English law), so act as to create connecting factors which attract to their transaction some other legal system under the normal choice of law rules, then the doctrine of the evasion of the law holds that the choice of law rules will not operate as normal, but that the evaded law will apply.

This general doctrine does not apply in English law; no regard is generally paid to the intention with which a connecting factor is created. This may be illustrated by the Gretna Green marriage cases: in the old days where a couple too young to marry without parental consent in England, but old enough to marry under Scots law, were determined to marry, they would elope to Gretna Green (the first village on the Scottish side of the England/Scotland border) and would marry there. (They were supposedly married by the village blacksmith.) Such marriages were held valid in England even although they were contracted in Scotland purely to evade the provisions of English law: *Compton* v *Bearcroft* (1769) 2 Hagg Con 83; (1767) 2 Hagg Con 444. Furthermore, French couples could come to England to marry to evade France's more stringent requirements of parental consent, and that marriage would be upheld (at least by English courts): *Simonin* v *Mallac* (1860) 2 Sw & Tr 67.

Professor J J Fawcett has, however, argued in 'Evasion of Law and Mandatory Rules of Private International Law' (1990) 49 *Cambridge Law Journal* 44 that English law tends to use various other devices in a pragmatic fashion to discourage or prevent evasion. Sometimes English choice of law rules have been moulded so as to restrict evasion. The clearest example of this is the role that the law of domicile plays in determining the essential validity of marriage (see Chapter 9). But in addition many English statutes override, expressly or impliedly, the usual choice of law rules and apply irrespective of choice of law. (See the discussion in Chapter 5, section 5.2 Statutes and the express choice of law.) Indeed, the legislature has even gone so far as to introduce a limited doctrine of evasion by s27(2)(a) of the Unfair Contract Terms Act 1977, which provides that the restrictions imposed by that Act on exemption clauses shall not be defeated by a choice of law 'imposed wholly or mainly for the purpose of enabling the party imposing (the choice of law) to evade the operation of the Act'.

## 2.3 The special conceptual problems: renvoi, characterisation and the incidental question

### Characterisation: general

We have already outlined this problem (sometimes called classification) and given a simple example of it in Chapter 1, section 1.3 *Classification or characterisation*; it is time now to look at it in more detail. We may illustrate the problem by looking at the famous Maltese Marriage case which led to the discovery of the problem of characterisation. (This case, *Anton* v *Bartolo*, is discussed fully by Cheshire, at 44.)

What had happened was that a husband and wife had married while they were both domiciled in Malta. The husband thereafter acquired a domicile in France where he bought some land. On his death his widow claimed a usufruct (a form of right known to civilian legal systems and similar to the life tenancy of English law) over the land. Under French law she was entitled to such a usufruct, but not under Maltese law.

Now the relevant choice of law rules of both Malta and France were identical.

The proprietary consequences of the marriage were determined by the lex domicilii at the time of the marriage (viz Maltese law), and succession to land was governed by the lex situs (law of the place) (viz French law). (Check that you have grasped the concept of the choice of law rule fully by analysing both these rules into their constituent parts of category and connecting factor.)

The difficulty was that it was unclear whether the widow's claim to a usufruct related to the proprietary consequences of marriage, or whether it was a matter of succession to land. And what were the principles to be used in deciding this question?

The problem of characterisation thus does not arise from the differences in the choice of law rules in various legal systems. It arises from the fact that different legal systems mean different things by the same rule, ie the French courts may consider that the claim for a usufruct is a matter of succession, while the Maltese courts may consider that such a question relates to the proprietary consequences of the marriage.

Characterisation has attracted the attention of innumerable academics who have constructed various subtle theories in an attempt to resolve the problem. The judges have, however, generally failed to recognise it or simply glossed over it when it has arisen. Thus, although there are many English cases in which the problem has arisen, it cannot be said that there is a clear or coherent judicial approach to the problem.

This judicial silence on the question of characterisation should not lead one to suppose that it is not an important problem. The academic concern with the problem arises for the following reason:

As we have seen, in the conflict of laws we are concerned with the selection of the appropriate legal system to govern a dispute. Now it would obviously be sensible if all legal systems could agree on the same legal system as the appropriate legal system to govern that dispute. If this were achieved then, wherever a dispute might be litigated, the same legal system would be used to resolve the dispute, and, in principle, the same result would be reached. There would be uniformity of decision, and there would be no need or reason to indulge in 'forum shopping', ie litigants trying to determine where to sue in accordance with their estimation of which court will select a legal system that favours their case. Such uniformity of decision is an important goal of any developed system of the conflict of laws, for it ensures that such injustices as persons married in one country and unmarried in another, or contracts valid in one country and not in another, etc, do not occur.

Now the obvious way in which such uniformity of decision could be achieved would be by unifying choice of law rules in all countries (or at least a large number of them), and as we shall see there are a number of occasions on which the English choice of law rules have been unified and so are identical with a large number of other countries. The point about characterisation, however, is that it shows that even if all choice of law rules were identical, uniformity of decision would not be achieved because different legal systems would still apply those identical rules differently!

Characterisation thus shows that uniformity of decision is an unattainable goal, and this is why it has played such an important part in academic writing.

## What is it that it is characterised?

The various attempts to solve the problem have centred upon the question of what principles the court should use in determining whether a matter falls into one category or another, and we shall consider the most important of these. But before we do this it is important to ask the question: what is it that is being characterised? What is it upon which the choice of law rule operates in order to select the lex causae?

Although there is a great deal of academic dispute about this question, the answer to it is, I believe, simple and straightforward: it is rules of law which are characterised. The reason for this is simply that when a characterisation dispute arises it is clear that one litigant asserts that there exists a rule (or rules) of law of some legal system which if applied to the dispute would allow him to win, while the other litigant denies that the rule (or rules) applies. Thus in the Maltese Marriage case it was the characterisation of the rules of French law that granted the widow a usufruct over her deceased husband's estate that was disputed. And all the characterisation cases can be analysed in this way to reveal that it is rules of law that are characterised.

It will be seen in what follows that this insight is useful in assessing the various approaches to the problem.

## Approaches to characterisation

### Characterisation by the lex fori
Characterisation by the lex fori is adopted widely in continental Europe, and by and large it is the approach adopted, usually unknowingly, by the English judiciary. (See, for instance, cases like *Ogden* v *Ogden* [1908] P 46 and *Huber* v *Steiner* (1835) 2 Bing NC 202.) The judge when faced with a characterisation dispute uses the lex fori to resolve the issue. Thus, to return to the Maltese Marriage case, a French judge would decide the case according to whether French law would consider the widow's usufruct a matter of succession or matrimonial property.

Characterisation by the lex fori is most popular with writers who consider that the object of characterisation is not a rule, or rules, of law by the facts of the case. The lex fori on this approach is simply applied to the facts of the case to reveal the answer. Once it is realised that it is rules of law which are characterised, such a crude resort to the lex fori is not possible, for it is clear that whatever else there may be in the categories of the lex fori, the rules of foreign law which have to be characterised are not to be found there!

Thus it is suggested in these circumstances the judge should characterise foreign rule according to the closest analogue to that rule in the lex fori. Sir Otto Kahn-

Freund has referred to this approach as that of the Procrustean bed: for if the lex fori attempts to characterise foreign rules it will end up either cutting them down to size or elongating them 'but in any case [will] deprive them of life' (op cit, 297). Of course, this approach whatever its other merits breaks down entirely when the lex fori is required to characterise a rule which has no analogue at all in the lex fori.

Although the facts of *G & H Montage GmbH v Irvani* [1990] 1 WLR 667 deal with some very technical aspects of negotiable instruments (and are not worth setting out here), the case is worth noting because Mustill LJ discussed the problem of characterisation more extensively than English judges usually do and gave some support to characterisation by the lex fori. He said:

> 'Some law has to be invoked to tell the English court whether the document is a bill [of exchange], whether a signatory is an indorser, and so on. All are agreed that this must be English law; no other law can be chosen without begging the question ... something more than a fleeting resemblance between the concepts [from the foreign law] which underlie the claim and those of English law will be necessary ... I can see no escape from the conclusion that the courts must examine the cause of action which the plaintiff asserts ... and then match them to see whether his asserted claim corresponds to the kind of cause of action contemplated [in the English choice of law rule].'

This may look like strong support for the lex fori, but it may be doubted whether this is actually what the judge intended. The reason for this is that the judge then in fact created a category for the concept of an aval – a kind of guarantee on a bill of exchange that is recognised under the civilian legal systems but which is unknown to English law. This must be something like Kahn-Freund's 'enlightened' lex fori discussed below.

**Characterisation by the lex causae**
An alternative is to characterise the foreign rule by the legal system to which it belongs. This was essentially what the Court of Appeal did in *Re Maldonado* [1954] P 223. The issue there was whether the Spanish state or the Crown was entitled to the movables left by a Spanish domiciled intestate who died without next of kin. Since succession to the movables of an intestate is governed by the lex domicilii, the question was whether the Spanish state was claiming as a successor, or whether it was claiming a ius regale – a right of the state to own whatever was not owned by someone else, such as the Crown's right to bona vacantia in English law. Jenkins LJ said: 'In accepting the foreign state's law of succession [because of the choice of law rule], English law recognises the foreign state as being the arbiter of what the succession is to be.' This is a clear recognition of the lex causae's role in determining how particular rules of that system should be treated.

Characterisation by the lex causae has its own difficulties. First of all, one needs to know which system of law has been selected as the lex causae before the lex causae can be used to characterise. However, we do not know, until the choice of law process is complete, what the lex causae is, so how can it be used in part of that choice of law process? This difficulty can be avoided by characterising by the potentially applicable lex causae instead of the lex causae itself, but this points to a second and more fundamental difficulty: where there is more than one potentially applicable lex causae, the process may simply not work. The different rules drawn from each of the potential leges causae may, when characterised by the appropriate potential leges causae, each claim to be applicable! If this is so the choice of law process has obviously failed to select a single lex causae.

### Falconbridge's via media

Given the flaws with both the approaches considered so far, Falconbridge developed (first in an article 'Conflicts Rule and Characterisation of Question' (1952) 30 *Canadian Bar Review* 103 and 264) an approach to characterisation that required first a provisional characterisation in which the leges causae were predominant, followed by a final stage in which the lex fori was predominant. This approach is non-mechanical, ie the judge does not blindly follow the rules of either the lex fori or the lex causae in making an appropriate selection.

Morris (op cit, 485) claims that something very like Falconbridge's via media was adopted by the English courts in *Re Cohn* [1945] Ch 5. What happened there was that a mother and a daughter, both domiciled in Germany, were killed during an air raid on London during the war. Under the mother's will the daughter was entitled to the mother's movables provided she survived her mother. But did she? The medical evidence did not resolve this question, but s184 of the Law of Property Act 1925 provided that the presumption was that the mother died first; on the other hand, article 20 of the BGB 1900 (the German Civil Code) said that they should be presumed to have died simultaneously. So which was applicable: s184 or article 20?

The applicable choice of law rules were clear: succession to movables was governed by the lex domicilii, while matters of procedure were governed by the lex fori (this is the usual rule, and this principle is discussed more fully below in section 2.4). Thus German law would govern matters of substance, while English law would govern the procedural matters. But was s184 substantive (in which case it did not apply) or was it procedural (in which case it did apply)? On the other hand if article 20 was procedural it did not apply, while if it was substantive it did apply. (Note how it emerges naturally that it is rules of law which are characterised.)

Now in *Re Cohn* Uthwatt J characterised both s184 and article 20 in the context of the legal systems from which they came, and came to the initial impression that s184 was substantive and that article 20 was also substantive. This was a convenient result to reach as it left only article 20 applicable, so this initial impression was confirmed. This, Morris feels, was an example of Falconbridge's via media in practice.

*Re Cohn* can be used to illustrate another problem that often lurks in characterisation cases. What if the conclusion had been reached that s184 was procedural and article 20 was substantive? The brief answer is that both would be applicable! This is known as the problem of 'cumulation', and Falconbridge's via media (as well as the other approaches to the problem) provides no easy solution.

Yet the result is unacceptable: two conflicting presumptions, both of which are applicable. Related to 'cumulation' is the problem of 'gap'. This would arise if s184 were characterised as substantive (and thus not applicable), and article 20 were characterised as procedural (and thus not applicable), ie there would be no law applicable to that aspect of the case at all! There is really no solution to these problems other than the consilium desperationis that when these problems arise one should have recourse to the lex fori and apply its rules.

### Kahn-Freund's enlightened lex fori

The late Sir Otto Kahn-Freund recently advocated characterisation by an enlightened lex fori (op cit, 227ff). He argues that there is nothing to stop the lex fori developing its own principles of characterisation for use in conflict of laws cases which were different from the categories used in the lex fori. Such special principles of characterisation would be 'enlightened' and thus would take into account the different attitudes of different legal systems to the question and the need to strive to achieve uniformity of decision.

Such principles, Sir Otto argues, have already been adopted in some cases by English judges (but again unknowingly). There are two clear examples of this: first, the adoption of the distinction between movables and immovables in the English conflict of laws instead of the distinction between realty and personality. And, secondly, the English courts are willing to characterise – for the purposes of the conflict of laws only – agreements unsupported by consideration as contracts (see *Re Bonacina* [1912] 2 Ch 394).

Sir Otto's 'enlightened lex fori' has, it is submitted, the elements of the most useful approach: it is non-mechanical, allowing the judge to shape his decision according to the wider considerations of the case, it takes into account the view of the potentially applicable leges causae, yet it recognises that it is ultimately up to the lex fori to resolve the problem. All that is necessary is for the judges to adopt this approach expressly.

### Characterisation according to the 'accepted international interpretation'

In *In re State of Norway's Application (No 2)* (1988) The Times 8 January, the Court of Appeal in interpreting the phrase 'civil and commercial' matters in an English statute sought out the 'accepted international interpretation' of that phrase in the Brussels Convention (see Chapter 4, section 4.3 The scope of the convention). Although this case dealt purely with English law, it shows a distinct move away from the usual attitude of the English courts of simply characterising by the lex fori. It will be interesting to see whether this same attitude is adopted when the courts are not seeking to interpret the provisions of an English statute but to characterise the provisions of a foreign law. However, in the House of Lords this approach was abandoned and the question was seen purely as a matter of English law.

## *Renvoi*

We have already outlined what renvoi is and how it arises in Chapter 1, section 1.3 Renvoi. To some writers and judges renvoi represents the very worst of academic theorising about the conflict of laws. To them it seems ridiculous that so much effort should be put into selecting a lex causae by the application of the choice of law rule, only to find that, once this process is complete, the same effort now has to be put into deciding which legal system the chosen law would apply to the dispute. These writers dismiss renvoi out of hand; they hold that once the lex causae has been selected using the lex fori's choice of law process that should be an end of the matter and the domestic rules of the chosen law should be applied.

### The internal or domestic law approach to renvoi

This view would be popular with students by relieving them of the task of mastering a tricky area of law and, moreover, it has commended itself to some English judges. Consider *Re Annesley* [1926] Ch 692, for example. Here, an Englishwoman had died domiciled in France (at any rate in terms of English law she was domiciled in France; French law held that she was not domiciled there, but as we have seen it is English law that matters in this context). In her will she disposed of her estate in a manner contrary to the law of France, but not of England. The relevant English choice of law rule was that the validity of this disposition was to be determined by the law of her domicile, while the relevant French choice of law rule was that the estate of persons not domiciled (in the French sense) in France were to be distributed according to the law of their nationality (the lex patriae). Thus the renvoi was clear and it arose in the form of the endless circle or circulus inextricabilis. English law referred the case to French law (as lex domicilii); French law referred the case to English law (as lex patriae); but English law referred the case to French law (as lex domicilii) and so on endlessly.

Faced with such a prospect it is not surprising that Russell J asked:

> 'When the law of England requires that the personal estate of a British subject who dies domiciled ... in a foreign country shall be administered in accordance with the law of that country, why should this not mean in accordance with the law which that country would apply, not to the propositus, but to its own nationals legally domiciled there? In other words when we say that French law applies to the administration of the personal estate of an Englishman who dies domiciled in France, we meant that French municipal law which France applies in the case of Frenchmen. This appears to me a simple and rational solution which avoids altogether the endless oscillation which otherwise would result ...'

Unfortunately for law students these views do not accurately reflect the law of England; indeed these remarks were obiter, and Russell J himself applied a different approach in *Re Annesley*. They show, however, how deeply ingrained the feeling is that renvoi is simply a subtle waste of time; and how important it is to stress that it does have an important role to play in the conflict of laws. (See also *Re Askew* [1930] 2 Ch 259 at 278 per Maugham J.)

### The role of renvoi

Renvoi, it seems to me, has an important role to play for at least two reasons. First, if it is rejected altogether (as Russell J suggests) then uniformity of decision will have been abandoned as a goal. Take *Re Annesley*, for example. If both the French court and the English court had rejected renvoi, then French law would have been applied had the case been litigated in England, while English law would have been applied had the case been litigated in France. Thus the outcome of the case would depend, not upon the rational application of legal principles, but upon such chance factors such as, for example, whether the dispute was over money in a Paris bank account in which case it might be litigated in France, or whether the money was in England in which case it would be fought out before the English courts. That could not be right, and one of the major goals of conflict of laws must be achieving as far as possible the uniformity of decision that avoids such irrational outcomes.

Secondly, renvoi has an altogether more mundane and pragmatic role to play in providing an escape mechanism when otherwise English law would force a judge to give a ridiculous or patently unjust judgment. This point is best illustrated by one of the first cases on renvoi in English law: *Collier v Rivaz* (1841) 2 Curt 855. At this time the English choice of law in regard to the formal validity of wills was very rigid; only the law of the testator's last domicile (lex ultimi domicilii) could be used to determine this question. In *Collier v Rivaz* an Englishman had died domiciled in Belgium leaving a will (made according to the Belgian form) and a range of codicils, some of which had been executed according to the Belgian form and some according to English law. There was no dispute over the will and those of the codicils executed according to the Belgian form. But what of those made according to the English form? Prima facie they were invalid, for the testator had died domiciled in Belgium and thus only Belgian law could be used to test formal validity.

However, Sir Henry Jenner pointed out that Belgian law in such a case would have referred the validity of the codicils to the law of the foreigner's own country; he, therefore, accepted the renvoi from Belgium and applied English law to test the validity of the codicils.

This was obviously a sensible result, for the rigid English choice of law rule would otherwise lead to injustice. Indeed, in 1861 the law in regard to the formal validity of wills was reformed (after *Collier v Rivaz* had been disapproved of in *Bremer v Freeman* (1857) 10 Moo PC 306 at 374), and the rules in force today are very liberal (see Chapter 7, section 7.8). However, this kind of reasoning should not be pressed too far. After all, if adopted consistently in *Collier v Rivaz* it would have meant that the will (and codicils) executed according to the Belgian form were invalid for Belgian law would have applied English law to test their validity! Moreover, the extent to which it is proper for a judge to manipulate the law in order to achieve justice in the particular case, rather than simply apply the law as it is without regard to the justice of the outcome, is a profound and controversial one. None the less, it is clear that renvoi has played a useful role as such an escape device. (See further Morris, op cit, 471–474.)

If it is accepted that renvoi has a useful role to play (and this is by no means a universal view) then it has to be decided which of the two approaches to renvoi which are to be found in the English decisions should be adopted. The two theories are that of single or partial renvoi and that of double renvoi or the foreign court theory.

## Single or partial renvoi

Until the decision in *Re Annesley* this approach could be seen as being the orthodox view of renvoi in English law. When the case was referred by the choice of law rules of the lex fori to another legal system, then one looked at the choice of law rules of that system; and if that legal system referred the matter back to the lex fori then judge of the lex fori 'accepted the renvoi' and applied the lex fori. *Collier v Rivaz* may serve as an example of such a case. (Such cases are known as 'remission' because the lex causae remits the matter back to the lex fori; but cases of 'transmission' can also occur. In such cases the choice of law rules of the lex causae transmit the case on to a third legal system.)

This approach to renvoi can operate arbitrarily and does not necessarily advance uniformity of decision. First, it is arbitrary for the following reason. Single or partial renvoi amounts to allowing the relevant choice of law rules to refer the case on twice: the choice of law rules of the lex fori refer the case to the lex causae, and the choice of law rules of the lex causae refer the case on once more (back to the lex fori (in the case of remission) or on to a third legal system (in the case of transmission)). But there is no magic in the number two; why should three onward references not be allowed (to a fourth legal system in the case of transmission or back to the lex causae in the case of remission) or four? Or indeed, why should one not decide to allow only one onward reference, ie reject renvoi altogether?

Moreover, partial renvoi does not necessarily advance uniformity of decision, and this can be seen in the following way. Suppose in a case like *Collier v Rivaz* both Belgian law and English law adopted partial renvoi. Then, if the matter were litigated in Belgium, Belgian law would apply, while if it were litigated in England then English law would apply. (Check that you have mastered the principle of partial renvoi by working through *Collier v Rivaz* until you reach this result.) Partial renvoi does have the advantage of allowing the judge in case of remission always to apply his own law; but although judges have a natural preference for their own law, for they know and understand it best, this 'homeward trend' should be guarded against and not elevated to a principle determining the correct attitude to renvoi.

## The foreign court theory or the 'double renvoi' approach

In *Re Annesley* it seems a change in approach to renvoi took place even although Russell J (as we have seen) would have preferred a 'no renvoi' solution. (The reader should, at this stage, refresh his or her memory as to the facts of this case.) In these circumstances it is a bit of a puzzle why the learned judge without reference to English authority (although *Collier v Rivaz* itself can be read in support of the foreign court theory) went on to introduce a new approach to the subject. None the less, this is what he did. And the way that he did it was to make the outcome of the case depend upon the attitude of the French courts to the question of renvoi. He said:

'I ... decide that the domicile of the testatrix at the time of her death was French. French law accordingly applies, but the question remains: what French law? According to French ... law, the law applicable in the case of [such] a foreigner ... is the law of that person's nationality, in this case British. But the law of that nationality refers the question back to French law, the law of the domicile; and the question arises, will the French law accept this reference back, or renvoi, and apply French [domestic] law? ... after careful consideration ... I have come to the conclusion that ... the French courts ... will apply French [domestic] law [ie would accept the renvoi].'

In other words the English judge when dealing with such cases should in effect don the mantle of the foreign judge and decided the case just as he would have. If that judge would have rejected renvoi then the English judge rejects renvoi; if that judge would have applied partial renvoi (as Russell J found the French courts would have in *Re Annesley*), then partial renvoi is applied.

The great merit of this approach to renvoi is that it advances uniformity of decision; whether the matter is litigated in the one court or the other they should end up applying the same law to that case. Unfortunately, it has other disadvantages. Suppose the foreign judge also adopts the double renvoi approach; then it does not work at all. The English judge asks how the French judge would decide the case; but the French judge says that he would decide it just as the English judge would, who as we know would do what the French judge would, etc, etc! One should not exaggerate this difficulty, for frequently the foreign court will have a clear approach to renvoi (either rejecting it or adopting partial renvoi), usually laid down in a civil code or similar statute. In these circumstances the theory works, and it works well to promote uniformity of decision. However, equally frequently the foreign court itself has no clear attitude to renvoi, or its attitude to renvoi cannot be proved; and, as we know, in such cases the foreign law is presumed to be the same as English law, ie double renvoi is presumed to be the foreign court's attitude to renvoi!

In any event, since *Re Annesley* double renvoi has emerged as the orthodox English approach (see *Re Ross* [1930] 1 Ch 377; *Re Askew* [1930] 2 Ch 259, cf *Kotia v Nahas* [1914] AC 403); but the matter is hardly free from doubt, for the cases are open to varying interpretations.

### The scope of renvoi

Although the precise approach to renvoi as well as the usefulness of the concept may be open to debate, it is clear that there are some areas of the law in which the technique of renvoi will not be applied. For instance, in *Amin Rasheed Shipping Corp v Kuwait Insurance Co* [1983] 2 All ER 884, Lord Diplock said that the proper law of a contract (ie the law governing most aspects of that contract (this will usually be the law which the parties have chosen to govern their contract (see Chapter 5, section 5.2 *General principles* and *Ascertaining the proper law*) was the 'substantive law of the country which the parties have chosen as that by which the mutual legally enforceable rights are to be ascertained, but excluding any renvoi, whether of remission or transmission, that the courts of that country might themselves apply if the matter were litigated before them'. Similarly, the EC Convention on the Law Applicable to Contractual Obligations, which is now part of English law, specifically excludes the application of renvoi. And although renvoi may have entered English law in the field of the formal validity of wills, the Wills Act 1963 in effect excludes renvoi from this area (not that this is likely to lead to any wills failing, for a wide range of different laws can be used to test formal validity under the 1963 Act (see Chapter 7, section 7.8)).

On the other hand the doctrine has been used widely in the field of succession, including the following areas: intestate succession (*Re Johnson* [1903] 1 Ch 821; *Re O'Keefe* [1940] Ch 124), and intrinsic validity of wills (*Re Trufort* (1887) 36 Ch D 600; *Re Ross* [1930] 1 Ch 377). Furthermore, the doctrine has been applied to questions of capacity to marry (*R v Brentwood Superintendent Registrar of Marriages, ex parte Arias* [1968] 2 QB 956), and a very similar principle operates in the field of the recognition of foreign divorce decrees (*Armitage* v *Attorney-General* [1906] P 135). There are signs that renvoi also applies in the field of formal validity of marriage (*Taczanowska* v *Taczanowski* [1957] P 301). Morris (op cit, 476–477) argues cogently that the doctrine also has a role to play in the law of property. If, for instance, title to immovable property is in question (and this is governed by the lex situs, see Chapter 7, section 7.3), and if the lex situs would apply the law of some other country, then it is only sensible for the English court to apply the law of that other country. Since only the lex situs can ultimately determine title to immovable property within its jurisdiction, uniformity is crucial in such areas.

## The incidental question

A further problem, which like renvoi arises from the differences between the conflict rules of different countries, is the incidental question. Different legal systems may decide the same choice of law question in different ways. Suppose, for example, that H, a national of Utopia, dies intestate leaving securities deposited in a bank in London. At the time of his death H is domiciled in Hades. Now in terms of the English conflict rule, intestate succession to movables is governed by the law of the last domicile, viz, Hades law (see Chapter 7, section 7.7).

One of the claimants for H's securities is W, who claims to be his wife, and under the law of Hades the spouse of an intestate is entitled to one third of the estate. However, is W H's wife? Under the English choice of law rule the formal validity of marriage is governed by the law of the place where the marriage is celebrated (the lex loci celebrationis) (see Chapter 9), and H has gone through a ceremony of marriage with W with all the usual formalities in England. But under the law of Hades, the formal validity of marriage is governed by the national law (the lex patriae), ie Utopian law, and no marriage (even celebrated outside Utopia) is valid under the law of Utopia unless accompanied by the eating of lotus leaves. No leaves were eaten at H & W's 'marriage' since the lotus plant was unobtainable in England.

Now the incidental question can be understood: incidentally to the question of the intestate succession to movables (which is clearly governed by the law of Hades) the question of the formal validity of marriage arises. But which law governs that issue: the law which the lex causae (Hades law) would apply, viz, the law of Utopia, or the law which the lex fori would normally apply to that issue, viz, English law (the lex loci celebrationis)?

The academic writers are divided about how the incidental question should be resolved. The obvious point may be made that if the incidental question is governed by the lex causae (ie in our example it would be decided as the law of Hades would decide it, viz, Utopian law would be applied) then uniformity of decision will be advanced; whether the matter is litigated in England or Hades the same result will be reached.

On the other hand, there may be difficulties with this approach: first, it will sometimes be unclear which is the incidental question and which is the main question, and different results would be reached depending upon which was which. Secondly, suppose in our example before his death H approached the English courts seeking a declaration that he was validly married to W. There could be little doubt that in these circumstances the English courts would test formal validity by the lex loci celebrationis and declare that the marriage was formally valid. Should H then die intestate and the incidental question arise, it seems inconceivable that the courts would hold the marriage was invalid in an application of the Utopian law!

Given these difficulties it is not surprising that most academic writers differ in the suggested solutions to the problem; some support the application of the lex causae as advancing uniformity, other support the application of the lex fori, and others suggest a non-mechanical solution to the problem, solving it on a case by case basis. (See Morris, op cit, 492, and Gotlieb (1955) 33 *Canadian Bar Review* 523 and (1977) 26 *ICLQ* 734 for an introduction to the academic debate.)

In England, the incidental question has not been discussed by name in the cases although there are a number of decisions that raise questions very similar to the incidental question. The best known of these is *Lawrence* v *Lawrence* [1985] Fam 106 which we will discuss in more detail in Chapter 9. What had happened was that a woman (Mrs Lawrence), domiciled in Brazil according to the ordinary rules of English law (see Chapter 3), had divorced her first husband in Nevada, and the next day she had married her second husband in Nevada. The couple came to live in England. An English court was asked: was her second marriage valid?

Now the orthodox rule for testing the validity of marriage (see Chapter 9) was that formal validity was tested by the lex loci celebrationis (Nevada), and essential validity (including capacity) was tested by the parties' ante-nuptial domicile (viz Brazil as far as W was concerned). The snag was that the law of Brazil did not recognise divorce and in particular would not recognise the divorce decree obtained in Nevada. On the other hand, the Nevada decree of divorce was bound to be recognised under the relevant legislation applicable in England (see Chapter 9).

Analysing these facts in terms of the incidental question we can say that the primary question was: did Mrs Lawrence have capacity to marry? And the lex causae to govern that question was her domiciliary law, viz Brazilian law. Incidental to this question arose the issue of whether the Nevada divorce had put an end to her first marriage. If the lex causae was applied by the English court to that issue, uniformity would be advanced in that the same conclusion would be reached in England as would be reached in Brazil (her second marriage would be held void). On the other hand, if the lex fori (English law) were applied to the incidental question, a different result from that reached by the Brazilian courts would be reached; the second marriage would be upheld. In the event, in a criticised decision, the Court of Appeal upheld the second marriage; and although the judges never analysed the case as one raising the incidental question, *Lawrence* v *Lawrence* can perhaps be seen as support for the lex fori as the governing law for the resolution of the incidental question.

On the other hand, in the Canadian case of *Schwebel* v *Ungar* (1963) 42 DLR (2d) 622, affirmed (1964) 48 DLR(2d) 644, the court, in effect, applied the lex causae to a similar situation. (Parties domiciled in Hungary, divorced by extra-judicial ghett, which was not recognised in either Hungary or Canada, but was recognised in Israel where the parties acquired a domicile and then remarried; was the second marriage valid? Yes: the lex causae for essential validity of marriage was Israeli law, and using that law to resolve the incidental question (was the ghett recognised?) led to upholding the second marriage). But note that in both these cases the conclusion of the court was that the disputed marriage was valid. Perhaps then these cases tell us more about the courts' policy of upholding marriage wherever possible than they do about the incidental question.

## 2.4 Substance and procedure

As we have seen, an English court will, when so directed by a choice of law rule, apply to the dispute before it the rules of a foreign legal system. But it would be quite impractical for the procedural aspects of that litigation to be governed by any law other than English law (the lex fori). After all it is frequently not known until the end of a case that some foreign law is applicable, and if so which foreign law is to be applied. In these circumstances the procedural aspects of the dispute must be governed by the lex fori. Thus it is beyond dispute that matters of procedure are governed by the lex fori.

The difficulty is that there is no innate distinction between substance and procedure. As Cheshire (at 77) says: 'There is no pre-ordained dividing line between the two, having some kind of objective existence discoverable by logic.' Setting procedure and substance asunder, therefore, is a difficult task that involves a measure of artificiality. The astute will readily recognise that the problem of distinguishing between procedure (governed by the lex fori) and substance (governed by the lex causae) is an old friend of ours; the problem of characterisation is, does a particular potentially applicable rule fall into the category substance or does it fall into the category of procedure? Thus the non-mechanical techniques discussed above all apply here mutatis mutandis. And one should bear in mind the much cited words of Cook (in *Logical and Legal Basis of the Conflict of Laws*, 166) stressing that the crucial purpose for applying this distinction is the convenience of the court. Thus one should ask: 'How far can the court of the forum go in applying the rule taken from the foreign system of law without unduly hindering or inconveniencing itself?' This consideration argues for a narrow rather than a wide view of procedure (this is not always the attitude of the judges), and a pragmatic attitude to the question.

It is now useful to set out here the characterisations of particular rules that have been adopted in the past as well as some of the characterisations which have been imposed by statute.

## Statutes of limitation

We may begin the discussion by drawing a distinction between two kinds of statute of limitation. First, there are those statutes – we may call them 'weak' statutes of limitation – which merely specify that after a certain period of time a legal right cannot be enforced. And, secondly, there are 'strong' statutes of limitation which specify that after a period of time a legal right is extinguished altogether and not simply that the right can no longer be enforced.

The English common law on the characterisation of 'weak' statutes of limitation was clear if unsatisfactory: such statutes were procedural. Moreover, English law statutes of limitation were generally of the 'weak' variety. The result of this was that when a matter was litigated in an English court, the English limitation rules were characterised as procedural and were applied, while the limitation rules of the lex causae were disregarded. Thus even if an action could still be maintained under the lex causae, the English statute of limitation would provide a good defence before an English court (*British Linen Company* v *Drummond* (1830) 10 B & C 903). And if an action is out of time under a 'weak' statute of limitation from the lex causae, it may still be enforced in England provided it is within the English limitation period (*Huber* v *Steiner* (1835) 2 Bing NC 202 (although the court was almost certainly wrong to conclude that the foreign statute was 'weak' rather than 'strong').

Where the foreign statute of limitation is 'strong' then it is generally characterised as substantive, and it may be successfully pleaded before an English court (see dicta in *Harris* v *Quine* (1869) LR 4 QB 653; see also *Black-Clawson International* v *Papierwerke Waldhof-Aschaffenburg* [1975] AC 591 at 630).

This attitude to statutes of limitation was out of step with many other legal systems (which considered such matters as substantive). The Law Commission recommended a change (*Report on Classification of Limitation in Private International*

*Law* (Law Com No 114, Cmnd 8570, 1982) and the substance of their recommendations was enacted into law in the Foreign Limitation Periods Act 1984.

The central provision of this measure is s1(1) which imposes a classification upon foreign limitation rules as substantive rather than procedural. It reads as follows:

> 'Subject to the following provisions of this Act, where in any action or proceedings in a court in England and Wales the law of any other country (falls in accordance with rules of private international law applicable by any such court) to be taken into account in the determination of any matter –
> a) the law of that other country relating to limitation shall apply in respect of that matter for the purposes of the action or proceedings; and
> b) except where that matter falls within subsection 2 below, the law of England and Wales relating to limitation shall not so apply.'

While it is clear that henceforth foreign limitation rules will be regarded as substantive rather than procedural, the Foreign Limitation Periods Act 1984 is set about with a range of rather more technical issues that we need to explain.

First, subs 2 (read with s1(1)(b)) provides that the limitation of rules of the law of England and Wales shall continue to apply to cases where 'both the law of England and Wales and the law of some other country fall to be taken into account'. The reason for this odd provision is that (as we shall see in Chapter 6, section 6.2) the English choice of law rule for tort requires actionability under both the lex fori and the lex loci delicti (the place where the tort was committed). Had the qualification in subs 2 not applied, then a tort which was not actionable in England, because it was out of time under the lex fori, would none the less have been recoverable in England. Parliament did not intend to change the choice of law rules in regard to tort in this way; hence this provision.

Secondly, s1(3) provides that the law of England and Wales, rather than the foreign law, shall determine when time begins to run. The reason for this is that Parliament did not wish to impose upon the courts the burden of investigating the details and complex foreign rules in regard to these matters. Given the complex foreign rules that English courts are expected to master on other occasions, it is difficult to see why they should have this burden lifted from them in this case.

Thirdly, s1(4) specifically provides that, where the foreign law allows the exercise of a discretion in regard to limitation, the English court acting in terms of s1(1) shall exercise that discretion 'so far as practicable … in the manner in which it is exercised in comparable cases by the courts of that other country'. English courts do not in general exercise discretions vested in foreign courts; hence the necessity for this provision.

Fourthly, s1(5) excludes the operation of renvoi in this area. Thus in applying a foreign rule in terms of s1(1) one does not need to ask: how would the foreign court deal with this matter?

Fifthly, s2(1) provides that where 'the application of s1 above would to any extent conflict … with public policy, that section shall not apply to the extent that its application would so conflict'. It is difficult to see why this provision was necessary, for the courts retain, it is submitted, irrespective of statute, the power to exclude the application of foreign law that is contrary to public policy, and the wide terms of this exclusion may encourage courts to exclude in other than exceptional cases. Section 2(2) goes on to provide that the application of s1 'shall conflict with public policy to the extent that its application would cause undue hardship to a person who is, or might be made, a party to the action or proceedings'. Future litigation may clarify the meaning of 'undue hardship'. Section 2(3) further provides that rules of foreign law which provide that the limitation period shall be interrupted by 'the absence of a party ... from any specified jurisdiction or country ... shall be disregarded'. English law, for instance, had a long-abolished rule that where a party was 'beyond the seas' limitation would not run; s2(3) is designed to ensure that such provisions in foreign laws are not applied by English courts.

Sixthly, s4(1) and (2) spell out what is implicit in s1: that, save where otherwise provided, the foreign rules in regard to the application, extension, reduction or interruption of the limitation period shall apply.

Finally, s4(3) allows the English court notwithstanding that it may be applying a foreign law to refuse to grant relief on equitable grounds, such as the plaintiff having been guilty of laches or acquiescence. However, in applying these principles the court is specifically enjoined to have regard to the foreign law's limitation periods.

## *Evidence*

Again it is perfectly clear that matters of evidence are for the lex fori. Thus in *Bain v Whitehaven and Furness Railway* (1850) 3 HLC 1 at 19 it was held that 'whether a witness was competent or not, whether a certain matter requires to prove by writing or not, whether certain evidence proves a certain fact or not ... is to be determined by the law of the country where the question arises'.

But the breadth of this principle has inconvenient results especially where the question of writing arises. Thus, for example, if the lex fori requires that a particular matter shall be proved by writing, it follows that that matter cannot be proved orally even if oral proof would have been acceptable under the lex causae. This reasoning has been upheld in the case of *Leroux v Brown* (1852) 12 CB 801, where it was held that s4 of the Statute of Frauds 1677, which provided that 'no action shall be brought on various contracts unless the agreement was evidenced in writing', was procedural. In this case an oral contract of employment valid under the lex causae (French law) was denied enforcement in England because it could not be proved by writing.

Although this result is much criticised, for it can so easily lead to injustice, it remains the law in England. In California, however, in *Bernkrant v Fowler* (1961) 55 Cal 2d 588, when the same point arose, the Californian Supreme Court refused to apply the Statute of Frauds from the lex fori to an oral contract governed by the law of Nevada because it was held that that statute, properly interpreted, did not apply to foreign contracts. This appears to be a far more apt rule, for there is no reason why the strictures of the lex fori need apply to contracts governed by another law.

There is, however, one helpful distinction to be drawn in this area: that between interpretation of a document (which is governed by the lex causae) and proof of the existence of a contract by tendering a document in evidence (this is governed by the lex fori).

## The nature and extent of the remedy

### Remedy not known to the lex fori

Where the plaintiff seeks a remedy unknown to the lex fori he will be unsuccessful. Thus in *Phrantzes* v *Argenti* [1960] 2 QB 19, Lord Parker refused the plaintiff (the daughter) the remedy available under Greek Law to require a father to enter into a dowry contract on behalf of his daughter. The daughter failed because such an order 'condemning someone to enter into a contract in a particular person not even a party to the proceedings' was not known to English law.

### Damages

Although authority is sparse and often confusing, questions about damages should not cause great difficulty provided the distinction between remoteness of damage and the quantum (or amount) of damages is kept clearly in mind. Where the question is one of remoteness, then it is plainly substantive and governed by the lex causae. On the other hand where the question is one of the quantification of damages, then the matter is for the lex fori. This distinction has been recognised in the decided cases. Thus in *D'Almaida Araujo Lda* v *Sir Frederick Becker & Co Ltd* [1953] 2 QB 329 a contract for the sale of palm oil governed by Portuguese law was breached. Certain damages were irrecoverable under English law but not under Portuguese law. It was held that these damages (arising from an indemnity that the plaintiff (the vendor) had to pay to his supplier of oil as a result of the defendant's breach) were substantive not procedural; and thus that the plaintiff could recover. Remoteness of damage has been recognised as substantive in both contractual and tortious claims (*Boys* v *Chaplin* [1971] AC 356, discussed fully in Chapter 6, section 6.3).

### Judgments in foreign currency

For hundreds of years it was clear that English courts would give judgment only in sterling, and this was confirmed in 1961 by the House of Lords in *Re United Railways of Havana and Regla Warehouses* [1961] AC 1007. Thus where a claim was made for an amount of foreign currency that sum had to be converted into sterling before judgment was given. Moreover, it was clear that the date for the conversion into sterling was the date the cause of action arose.

This rule has now been overturned by the House of Lords in *Miliangos* v *George Frank (Textiles) Ltd* [1976] AC 443. In this case the plaintiff sold polyester yarn to the defendants, an English company. The price was payable in Swiss francs, and the contract was governed by Swiss law. The defendants refused to pay for the yarn, and the plaintiff, a Swiss national, sued in the English courts for the agreed price.

The problem was that, between the time that the price was due and the date of the hearing of the case, sterling had depreciated against the Swiss franc. The price was the equivalent of £42,000 when it fell due but £60,000 at the date of the hearing. In these circumstances the rule of *Re United Railways* operated harshly against the Swiss plaintiff, and in response to this the House of Lords abandoned the earlier rule. Lord Wilberforce said:

> 'Justice demands that the creditor should not suffer from fluctuations in the value of sterling. His contract has nothing to do with sterling; he has bargained in his own currency and only in his own currency. The substance of the debtor's obligations depends upon the proper law of the contract ... and though English law ... prevails as regard procedural matters, it must surely be wrong in principle to allow procedure to affect, detrimentally, the substance of the creditor's rights.'

Thus henceforth it would be possible for judgment to be given in an amount of foreign currency.

For procedural reasons, however, the English courts, although they will now give judgment for sums of foreign currency, will only execute judgments that have been converted into sterling. This sounds odd but is sensible. If property is to be seized to satisfy the judgment then the court officials must know the sterling value of the judgment, otherwise they might seize too much or too little. In *Miliangos*, however, it was held that the date for such conversion was the date on which the court authorises the enforcement of the judgment in terms of sterling. This, said Lord Wilberforce, 'gets nearest to securing the creditor exactly what he bargained for'. In some cases a different date is still used. Thus where a company is in compulsory liquidation the date of the winding-up order is used (since otherwise the creditors would be unequally treated), and in claims against a deceased's estate the date of the administration order will be used.

Although *Miliangos* v *George Frank* strictly speaking was confined to claims for liquidated sums, the principle of the case was soon applied in other areas. Thus in regard to tortious claims it was held in *The Despina R* [1979] AC 685 that judgment could be given in foreign currency, but that would usually be the currency which the plaintiff normally used in the course of his business and not necessarily the currency in which the loss was immediately suffered. Similarly judgment could be given in a foreign currency in a claim for breach of contract (for unliquidated damages); this currency would be that which most fully expresses the plaintiff's loss (*Services Europe Atlantique Sud* v *Stockholms Rederiaktiebolag Svea* [1979] AC 685). Thus in principle judgment could be given in a foreign currency even where the proper law of the contract was English. Thus it now seems that in any proper case the English courts have power to give judgment in foreign currency.

## Judgments in foreign currency

The interest payable on judgments in foreign currency has in the past been paid at the appropriate statutory rate for judgment debts in sterling (*Practice Direction*

[1976] 1 WLR 83; amended by [1977] 1 WLR 197). Part I of the Private International Law (Miscellaneous Provisions) Act 1985 now states (in accordance with the recommendation of the Law Commission (Report No 123, 1983)) that the rate of interest should be 'such rate as the court thinks fit' (s1(1)). This power to fix the rate of interest extends to county court judgments and arbitral awards (ss2 and 3). The reason for this power is that the prescribed rate for English judgments varies according to the strength or weakness of sterling, whereas the rate that foreign currency judgments should bear should vary according to the strength or weakness of the currency of the judgment. Part I is to be brought into force by order. At the date of writing no such order has been made.

## Priorities

These are governed by the lex fori: see *The Halcyon Isle* [1981] AC 221. Thus a form of security such as a maritime lien recognised under the lex causae of the debt (which the lien is supposed to secure) will be of little use if liens of that type are not recognised under the lex fori.

## 2.5 Public international law and the conflict of laws

As we have seen (Chapter 1, section 1.1 *The nature of the conflict of laws*) the conflict of laws is part of English law, not public international law. However, there are two areas in which the conflict of laws and public international law overlap, and these we will consider here.

## Sovereign and diplomatic immunity

It has long been a recognised principle of public international law received into the common law that a foreign sovereign state could not be sued in the English courts unless it submitted to the jurisdiction of the English courts (*Duke of Brunswick* v *King of Hanover* (1844) 6 Beav 1; (1848) 2 HLC 1). For many years this was an absolute immunity, ie the foreign state was immune from the jurisdiction of the English courts in all circumstances. In a series of cases in the 1970s, however, the courts began to recognise a distinction between acta jure imperii (or acts of government) and acta jure gestionis (or commercial acts) and to hold that sovereign immunity only applied to acta jure imperii (*The Philippine Admiral* [1977] AC 373 (no immunity in an action in rem against a ship used to trade) and *Trendtex Trading Corporation* v *Central Bank of Nigeria* [1977] QB 529 (no immunity when state involved in ordinary commercial transactions)).

This development has been fortified and extended by the State Immunity Act 1978 (which implements the European Convention on State Immunity). The scheme of the Act is to enact the general rule that a sovereign 'State is immune from the jurisdiction of the courts of the United Kingdom' (s1(1)) but then to go on to specify a wide range of exceptions to this principle.

The major exceptions are in brief:

1. where the State has submitted (and it can now submit more easily and in a wider range of circumstances than was previously the case); prior written agreements to submit are now binding, and the institution of proceedings will generally amount to submission (s2);
2. a State is not immune in regard to commercial transactions (which has a wide definition including supply of goods and services, loans and other transactions 'into which the State enters ... otherwise than in the exercise of sovereign authority' (s3));
3. a State is also not immune in regard to contracts (whether commercial transactions or not) to be performed wholly or partly in the United Kingdom (unless the parties have agreed otherwise), nor is it immune regarding employment contracts where the contract was made in the United Kingdom or the work is to be done here unless the parties agree otherwise, or the employee is a national of the State or not a national of the United Kingdom (ss3 and 4);
4. a State is not immune from proceedings in respect of death or personal injury or damage or loss of tangible property caused by an act or omission within the United Kingdom (s5);
5. nor is a State immune from proceedings regarding possession or use or related issues regarding immovable property in the United Kingdom (s6);
6. nor is a State immune in matters of trade marks and patents registered in the United Kingdom (s7);
7. nor is a State immune from proceedings relating to its membership of a body corporate or an unincorporated association or a partnership incorporated in the United Kingdom or controlled, or having its place of business, in the United Kingdom (s8);
8. nor is a State immune from Admiralty actions in rem in regard to ships used for commercial purposes and this extends to in rem proceedings against the cargo (s10);
9. a State is not immune from proceedings in regard to taxes due and rates due on premises occupied for commercial purposes.

The State Immunity Act 1978 has most recently been under consideration in *Al-Adsani* v *Government of Kuwait and Others* (1996) The Times 29 March. Here the plaintiff, a British national and a citizen of Kuwait, claimed to have been subjected to torture while he was in Kuwait. The plaintiff claimed that despite the express wording of s1 of the State Immunity Act, which prima facie granted sovereign immunity to the defendant, the section had to be read subject to the implication that a State was only to be granted immunity if it was acting within the law of nations. International law against torture was so fundamental that it overrode all other principles of sovereign immunity. However, the Court of Appeal held that the

1978 Act was a comprehensive code and was not subject to any overriding considerations.

Separate entities closely associated with the State may also be immune from jurisdiction if they act in the exercise of sovereign immunity and the circumstances are such that a State would have been immune (s14(2)). For example, in *Kuwait Airways Corporation* v *Iraqi Airways Co and Another* (1995) The Times 25 July, the Iraqi Air Corporation (IAC) was ordered by the Iraqi Minister for Civil Aviation to seize the aircraft of the Kuwait Aircraft Corporation (KAC). By order of the Iraqi government the KAC was dissolved and the IAC pursuant to a legislative decree incorporated the aircraft. On appeal, the principal substantive issue was whether IAC, as a separate entity, was entitled to immunity under s14(2) State Immunity Act 1978.

While the House of Lords agreed that the seizure of the aircraft was in the exercise of sovereign authority (by order of the Iraqi government), only a bare majority agreed that the incorporation of the aircraft pursuant to the legislative decree was not such an exercise of sovereign authority.

The Act also makes detailed provision for the service of process on foreign states and the execution of judgments. It should be noted that the property of foreign central banks will, unless the bank agrees otherwise, remain immune from execution (s14(3) and (4)).

Diplomats have also long enjoyed a similar immunity, and the present law is contained in the Diplomatic Privileges Act 1961 (which implements the Vienna Convention on Diplomatic Relations 1961). Consuls only enjoy immunity in respect of their official acts (see the Consular Relations Act 1968). As with sovereign immunity diplomatic immunity can be waived by the state which the diplomat is representing.

International organisations may, in terms of the International Organisations Act 1968, be accorded immunity from suit and legal processes by the Crown. The extent of this immunity was tested in the extensive litigation arising out of the collapse of the International Tin Council in the mid 1980s. The council had entered into an agreement with the United Kingdom government and had been accorded a certain immunity under the International Tin Council (Immunities and Privileges Order) 1972. Article 6(1)(a) of the Order provided that the ITC was to enjoy 'immunity from jurisdiction and execution except ... to the extent that [ITC] shall have expressly waived such immunity in a particular case'.

In *Standard Chartered Bank* v *International Tin Council and Others* [1986] 3 All ER 257 the ITC sought to rely upon this immunity when sued by the Standard Chartered Bank who had loaned it £10,000,000. However, in terms of the loan agreement the ITC submitted irrevocably to the English courts. The ITC sought to avoid the consequence of this undertaking by arguing that article 6(1)(a) meant that it could only submit to the jurisdiction of the courts once the dispute had arisen; it could not submit in advance. Although there is support for this proposition in the common law, it is rejected, as we have seen, in the State Immunity Act 1978, and was rejected by Bingham J too. He held that international organisations did not enjoy sovereign or diplomatic immunity except where such immunity was granted by legislative instrument; and that on a true construction article 6(1)(a) meant that there could be submission in advance.

However, the liabilities of the Tin Council far exceeded its assets, so the creditors wished to establish that the states which were members of the Tin Council were liable for its debts. The House of Lords settled this issue in *J H Rayner (Mincing Lane)* v *Department of Trade and Industry* [1989] 3 WLR 969, where it held that:

> 'The municipal courts were not competent to adjudicate upon or to enforce the rights arising from transactions entered into by ... sovereign states on the international law plane ... [and] ... without the intervention of Parliament [the rights of individuals could not be changed, because] a treaty was not part of English law unless and until it had been incorporated into it by legislation ...'.

It followed (putting the issue much more simply than it was in the litigation) that even if there was a principle in international law that the member states of an international organisation were liable for the debts of that organisation, since that principle had not been incorporated into English law there could be no remedy through English courts against the member states for the unpaid debts of the International Tin Council.

In the tin litigation no problem arose over the existence of the International Tin Council even although it was an international organisation set up on the international law level, because the ITC had been created a legal person in English law by the ITC Order in Council 1972 made under the International Organisations Act 1968. But obviously a problem could arise with other international organisations, which existed under international law but which had not been given that status under English legislation. Could they sue or be sued in England? The point arose recently in *Arab Monetary Fund* v *Hashim and Others* [1992] 2 WLR 729 (HL). The Arab Monetary Fund (AMF) was set up by agreement between various Arab states, and it sought the aid of the English courts to recover funds allegedly misappropriated from it by its former Director-General now resident in England. The Court of Appeal applied the reasoning of *J H Rayner* v *DTI* and held that the English courts could not adjudicate upon or enforce the rights of an international organisation unless it had been 'touched by the magic wand of an Order in Council' (made under the International Organisations Act 1968). However, the agreement conferred on the fund 'independent juridical personality'. A decree of the United Arab Emirates established the fund as an 'independent juridical personality' in the UAE and, in particular, in Abu Dhabi (where the fund had its headquarters); should this not be recognised by the English courts? In the end the House of Lords overruled the Court of Appeal. The comity of nations required that the courts of the UK should recognise a corporate body created by the law of a foreign state recognised by the Crown (like the UAE). Thus, since on a true construction of the

UAE decree corporate personality was established not just under international law but under the law of the UAE, the fund was entitled to sue.

This result is consistent with the other recent case on the subject. This case is *Bumper Development Corporation* v *Commissioner of Police of the Metropolis* [1991] 1 WLR 1362, and it concerned a dispute in London over a 12th-century bronze idol representing the Hindu god Siva. The idol had been stolen from a ruined temple in the Indian state of Tamil Nadu, brought to England and then sold in good faith to the Bumper Development Corporation. There were several claimants including the temple, suing through its representative. But was the ruined temple, although recognised under the law of Tamil Nadu, entitled to sue in England?

The Court of Appeal held that since the temple was entitled to sue under the law of Tamil Nadu, and it would not offend English public policy to allow the temple to sue, the duly authorised representative of the temple was entitled to sue in England. Although *Arab Monetary Fund* v *Hashim* was not referred to in Bumper, and the facts of the two cases are very different, they are consistent, the crucial question being whether the body in question was recognised under the law of a recognised state.

## The laws of unrecognised states and governments

It is well recognised that unrecognised states cannot sue or be sued in English courts (*City of Berne* v *Bank of England* (1804) 9 Ves 347), and that the governmental acts and laws of such unrecognised states cannot be recognised in an English court (*Luther* v *Sagor* [1921] 1 KB 456 and *Hesperides Hotels Ltd* v *Aegean Turkish Holidays Ltd* [1978] 1 QB 205(CA)). This principle may be subject to exception where the act of an unrecognised state affects the family or property rights of individuals (*Re James (An Insolvent)* [1977] 1 All ER 364 and *Carl Zeiss Stiftung* v *Rayner & Keeler (No 2)* [1967] 1 AC 853 at 954). The Foreign Secretary issues a certificate (which is regarded as conclusive by the court) indicating whether a particular state is recognised or not by Her Majesty's government.

This rule can operate harshly where individuals are involved, for it is unjust that individual rights should depend upon the vagaries of international politics. Thus the courts have created the *Carl Zeiss Stiftung* exception. This holds that even where the United Kingdom does not recognise the state in question, it may recognise another state as entitled to exercise sovereign authority there. The courts may then consider the unrecognised state as being a subordinate body to that recognised to exercise authority, and recognise its decrees. Thus in *Carl Zeiss Stiftung* the Foreign Office certified that Her Majesty's Government did not recognise the 'German Democratic Republic' (East Germany); it did, however, recognise the USSR as entitled to exercise authority in East Germany. The House of Lords then recognised various East German decrees on the basis that the East German government was a 'subordinate body which the USSR had set up to act on its behalf'.

In 1980 the United Kingdom changed its practice in this regard. It decided that while it would continue to recognise states in accordance with the usual rules, it would no longer recognise governments. When the question of whether a government was recognised arose in legal proceedings, the Foreign Office would no longer issue a certificate, and the nature of HMG's view of a new regime (in a recognised state) would have to be inferred from HMG's dealings, if any, with that government. This change of practice caused some difficulty in *GUR Corp v Trust Bank of Africa Ltd (Government of the Republic of Ciskei, Third Party)* [1986] 3 All ER 449. The case arose from a commercial dispute in which it was sought to make the Republic of Ciskei one of the parties. The Republic of Ciskei is part of South Africa and is considered by South Africa, but by no other state, to be an independent state. The Foreign Office certified that it did not recognise the Republic of Ciskei as a state (either de jure or de facto), but it had 'no formal position regarding the exercise of governmental authority over the territory of Ciskei ... but it made certain representations to the South African government in relation to certain matters that had occurred in Ciskei'. Steyn J at first instance felt that this certificate did not entitle him to hold that HMG recognised the South African government as having sovereign authority over Ciskei, and apply the *Carl Zeiss Stiftung* exception; the Court of Appeal differed and applied the exception. The Court of Appeal felt that it was possible to conclude that the view of HMG was that the South African government was entitled to exercise sovereign authority over Ciskei, and that the various legislative bodies set up in Ciskei were subordinate to South Africa in the same way as the German Democratic Republic was subordinate to the USSR.

*Republic of Somalia v Woodhouse, Drake and Carey (Suisse) SA and Others* (1992) The Times 23 March (QB) (also reported as *The Mary* [1992] 2 Lloyd's Rep 471) established that the courts would *in marginal cases* consider the extent of international recognition (ie by governments other than HMG) that had been extended to the government of that state.

The area of the law has been affected recently by the Foreign Corporations Act 1991. This Act, which has slipped almost unnoticed on to the statute book (it came into force on 25 August 1991), tackles the question of whether the legal personality of a body established or disestablished under 'the laws of a territory which is not at that time a recognised state' should be recognised by the courts of the United Kingdom. Section 1 provides that:

> 'if ... it appears that the laws of that territory are at that time applied by a settled court system in that territory, the question [of the recognition of the corporate status of that body] and any other material question ... shall be determined [and account shall be taken of those laws] as if that territory were a recognised state'.

While this Act is doubtless welcome (for it is unjust that matters of private right should be determined by the vagaries of international politics that in practice govern the recognition of states), it is difficult to see why the Act should be limited in the way that it is. Why should the laws of such territories not be recognised generally? (Cf s1(2) and the wide definition of 'material question'.)

## 2.6 The time factor

Legal systems are dynamic, and the content of their rules will change over time. When a lex causae is chosen through the operation of a choice of law rule, the question arises at what time is the lex causae to be determined. Let us illustrate the point with an example. Suppose the issue is the essential validity of a will of movables: the lex causae is plainly the lex domicilii at the time of death (see Chapter 7, section 7.8 *Essential validity of a will*). But it may be that that legal system has changed its rules since the testator made his will. Now should one 'freeze' the law at the time of execution or apply the changed law to the distribution of the movables?

In principle the position is quite plain: the lex causae as it changes applies. After all, that is the rule that would apply in an entirely domestic case. Frequently, of course, the most significant changes may not be intended to be applicable retrospectively, and then, of course, they will not apply. Furthermore, public policy is the ever-present check to ensure that the local court is not forced to uphold a result that is offensive to the deeply held principles of the lex fori (see section 2.2).

Unfortunately, this principled and clear approach has been rather muddied by the judges who have formulated the applicable rules ambiguously and by writers who have argued that the apparently conflicting cases can be reconciled by the adoption of various complicated theories.

Let us look at some of these cases. *Nelson v Bridport* (1846) 8 Beav 547 supports the principles set out above. The case concerned land in Sicily granted by the King of the Sicilies to Admiral Nelson. Nelson left the land on trust to certain trustees. The applicable law was plainly the lex situs (see Chapter 7, sections 7.8 and 7.9), and the court took it for granted that the relevant changes in the Sicilian law made after Nelson's death applied. In *Phillips v Eyre* (1870) LR 6 QB 1 (see Chapter 6, section 6.2) it was also taken for granted that the lex causae as it changed applied. Similarly, a change in the proper law of the contract discharging or altering the contractual obligations has been upheld in *R v International Trustee for the Protection of Bondholders AG* [1937] AC 500.

But now let us look at some of the more difficult cases: first, *Lynch v Provisional Government of Paraguay* (1871) LR 2 P & D 268. The dictator of Paraguay by will left movable property in England to his mistress. He was domiciled in Paraguay so the matter was governed by Paraguayan law. After his death there was a revolution in Paraguay, and the new government passed a decree depriving the dictator's will of all force. Would the English courts give the mistress the money? They did, but Lord Penzance said that this was because English law applied the law of the domicile 'as it stands at the time of the death'.

This is plainly wrong; the decree should have been denied applicability because it was penal and contrary to public policy, not because the law was 'frozen' at the time of death (see Chapter 2, section 2.2 *Penal laws*). However, *Lynch* was followed in *Re Aganoor's Trusts* (1895) 64 LJ Ch 521 although no clear public policy issue was involved. A testatrix was domiciled in Padua and made a will of movables valid under the law then prevailing there, but after her death the Italian civil code came into force in Padua and forbade the kind of trust substitutions contained in her will. *Lynch* was followed, and the law of Padua frozen at the time of her death was applied. But it seems to me that a fuller analysis of the change in legal regime might have revealed that the Italian law was not intended to apply to existing trusts; but if it was intended to apply, then, apart from public policy (for instance if it was penal), it should have been held to apply. (Note that some writers attempt to explain *Lynch* and *Aganoor* on the ground that they concerned 'once and for all' events (such as making a will), not continuing relations such as a long term contract, for instance, the *Bondholders* case. See Collier, *The Conflict of Laws*, 34–35, adopting Professor Lipstein's views.)

Consider now a further interesting case: *Starkowski v Attorney-General* [1954] AC 155. H1 and W both domiciled in Poland were married by a Roman Catholic priest in Austria in 1945 during the chaos surrounding the end of the war. Such a marriage was not, at the time, valid under Austrian law (because there was no civil ceremony), but a retrospective law was passed in Austria later in 1945 validating such marriages if they were duly registered. The marriage was registered in 1949, but by then the parties had acquired a domicile in England and had separated. In 1950 W married H2, another Pole domiciled in England. Was this second marriage valid or was it bigamous?

The House of Lords held that the first marriage was valid and distinguished, rather equivocally, *Lynch*, restricting it to its different facts. Lord Reid said: 'There is no compelling reason why the reference [in the choice of law rule] should not be to that law as it is when the problem arises for decision.' This is in principle right. But we should never forget public policy. Morris, op cit, 502–503 sets out some of the difficulties:

1. Suppose that the Austrian legislation had invalidated the marriage rather than vice versa; it would probably not have been applied because of the policy to uphold marriages.
2. Suppose that before the marriage had been registered one of the parties had sought an English nullity decree. That would have been readily granted in the circumstances, and the subsequent registration would not render the marriage valid.
3. Suppose that the English marriage had taken place before the Austrian registration? This was left open in *Starkowski*, but it is unlikely that the registration would be effective to validate the first marriage and thus invalidate the second. But in the Canadian case *Ambrose v Ambrose* (1961) 25 DLR (2d) 1 in similar circumstances, *Starkowski* was distinguished.

# 3

# A Special Connecting Factor: Domicile

3.1  What is domicile and why is it important?

3.2  Principles of the law of domicile

3.3  The domicile of dependence

3.4  The domicile of choice

3.5  The domicile of origin

3.6  The domicile of corporations

3.7  The reform of the law of domicile

3.8  Habitual residence and nationality

## 3.1  What is domicile and why is it important?

In our earlier discussion (see Chapter 1, section 1.2) we said that 'domicile' meant simply 'permanent home'. This was an inaccurate statement (although adequate for our purposes then) for domicile means rather 'that legal relationship between a person ... and a territory subject to a distinctive legal system which invokes [that] system as [his] personal law' (per Sir Jocelyn Simon in *Henderson* v *Henderson* [1967] P 77 at 79). It is simply that place considered by the law to be a person's permanent home. Domicile, then, is a legal concept, created by the law and serving the law's purposes. Inevitably, therefore, it tends to be an artificial concept. Thus it will come as no surprise to learn that persons may be domiciled in places other than their actual permanent homes; indeed, a person may be domiciled in a country to which he or she has never been! Moreover, the rules of the law of domicile are sometimes difficult to apply. (The difficulty and complexity of the rules should not be over-estimated, and once the rules are mastered then you should be able to deal with the standard 'domicile tracing' examination question accurately and quickly.)

The prime purpose which the concept serves is to provide a link between an individual and a place, and this allows the law governing at that place to be held applicable to that individual. Domicile, therefore, is simply a particular connecting factor; in many areas of the law the choice of law uses domicile as a connecting factor, and the domicile of the persons concerned (once ascertained) acts as the signpost pointing to the lex causae. One choice of law rule (which we have already discussed: see Chapter 2, section 1.2) that uses domicile as a connecting factor is 'succession to movables of an intestate is governed by the law of his domicile at the time of his death', but domicile is very widely used as a connecting factor. In this book we shall see domicile being used as a connecting factor in the law of succession, in questions of contractual capacity and other aspects of contract. In addition it is widely used in matrimonial and family law. Furthermore, domicile has important fiscal implications, for a person not domiciled in the United Kingdom enjoys a partial immunity from the United Kingdom's tax system. So the concept, and the rules defining it, are obviously important.

There are three types of domicile and although we will be looking at each in detail, this is a useful place to introduce you to them:

1. The domicile of dependence. When a child is born it will usually take as a domicile of dependence the same domicile as its father if it is legitimate and its mother if illegitimate. (This rule has been modified by statute, see section 3.3 below.) Married women used to take the domicile of their husbands as a domicile of dependence, but this rule has been abolished.
2. The domicile of choice. Once the child reaches the age of 16 it can acquire its own domicile by choice. What is required, very broadly, is that the person should take up residence in the new domicile with the intention of residing there permanently.
3. The domicile of origin. This final type of domicile is a curious creature. It is assigned to the child at birth, and it is the domicile of the father, if legitimate, or the domicile of the mother, if illegitimate. At first sight this may appear identical to the child's domicile of dependence (at any rate prior to the statutory modifications to that concept). However, this is not so, for the domicile of origin has an additional quality: the domicile of origin will revive should the person concerned cast off his domicile of choice or dependence. Thus if all else fails, the domicile of origin will be there to ensure that the person concerned is domiciled somewhere. The revival of the domicile of origin is one of the most controversial aspects of the law of domicile, and we will discuss it in full in due course.

You should now have a clear idea of what domicile is, what it is used for, why it is important, as well as the three types of domicile that you will have to master.

## 3.2 Principles of the law of domicile

Morris, *The Conflict of Laws*, 3rd ed, 15–19, isolates four general principles of the law of domicile. If you understand these principles, the law of domicile will become much clearer.

First, the principle that no person can be without a domicile. If persons were so able to contrive their affairs that they were not domiciled anywhere, the choice of law rules that used domicile as a connecting factor would be unworkable. Thus 'it is a settled principle that no man shall be without a domicile' (per Lord Westbury in *Udny* v *Udny* (1869) LR 1 Sc & Div 441). And as we have seen the law goes so far as to create the domicile of origin which is ever ready to revive and fill any gap that may arise.

Secondly, no person can have at the same time more than one domicile. Again, the reason for this principle is clear: if domicile is called upon to play the part of selecting the appropriate legal system to govern a person's affairs, then at any one time he cannot have more than one domicile or else the selection process cannot work.

This principle may have to be qualified slightly. It is possible, for instance, for an English domicilary to decide that he wishes to reside permanently in Australia or other federal state and to take up residence there, without deciding in which of the Australian states he will put down his roots. In principle, such a person remains domiciled in England until he decides in which state he is going to settle (*Bell v Kennedy* (1868) LR 1 Sc & Div 307).

Some Australian statutes (eg the Family Law Act 1975), however, refer to persons being 'domiciled in Australia'. There is no authority on this point, but it may be that in a proper case the courts will hold that such a person was domiciled in England for most purposes, but was domiciled in Australia for the purposes of the Family Law Act 1975 (see Dicey and Morris, 104–105). There are also United Kingdom statutes which refer to 'domicile in the United Kingdom', so the question could easily arise in an acute form before an English court. However, it may be that such statutes will be interpreted as meaning 'domiciled in either England and Wales, Scotland or Northern Ireland'.

Thirdly, the burden of proving a change of domicile lies on those who assert that there has been a change of domicile. The problem is that the burden seems to vary with the type of domicile that is in question. In practice the domicile of origin is very difficult to cast off, while a domicile of dependency is rather easier, and a domicile of choice lies between the two. Moreover, there are dicta that suggest that in proving a change of domicile a higher standard of proof is required than the usual balance of probabilities of ordinary civil proceedings (see *Henderson* v *Henderson* [1967] P 77 at 80). This is unfortunate, for there is little reason for this attitude by the courts; the proof of domicile is an ordinary civil matter and should be governed by the ordinary standard of proof. The upshot of all this is 'that an existing domicile is presumed to continue until it is proved that a new domicile has been acquired' (Morris, op cit, 17).

Fourthly, 'for the purposes of a rule of the conflict of laws, domicile means domicile in the English sense' (Morris, op cit, 18). Thus it is quite possible for an English court to hold that a person is domiciled in France, notwithstanding that the law of France holds that he is domiciled elsewhere. But this is simply an aspect of the general proposition (discussed in Chapter 1, section 1.3 Determination of the connecting factor) that connecting factors are determined by the lex fori.

## 3.3 The domicile of dependence

### Married women

At common law a married woman took the domicile of her husband as a domicile of dependence, and as her husband changed his domicile so her domicile changed irrespective of her wishes and intentions and irrespective of whether she continued to live with her husband or not (*Lord Advocate* v *Jaffey* [1921] 1 AC 147). Indeed, it applied even if the couple where judicially separated (but not divorced) (*Attorney-General for Alberta* v *Cooke* [1926] AC 444). In well-known words Lord Denning called this rule 'the last barbarous relic of a wife's servitude' (*Gray* v *Formosa* [1963] P 259 at 267). Fortunately, the rule has been abolished by s1(1) of the Domicile and Matrimonial Proceedings Act 1973, which provides that:

> 'the domicile of a married woman as at any time after the coming into force of this section [1 January 1974] shall, instead of being the same as her husband's by virtue only of marriage, be ascertained by reference to the same factors as in the case of any individual capable of having an independent domicile.'

The statute is not retrospective (cf Morris, op cit, 28); thus if it is necessary to determine the domicile of a married women at a time prior to 1 January 1974 then the old rule continues to apply. But what about the domicile of a married woman who was married prior to 1 January 1974? Prior to that date she obviously takes the domicile of her husband, and after that date she will be treated as 'an individual capable of having an independent domicile'. But will her domicile change immediately on 1 January 1974? The point may be illustrated by an example. A woman lives happily in England with her husband (who is domiciled in England) until 30 December 1973; she decides to flee with her lover to New Zealand and live there for the rest of her life. Unfortunately, she dies in a car crash on 2 January 1974 on the way to the airport to take a plane to New Zealand. Where does she die domiciled? She has not acquired a domicile of choice in New Zealand (for that requires actual residence there and she has not yet arrived (see section 3.4 below)) but she no longer takes her husband's domicile (in England) as a domicile of dependence.

Such transitional cases are dealt with in s1(2) which provides that where:

> 'immediately before this section came into force a woman was married and then had her husband's domicile by dependence, she is to be treated as retaining that domicile (as a domicile of choice, if it is not also her domicile of origin) unless and until it is changed by acquisition or revival of another domicile either on or after the coming into force of this section'.

Thus in broad terms s1(2) provides that the husband's domicile persists as a domicile of choice until she acquires a new domicile. In our example, therefore, the woman would die domiciled in England. On the other hand, if the woman had had a domicile of origin in New Zealand and had left England on 30 December 1973 intending never to return but had died on 2 January in a plane crash at Singapore on her way to New Zealand then her domicile of origin would revive and she would die domiciled in New Zealand. This would be an example of a change in domicile by 'revival of another domicile either on or after the coming into force of this section'.

Section 1(2) has been before the courts in *IRC v Duchess of Portland* [1982] Ch 314. What had happened there was that a woman with a domicile of origin in Quebec had married the Duke of Portland who was a domiciled Englishman. She maintained strong links with Quebec, returning there for summer holidays, kept a house there and remained a Canadian citizen. She intended to return permanently to Quebec should her husband predecease her, and her husband had agreed to retire to Quebec. In a dispute with the Inland Revenue she claimed that she had acquired a domicile of choice in Quebec during her summer visit in 1974, but the Revenue insisted that she remained domiciled in England (and therefore liable to more tax). Nourse J held that the clear terms of s1(2) required him to treat the Duchess as if she had a domicile of choice in England, and a domicile of choice can only be abandoned by ceasing to reside there and by ceasing to intend to reside there. But the Duchess did not cease to reside in England simply by taking a summer holiday in Quebec, and although she intended to return permanently to Quebec in due course her intention in 1974 was just to spend the summer there. So she retained her domicile in England.

Had the Duchess been married after 1 January 1974 then almost certainly she would not have had the necessary intention to remain in England permanently to acquire a domicile in England; she would have remained domiciled in Quebec. Thus women married before 1 January 1974 are less favourably treated than women married after. Another difficulty faced by the Duchess was the fact that the statute specified that the previous domicile of a person in her position persisted as a 'domicile of choice'; had it persisted as a domicile of dependence then she would have been able more easily to rid herself of it, for as we have seen domiciles of dependence are more easily cast off than domiciles of choice.

## Children: the common law

The general rule of the common law is that a child acquires upon birth the domicile of its father, if legitimate (*Re Duleep Singh* (1890) 6 TLR 385; *Henderson* v *Henderson* [1967] P 77), or the domicile of its mother, if illegitimate (*Potinger* v *Wrightman* (1817) 3 Mer 67), as a domicile of dependence. This domicile will coincide with the child's domicile of origin, but whereas the latter is fixed at birth for all time, the domicile of dependence will change as the domicile of the person upon whom the child is dependent changes. Thus, to give an example, a legitimate child born in England of a father domiciled in France will acquire a domicile of origin in France and a domicile of dependence in France. But should the father acquire a domicile of choice in New York, the child will acquire a domicile of dependence in New York although its domicile of origin will remain French.

Other than in the special cases to be discussed below this general rule is not subject to any common law exception. However, there are two points to be noted. First, although there is no English authority, there is the Northern Irish case of *Hope v Hope* [1968] NI 1 in which it was held that where a father has totally abdicated his responsibility for the child and custody had been granted to the mother, the child should cease to follow the father's domicile.

Secondly, this general rule begs the question of how is it to be determined whether a child is legitimate or not. In principle, legitimacy is a matter for the personal law, and that is generally governed by the lex domicilii. But how can we use the lex domicilii to determine domicile? You should be aware of this slippery logical problem. There is no English authority dealing with it, but the best way of tackling it is probably to determine the validity of the parents' marriage in accordance with the normal rules (which depend inter alia upon the domicile of the parents, not that of the child), and then to hold the child legitimate if the marriage is valid and illegitimate otherwise. This is not an ideal solution, however, for there are occasions upon which the child is legitimate even though the parents' marriage is not valid.

Of course, the general rule did not cover all cases; and we must deal with some special cases:

1. Legitimated children, ie children who are born illegitimate but become legitimate through the subsequent marriage of their parents, are thought to take the domicile of their mothers until the legitimation takes effect after which they take the domicile of their father. There is scant judicial authority on this point but this is the view favoured by Dicey and Morris (at 143–145).

2. Fatherless children, ie legitimate children whose father has died, are treated as illegitimate; they follow the domicile of their mother. However, this rule is less strictly applied than the rule that legitimate children whose fathers are still alive follow the domicile of their father.

   Thus in *Re Beaumont* [1893] 3 Ch 490 it was said:

   'The change in the domicile of an infant which ... may follow from a change of domicile on the part of the mother, is not to be regarded as a necessary consequence of a change of the mother's domicile, but as the result of the exercise by her of a power vested in her for the welfare of the infants, which, in their interest, she may abstain from exercising, even when she changes her own domicile.'

   What happened in *Re Beaumont* was that a widow who (with her first husband) was domiciled in Scotland remarried and with her second husband moved to England where he was domiciled. Her domicile thus changed from Scotland to England. However, the court held that the one child of the first marriage who did not move south to England but was sent by its mother to live with an aunt in Scotland continued to be domiciled in Scotland.

This is an awkward and ill-defined rule. It is not clear whether a mother can by means of this exception only preserve a domicile that would otherwise change (as was the case in *Re Beaumont* itself) or whether the mother could by sending a child away change the domicile of the child. Furthermore, it seems to be illogical that the wife should have this power to exercise in the interests of the child, but the father should have no such power – the child being bound to follow his domicile.

3. Orphans and illegitimate children whose mother has died: the rule here is far from clear, but it appears to be that the child's domicile cannot be changed; it remains as it was when the parent upon whom it depended for its domicile died. There are suggestions that its guardian may have the power to change its domicile, but this is mere speculation. (See Dicey and Morris, 135–136).
4. Adopted children are treated as the legitimate children of their adoptive parents (Children Act 1975, s8; Adoption Act 1976, s39).

## Children: the s4 exception and miscellaneous matters

The rules outlined above have been substantially modified by the provisions of s4(1) and (2) of the Domicile and Matrimonial Proceedings Act 1973. Let us illustrate the mischief that this act aimed to rectify. H and W, both domiciled in Quebec, might marry and have a child, C. H and W might then divorce, and W, taking C, with her may come to England and acquire a domicile here. H may then also change his domicile to New York. If the rules were strictly applied, C would be domiciled in New York – a place he or she had never been to – and would have a different domicile to that of his or her mother (with whom he or she lived). This sort of problem was made more acute by the enactment of s1 (discussed above) for now it was no longer necessary for H and W to divorce before they acquired different domiciles.

Thus s4 creates special rules for determining the dependent domiciles of children whose parents are living apart or were living apart when the mother died. The scheme of the section is to make the domicile of such a child depend upon the parent where the child has its home. The central provision, thus, is the following: a child whose parents are 'living apart' shall have the same domicile as his mother, if 'he then has his home with her and has no home with his father'. This maternal domicile persists, even after the child has ceased to have a home with his mother, provided that 'he has not since had a home with his father'. Where the mother has died, the child, if he has had a s4 domicile, retains his dead mother's domicile provided that 'he has not since had a home with his father'.

Where s4 does not apply (because for instance the parents are not living apart, or because the child has never had a home with either parent) then the common law rules outlined above continue to apply. In fact the slight bias in favour of the mother is fortified by s4(4) which provides that nothing 'in this section prejudices any existing rule of law ... in which a child's domicile is regarded as being, by dependence, that of his mother'. It should be noted too that the principle of *Re Beaumont* survives s4. (Check that you understand why this is so.)

Section 4 is not retroactive, so the domicile of children prior to 1 January 1974 is determined using the common law rules alone. And s3(1) provides that a person ceases to be a child and becomes capable of having an independent domicile when 'he attains the age of sixteen or marries'.

## The insane

The rule is that the insane retain the domicile that they had when they became insane. The reason for this is that they cannot on account of their condition exercise their will and thus cannot discard or acquire a domicile. This reasoning does not apply to insane persons who have domiciles of dependence – eg an insane child – so their domiciles can be changed in the normal way. Indeed, some of the cases go further and hold that the parent retains the power to change the insane child's domicile even after he or she has reached the age of sixteen (*Re G* [1966] NZLR 1028). Given modern recognition of the range and complexity of mental disorders, it is surely true that this crude rule is due for reform; it is more difficult to say, however, how it should be reformed.

## 3.4 The domicile of choice

Every independent person (that is someone over the age of 16 or any married person (s3 of the Domicile and Matrimonial Proceedings Act 1973) and who is not insane) can acquire a new domicile, a domicile of choice, by his or her own actions. What is required is that he or she should take up residence in the new domicile with the intention of remaining there permanently. (As we shall see, it may be that the intention to remain there indefinitely rather than permanently may be sufficient.) Each of these elements, residence and intention, needs to be analysed separately, although they are sometimes difficult to keep apart.

### The requirement of residence (sometimes called factum)

It is not necessary to establish a residence of any length to acquire a domicile of choice, but it must be residence in pursuance of the intention to settle permanently. As Lord Chelmsford said in *Bell v Kennedy* (1868) LR 1 Sc & Div 307 at 319, 'If the intention of permanently residing in a place exists, [then] residence in pursuance of that intention, however short, will establish a domicile.' One spectacular example of this is the American case of *White v Tennant* 31 WVa 790; 8 SE 596 (1888).

There residence in the new domicile of one afternoon (before returning to his old domicile because of illness) was held sufficient. Thus an immigrant (provided that he intends to settle permanently in the new country) acquires his new domicile as soon as he steps onto that new country's soil. It is not necessary that he buy or rent a home. It seems clear, however, that the residence must be lawful (*Puttick* v *Attorney-General* [1980] Fam 1). The illegal immigrant, therefore, cannot acquire a domicile of choice in the country to which he emigrates.

In *Plummer* v *IRC* [1988] 1 WLR 292; [1988] 1 All ER 97 the domicile of a person who was resident in two places was discussed. Elizabeth Plummer's domicile was in issue for income tax purposes. She had been born in England of English parents in 1965, but in 1980 her mother and young sister had moved permanently to Guernsey, and her father, who worked in London, spent the weekends and holidays in Guernsey as well. Elizabeth Plummer remained in England first as a schoolgirl and then as a student at London University. However, whenever possible she went to Guernsey for weekends and holidays and formed a strong attachment to the island, intending to settle there permanently once her education was complete. She had a Guernsey bank account, a Guernsey driver's licence and a Guernsey passport. She seemed to be resident in both Guernsey and England. But where was she domiciled: England or Guernsey? Although it was possible for a person to acquire a new domicile of choice in a new country (ie Guernsey) without ceasing to be resident in their domicile of origin (ie England), that person had to establish that their residence in the new country was their chief residence (Hoffman J held). This Ms Plummer had failed to do.

## The requirement of intention (sometimes called animus)

The intention of a person in regard to future residence in a country in which he is presently residing will be found to be one of the following four types:

First, an intention to reside for a definite period, eg for the next six months, and then leave.

Secondly, an intention to reside in the country until a definite purpose is achieved, eg until a particular piece of work is completed, and then to leave.

Thirdly, an intention to reside in the country for an indefinite period, ie until and unless something, the happening of which is uncertain, occurs to induce that person to leave.

Fourthly, an intention to reside forever come what may.

(This analysis is based on that of Walter Pollack QC in (1933) 50 *SALJ* 449, (1934) 51 *SALJ* 1.)

Now it is quite plain that the first two states of mind are insufficient to acquire a domicile of choice (*Attorney-General* v *Rowe* (1862) 1 H & C 31 (first state) and *Qureshi* v *Qureshi* [1972] Fam 173 (second state)), and that the fourth state of mind is sufficient. The question is whether the third state of mind is sufficient to acquire a domicile of choice.

The orthodox English law view is that the third state of mind is not sufficient, but there are some indications that certain types of third state may not prevent the acquisition of a domicile of choice. The leading case is still the bizarre one of *Winans* v *Attorney-General* [1904] AC 287. Winans was an eccentric American millionaire who hated England. He had, for instance, worked against British interests in the Crimean war. This dislike of England did not, however, prevent him from spending most of the last 37 years of his life in England. But he spent that time caring for his health and plotting to wrest Britain's predominance in shipping away from her. He worked hard at designing a huge fleet of cigar-shaped vessels, which would fly the United States flag and dominate the shipping world. He dreamt of returning to the United States to direct and control this fleet from a dock in Maryland. The House of Lords (Lord Lindley dissenting) held he had not acquired a domicile of choice in England. Lord Macnaghten said that when Winans came to England 'he was a sojourner and a stranger, and he was ... a sojourner and stranger in it when he died ... I think up to the very last he had an expectation or hope of returning to America and seeing his grand schemes inaugurated ...'. Thus Winans's belief that his grandiose schemes might triumph, and that then he would return to America, prevented him from acquiring a domicile in England.

A further case which is strongly against the third state of mind as being sufficient is *Ramsey* v *Royal Liverpool Infirmary* [1930] AC 588. This was the case of George Bowie, a Scot, who lived in Liverpool for 35 years and did not even return to Scotland to attend his mother's funeral, but was held to have died domiciled in Scotland! These are old cases, but the attitude evinced by them lives on. Thus in *IRC* v *Bullock* [1976] 1 WLR 1178 the Court of Appeal held that Group Captain Bullock had not acquired a domicile of choice in England (but retained his domicile in his native Canada) notwithstanding residence in England for nigh on 40 years, because he intended to return to Canada on the death of his wife, who was English.

From these cases it appears that the contemplation of any event, however remote, upon which residence would cease, will prevent the acquisition of a domicile of choice.

On the other hand, in *Attorney-General* v *Pottinger* (1861) 30 LJE 284 at 292 Baron Bramwell said:

> 'There is not a man who has not contingent intentions to do something that would be very much to his benefit if the occasion arises. But if every such intention or expression of opinion prevented a man from having a fixed domicile, no man would ever have a domicile at all except his domicile of origin.'

Thus there are cases in which the contemplation of a remote or doubtful contingency upon the occurrence of which residence would cease has not prevented the acquisition of a domicile of choice. An intention to move, if he made a fortune, did not prevent the propositus (simply the person we are talking about) from acquiring a domicile in *Doucet* v *Geoghegan* (1878) 9 Ch D 441; nor did an intention to move if his mistress died prevent the propositus from acquiring a domicile in

*Anderson* v *Laneuville* (1854) 9 Moo PC 325. And more recently, in *Re Furse* [1980] 3 All ER 838, an American who had worked on a farm in England for 39 years, but who intended to return to America if his health prevented him from working on the farm, was held to have acquired a domicile in England.

These cases show how difficult it is to determine whether a particular contingency is sufficiently clear and definite to prevent the acquisition of a domicile of choice. *In the Estate of Fuld* [1968] P 675 Scarman J said that what was required was 'a clearly foreseen and reasonably anticipated contingency'. But with respect this is not very helpful: were Winans's dreams of return to the United States reasonably anticipated, and was the death of a mistress not clearly foreseen?

## Proof of intention

In *Drevon v Drevon* (1834) 34 LJ Ch 129 at 133 Kindersley V-C said:

'There is no act, no circumstances in a man's life, however trivial it may be in itself, which ought to be left out of consideration in trying the question whether there was an intention to change domicile. A trivial act might possibly be of more weight with regard to determining this question than an act which was of more importance to a man in his lifetime.'

The result is, as we have seen in cases such as *Winans,* that determination of the necessary intention requires long and frequently fruitless investigations into all aspects of a person's life. What were his hopes, ambitions, desires and dreams?

Some points, though, are clear. First, long residence will of itself not provide sufficient evidence of the requisite intention, and secondly, the declarations of the propositus, either in oral evidence before the court or in written evidence admissible under one of the exceptions to the hearsay rule, are treated with some scepticism. The reason for this is simply that the propositus may easily be speaking in his own interests, ie he will have an ulterior reason for wishing to be domiciled in one place rather than another. So such declarations are best backed up with other consistent evidence.

## Abandonment of a domicile of choice

Dicey and Morris's rule 13(1) puts the position clearly:

'A person abandons a domicile of choice in a country by ceasing to reside there and by ceasing to intend to reside there permanently or indefinitely, and not otherwise.'

(This rule was specifically approved in *IRC* v *Duchess of Portland.*)

Thus it is clear that when a person ceases to reside in his country of domicile he does not cease to be domiciled there for so long as he intends to return for permanent residence; and on the other hand, even if he decides to leave and settle elsewhere, he remains domiciled there until he actually leaves and ceases to reside. This last point may be illustrated by *In the Goods of Raffenel* (1863) 3 Sw & Tr 49.

There a woman with a domicile of origin in England acquired a domicile in France (not in fact a domicile of choice but a domicile of dependency through her marriage, but the principle is the same). On the death of her husband she decided to leave France and return permanently to England, but she died as she was about to board the Channel steamer for England. She was held not to have abandoned her French domicile.

When a domicile of choice is abandoned then one of two things happens. Either a new domicile of choice is acquired, or the domicile of origin revives; we will return to this in discussing the domicile of origin.

## Domicile of choice: special cases

Thus far we have discussed the domicile of choice on the assumption that the person concerned was free to move and to form his intentions as he wished. As Lord Westbury said in *Udny* v *Udny* (1869) LR 1 Sc & Div 441 (at 458):

> 'There must be a residence freely chosen, and not prescribed or dictated by any external necessity, such as the duties of office, the demands of creditors, or the relief of illness.'

We now move on to discuss the domicile of choice of persons whose freedom is impinged upon by external factors. The harsh approach of Lord Westbury would appear to have been tempered in the more modern cases.

1. Prisoners apparently, unless transported or exiled for life, retain the domicile they had prior to confinement and do not acquire a domicile in their place of imprisonment (*Re the late Emperor Napoleon Bonaparte* (1853) 2 Rob Eccl 606). This seems harsh; if the prisoner is so impressed by the place where he is imprisoned there seems to be no reason why he should not be able to form the intention to acquire a domicile there, ie he intends to remain there after his release.

2. Refugees depend upon circumstances. If they intend to return to the country from which they have fled once political conditions change, then they retain their domicile there (*Re Lloyd Evans* [1947] Ch 695). Of course, they may give up all hope of returning home and intend to settle in the country to which they have fled, in which case they acquire a domicile there (*May* v *May* [1943] 2 All ER 146).

3. Fugitives from justice have not voluntarily chosen their new countries of residence. In *Re Martin* [1900] P 211 a French professor who had committed a crime in France fled to England and remained there for 20 years. Two years after the French period of prescription for that crime had expired he returned to France. It was held by the Court of Appeal (Lindley LJ dissenting) that he acquired a domicile in England six years after he arrived here. Persons fleeing to escape their creditors are treated similarly.

4. Invalids pose a difficult problem. A mortally ill person may move to a different country because he is told that his suffering will be less in that climate or that he

will live longer. Such a person fulfils all the requirements for acquiring a domicile of choice in that different country; he resides there and intends to do so for the rest of his life. But to accord him a domicile there has been described as 'revolting to common sense and the common feelings of humanity' (*Moorhouse* v *Lord* (1863) 10 Cas 272 at 292). On the other hand, in *Hoskins* v *Mathews* (1855) 8 DM & G 13 a man who settled in Tuscany because he thought that the warm climate would benefit his spinal injury was held to be 'exercising a preference and not acting upon a necessity'; thus he acquired a domicile in Tuscany.

5. Employees, diplomats, and soldiers: such persons who have to reside in a particular country at the whim of their employer or commanding officer used to be thought to be unable to change their domicile to that country. However, the better view (confirmed by cases such as *Donaldson* v *Donaldson* [1949] P 363 and *Naville* v *Naville* 1957 (1) SA 280) is that it depends upon the circumstances. Where, for instance, a soldier becomes very fond of the place where he is posted there is no reason why he should not be domiciled there even if he knows that he may be posted elsewhere (and will then face the choice of leaving the army or only being able to return on his retirement).

## 3.5 The domicile of origin

The first important thing to understand about the domicile of origin is that while everyone has a domicile of origin, that domicile is frequently inoperative, ie it is not used as a connecting factor to select the appropriate legal system. The reason for this is that generally the person concerned will have a domicile of dependence or a domicile of choice to which reference will be made in preference to the domicile of origin. The domicile of origin therefore is the domicile of 'last resort'; it is only used when there is no other domicile available. None the less, as we shall see, it is often difficult to shake off an operative domicile of origin and acquire some other domicile.

The central rule about the domicile of origin is that a legitimate child acquires as a domicile of origin the domicile of his father at the time of his birth, while an illegitimate child acquires the domicile of his mother. This rule is subject to the same logical difficulty discussed in regard to the domicile of dependence of children (see section 3.3 *Children: the common law*), in that one may wish to know the domicile of the propositus in order to determine whether he is legitimate or not. It is suggested that this difficulty should be resolved in the same way.

This central rule will, of course, not work in the case of foundlings or other children whose parents' domicile is quite unknown. Thus here the consensus seems to be that the child takes as a domicile of origin the country in which it is found (Dicey and Morris, at 108–109). Unlike the domicile of dependence the domicile of origin is fixed for all time and cannot be changed. There is, however, one exception to this rule: adopted children are treated as if born to the adoptive parents in wedlock (Children Act 1975, s8 and Schedule 1); thus the adopted child will on adoption have its domicile of origin changed to that of its adoptive father at the time of its birth.

## The tenacity of the domicile of origin

Both *Winans* v *Attorney-General* and *Ramsey* v *Royal Liverpool Infirmary* were cases in which what was in dispute was whether a particular person had successfully abandoned a domicile of origin and acquired a domicile of choice elsewhere. And we can see from those cases how reluctant the courts were to allow such a change. In fact it is clear that once a propositus has acquired a domicile of choice, it is easier for him to discard that domicile and acquire another domicile of choice than it is for him to discard a domicile of origin and acquire a domicile of choice. As Lord Macnaghten said in *Winans* the 'character [of the domicile of origin] is more enduring, its hold stronger, and less easily shaken off'.

The reason for this great tenacity of the domicile of origin is to be found in the history of the British Empire. During the 19th century (and for much of the 20th) men and women with English domiciles of origin would spend most of their lives in far-flung corners of the globe in the service of the Crown or British commercial interests. Yet they would expect that English law would continue to govern their personal affairs, rather than the law of the country in which they had spent most of their lives. The tenacity of the domicile of origin achieved this end by ensuring that they only rarely lost the English domicile, and thus the mantle of English law was cast over those distant children of Empire. Of course such tenaciousness is unnecessary in the changed circumstances of the 20th century, although there is little sign that the judges are bringing about the requisite changes in the law.

One aspect of the tenaciousness of the domicile of origin is the rule that it cannot be abandoned, but can only be lost by the acquisition of a domicile of choice (*Bell* v *Kennedy* (1868) LR 1 Sc & Div 307). But although some of the textbooks make great play of this rule (cf Morris, op cit, 16) it is in fact simply the obverse of the rule that where there is no other domicile applicable the domicile of origin will revive. The reason for this is that unless a domicile of choice is acquired to displace the domicile of origin, there is no domicile that can govern the propositus, hence his domicile of origin would in any event revive. It is thus now time to discuss the revival of the domicile of origin in detail.

## The revival of the domicile of origin

In *Udny* v *Udny* Lord Westbury held that:

> 'As the domicile of origin is a creature of law, and independent of the will of the party, it would be inconsistent with the principles on which it is by law created and ascribed, to suppose that it is capable of being by the mere act of the party, entirely obliterated and extinguished. It revives and exists whenever there is no other domicile ...'.

Since then it has been clear that in English law, the domicile of origin has this 'gap-filling' role and ensures that the principle that no man is ever without a domicile is upheld (see Chapter 2, section 2.2 above).

The doctrine of revival, however, has been much criticised as artificial. As Morris writes (op cit, 16):

> 'If, for instance, an Englishman emigrates to New York at the age of twenty five, remains there for the next forty years and then decides to retire to California, but is killed in an air crash en route, it does not make much sense to hold that he died domiciled in England, [because he has clearly cast off his New York domicile (if he ever had one), his English domicile of origin revives] especially as an American court would undoubtedly hold that he died domiciled in New York.'

It is easy to construct further examples in which a propositus has no substantial connection with his domicile of origin and it is quite plainly an even more inappropriate law to govern his affairs. Take Morris's example and suppose that the propositus was actually born in New York but at that time his father was still domiciled in England (because although he had decided to settle in the United States he was uncertain which state he was going to make his permanent home); that propositus dies domiciled in England although he might never have been there and although even his father's connections with England were tenuous and ancient.

As an alternative it is sometimes suggested that the American rule of the persistence of the last domicile (even if a decision has been taken to leave that place and never to return) should apply. This rule may be illustrated by the case of *Re Jones' Estate* (1921) 192 Iowa 78. Here Jones, who had a Welsh domicile of origin, emigrated to the USA in flight from a girl who was pregnant by him. There he acquired considerable property and a domicile of choice in Iowa. After the death of his wife (not the Welsh girl) he decided to return to Wales for good but, as luck would have it, took passage to England in the Lusitania. He drowned when that vessel was torpedoed by German submarines. Had an English court had to decide where he was domiciled, it would have said that he had cast off his Iowa domicile of choice and that his Welsh domicile of origin revived; hence he died domiciled in Wales. The Iowa court, however, held that his domicile of choice in Iowa persisted notwithstanding his clear intention to cast it off, and thus he died domiciled in Iowa. It is far from obvious that this domicile was, in the circumstances, more appropriate than the Welsh domicile of origin. (Although it did have the serendipitous outcome that his illegitimate Welsh daughter was entitled to his property!)

Two points may be made. First, both the rule of persistence and the rule of revival are artificial and may sometimes lead to inappropriate results. But this is inevitable, because we are concerned with the filling of gaps when the ordinary rules have failed. But, secondly the propositus must have some substantial link with his last domicile (even if he has decided to leave) while he may have no link at all with his domicile of origin. Thus on balance the rule of persistence is likely to lead to more appropriate results.

## 3.6 The domicile of corporations

Corporations are domiciled in their place of incorporation. This domicile cannot be changed, even if the corporation carries on its business elsewhere (*Gasque* v *IRC* [1940] 2 KB 80).

## 3.7 The reform of the law of domicile

The rules that have been outlined in this chapter have been much criticised by academic writers and by judges, yet little has been done to change them. The major grounds of criticism have been the obvious ones: first, it is often difficult to tell where a particular person is domiciled. It can also be very expensive (especially when one has to go through his entire life history in an attempt to find out). Secondly, the application of these rules often means that persons are assigned artificial domiciles in countries with which they have very few links. This consideration should not be overestimated; the cases that reach the law reports are the unusual or bizarre ones, and in many cases the rules work well.

Various attempts have been made to reform the law of domicile, and the Domicile and Matrimonial Proceedings Act 1973 has made substantial progress. However, attempts to tackle the domicile of choice and to render it easier to acquire have always failed, chiefly because the foreign business community in London (the members of which are seldom domiciled in England even if they have lived here for a very long time) makes strong representations about the fact that if it were easier to acquire domiciles of choice it would lose their partial immunity from the United Kingdom's taxation laws.

The most recent proposals for reform will be found in Law Commission Working Paper No 88 (1985). The recommendations in the Working Paper are in broad terms as follows:

1. That the domicile of origin should be abolished (and with it the doctrine of revival).
2. The domicile of any person under sixteen shall be the mother's domicile if the child has its home with both parents; but if it has its home with only one parent, then the domicile of that parent; if the child has its home with neither parent then it is domiciled in the country with which it has the closest connection.
3. That the last domicile should persist until a new one is acquired (this fits in with the abolition of the revival doctrine), and that the intention necessary to acquire a new domicile should be that of indefinite residence, and that that intention should be presumed after continual residence for seven years after reaching the age of 16.
4. That the insane (and others incapax) should be domiciled in that country with which they have the closest connection.

Broadly speaking the Law Commission has accepted the recommendations in the above Working Paper and has prepared a draft Domicile Bill. It appears, therefore, that we are moving towards reform in this area along the lines suggested.

## 3.8 Habitual residence and nationality

The above two concepts are sometimes put forward, and have been adopted in some legal systems, as alternatives to domicile as the determinants of the personal law. Furthermore, specific reference is made to them in particular English statutes. Thus we may consider each in turn.

Nationality has the distinct advantage over domicile that it is usually easy to determine what a person's nationality is by simply applying the law of the particular state that grants, or is alleged to grant, nationality to that person. However, there are stateless persons who have no nationality but there must be some law that applies to them. Here domicile has the edge, for no man (or woman) can be without a domicile (see section 3.2 above). Moreover, it is quite possible for a person to be a national of more than one country; thus using nationality in these circumstances will not work. Furthermore, the fact that a person is, say, a United States citizen does not indicate whether the law applicable to him is that of New York, California or one of the other 50 states. These are the obvious practical difficulties to replacing domicile by nationality, but there is the further point of policy: does English law as a matter of policy wish to have political allegiance (viz nationality) determining matters of personal law?

The concept of 'habitual residence' has been much used since the Second World War in the Hague international conventions designed to unify the rules of the conflict of laws in different countries. The concept makes an appearance in a number of English statutes (see Chapter 7, section 7.8). Morris 'hazard[s] the guess that it means much the same thing as domicile minus the artificial elements of that concept' (at 35). It was defined, not very usefully, in *Cruse v Chittum* [1974] 2 All ER 940 as 'regular physical presence which must endure for some time' but did not require the same intention that was necessary to acquire a domicile. It does not require continual presence and can continue despite absence for relatively long periods of time. In *R v Barnet London Borough, ex parte Nilish Shah* [1983] 2 AC 309 the House of Lords equated 'ordinary residence' and 'habitual residence'.

# 4

# Jurisdiction in Personam

## 4.1 General principles

### The meaning of jurisdiction

There are some disputes, for example a dispute between two Tibetans over a contract to be performed in Tibet, that concern parties and matters so remote from England and the English legal system, that English law denies to the courts the right to decide such cases (save in special circumstances). In this chapter we will be seeking to determine when the English courts have the right to decide certain disputes; or, in other words, what are the limits of their jurisdiction? The topic is crucial to the conflict of laws, for problems of jurisdiction generally only arise in cases with an international element, and, moreover, unless the court has jurisdiction, then there is no point in going into questions of choice of law.

In this chapter we will be concerned with jurisdiction in personam, ie jurisdiction that is exercised against a particular person (for example, the defendant in a tort claim or action for breach of contract) and not with the jurisdiction in rem (where the dispute is over a particular thing such as a ship in an Admiralty action in rem). Nor will we be concerned with jurisdiction in matters such as probate, administration of estates, matrimonial causes and the like. Save for Admiralty actions in rem (which lie beyond the scope of this book), English law always exercises jurisdiction over persons rather than things. Note, however, that the courts sometimes refuse to exercise their jurisdiction over property outside England even though they have jurisdiction over the persons involved. This is discussed in Chapter 7, section 7.2.

## *The liberality and simplicity of the common law of jurisdiction*

Until relatively recently, the law of jurisdiction in personam in England was liberal and relatively simple. It was liberal in the sense that the English courts would exercise jurisdiction over a wide range of persons in circumstances in which the courts of most other countries would deny that they had jurisdiction. The essential proposition was that the English courts had jurisdiction over anyone who was present within the realm, and in practice this means that the High Court had jurisdiction over anyone who is validly served with a writ within England. It was not necessary that the matter in dispute should have anything to do with England or English law; and it was not necessary that either of the parties should be resident or domiciled in England: they simply had to be in England when the writ was served. The liberality of this principle may be illustrated by the case of *Maharanee of Baroda* v *Wildenstein* [1972] 2 QB 283. Here the plaintiff was an Indian princess resident in France and the defendant was an international art dealer; the dispute was over a sale (whose proper law was French) of a picture reputed to have been painted by the French artist Bouchier. Obviously neither of the parties nor the dispute had anything to do with England. However, the defendant came to England briefly in order to attend the races and he was served with a writ while at the race course. It was held that the English court had jurisdiction.

The liberality of the approach of the English courts is shown by two further principles. First, where the parties submit to the jurisdiction of the English courts, then the courts generally have jurisdiction even if the dispute and the parties have nothing to do with England. And, secondly, where the defendant was outside England (so that a writ could not be served on him in the ordinary way) the plaintiff could apply to the court for leave (under RSC O.11) to serve the writ outside the jurisdiction. Whether leave was granted was a matter in the discretion of the court, but if the court granted leave and the writ was served outside the jurisdiction then, once more, the English court had jurisdiction. Some quite complex rules determine how the court will exercise its discretion to allow service outside the jurisdiction. We will consider them below in section 4.2 *Where leave is given under RSC O.11 r1(1)* below.

The liberality of the English jurisdictional rules is characteristic of English law. Most other legal systems require that there should either be some substantial link between the defendant and the forum (in the form of residence or domicile) or between the dispute and the forum (in that crucial events in the dispute took place within the forum) before the courts of the forum have jurisdiction. They do not consider mere presence within the jurisdiction as sufficient of a link to give the courts jurisdiction. This point should not, however, be over-stressed, for other legal systems also have 'exorbitant' rules of jurisdiction and exercise jurisdiction where the matter in dispute has little link with the forum. French law, for instance, gives French courts jurisdiction in any case where the plaintiff is French.

## *The Civil Jurisdiction and Judgments Act 1982*

The relative simplicity of the English rules is shown by the fact that it has been possible to outline the basic principles in two short paragraphs. However, for good or ill, this simplicity has now been stripped away by the coming into force of the Civil Jurisdiction and Judgments Act 1982. The prime purpose of this Act is to implement the Brussels Convention of 1968 on Jurisdiction and the Enforcement of Judgments in Civil and Commercial Matters as amended by the Accession Convention of 1978.

A few words of explanation about these various conventions seems required. The Brussels Convention was agreed between the original six members of the EEC. These states were in fact bound by article 220 of the Treaty of Rome (the treaty that set up the EEC (now the EC) to enter into such a convention in regard to the recognition of foreign judgments (see Chapter 1, section 1.1 *The scope of the conflict of laws*), but the Brussels Convention went further than this and for reasons that will become clear in due course extended far into the area of jurisdiction too. Hence its present importance to us.

It was laid down in the Brussels Convention that any state which subsequently joined the community (such as the UK, Eire, Denmark and Greece (and now Spain and Portugal too), was to be bound by its terms. However, when the UK, Eire and Denmark joined, an Accession Convention was negotiated which made a number of changes to the Brussels Convention.

A further international document that should be mentioned here is the Protocol on Interpretation of 1971 which sets out how the Convention is to be interpreted. The mechanism created to ensure uniform interpretation throughout the EC is that of referring questions of interpretation to the European Court in Brussels.

There have been two recent developments affecting the legislative background to the Brussels Convention; we should note both of them. First was the enactment of the Civil Jurisdiction and Judgments Act 1991. This Act (by s1(1)) gives force of law to the Lugano Convention of 1988, and it came into force in May 1992 (SI 1992/745).

The purpose of the Lugano Convention (which is now (as a result of s1(3) of the 1991 Act) to be found in Schedule 3C of the Civil Jurisdiction and Judgments Act 1982) is to extend the principles of the Brussels Convention to the European Free Trade Association (EFTA), so that the advantages of a uniform law of jurisdiction and the easy enforcement of judgments would extend beyond the EC to the EFTA states too. (The EFTA states are Austria, Finland, Norway, Iceland, Sweden and Switzerland.) The central provisions of the Lugano Convention are essentially similar (indeed, often identical) to those of the Brussels Convention, but there are important differences. There is, for instance, no mechanism (such as reference to the European Court similar to that set up in the 1971 Protocol (to the Brussels Convention) on Interpretation) to ensure that the Convention is uniformly interpreted. However, in Protocol 2 of the Lugano Convention the parties undertake to 'pay due account to the [relevant] principles laid down ... by the courts of other Contracting States'. Moreover, a mechanism is set up for the exchange of information about relevant judgments concerning the Lugano Convention and the Brussels Convention. Such significant differences as remain between the Brussels Convention and the Lugano Convention are dealt with below in Chapter 4, section 4.3 *The remaining differences between the Brussels and Lugano Conventions ...*, as well as the relationship between them.

The second important legislative change (which came into force on 1 December 1991), was the amendment of the Brussels Convention by the San Sebastian Convention of 1989. This Convention agreed between the 12 members of the EC was designed to 'make adjustments' to the Brussels Convention so that Spain and Portugal could accede to the Brussels Convention. These 'adjustments' would in the normal course of events be technical and transitional and of no particular interest to us. However, the San Sebastian Convention goes somewhat further than this for the following reason: the Lugano Convention (which was agreed in 1988 before the San Sebastian Convention in 1989) followed the principles of the Brussels Convention but incorporated improvements to several of the central articles of the Brussels Convention. Rather than have unnecessary divergencies between the Lugano and Brussels Conventions the opportunity was taken to incorporate those improvements into the Brussels Convention by the San Sebastian Convention. In the text that follows we will deal with the amended text of the Brussels Convention.

However, it remains now to explain the mechanism by which these amendments were made. After all, the Brussels Convention has force of law in England because of s2(1) of the Civil Jurisdiction and Judgments Act 1982; how can it be amended without the intervention of Parliament? Well, s14 of the Civil Jurisdiction and Judgments Act 1982 provides that where the UK government has agreed to a revision of the Conventions then the Crown may by Order in Council (which has to be laid before Parliament and approved by resolution in both Houses) make appropriate modifications to the 1982 Act 'or any other statutory provision'. It was by this route that the amendments to the Brussels Convention were made.

Naturally, since the Brussels Convention was originally negotiated between six states with civilian legal systems it contains much that is foreign to English law. Its adoption in England has meant abandoning much of the liberality of English law and it has made the English law of jurisdiction much more complicated. It has also made studying this part of the conflict of laws much more difficult. By the time you have mastered the Civil Jurisdiction and Judgments Act 1982 you may well wish that it had never been enacted. However, it ought to be recognised that the basic scheme of the Brussels Convention is both grand and sensible. The essential idea being that where a defendant was 'domiciled' in an EC country, then the court of that country, the court of his 'domicile', and not others would have jurisdiction; and, most importantly, once that court had given judgment then that judgment would be able to be enforced easily against the defendant throughout the EC. The efficient working of such a scheme is obviously of great value to all EC countries and their citizens. Moreover, the extension of these principles to the EFTA states through the Lugano Convention is similarly beneficial. But part of its price is the increased complexity of the English law of jurisdiction.

It is interesting to note that the ease and simplicity with which judgments may be enforced under the Brussels Convention (see Chapter 8, section 8.3) has begun to have an impact on other areas of the law. For instance, in *De Bry* v *Fitzgerald* [1990] 1 WLR 554 the Court of Appeal held that in deciding whether to order a foreign plaintiff (who was domiciled in the EC) to provide security (in terms of RSC O.53 r1(1)(a)) for the costs that may be awarded against him the court should have regard to the simplicity of the improved rights of enforcement under the Brussels Convention and should not order foreign plaintiffs to provide security because of a supposed difficulty of enforcing a judgment for costs elsewhere in the EC. (To like effect see *Carlo Silvera* v *Faleh Al-Rashidi* [1994] ILPr 332 (CA).)

Similarly, the Brussels Convention may affect the reach of article 7 of the Treaty of Rome (which prohibits discrimination on grounds of nationality). For instance, in *Hatrex International Transport* (Case C398/92) [1994] ILPr 264 the ECJ held a provision of German law (section 917(2) of the Zivilprozessordnung) which allowed national courts to require security for compliance from a foreign defendant established elsewhere in the EU but who had no assets within the jurisdiction (so any judgment would have to be enforced abroad), was contrary to article 7 EEC (Treaty of Rome) which prohibits discrimination on grounds of nationality. Such discrimination was prohibited unless justified by objective circumstances, and those circumstances did not exist where, given the Brussels Convention, the territory of all the EU states could be considered one entity for the purposes of the enforcement of judgments.

We have just mentioned the concept of 'domicile' for the first time in this chapter, and in order to avoid any possibility of confusion it should be made clear that the concept of 'domicile' used in the Brussels Convention and the Civil Jurisdiction and Judgments Act 1982 is not the same as the concept of domicile that we have just discussed in Chapter 3. In due course we will discuss its meaning fully, but for the present it is enough to say that speaking very broadly it means residence for about three months (see section 4.3 below). To avoid any confusion, when 'domicile' in terms of the Civil Jurisdiction and Judgments Act 1982 is meant inverted commas will be used.

Although the scope of the Brussels Convention is wide it does not generally apply where the defendant is 'domiciled' elsewhere than in the EC. Thus, in addition to all the new and complicated rules from the Civil Jurisdiction and Judgments Act 1982, we must still understand and master the traditional common law of jurisdiction. To this task we now turn.

## 4.2 Actions in personam where the defendant is not 'domiciled' in the EC

### Where the defendant is present in England

As we have seen, the applicable principle is that the court has in personam jurisdiction over anyone who has been served with a writ in England. As was said in *John Russell & Co Ltd* v *Cayzer, Irvine & Co Ltd* [1916] 2 AC 298 at 302, 'whoever is served with the King's writ and can be compelled consequently to submit to the decree made is a person over which the courts have jurisdiction'. The only possible exception to this principle is where the defendant is lured by the plaintiff by some trick into the jurisdiction (*Watkins* v *North American Timber Co* (1904) 20 TLR 534).

The writ can be served on an individual either by post (RSC O.10) or by personal service (RSC O.65 r2). Where there is service by post the date of service (unless the contrary is shown) is deemed to be seven days after posting (RSC O.10 r1(3)). In cases where the defendant may only be in England for a short time, it will usually be wise to effect personal service. Personal service on an individual is effected by handing over to the defendant a copy of the writ (sealed by the Central Office of the Law Courts). If the defendant refuses to accept the copy of the writ, then it can simply be left near to him after telling him about the nature of the document. Personal service on a partnership may be effected either by personal service on a partner or by service on the person having control of the business at the principal place of business (RSC O.81). Service in either of these ways gives the court jurisdiction over all the partners, even those who are not in England at the time (*Worcester City and County Banking Co* v *Firbank, Pauling and Co* [1894] 1 QB 784 and *Lysaght Ltd* v *Clark & Co* [1891] 1 QB 552). In addition, the defendant can authorise solicitors to accept service on his behalf (RSC O.10 r1(4)). In *Barclays Bank of Swaziland* v *Hahn* [1989] 1 WLR 506 there was held sufficient service in the following circumstances: the writ had been pushed through the letter box of the defendant's flat in London at 15.30 on 14 April 1987. The defendant arrived at Heathrow at 17.27 but was warned of the writ and so did not go to the flat but returned to Geneva the next day. The House of Lords decided that it was enough that *while* in the jurisdiction the defendant should have known about the existence of the writ.

Where the defendant is a company, different principles apply. The crucial question remains, though, whether a writ has been properly served within the jurisdiction. Where the company is registered in England then it will have a registered office and the writ can be served either by leaving it at the office or by post. Where the company is registered in Scotland but carries on business in England and Wales, the writ may be served by leaving it at or sending it by post to the company's principal place of business in England and Wales, but in addition a copy of the writ must be sent to the company's registered office in Scotland. (These matters are all dealt with in s725 of the Companies Act 1985.)

Foreign incorporated companies (or overseas companies) are considered to be present in England if they carry on business in England. Section 691(1)(b)(ii) of the Companies Act 1985 requires such a company to deliver to the Registrar of Companies the name and address of one or more persons resident in Great Britain who are authorised to accept service on the company's behalf, and s695 provides that a writ will be sufficiently served on an oversea company if it is posted to one of the persons referred to above or left at his address. Should the company fail to provide the name of a person as required by s691(1)(b)(ii), or should those persons be dead or have ceased to reside at that address, then the writ can be served by leaving it at or sending it by post to any place of business established by the company in Great Britain. In *Rome and Another* v *Punjab National Bank* [1989] 1 WLR 1211 it was held that it was sufficient in serving a writ on an oversea company to leave or post the writ to the address that had been notified to the Registrar even if the company had ceased to carry on business in Britain.

The meaning of the phrase 'established place of business' in the predecessor of s695 was the subject of judicial determination in *South India Shipping Corp Ltd* v *Export-Import Bank of Korea* [1985] 2 All ER 219 (CA). The defendant bank did not carry on any banking business in Great Britain (ie it did not accept deposits and make loans) but it had both premises and staff within the jurisdiction, it conducted external relations with other banks, it carried out preliminary work in relation to the granting or obtaining of loans, it sought to publicise its bank and it encouraged trade between the United Kingdom and Korea. In reliance upon *A/S Dampskib 'Hercules'* v *Grand Trunk Pacific Railway Co* [1912] 1 KB 222, Ackner LJ held that a 'company established a place of business within Great Britain if it carried on part of its business activities within the jurisdiction and it was not necessary for those activities to be either a substantial part of or more than incidental to the main objects of the company'. Accordingly the Export-Import Bank of Korea had established a place of business in Great Britain.

The statutory methods of effecting service on the overseas company are, it appears, the only way in which process can be served. Thus personal service upon the president (or other officer) of the overseas company who happens to be in England will not give the courts jurisdiction over the company (*The Theodohos* [1977] 2 Lloyd's Rep 428), although on general principles it will give the court jurisdiction over the president. In the case of domestic companies personal service on the chairman, president, treasurer or secretary is available as an alternative to the statutory procedure (RSC O.65 r3).

## Where the defendant has submitted to the jurisdiction of the court

As was mentioned earlier, a defendant who would not otherwise be subject to the jurisdiction of the court may submit to the court's jurisdiction. Submission can take place in a variety of ways, but the major ones are: where a plaintiff institutes an action against a particular defendant, he generally submits to any counterclaim that the defendant may institute against him (RSC O.15 r2; *High Commissioner for India v Gosh* [1960] 1 QB 134); where a defendant instructs his solicitor to accept service on his behalf, and the solicitor indorses the writ with a statement that he has done so, then the writ is deemed to have been duly served upon the defendant (RSC O.10 r1(4)) and the court has jurisdiction; where the defendant appears and contests the case on its merits he will be taken to have submitted to the jurisdiction of the court (*Boyle v Sacker* (1888) 39 Ch D 842), and an acknowledgement of service will be deemed, unless the contrary is shown, to have been served on him (RSC O.10 r1(5)). However, an appearance solely to protest that the court does not have jurisdiction does not constitute submission (*Re Dulles's Settlement (No 2)* [1951] Ch 842).

The above have been cases of submission by conduct, ie from the conduct of the defendant the court draws the conclusion that he has submitted to the jurisdiction of the court. In addition there is submission by agreement, ie the defendant contracts, either expressly or impliedly, to submit to the court's jurisdiction in circumstances in which he would not otherwise be subject. Usually such an agreement will form but one clause of a contract with one or more international elements. In order that there might be certainty about which court has jurisdiction, or because one of the parties wishes that the English courts should have jurisdiction, the parties may provide as part of the major contract that any disputes under the contract shall be settled by the English courts. Once a party has consented to the jurisdiction of the English courts, he is bound by that agreement. Thus service can either be effected on his agent within the jurisdiction (RSC O.10 r3(1); *Montgomery, Jones & Co v Liebenthal & Co* [1898] 1 QB 487), or an application may be made under RSC O.11 r1(1)(d)(iv) for leave to serve the writ outside the jurisdiction. This is the first time that we have encountered a detailed provision of RSC O.11, so this seems an appropriate point to consider it in detail.

## *Where leave is given under RSC O.11 r1(1)*

The common law rule that we have been discussing so far, viz, that the court does not have jurisdiction unless a writ has been served on the defendant in England or the defendant has submitted to the court's jurisdiction, is not a convenient one. A defendant who has not submitted to the jurisdiction and is not present in England is not able to be sued in England, even although the English courts may be the most convenient or appropriate forum in which to resolve the dispute. England may be the best forum in which to hear the case for a variety of reasons: the dispute may have arisen in England and all the witnesses may be in England, the lex causae may be English law, and all the parties may be domiciled in England (even although the defendant is not present in England). Moreover, from the plaintiff's point of view England may be the best forum because the defendant may have substantial assets in England which could be used to satisfy any judgment that might be given against him!

For these reasons the Common Law Procedure Act 1852 introduced the principle of an 'assumed' or 'extended' or 'exorbitant' jurisdiction. This gave the court a discretionary power to summon before it defendants (whether English or foreign) who were not present in England, by having them served with the writ or notice of the writ. The relevant rules are to be found today in RSC O.11 r1(1). It should be stressed that service of the writ outside the jurisdiction is discretionary. Thus it is not enough that the case is one within O.11 r1(1); the court may none the less refuse leave. We will consider below (see *The discretion to grant leave*) the detail of the exercise of that discretion.

We may now look at some of the specific circumstances in which leave may be granted. RSC O.11 r1(1) lists some fourteen sub-sub-rules which specify specific circumstances in which leave may be granted 'in actions begun ... by writ', and one of those sub-sub-rules (RSC O.11 r1(1)(d) (dealing with contracts) contains four sub-sub-sub-rules. So the position is complicated. You should also be aware that reading the cases about RSC O.11 is made more confusing by the fact that when the Order was amended to take account of the Civil Jurisdiction and Judgments Act 1982 (none of which amendments are relevant to us presently because we are considering cases where the defendant is 'domiciled' outside the EC) the numbering and lettering of the rule was rearranged; thus the cases decided before this latest amendment (in 1983) refer to different numbers and parts of the rule from the ones presently in force. All in all you are in for a complicated read before you master the provisions of RSC O. 11 r1(1). We shall now consider the various provisions in turn.

One further preliminary point: in determining where a particular case falls within a particular head of O.11 r1(1), various questions of fact may need to be determined, eg, whether a contract is governed by English law or made in England or whatever. And in *Attock Cement Company Ltd* v *Romanian Bank for Foreign Trade* (1989) The Times 13 January, the Court of Appeal laid down the correct attitude to be adopted where there is a disputed question of fact which was essential to the application of O.11 r1. Staughton LJ laid down that where such facts are disputed 'the judge must reach a provisional or tentative conclusion that the [plaintiff's version of the facts] was probably right before the court allowed service to stand'. In making this decision the court is not exercising a discretion (that comes later) but simply deciding a question of fact. Moreover, voluminous evidence and prolonged argument on such matters should be discouraged. (See Lord Templeman's dictum in *The Spiliada* [1986] 3 All ER 843 cited in section 4.4 Forum conveniens in general, below.)

## RSC O.11 r1(1)(a)

Where the defendant 'is domiciled within the jurisdiction' leave may be granted. Domiciled here (and elsewhere in RSC O.11 r1 (see RSC O.11 r1(4)) means domiciled in accordance with the rules laid down in ss41–46 of the Civil Jurisdiction and Judgments Act 1982, ie in accordance with the convention adopted earlier it means 'domicile'. We will discuss these rules in section 4.3. The old rule (RSC O.11

r1(1)(c)) spoke of a person 'domiciled or ordinarily resident within the jurisdiction'. As we shall see when we look at the rules of 'domicile' under the Civil Jurisdiction and Judgments Act 1982, there is not a great difference between the old and the new rules on this point.

## RSC O.11 r1(1)(b)

This sub-sub rule provides that leave may be granted where 'an injunction is sought ordering the defendant to do or refrain from doing anything within the jurisdiction'. The idea here is that the court should not be prevented, by the defendant's absence from the jurisdiction, from being able to issue an injunction to prevent something unlawful being done in England. Although claiming damages in addition to the injunction does not prevent reliance upon this sub-sub-rule, the injunction must be the substantial issue between the parties; thus where the injunction is sought simply to bring the case within this sub-sub rule, leave will be refused (*Watson* v *Daily Record* [1907] 1 KB 853; *Rosler* v *Hilbery* [1925] Ch 250).

In accordance with this principle, where a Mareva injunction is sought (ie an interlocutory injunction as developed in *Mareva Compania Naviera SA* v *International Bulkcarriers SA* [1980] 1 All ER 213; [1975] 2 Lloyd's Rep 509 to restrain a defendant from removing his assets from the jurisdiction until the dispute is resolved) then the defendant must be subject to the jurisdiction of the court other than through the operation of this sub-sub rule (The *Siskina* [1977] 3 WLR 818).

## RSC O.11 r1(1)(c)

Here leave may be granted to serve outside the jurisdiction on a 'person ... [who is] ... a necessary and proper party' in an action against a person 'duly served within or out of the jurisdiction'. The purpose of this sub-sub rule is clear: it is to ensure that all the necessary and proper parties can have their dispute resolved in one trial. But, again, leave will be refused if the service of the first defendant is a sham, designed simply to bring the second defendant within this sub-sub rule (*Witted* v *Galbraith* [1893] 1 QB 577). Moreover, it was decided in *The Brabo* [1949] AC 326 that if the action against the first defendant is bound to fail, then leave will be refused. This was confirmed in *MB Pyramid Sound NV* v *Briese Schiffarts GmbH & Co* [1993] 2 Lloyd's Rep 192.

It seems clear that the person sought to be served can be either a necessary or a proper party; he does not need to be both.

## RSC O.11 r1(1)(d)

This is one of the most important of the sub-sub rules and it is the one that is further broken down into four sub-sub-sub rules. It deals with 'claims brought to enforce, rescind, dissolve, annul or otherwise affect a contract, or to recover damages or obtain other relief in respect of the breach of a contract'. In *Gulf Bank KSC* v *Mitsubishi Heavy Industries Ltd* (1993) The Times 24 August Hobhouse J held even where the underlying contract has been declared void a claim may still fall within r1(1)(d) in that it may be brought to 'otherwise affect a contract'. Thus, where a contract governed by Kuwaiti law for the supply of plant to the Kuwaiti Ministry of Electricity and Water was declared void after the Iraqi invasion of Kuwait, a counter indemnity for payment under the contract given by the defendants to the plaintiff still fell within r1(1)(d).

Sub-sub-sub rule (i) provides that leave may be granted where the contract in question 'was made within the jurisdiction'. It may on occasion be difficult to determine where a contract is made, but these are the standard rules: where the contract is made by post or telegram, the contract is made where the acceptance is posted (*Benaim* v *Debono* [1924] AC 514 (at 520) and *Cowen* v *O'Connor* (1888) 20 QBD 640). On the other hand, where the parties deal with each other instantaneously, eg by telephone or telex, the contract is made where the acceptance is communicated to the offeror (*Entores Ltd* v *Miles Far East Corporation* [1955] 2 QB 327). Note however that in *Brinkibon Ltd* v *Stahag Stahl* [1982] AC 34 Lord Wilberforce considered that these rules in regard to telexes might in the future be more flexibly applied. He said:

'Since 1955 [and the *Entores* case] the use of telex communication has been greatly expanded, and there are many variants on it. The senders and recipients may not be the principals to the contemplated contract. They may be servants or agents with limited authority. The message may not reach, or be intended to reach, the designated recipient immediately: messages may be sent out of office hours, or at night, with the intention, or on the assumption, that they may be read at a later time ... No universal rule can cover all such cases; they must be resolved by reference to the intentions of the parties, by sound business practice and in some cases by judgement where the risks should lie ...'.

Although Lord Wilberforce's argument is obviously cogent, the introduction of flexibility into these rules may make it difficult to predict when leave to serve outside the jurisdiction will be granted.

One final problem arises in this area. A contract may be made in one place, and then its terms may be altered by agreement in another place. The approach in *BP Exploration (Libya) Ltd* v *Hunt* [1976] 1 WLR 788 was to hold that leave could be granted where the contract was made in England, even if there was an alteration elsewhere. Obviously, difficult cases can arise in determining whether the contract has been altered or whether the old contract has been terminated and a fresh one agreed.

Sub-sub-sub rule (ii) provides that where the contract was 'made by or through an agent trading or residing within the jurisdiction on behalf of a principal trading or residing out of the jurisdiction', leave may be granted. The word 'through' bears a wide meaning and includes cases where the agent does not make the contract but simply passes on orders to his principal to accept or reject. In *National Mortgage and Agency Co of New Zealand* v *Gosselin* (1922) 38 TLR 832 the London agent of a Belgian firm sent a price list to the plaintiff and in due course sent the plaintiff's order (which was treated as an offer) to the Belgian firm, which accepted the order by post. Although the agent did not make the contract with the plaintiff (that was made directly with the firm) the agent did negotiate the terms (by sending the price list and passing on the order); thus leave to serve the writ outside the jursidiction was granted.

It has been made clear by *Union International Insurance Co Ltd* v *Jubilee Insurance Co Ltd* [1991] 1 WLR 415 that the agent referred to in RSC O.11 r1(1)(d)(ii) had to be the agent of the defendant. Thus the plaintiff – a Bermudan insurance company trading and residing outside the jurisdiction – could not rely upon r1(1)(d)(ii) in the following circumstances: the plaintiff had, through its agents (a firm of London insurance brokers), entered into a contract with the defendant, a Kenyan insurance company. Leave under r1(1)(d)(ii) to serve the Kenyan company outside England was refused. The plaintiff argued that its agent traded and resided in England, while it traded and resided outside the jurisdiction; thus the requirement of the rule were satisfied and the court could grant leave. However, the court held that, in order to give a sensible interpretation to the rule, words were to be implied into it restricting the agent to being the agent of the defendant.

In many cases the plaintiff may have a choice of either seeking leave under this sub-sub-sub rule to serve the writ outside the jurisdiction, or utilising the provisions of RSC O.10 r2 and serving the writ on the agent. RSC O.10 r2 provides that where 'a contract has been entered into within the jurisdiction with or through an agent' (who is either an individual resident or carrying on business within the jurisdiction or a company with a place of business or a registered office within the jurisdiction) acting on behalf of a foreign principal (ie an individual or company not resident or registered or carrying on business within the jurisdiction) then the court can authorise the service of the writ on the agent provided the agent's authority has not been determined by the principal when the application is made for authorisation. When authorisation is granted then, in addition to serving the writ on the agent, the principal must be notified by post at his address outside the jurisdiction. Note that the RSC O.10 r2 power is a little narrower than that under RSC O.11 r1(1)(d)(ii), for (a) the contract must be made in the jurisdiction and (b) the agent's authority must not have been determined.

Sub-sub-sub-rule (iii) provides that leave may be granted where the contract 'by its terms, or by implication, [is] governed by English law'. For present purposes we can take this simply as meaning that the proper or governing law of the contract is English law. In Chapter 5 we go into detail about how the proper law of the contract is to be determined. For the present it is sufficient to note that a contract may have English law as its proper law although it is not made in England, and that even if it is made in England a contract may have a proper law other than English law. Thus we are here dealing with a completely different question to that discussed under sub-sub-sub rule (i).

Sub-sub-sub rule (iv) provides that leave may be granted where the contract contains a term 'to the effect that the High Court shall have jurisdiction to hear and to determine any action in respect of the contract'. This sub-sub-sub rule is designed simply to deal with the situation where a defendant has submitted by contract to the jurisdiction and it is necessary to serve the writ on him outside England.

One important point that applies generally to RSC O.11 r1(1)(d) (and perhaps also to RSC O.11 r1(1)(e), which is about to be discussed) is the effect of a foreign jurisdiction clause, ie a clause in the contract that provides that disputes under the contract are to be determined by the courts of some foreign country. Provided that the clause is not void ab initio, leave will generally not be granted even if the case was otherwise within RSC O.11 r1(1)(d), for example, if the contract had been made in England. Thus in *Mackender v Feldia AG* leave was refused because a clause in a contract made in England gave the Belgian courts exclusive jurisdiction. It was an insurance contract, and the defendants argued that there had been non disclosure which rendered the contract (including the foreign jurisdiction clause) voidable, but this was not enough; the clause had to be void not voidable.

## RSC O.11 r1(1)(e)

This sub-sub rule provides that leave may be granted where a contract is breached within the jurisdiction. It provides that it makes no difference whether the contract was made within or outside the jurisdiction and that the breach within the jurisdiction 'was preceded or accompanied by a breach committed out of the jurisdiction that rendered impossible the performance of so much of the contract as ought to have been performed within the jurisdiction'.

The extension contained in the last part of the sub-sub rule is designed to meet the difficulty of *Johnson v Taylor* [1920] AC 144. Here, although it was held that the vendors under a cif contract for the sale of certain goods had breached their contract in failing to deliver shipping documents in England, leave was not granted for there had been a prior breach in Sweden, where they had failed to ship the goods to England at all.

The extension apart, it is clear that there must be a contract that is breached in England. (It matters not that its proper law is not English.) This seems straightforward, but it is sometimes difficult to know whether the sub-sub rule is satisfied. For instance, where is a contract breached if one party writes a letter of repudiation in one country to the other party in another country? It appears that the contract is breached where the letter of repudiation is posted, not where it is received (*Martin v Stout* [1925] AC 359 at 368 approving *Holland v Bennett* [1902] 1 KB 867). Thus if A in France writes to B in England repudiating their contract, the contract is breached in France, not England. However, if A sends his agent to England with instructions to repudiate or writes to his agent in England instructing him to repudiate the contract, then when the agent does so the contract is breached in England and leave may be granted (*Oppenheimer v Louis Rosenthal & Co A/G* [1937] 1 All ER 23).

Where the breach takes place not through repudiation but through a failure of a party to perform his obligations under the contract, then the breach takes place where the party ought to have performed his obligation. It is not necessary for the contract to provide expressly that the obligation is to be performed in England, but it must be possible for the court to determine from the contract as well as from the surrounding circumstances that this was the intention of the parties (*Charles Duval*

*& Co Ltd* v *Gans* [1904] 2 KB 685). But if the obligation could be performed either in England and elsewhere then the sub-sub rule is not satisfied; what is necessary is that the party in breach must have failed to perform an obligation, part of which at least was required by the contract to be performed in England (*Cuban Atlantic Sugar Sales Corporation* v *Compania de Vapores San Elefetrio* [1960] 1 QB 187).

Where there is no express agreement as to where a party is to perform, the courts often are able to infer where the performance was to be. Thus wages usually have to be paid where the services are performed, and goods usually have to be paid for where the seller is in business. And a debtor (someone under an obligation to pay money) usually has to seek out the creditor; but this does not mean that the creditor, by going to England, can force the debtor to breach the contract in England. (For more detail of these rules see either general texts on contract or Morris, *The Conflict of Laws*, 73–74).

## RSC O.11 r1(1)(f)
Leave may be granted where 'the claim is founded on a tort and the damage was sustained, or resulted from an act committed, within the jurisdiction'. The old rule (RSC O.11 r1(1)(h)) provided only that the tort had to be 'committed within the jurisdiction', and this created difficulties where the wrongful act was committed in one country and the harm occurred in another country. Fortunately, since the change in the rule this problem of determining the locus of a tort is not likely to arise again. Those interested may consult Cheshire, 199–201, 553–560. In broad terms the predominant view is that the place where the tort is committed is the place where the 'substance of the tort' is committed (*Distillers Co (Biochemicals) Ltd* v *Thompson* [1971] AC 458 and *Metall und Rohstoff AG* v *Donaldson Lufkin & Jenrette Inc* [1989] 3 WLR 563; [1986] 3 All ER 116). Thus in the *Distillers* case, where a drug containing thalidomide was manufactured in England but sold and distributed in New South Wales, it was held by the Privy Council that 'in substance ... the cause of action' arose in New South Wales.

## RSC O.11 r1(1)(g)
Leave may be granted if 'the whole subject-matter of the action is land situate within the jurisdiction (with or without rent or profits) or the perpetuation of testimony relating to land so situated'. (Perpetuation of testimony is a Chancery procedure that allows evidence which is likely to be lost because of a witness's age or health or intention to go abroad to be taken to preserve and perpetuate it.)

## RSC O.11 r1(1)(h)
Leave may be granted if 'the claim is brought to construe, rectify, set aside or enforce an act, deed, will, contract, obligation or liability affecting land situate within the jurisdiction'. 'Enforce' here has a wider meaning than 'specifically performed' (*Official Solicitor* v *Stype Investments* [1983] 1 WLR 214).

## RSC O.11 r1(1)(i)
Leave may be granted if 'the claim is made for a debt secured on immovable property or is made to assert, declare or determine proprietary or possessory rights,

or rights of security, in or over movable property, or to obtain authority to dispose of movable property, situate within the jurisdiction'. This provision, which is a wider form of the old rule (RSC O.11 r1(1)(k)), is designed to ensure that the court is not precluded by the absence of the relevant parties from the jurisdiction from dealing with property situated within the jurisdiction.

### RSC O.11 r1(1)(j)

Leave may be granted if 'the claim is brought to execute the trusts of a written instrument being trusts that ought to be executed according to English law and of which the person to be served with the writ is a trustee, or for any relief or remedy which might be obtained in any such action'. Under the old rules the trust property had to be situate in England.

### RSC O.11 r1(1)(k)

Leave may be granted if 'the claim is made for the administration of the estate of a person who dies domiciled within the jurisdiction or for any relief or remedy which may be obtained in any such action'.

### RSC O.11 r1(1)(l)

Leave may be granted if 'the claim is brought in a probate action within the meaning of Order 76'.

### RSC O.11 r1(1)(m)

Leave may be granted if 'the claim is brought to enforce any judgment or arbitration award'. This sub-sub rule will become clear when we consider the enforcement of foreign judgments in Chapter 8.

### RSC O.11 r1(1)(n)

Leave may be granted if 'the claim is brought against a defendant not domiciled in Scotland or Northern Ireland in respect of a claim by the Commissioners of Inland Revenue for or in relation to any of the duties or taxes which have been, or are for the time being, placed under their care and management'.


## The discretion to grant leave

As stressed above the grant of leave is discretionary. O.11 r1(1) speaks simply of service being 'permissible' and O.11 r4(2) says that no leave 'shall be granted unless it shall be made sufficiently to appear [by affidavit] to the Court that the case is a proper one for service out of the jurisdiction ...'. In the past there has been considerable uncertainty about what the plaintiff had to show in order for the court to grant leave. It was frequently said that since the jurisdiction to serve outside was 'exorbitant' (*Amin Rasheed Shipping Corporation v Kuwait Insurance Co* [1984] AC 50) and the discretion should be sparingly exercised 'with extreme caution' (*Cordova Land Co Ltd v Victor Brothers Inc* [1966] 1 WLR 793) and only where the plaintiff showed 'a good arguable case' (*Vitkovice Horni a Hutni Tezirstvo v Korner* [1951] AC

869). This did not make the position much clearer but suggested that the plaintiff had to discharge a heavy burden before leave would be granted.

However, the House of Lords has recently clarified the position in *Seaconsar Far East Ltd v Bank Markazi Jomhouri Islami Iran* [1993] 3 WLR 756, which now dominates the law in this area. Lord Goff's speech should be read with care; it suggests that, other things being equal, it will now be easier for leave to be granted.

One aspect of this question we can immediately set to one side: where there is some other more appropriate forum, then leave will generally not be granted. We will discuss this in detail below (see **4.4 Forum conveniens**), but for the present we will assume that England is an appropriate forum for trial of the action.

The next point to make is that a distinction should be drawn between establishing that the case is one that falls under one head or another of O.11 r1(1), for instance, establishing that the defendant was 'domiciled' within the jurisdiction in terms of r1(1)(a) (this is the jurisdiction point) and establishing that the plaintiff's case is strong enough to justify service outside the jurisdiction (this is the merits point).

The jurisdiction point and the merits point often overlap. For instance, a plaintiff who seeks to establish that his case is within O.11 r1(1)(e) will need to establish (i) that there was a contract made within or outside the jurisdiction, (ii) that it was breached, and (iii) that it was breached *within* the jurisdiction. A plaintiff who establishes that his case falls within r1(1)(e) (the jurisdiction point) would also have made a strong case to justify service outside the jurisdiction (the merits point). But they need not overlap at all: the plaintiff who relies on r1(1)(a) and establishes that the defendant is 'domiciled' within the jurisdiction (the jurisdiction point) will have made no progress with the merits point.

Lord Goff makes clear, however, that establishing the jurisdiction point is governed by r4(2); and 'a good arguable case' that the case fell within O.11 r1(1) had to be shown.

However, when considering the merits point different considerations applied. It was important that there should not be 'premature consideration' of the merits; and it would be sufficient for the plaintiff to shown that there was a serious issue to be tried in that there was a substantial issue of fact or law between the parties. Lord Goff approved the following dictum from Stuart-Smith LJ's judgment in the same case in the Court of Appeal:

> 'It seems to me to be wholly inappropriate once the question[s] of jurisdiction [ie the jurisdiction point] and forum [conveniens (to be discussed later)] are established for there to be prolonged debate and consideration of the merits of the plaintiff's claim at the · interlocutory stage.'

Thus, it was not necessary for the plaintiff to establish 'a good arguable case on the merits'. Lord Goff also rejected any suggestion that the strong the plaintiff's case was the easier it would be to establish forum conveniens and vice versa.

Thus, in the end, Lord Goff was preserving the traditional strict approach to the jurisdiction point but has significantly eased in his cogent judgment the test of the merits point.

### *Where leave is not required to serve the writ on a defendant who is not present within the jurisdiction*

A number of statutes provide that the High Court has the power to determine certain claims notwithstanding that the defendant may not be in England. For example, the Carriage by Air Act 1961 implements the Warsaw Convention of 1929 (as amended) governing carriage by air, and under the Convention a passenger has the right to sue a carrier in the courts of the place of destination of the relevant flight. Thus if a plaintiff suffers damage on a flight whose destination was London, the High Court has jurisdiction. However, if the airline is foreign, it may not be subject to the jurisdiction of the English courts.

None the less, the plaintiff can exercise his rights under the Convention and sue the airline in England because RSC O.11 r1(2)(b) provides that the defendant can be served outside the jurisdiction without leave where 'by virtue of any ... enactment the High Court has power to hear and determine notwithstanding that the person against whom the claim is made is not within the jurisdiction of the Court or that the wrongful act, neglect or default giving rise to the claim did not take place within the jurisdiction'.

Most of the statutes which fall within this category implement international conventions relating to international transport (eg the Carriage of Goods by Roads Act 1965 and the Civil Aviation Act 1982), but this is not essential (see the Protection of Trading Interests Act 1980).

Note also that RSC O.11 r1(2)(a) provides that subject to certain conditions leave is not required where the English courts have jurisdiction under the Civil Jurisdiction and Judgments Act 1982. So we turn now to consider jurisdiction under the Civil Jurisdiction and Judgments Act 1982.

## 4.3 Actions in personam where the defendant is 'domiciled' in the EC

### *The status, nature and interpretation of the Brussels Convention, the Civil Jurisdiction and Judgments Act 1982 and related documents*

We have already outlined something of the nature and origins of the Brussels Convention and the Civil Jurisdiction and Judgments Act 1982 in section 4.1 *The Civil Jurisdiction and Judgments Act 1982* above. Now we must go into a little more detail on these topics.

### The Conventions have force of law in the United Kingdom

The first point to note is that s2 of the Civil Jurisdiction and Judgments Act 1982 provides that 'the Conventions shall have the force of law in the United Kingdom, and judicial notice shall be taken of them.' By s1(1) 'the Conventions' means the Brussels Convention of 1968, the Protocol on Interpretation of 1971, and the Accession Convention of 1978. Authentic texts of the Conventions are found in schedules to the Civil Jurisdiction and Judgments Act 1982.

### The intepretation of the Convention

The interpretation of the Convention by English courts takes place according to the principles laid down by the European Court, and questions of interpretation can and sometimes must be referred to the European Court.

One important consequence of the Conventions having the force of law is that English courts are sometimes entitled and at other times are obliged to refer questions of the interpretation of the Conventions to the Court of Justice of the European Communities (articles 1–4 of the Interpretation Convention). Moreover, in English courts 'questions as to the meaning or effect of any provision of the Conventions shall, if not referred to the European Court in accordance with the 1971 Protocol, be determined in accordance with the principles laid down by and any relevant decision of the European Court'.

In addition, two reports (the Jenard report on the 1968 Convention and the 1971 Protocol, and the Schlosser report on the Accession Convention of 1978) are given by s3(2) of the Act a special status as aids to interpretation. They 'may be considered in ascertaining the meaning or effect of any provision of the Convention and shall be given such weight as is appropriate in the circumstances'. You will readily appreciate that these, from the traditional point of view of English law, are remarkable and novel aids to interpretation. Yet they are important, for as Morris points out: 'Many of the amendments sought by the United Kingdom during the accession negotiations were given effect to by "undertakings" recorded in the Report and not by formal amendments to the Convention.' (op cit).

Apart from various matters concerning the enforcement of foreign judgments (which we will consider in Chapter 8) rather than jurisdiction, the House of Lords is the only court which must refer the matter to the European Court (article 3(1), and see Hartley, *Civil Jurisdiction and Judgments*, 1984, at 102–103). The courts which are entitled to refer the matter to the European Court are (apart from matters concerning the enforcement of judgments) courts sitting in an appellate capacity (articles 3(2), 2(2) and (3) and Hartley, op cit, 103).

In the cases on the Convention that have come before the European Court, the Court has generally interpreted the Convention independently of the national law of the court that has made the reference to it (see, for instance, *LTU* v *Eurocontrol* [1976] ECR 1541). On the other hand, in one case, which we will discuss more fully later, *Tessili* v *Dunlop AG* [1976] ECR 1473, the national law was referred to.

However, uniformity throughout the community is obviously an important goal of the Conventions; thus references to the national laws rather than community principles are likely to be rare.

It is important to realise that the whole approach of the English courts to the interpretation of Community Law is different from their approach to the interpretation of English statutes. This has been made clear, with regard to the Brussels Convention in particular, by the recent case of *New Hampshire Insurance Co v Strabag Bau AG* [1990] ILPr 334. Here Potter J said that the proper approach to the interpretation of the Brussels Convention was 'to seek to give effect to its purpose and not to give it "a narrow literalistic construction"'. Potter J also adopted a dictum from *Henn & Derby* v *DPP* [1980] AC 850 where Lord Diplock had said (at 950) that:

'The European Court, in contrast to English courts, applies teleological rather than historical methods to the interpretation of the Treaties and other Community legislation. It seeks to give effect to what it conceives to be the spirit rather than the letter of the Treaties: sometimes, indeed, to an English judge it may seem to the exclusion of the letter. It views the Communities as living and expanding organisms and the interpretation of the provisions of the Treaties as changing to match their growth.'

Those therefore accustomed only to the interpretation of the standard English statute will sometimes find following the reasoning of the European Court difficult and the results reached awkward. Yet this is a course upon which the English courts are now irrevocably committed, and the interpretation of the Community legislation is coming to dominate many aspects of the English conflict of laws.

### The scope of the Convention

Article 1 lays down the scope of the Convention. It applies to 'civil and commercial matters'. This is obviously very wide, but the article then goes on to specify matters to which the Convention does not apply. These are 'revenue, customs or administrative matters', and in addition the Convention does not apply to:

1. matters of 'status or legal capacity of natural persons, rights in property arising out of the matrimonial relationship, wills and succession';
2. bankruptcy proceedings and like matters;
3. social security;
4. arbitration.

There has been litigation before the European court over the meaning of the phrase 'civil and commercial matters' and in particular about whether litigation with a public authority is such a matter. It appears from *LTU* v *Eurocontrol* [1976] ECR 1541 that 'unless the public authority was acting as an ordinary citizen and not claiming any special prerogatives' (Hartley, op cit, 13) it will lie outside the scope of the Convention. Moreover, as we have seen above, the court made it clear that the concept 'civil and commercial matters' would be given its meaning from the Convention and not from the provisions of the national laws involved in the litigation. (See also *The Netherlands* v *Ruffer* Case 814/79 [1980] ECR 3807 and Hartley, op cit, 13–16.)

A wide range of matters is considered in the Schlosser report to fall within 'status or legal capacity of natural persons' including nullity of marriage, judicial separation, dissolution of marriage, death, status and capacity of a minor, legal representation of the mentally ill, nationality and domicile, care and custody of children and adoption. It is clear from *De Cavel* v *De Cavel (No 1)* [1979] ECR 1055 that if certain substantive rights are outside the Convention, eg those of matrimonial property, then so too are interim measures designed to protect those substantive rights (eg orders freezing bank accounts, etc, while the court determines how the matrimonial property should be divided).

Three recent cases add to the law about the scope of the Convention. First, in *Menten* v *The Federal Republic of Germany* [1991] ILPr 259 the meaning of the phrase 'civil and commercial matters' in article 1(1) was considered by the Court of Appeal in The Hague. What had happened was that Menten had fraudulently made compensation claims against Germany, and DM550,000 was paid to him and his wife. When this was discovered the German government sought restitution of these sums and was granted several judgments in the German courts. The German government now sought to enforce these judgments against Menten in the Netherlands, but the procedure to be adopted as well as the circumstances in which enforcement might be stayed depended upon whether the judgment was being enforced under the Brussels Convention or not. This depended upon whether the claim for repayment was a 'civil and commercial matter'. The Dutch court held that an action between a public authority and an individual that was governed by private law could come within the Convention, while if the dispute concerned the exercise by the public authority of its public authority powers then the matter could not be 'civil and commercial'. In this case, the claim for repayment of the money whose original payment was induced by fraud was 'rooted in private law' and had nothing to do with public authority powers. Hence the matter was 'civil and commercial'.

Secondly, in *Marc Rich & Co AG* v *Societa Italiana Impianti pA* [1991] ILPr 524 the European Court of Justice interpreted article 1(4) of the Convention. This provides that 'the Convention shall not apply to ... arbitration', but in this case it was argued that whether an arbitration agreement existed was a matter within the Convention and so governed by the Convention's rules in regard to jurisdiction. What had happened was that a dispute had arisen between the Swiss purchaser and the Italian seller of a cargo of oil (which turned out to be contaminated). The Swiss purchaser had sent a telex setting out the terms of the contract, one of which subjected the contract to English law and provided for arbitration in London. But no reply to this telex was received. A central part of the dispute was whether these terms were part of the contract, but the concrete way in which the matter arose was when the purchaser sought the aid of the English courts to appoint an arbitrator. Did that question fall within the Convention? Impianti (the Italian seller) alleged that it did because otherwise it would be possible to evade the application of the Convention simply by alleging the existence of an arbitration clause. However, the European Court rejected this; in order to determine whether a dispute fell within the Convention one looked to its subject matter. If that subject matter – eg the appointment of an arbitrator – fell outside the Convention, that was that. And the mere fact that a different preliminary issue (was the arbitration agreement valid) had to be determined before that concrete issue was addressed did not bring the matter within the Convention.

Note that this judgment seems to leave open the question of what the position would be if the validity of the arbitration agreement were the only issue in dispute, not just a preliminary one.

In *Volker Sonntag* v *Waidmann* [1993] ILPr 466 the European Court of Justice held that damages awarded in criminal proceedings to a deceased next of kin came within the concept of a 'civil matter' for the purposes of the Convention. What had happened was that a German schoolteacher had been responsible for the death of one of his pupils during a school excursion to the Italian Alps, and he had been found guilty of culpable homicide in Italy. The deceased's next of kin were represented as parties civiles in those proceedings and a damages award was made in favour of those next of kin. That damages award was held to be a 'civil matter', thus within the Convention and enforceable against the schoolteacher in Germany. The fact that he held a public office (schoolteacher) made no difference. Note that article 5(4) clearly grants special jurisdiction to the criminal court that makes a civil damages award provided that is possible to do so under its own law, so the concept exemplified by *Sonntag*'s case is not that novel (see also *Black* v *Yates* [1991] 3 WLR 90).

## The concept of 'domicile' under the Conventions and the Civil Jurisdiction and Judgments Act 1982

### The concept under the Convention
The concept of 'domicile' is crucial to the Convention because, as we have seen, it forms the basic jurisdictional link determining whether and if so which court in the EC has jurisdiction. Yet, remarkably, the Convention does not define 'domicile'; all that it does is to specify which legal system is to be used in determining where a person is domiciled.

Thus article 52 of the Convention provides, first, that 'in order to determine whether a party is domiciled in the Contracting State whose courts are seised of the matter, the court shall apply its internal law'.

The article goes on, secondly, to provide that 'if a party is not domiciled in the State whose courts are seised of the matter, then, in order to determine whether the party is domiciled in another Contracting State, the court shall apply the law of that State'.

Then, thirdly, the article provides that 'the domicile of a party shall, however, be determined in accordance with his national law if, by that law, his domicile depends upon that of another person or on the seat of an authority'.

Although there are some complexities, the basic scope of the article is clear. In determining where a person is 'domiciled' the court first uses its own rules to determine whether that person is 'domiciled' within its territory. If it decides that that person is not 'domiciled' the court then uses the law of the other relevant community states to determine whether that person is 'domiciled' in any one of those states under the laws of those states.

Two important points arise from what we have said so far. The English concept of domicile with all its artificial rules that we discussed in Chapter 3 is obviously unsuitable for use for Convention purposes. Thus a special Convention 'domicile', which has nothing to do with the concept of domicile discussed in Chapter 3, is created in ss41–46 of the Civil Jurisdiction and Judgments Act 1982. We shall discuss the details of the Convention 'domicile' shortly. For the present it is sufficient to note that the rules will need to specify whether a person is 'domiciled' in a part of the United Kingdom (ie England and Wales, Scotland or Northern Ireland) and, more rarely, whether a person is 'domiciled' in a particular place in the United Kingdom.

Secondly, using the laws of the individual states to determine where a person is 'domiciled' has the consequence that a person may be held to be 'domiciled' in more than one EC state. This means that, in principle, a person who is 'domiciled' in more than one EC state can be sued in any of them. However, this is not likely to be a major problem for an English court. If the person has a 'domicile' in England then, in principle, the English court has jurisdiction and need not consider any other community state's law. If, however, the person is not 'domiciled' in the United Kingdom, but is, perhaps 'domiciled' in both France and Germany (according to the respective laws of those countries), the English court will, in principle, decline jurisdiction for it will only hear cases against persons 'domiciled' within its territory.

Thus far we have been concerned with the 'domicile' of individuals. But article 53 contains cognate provisions about the 'domicile' of corporations and trusts. A company is to be 'domiciled' where it has its 'seat', and the question of where that is will be determined by the court applying its rules of private international law.

Alas, the private international law of England does not know the concept of the 'seat' of a company, so s42(3) and (4) of the Civil Jurisdiction and Judgments Act 1982 was enacted to provide an answer. A company (or corporation) has its 'seat' in the United Kingdom if it is 'incorporated in the United Kingdom and has its registered office or some other official address in the United Kingdom ... or its central management and control is exercised in the United Kingdom'. A company has its 'seat' in a particular part of the United Kingdom (ie England and Wales, Scotland or Northern Ireland) if, and only if, 'it has its registered office or some other official address in that part ... or ... its central management and control is exercised in that part; or ... it has a place of business in that part.' Essentially analogous provisions also define when a company will be 'domiciled in a place in the United Kingdom'. Note that these provisions mean that it is possible for a company to have 'seats' in a number of different parts of the United Kingdom. A company registered in England is 'seated' in England, but if its central management and control is exercised from Scotland it is also 'seated' there; and it may also be 'seated' in Northern Ireland if it has a place of business there. (The example is Morris's: op cit, 80).

A company has a 'seat' outside the United Kingdom 'if and only if ... it was incorporated ... under the law of that state and has its registered office or some other official address there or its central management and control is exercised in that state' (s42(7)). However, a company shall not be regarded as having its seat in another EC state if 'the courts of that state would not ... regard it as having its seat there' (s42(8)).

The 'domicile' of trusts is to be determined again by the court applying its own rules of private international law. The relevant rules have been specified in s45 of the Civil Jurisdiction and Judgments Act 1982, which states that 'a trust is domiciled in a part of the United Kingdom if and only if the system of law of that part is the system of law with which the trust has its closest and most real connection', and a trust 'is domiciled in the United Kingdom if and only if it ... domiciled in a part of the United Kingdom'.

### The concept under s41 of the Civil Jurisdiction and Judgments Act 1982

Section 41(2) of the Civil Jurisdiction and Judgments Act 1982 provides that a person 'is domiciled in the United Kingdom, if and only if ... he is resident in the United Kingdom; and the nature and circumstance of his residence indicate that he has a substantial connection with the United Kingdom'. Under s41(6) a presumption of 'substantial connection' arises where a person has been resident in the United Kingdom for the last three months. The presumption is rebuttable by proof that there is no 'substantial connection'.

Of course, it is not enough to know that a person is 'domiciled' in the United Kingdom; it is necessary to know in which part of the United Kingdom that person is 'domiciled'. Thus s41(3) provides that a person 'is domiciled in a particular part of the United Kingdom, if and only if ... he is resident in that part; and ... the nature and circumstances of his residence indicate that he has a substantial connection with that part'. A similar presumption of 'substantial connection' with that part applies.

When a person is 'domiciled' in the United Kingdom, but it is unclear whether he is 'domiciled' in any part of the United Kingdom under s41(3), then s41(5) provides that he 'shall be treated as domiciled in the part of the United Kingdom in which he is resident.'

Where it is necessary (as it rarely is) to know whether a person is 'domiciled' in a particular place in the United Kingdom, regard must be had to s41(4) which provides that a person is 'domiciled in a particular place in the United Kingdom if and only if he ... is domiciled in the part of the United Kingdom in which that place is situated; and ... is resident in that place'.

Finally, if a person is not 'domiciled' in the United Kingdom, where is he 'domiciled'? Well, he may be 'domiciled' in another EC state or states in accordance with the provisions of article 52. But, if article 52 does not provide the answer, s41(7) provides that a person 'is domiciled in a state other than a Contracting State [ie an EC state] if and only if ... he is a resident in that state; and ... the nature and circumstances of his residence indicate that he has a substantial connection with that state'. Note that under s41(7) there is no presumption of substantial connection.

## The central jurisdictional rules under the Convention

These are to be found in articles 2 and 4 of the Convention. Article 2 reads:

> 'Subject to the provisions of this Convention, persons domiciled in a Contracting State shall, whatever their nationality, be sued in the courts of that state ...'

And article 4 states:

> 'If the defendant is not domiciled in a Contracting State [ie EC state], the jurisdiction of the courts of each Contracting State shall, subject to the provisions of Article 16, be determined by the law of that state.'

If the Convention has a heart, it is to be found in these provisions. Basically, they state that a person is to be sued in the court of his 'domicile' (determined in the manner we have described above). But if he is not 'domiciled' in any EC state, then the ordinary jurisdictional rules of the EC state where he is sued apply. Article 16, referred to in article 4, contains certain provisions about exclusive jurisdiction which apply irrespective of the 'domicile' of the parties; we shall discuss it, and other, alas too numerous, exceptional cases, in full shortly.

This general position is made even clearer by article 3 which says:

> 'Persons domiciled in a Contracting State may be sued in the courts of another Contracting State only by virtue of the rules set out in sections 2 to 6 of this Title [this is a reference to the exceptional cases]'.

The article goes on to state that various provisions in regard to exorbitant jurisdiction in the laws of the Contracting States 'shall not be applicable' against persons 'domiciled' in the EC. English law's exorbitant jurisdiction based upon service of the writ and presence within the jurisdiction are specifically mentioned here; thus these heads of jurisdiction cannot now be relied upon where the defendant is 'domiciled' in the EC.

The jurisdictional rules that we have considered in this section so far relate to the position where a defendant is 'domiciled' in one of the EC states. When the defendant is 'domiciled' in the United Kingdom, a further problem arises. It is clear that he must be sued in the courts of the United Kingdom, but it is not clear whether the courts of England and Wales, of Scotland or of Northern Ireland, have jurisdiction. The answer to this question is to be found in s16 of the Civil Jurisdiction and Judgments Act 1982 and Schedule 4 to the Act. The schedule is the crucial provision, and you should take care to understand what it is and what it is doing here.

Schedule 4 consists of a modified version of articles 2–24 (Title II) of the

Convention. The modifications are designed with the following ends in mind: just as Title II of the Convention allocated jurisdiction on the basis of 'domicile' between the various states of the EC, subject to certain exceptions, so Schedule 4 allocates jurisdiction between the different parts of the United Kingdom on the basis of 'domicile' in that part, subject to exceptions which are analogous to those contained in Title II. (If you had any doubts earlier about why it was necessary to have rules determining both whether a person is 'domiciled' in the United Kingdom and also in which part of the United Kingdom, it should now be clear what the purpose of those rules was.)

As adumbrated the general provisions of Schedule 4 are similar, mutatis mutandis, to those contained in Title II. Even the numbers of the article of Schedule 4 are the same as the number of the analogous articles of Title II. Thus article 2 of Schedule 4 provides:

> 'Subject to the provisions of this Title, persons domiciled in a part of the United Kingdom shall be sued in the courts of that part.'

Thus it will not be necessary for us to examine the various provisions of Schedule 4 in detail; those differences that do arise will be dealt with in the detailed discussion of Title II.

By now the basic scheme of the Convention in regard to jurisdiction should be clear. First, the court determines where the defendant is 'domiciled' in accordance with the rules that we have discussed previously in section 4.3 *The concept of 'domicile' under the Conventions and the Civil Jurisdiction and Judgments Act 1982*, above. If the defendant is not 'domiciled' either in the United Kingdom or elsewhere in the EC, then the common law rules of jurisdiction discussed above in section 4.2 above apply and the court determines whether it has jurisdiction over the defendant according to those rules. If the defendant is 'domiciled' in one of the EC states excluding the United Kingdom, then the United Kingdom courts do not have jurisdiction. Should the conclusion be reached that the defendant is 'domiciled' in the United Kingdom, then the court determines which part of the United Kingdom he is 'domiciled' in; if the court that is seised of the matter has jurisdiction over that part of the United Kingdom, then it hears the case. If it has not, the court that has jurisdiction over that part should hear the case.

Unfortunately matters are not quite as simple as we would like them to be, for there are a number of matters in which the Convention departs from the principle that it is the court of the 'domicile' which has jurisdiction. Articles 5, 6 and 6A, for instance, deal with occasions upon which a person 'domiciled in a Contracting State' may be sued in another Contracting State. This is known as Special Jurisdiction. In addition article 16 provides that certain courts will in certain circumstances have 'exclusive jurisdiction, regardless of domicile'. This is known as Exclusive Jurisdiction. And, finally, there are specific rules dealing with insurance contracts and consumer contracts. We will consider these exceptions to the 'domicile' rule in turn.

## Special jurisdiction

Article 5 specifies seven occasions on which a court other than that of the defendant's 'domicile' shall have jurisdiction. (The court where the defendant is 'domiciled' retains jurisdiction even if another court has special jurisdiction.) Note that the defendant must be 'domiciled' in the EC before the question of special jurisdiction can arise. Article 5(1) has been amended by the San Sebastian Convention, and the relevant words from the amended version are given below. The words after the semi-colon have been added by the amendment.

### Contract: article 5(1)

'[In] matters relating to a contract ... the courts for the place of performance of the obligation in question can hear the case; in matters relating to individual contracts of employment, this place is that where the employee habitually carries out his work, or if the employee does not habitually carry out his work in any one country, the employer may also be sued in the courts for the place where the business which engaged the employee was or is now situated.'

This provision (in its unamended form) has been before the European Court on a number of occasions chiefly because it is sometimes uncertain where a particular obligation is to be performed and also because it is uncertain what law should be used to determine where the contract is to be performed. There are several important cases.

In *Tessili v Dunlop AG* [1976] ECR 1473 the court held that the national court using its own rules of private international law should determine where the contract was to be performed. This reliance upon the use of the national laws to interpret a provision of the Convention may be suspect in the light of such later cases as *LTU v Eurocontrol*, above, in which the court developed 'Convention concepts' independent of and different from those of national law. Obviously reliance upon national concepts will tend to undermine the uniformity that it is the intention of the Convention to advance. On the other hand, it may be possible to reconcile the *Eurocontrol* approach and that of *Tessili v Dunlop AG*. Even though the Brussels Convention should be uniformly interpreted (using Convention concepts), that was not in issue in *Tessili*; notwithstanding the Convention different contracts still have their different proper laws, and all that *Tessili v Dunlop* lays down is that that law, as determined by the lex fori's choice of laws rules, should determine where obligations are to be performed. It would be awkward, to say the least, if the Convention insisted that the contract should be performed in one country, when its proper law insisted that it should be performed elsewhere.

The European Court had the opportunity to reconsider the *Tessili v Dunlop* approach to this issue in *Custom Made Commercial Ltd v Stawa Metallbau GmbH* [1994] ILPr 516 where the Bundesgerichthof (German Federal Court), referred to the ECJ the question whether the phrase 'place of performance' in article 5(1) should be determined according to the *Tessili* approach or, if not, how is it to be decided. The circumstances were as follows: under German law, in the case of many international sales contracts, the rules of private international law are displaced in favour of the Uniform Law on International Sales which provides that such contracts were to be performed at the seller's place of business. To the German judges this seemed to give the seller an unfair advantage, since if *Tessili* were followed, seldom would any court other than the seller's domicile (which was already competent) have special jurisdiction, ie article 5(1) was effectively a dead letter. The ECJ, however, declined to depart from the *Tessili* approach.

It should perhaps be noted that recently the Court of Appeal in Paris has, in effect, applied *Tessili* v *Dunlop* although no cases at all were referred to! (This is not unusual in civil law cases.) What had happened in *Société Eureco* v *Société Confezioni Liviam di Crespi Luigi* [1990] ILPr 50 was that a dispute had arisen between a French firm (the plaintiff agent) and an Italian firm (the defendant principal) over the commission payable under an exclusive agency agreement. Could the French plaintiff sue in France or did he have to sue in the defendant's court, Italy? The Cour d'Appel applied its rules of private international law to decide that the proper law of the contract was French law and that under French law the commission was payable at the debtor's address, viz, in Italy. Thus 'the place of performance of the obligation in question' was in Italy, and the French courts did not have jurisdiction under article 5(1).

There was another straightforward application of these principles by the Italian court in *Spa OMV Officine Meccaniche Ventura* v *Prometal SA* [1990] ILPr 184. A contract for the sale of tubes was disputed between an Italian plaintiff (the seller) and the French defendant (the purchaser). The court applied the rules of Italian private international law to determine the law that governed the contract (broadly speaking Italian law holds that, in the absence of an express choice of law, the law of the place where the contract is made governs the contract). Since the contract was made in France the proper law of the contract was French law. Then the Italian court applied French law to determine where the 'obligation in question' was to be performed. Under French law the place where delivery of goods sold was to be performed was, in the absence of agreement otherwise, the place where the goods actually were at the time of the sale. Since the goods were in Italy at the time, the obligation to deliver them was to be performed in Italy; hence the Italian courts had jurisdiction under article 5(1).

The European Court of Justice has returned to the idea of Convention concepts in *Arcado SPRL* v *Haviland SA* (Case 9/87) [1988] ECR 1539 (see Hartley (1989) 14 *European Law Review* 172). Here it held, quite correctly, it is submitted, that the words 'in matters relating to a contract' in article 5(1) should be given a Convention meaning rather than a meaning drawn from the national law. This is consistent with the finding of the ECJ in *Jakob Handle GmbH* v *Traitements Mecano-Chimiques des Surfaces* (1992) The Times 19 August that product liability suits against the manufacturer (who had not sold the product to the plaintiff) were not within article 5(1): there had to be an undertaking, freely entered into, between plaintiff and defendant. And this was so notwithstanding that in some legal systems (in casu French law) such claims were seen as contractual.

In *De Bloos* v *Bouyer* [1976] ECR 1497 the court discussed the meaning of the phrase 'obligation in question'. These words did not make it clear which obligation – that of the plaintiff or of the defendant – was to be used in determining special jurisdiction. The court said that it was 'the place where the obligation which constitutes the basis of the claim was, or ought to be, peformed'. *De Bloos* v *Bouyer* has been followed in England in *Medway Packaging Ltd* v *Meurer Maschinen GmbH & Co Kg* [1990] ILPr 234. Here the defendants, a German firm that manufactured machinery, had agreed with the plaintiffs, an English firm, that the plaintiffs should have the exclusive right to distribute their machinery in England. A dispute arose over whether the defendants, in breach of this contract, had authorised another UK firm to distribute their products and whether the proper notice of termination of the agreement had been given. Applying *De Bloos* v *Bouyer* the Court of Appeal held that the obligation to give notice of termination 'could reasonably be regarded as the principal obligation in this case' and that notice had to be given in England. Thus the service of the writ on the German defendants was not set aside.

However, the court indicated how difficult the application of these rules might be: the obligation not to appoint another distributor required the grantor to act properly in both the UK and Germany, and 'it could not be said that the contract for the exclusive distributorship was wholly performable ... either in England or in Germany ... It was as much performable in the one country as in the other.'

There have been several recent cases dealing either with the identification of 'the obligation in question' or with determining its 'place of performance'. In *Union Transport Group plc* v *Continental Lines SA* [1992] 1 All ER 161, for instance, a charterparty required Belgian shipowners to nominate (in London) a vessel to carry telegraph poles from Florida to Bangladesh. The vessel was not nominated, and the dispute over this and other issues arose. Did the English court have jurisdiction under article 5(1)? The shipowners argued that 'the obligation in question' was to provide a vessel in Florida and that there was thus no article 5(1) jurisdiction in the English court. However, the House of Lords held, first, that where the dispute concerned a number of obligations under the same contract the principal obligation was 'the obligation in question'. But, secondly, in this case that was the obligation to nominate (to be performed in London) since such nomination was necessary to identify the subject matter of the contract and was an essential prerequisite for the performance of the other obligations under the contract.

The place of performance of 'the obligation in question' has been disputed in two further cases, one Scottish and one English; a similar issue arose in both, but while the English court was flexible in its approach the Scottish court was not. The cases are *Royal Bank of Scotland plc* v *Cassa di Risparmio delle Provincie Lombardi* [1991] ILPr 411 (English High Court) and *The Governor and Company of the Bank of Scotland* v *Wilfried Seitz* [1991] ILPr 426 (Court of Session, Scotland). Of course, it has been clear since *Tessili* v *Dunlop AG* (above) that the national court should use its own rules of private international law to determine the proper law of the contract, and that law should be used to determine where 'the obligation in question' should be performed. Now the general rule (of both English and Scottish law) is that in the absence of agreement otherwise the debtor must pay the creditor at the place of the creditor's business or residence. However, in the *Royal Bank of Scotland* case, in the context of inter-bank letters of credit (where it is possible for one bank to reimburse another by several different methods of payment), the English court was willing to apply the general rule flexibly. None the less, in this case there had been agreement that reimbursement would take place through certain American banks, thus the US was the place of performance of 'the obligation in question', so the English court (the creditor's place of business) did not have article 5(1) jurisdiction. On the other hand, in the *Royal Bank of Scotland* case, where a German guarantor had guaranteed the repayment of certain loans to the bank (which loans were to be repaid in Scotland), the guarantor's obligation too was to be performed in Scotland; thus the Scottish courts had article 5(1) jurisdiction.

Those familiar with the unamended article 5(1) will readily appreciate that spelling out in the amendment that in individual contracts of employment the place of performance of the obligation in question is the place where the employee habitually works, is pretty much the position that the European Court had already reached in its interpretation of article 5(1) in cases such as *Ivenel* v *Schwab* [1982] ECR 1891 and *Shenavai* v *Kreischer* [1987] ECR 239. In terms of those cases with contracts of employment the 'obligation in question' is the 'characteristic performance' of such a contract – work. So the employee will be able to sue his employer in the place where he works, even if his employer is domiciled elsewhere. This will not always be convenient for the employee. For instance, where the employee habitually works in one country but is 'domiciled' in another, he would generally prefer to sue in his domiciliary court – but that is not possible in terms of article 5(1).

The final part of the amended article 5(1) is designed to deal with problems akin to that which arose in *Six Constructions Ltd* v *Paul Humbert* [1990] ILPr 206. There a French-domiciled man had been employed by a Belgian-domiciled firm. During this employment he had worked in Libya, Zaire and Abu Dhabi. Could the dispute over his contract of employment be litigated in the French courts? There could plainly be no reliance on his habitual place of work for that, if it existed at all in the circumstances, was not in France. The European Court held that the French courts did not have jurisdiction; the firm would have to be sued in Belgium. However, the amended article 5(1) (which is consistent with both the Rome Convention and the Lugano Convention) would allow him to sue in the place where the business that engaged him 'was or is now situated' (which might be different from the place where it was domiciled).

See further, *Mulox IBC Ltd* v *H Geels* [1993] ILPr 668, where the ECJ (applying the unamended article 5(1)) in the case of a sales manager who sold in Germany, Belgium, Netherlands and Scandinavia but lived and had his office in France, held that only the courts of the place where he mainly discharged his obligations, viz, France since that was where his office was, had article 5(1) jurisdiction.

The related issue that arises in this context is what is a 'contract of employment'? Although decided under the unamended article 5(1), *Mercury Publicity Ltd* v *Wolfgang Loerke GbmH* (1991) The Times 21 October will prove to be useful in this context. An English firm had appointed a German firm sole advertising agent in Germany. When a dispute arose between the parties one of the issues argued before the English courts was that, since this was a contract of employment and the work was to be done in Germany, the English courts did not have jurisdiction under article 5(1). The English Court of Appeal held, quite correctly it is submitted, that the *Ivenel* principle was restricted to:

> 'those cases of a personal nature in the relationship between master and servant where inequality of bargaining power might well become critical and where [not to allow the doctrine to operate] might well deprive the employee or agent of the protection of restrictive agreements and of other statutory and union protection which had been negotiated for this benefit.'

This, of course, was a clear case, but there might be others in which it would be difficult to determine where a contract was 'an individual contract of employment' or not. It is submitted that this is a community concept, and that national laws will not be used in determining its content.

A different kind of problem relating to article 5(1) was considered in *Tesam Distribution Ltd* v *Schuh Mode Team GmbH and Commerzbank AG* [1990] ILPr 149 (CA). The plaintiff in this action was an English firm of shoe importers and the defendants were a German firm of shoe suppliers (Schuh Mode Team) and a German Bank (Commerzbank), and the plaintiff's claim alleged that both the defendants had breached a contract for the sale and delivery of certain shoes by failing to deliver the shoes as agreed and failing to accept payment therefor. It was clear that, if there was a contract between the parties, then the shoes were to be delivered in London. Thus the 'obligation in question' (the delivery of the shoes) was to be performed in London. This would plainly mean that under article 5(1) the English courts would have special jurisdiction, and the plaintiff did not need to sue the defendants in Germany.

But, although there had been considerable correspondence between the parties, there was doubt as to whether there was a binding contract between them. That question is a crucial one, for it could surely not be right that a plaintiff could, by simply asserting the existence of a contract, ensure that a court convenient for him had jurisdiction. On the other hand, the plaintiff could hardly be expected to provide conclusive evidence of the contract before the matter went to trial, for whether there was a contract or not might be (and was in this case) the most important issue to be decided at trial.

In the event the Court of Appeal decided that in the exercise of its article 5(1) jurisdiction:

'The court may determine the dispute whether a contract was entered into by the parties
... the court's jurisdiction ... is not dependent upon the court first satisfying itself that the
contract does exist. That is the subject matter of the dispute, and that is a subject matter
which *Effer* v *Kantner* Case 38/81 [[1982] ECR 825] established the court has jurisdiction
... [to determine]. If in due course the court finds that no contact was entered into, it will
dismiss the claim: but it had jurisdiction to determine that issue.'

Both judges (Nicholls and Stocker LJJ), however, stressed that it would not be
enough for the plaintiff simply to assert the existence of the contract; the court had
to be satisfied that there was 'evidence from which the conclusion could properly be
drawn that a contract existed and that the place of performance was the country in
which the action was brought'. Furthermore, it was for each Contracting State's
national law to determine the burden of proof of facts relevant to its jurisdiction. In
the event, on analysis of the correspondence that had passed between the parties, the
court held that it had jurisdiction to hear the claim in contract between the parties.
(See further discussion of this case at section 4.3 Tort: article 3, below, in regard to
special jurisdiction in tort claims under article 5(3).)

(Note that in *Rank Film Distributors Ltd* v *Lanterna Editrice Srl and Banca
Nazionale del Lavoro* [1992] ILPr 58 Saville J followed *Tesam Distribution Ltd* v
*Schuh Mode* and held that where there was a dispute as to the existence of 'the
obligation in question' the plaintiff must satisfy the court that his claim raised a
serious question which called for a trial for its proper determination and, if right,
brought the matter within article 5(1).

*Barclays Bank plc* v *Glasgow City Council* [1992] 3 WLR 827 (first instance
judgment); [1994] 2 WLR 466 (CA), although a rare example of a Schedule 4 case
(ie the question was whether the English courts or the Scottish courts had
jurisdiction), raises some important issues about the interpretation of article 5(1).
What had happened was that the plaintiff banks had conducted interest rate swap
transactions on behalf of various local authorities, including the Glasgow City
Council. These swap transactions had, after extensive litigation, been held ultra vires
and void (see *Hazell* v *Hammersmith and Fulham London Borough Council* [1992] AC
1 (HL); [1991] 2 WLR 372). The banks were now seeking recovery of sums paid
under these agreements by way of claims for restitution (instituted in England)
against the English and Scottish local authorities involved. The Glasgow City
Council contested the jurisdiction of the English court; the banks responded inter
alia that there was special jurisdiction under article 5(1) of Schedule 4 of the Civil
Jurisdiction and Judgments Act 1982 (but the relevant words of article 5(1) of
Schedule 4 were identical to those of the Brussels Convention) in that this was a
matter 'relating to contract' and the place of performance of 'the obligation in
question' was in England.

At first instance the banks failed and the action in England was stayed; the
Glasgow City Council had to be sued in Scotland where it was domiciled. Article
5(1), of course, created special jurisdiction 'in matters relating to contract' in the
courts for the place of performance of the obligation in question. But, since the

House of Lords had already said that the contracts were void, there was no contract and reliance could not be placed upon article 5(1). The reasoning of the court was based on the straightforward wording of the article, as well as the fact that the European Court has clearly laid down that special jurisdiction constitutes a derogation from the general principle of domiciliary jurisdiction and so should be strictly construed.

Note that the court was not persuaded by the argument that because in terms of article 10(1)(e) of the Rome Convention (see Chapter 5, section 5.3 The scope of applicable law as determined under the Convention) the applicable law governs 'the consequences of nullity of the contract', it followed that the consequences of nullity were included 'in matters relating to contract' under Schedule 4 of the Civil Jurisdiction and Judgments Act 1982. Moreover, the UK government has derogated from article 10(1)(e) of the Rome Convention and this fact was taken account of by Hirst J in reaching his conclusion. It is thus possible then that a different view may be taken in a pure Brussels Convention case and that the European Court may take a different view in such a case.

The European Court was then asked to make its views clear on this issue for the question of the interpretation of article 5(1) that seemed relatively clear to Hirst J in the court below were 'perplexing' to Lloyd LJ in the Court of Appeal. It was far from clear to him that a contract had to exist before the questions raised could be 'matters relating to a contract' in terms of article 5(1). The cases made it clear that a Convention concept of contract was to be used (*Peters Bauunternehmung GmbH* v *Zuid Nederlandse Aanmers Vereniging* (Case 34/82) [1983] ECR 987; *Arcado SPRL* v *Haviland SA* (Case 9/87) [1988] ECR 1539) and could not a claim for restitution be sufficiently close to a contractual claim to fall within article 5(1)? The logic of Hirst J's judgment is strong – since there was no contract how could there be a 'contractual matter'? – and Lloyd LJ did not refer to the fact that article 10(1)(e) of the Rome Convention was not part of the law of the UK. None the less, Lloyd LJ referred the question of the interpretation of article 5(1) of Schedule 4 to the European Court. This is a most surprising conclusion since it is difficult to see where the European Court gets jurisdiction to interpret Schedule 4 from. Schedule 4 is not part of the Brussels Convention or any of the other Conventions which the European Court has jurisdiction to interpret under the 1971 Interpretation Protocol. And the orthodox view is that, although the English courts are bound to have regard to the decisions of the European Court in interpreting Schedule 4 (s16(3) of the CJJA 1982), the Schedule is not subject to interpretation by the European Court (see, for instance, Cheshire, p336). The ECJ, not surprisingly, has now refused to rule on the interpretation of Schedule 4: *Kleinwort Benson Ltd* v *Glasgow City Council* (Case 346/93) [1995] All ER (EC) 514. Here, the European Court held that Schedule 4 to the 1982 Act took the Brussels Convention as a model only. The 1982 Act provides that when national courts apply provisions modelled on the Brussels Convention they are required only to have 'regard to' the case law of the European Court. The English court was therefore 'free to decide whether the interpretation given by it is equally valid for the purposes of the application of the national law based on the Convention'.

The saga in this very significant case continues, however, and the Court of Appeal, on appeal from the original judgment of Hirst J, and after the rejection by the European Court of jurisdiction to rule on the interpretation of article 5(1) following the reference from Lloyd J, has earlier this year reversed the judgment of Hirst J (*Kleinwort Benson Ltd* v *Glasgow City Council* [1996] 2 WLR 655). The Court held that a claim for restitution of money paid under a contract which was a nullity for want of capacity, was a matter relating to a contract within article 5(1). Millett LJ, in an important judgment, held that whether a claim was regarded as falling within article 5(1) depended on whether, for the purposes of the Convention, a defendant should broadly be regarded as being sued in a matter relating to a contract. It was thus wrong to ask whether the claim would be characterised as contractual under domestic law. He went on to say the words 'matters relating to a contract' were intentionally indefinite. While national laws differed, there was a general sense in which the word contract was understood by the signatories to the Convention as a consensual arrangement to create legal relations which was legally enforceable. Here, the parties purported to enter into a contract, assumed obligations to each other and intended them to be legally enforceable. When parties so acted, the intended place of performance was no less relevant a connecting factor because the contract was afterwards found to be void. Thus the Court of Appeal takes a broad sweep with respect to article 5(1) as it is incorporated into Schedule 1 of the Civil Jurisdiction and Judgments Act 1982. The judgment has considerable practical significance, not only with respect to the series of swap cases but in the wider practical world. It remains to be seen whether the European Court will endorse this approach, although it is suggested that they will follow the broad, teleological approach adopted by Court of Appeal.

In *Boss Group Ltd* v *Boss France SA* (1996) The Times 15 April, the Court of Appeal continued with this broad approach to article 5(1) in holding that the plaintiff who sought declaratory relief although denying existence of a contract, could establish that there were matters relating to a contract under article 5(1) of the Brussels Convention as incorporated in Schedule 1 to the Civil Jurisdiction and Judgments Act 1982 by relying on the defendants' assertion that a contract did exist between the parties. The defendants had commenced proceedings against the plaintiffs for breach of an exclusive distributorship, while the plaintiffs served an English writ seeking a declaration that there had been no breach as there had been no contract between themselves and the defendants. The Court of Appeal held that the word contract could not be read only as including cases where the existence of a contract was unchallenged. The fact that the plaintiffs asserted that no such contract existed did not make article 5(1) inapplicable.

Finally, note that it has been held in Ireland that a matter is not within article 5(1) if the obligation in question *could* have been, but did *not have to be*, performed in a Contracting State: *Hanbridge Services Ltd* v *Aerospace Communications Ltd* [1993] ILPr 778 Irish Supreme Court.

## Maintenance: article 5(2)

The courts of the maintenance creditor's 'domicile' or habitual residence have jurisdiction in addition to those of the debtor's 'domicile'. Furthermore, if the matter is ancillary to proceedings concerning the status of a person, then the court which has jurisdiction to entertain those proceedings also has jurisdiction in the maintenance matter, provided that the jurisdiction over the status is not based solely on the nationality of one of the parties.

## Tort: article 5(3)

In 'matters relating to tort, delict or quasi-delict ... the courts for the place where the harmful event occurred' have jurisdiction in addition to those of the defendant's 'domicile'. The difficulty here is that A may act wrongfully in one country and cause harm in another country.

The question came before the European Court in *Bier v Mines de Potasse* [1976] ECR 1735 and [1978] QB 708. Here a French firm discharged chloride into the Rhine (in France) and the discharge caused harm to Bier, a nurseryman in the Netherlands. Did the Dutch courts have jurisdiction? The court decided that the courts of both the place where the wrongful act was performed and that where the harm occurred had jurisdiction. This is obviously the solution most favourable to the plaintiff. RSC O.11 r1(1)(f), discussed above, effectively settles upon this solution for cases to which that part of the Order still applies. The harm must, however, be directly suffered. Thus in *Dumez France and Tracoba v Hessische Landesbank* (Case C220/88) [1990] ECR 49 (where the tortious cancellation on certain bank loans had a deleterious economic effect on certain German companies which were the subsidiary companies of a French company, Dumez France, which also suffered economic loss as a result) the ECJ held that there was no article 5(3) jurisdiction in France, since the parent company had not suffered direct harm. Now, with an application of this principle the Court of Appeal has held in *Kitechnology BV and Others v Unicor GmbH Plastmaschininen and Others* [1994] ILPr 568 that where there had allegedly been a breach of commercial confidence in Germany, but the plaintiff's commercial interests in England had not been harmed, there had been no 'harmful event' in England and so no article 5(3) jurisdiction.

Schedule 4, article 5(3), adds at this point that where the courts in one part of the United Kingdom have jurisdiction by virtue of the defendant's 'domicile' then, in addition to the court where the harmful event occurred, the court in that part of the United Kingdom where 'a threatened wrong is likely to occur' has jurisdiction. (If you have forgotten what Schedule 4 is and why it is relevant, refer back to section 4.3 *The central jurisdiction rules under the Convention* above (towards the end).)

In *Minster Investments Ltd v Hyundai Precision Industry and Another* (1988) The Times 26 January, article 5(3) was applied in a straightforward way. Steyn J held in reliance upon article 5(3) that the English courts had jurisdiction over a French company which had issued certain certificates about the quality of containers manufactured in Korea knowing that the plaintiffs, an English firm, would rely upon them. This meant that England was the place where the harmful event occurred.

The interpretation of article 5(3) came before the European Court in *Kalfelis* v *Schroder, Munchmeyer, Hengst & Co* (1988) The Times 5 October. The court held that the phrase 'matters relating to tort, delict and quasi-delict' in that article was an autonomous Convention concept whose meaning was not determined by the national laws of the various states involved. It was held at first instance in *Barclays Bank plc* v *Glasgow City Council* [1992] 3 WLR 827 that claims for restitution were not included within article 5(3) (as a form of 'quasi-delict'). However, the Court of Appeal ([1994] 2 WLR 466) was less certain and referred this question to the European Court. For the facts and discussion of this case see above (**Contract: article 5(1)**).

Moreover, article 5(3) (along with the other articles dealing with special jurisdiction, including article 6) should be given a restrictive interpretation because of deviation from the general jurisdictional principle of the Convention that defendants should be sued in the court of their domicile. Thus it followed that the mere fact that a particular court had jurisdiction under article 5(3) to deal with the tortious part of a claim did not mean that it had jurisdiction over the non-tortious part of that claim. Any inconvenience that might result from this state of affairs could always be resolved simply by suing the defendant in the court of his domicile.

Where a harmful or unlawful publication is printed and published in one country and bought and read in another, interesting questions arise about where the 'harmful event' occurred. For example, this is what happened in *Shevill* v *Presse Alliance SA* [1996] 3 All ER 929. An article had been published in the French newspaper *France Soir* alleging that a certain firm of Bureaux de Change operators, including its employees, was involved in the laundering of drug money. An English-domiciled employee of the firm (along with the firm) sued the French-domiciled owners of the newspaper for libel in England. But did the English court have jurisdiction? Only 250 copies of the offending paper had been sold in England. Purchas LJ held that where a libel had been published in England, that publication constituted a harmful event for the purposes of article 5(3). This was not because English law assumed special damage on the publication of a libel (that was an idiosyncratic rule of English law) but because the cause of action for libel arose when and where the publishee receives and reads the publication, and that was not an idiosyncratic rule of English law. Any state in which the libel had been published would have article 5(3) jurisdiction even if the harm suffered was minimal (although that might affect the quantum of damages).

On appeal, the House of Lords specifically referred to the European Court a question on the meaning of 'place where harmful event occurred', where the harmful event could have happened in a number of jurisdictions. The European Court held (Case C–68/93 [1995] All ER (EC) 2899) that a plaintiff in a libel action where the article was distributed in several Contracting States could bring an action, either where the publisher was established or in each State where the harmful article was distributed and where the victim claimed to have suffered damage to his reputation.

The European Court thereore accepted the likelihood of multiple fora having jurisdiction in a libel case and the possibility of forum shopping. Considerations of whether England was the appropriate forum were irrelevant.

The appeal then came back before the House of Lords, which found that it was abundantly clear from relevant parts of the European Court's judgment that what constituted a harmful event was to be determined by the national court applying its own substantive law. The House of Lords held that where, under English law, the publication of libellous material was regarded as harmful to the person libelled without specific proof, then this was a harmful event for the purposes of article 5(3). In this case the plaintiffs had made out a case entitling them to an inquiry as to the harm which they were alleged to have suffered in England as a result of the publication and thus article 5(3) applied and the English courts had jurisdiction.

*Shevill* is a straightforward application of the scope of article 5(3) as established by the European Court. It is clear that article 5(3) is not designed to harmonise substantive rules as to what harm is in the context of a libel action, but simply to unify the relevant jurisdictional rules and, accordingly, it is logical that the determination as to what harm entails in the context of a libel action is best left to the court seised under article 5(3).

Contrast this, however, with the German case of *Re the Unauthorised Publication of Approved Photographs* [1991] ILPr 468. Here a photograph of the plaintiff (a German domiciliary) had been published without his consent in a Dutch pornographic magazine. He sued the publisher (a Dutch domiciliary) in Germany, but did the German courts have jurisdiction in terms of article 5(3)? The German court held that no harmful event had occurred in Germany even though the Dutch magazine could be bought in Germany. Relying on a provision of German law (article 24 of the Unfair Competition Act), the court held that the publication had to circulate to a significant extent or to be distributed regularly even if only in small numbers before the German courts would have jurisdiction. The court said that if one regarded the German courts as having jurisdiction 'simply on the ground that the publication could be bought in Germany, that would produce the result that this Court would have jurisdiction over all injury caused by newspapers and periodicals anywhere in the world, since it is possible eventually to buy any newspaper appearing in the world in Germany'.

Perhaps the two cases may be reconciled on the ground that in *Shevill* it was clear that *France Soir* circulated regularly in England (although in small numbers). More pertinently, one may ask whether the German court was right to rely on German law in deciding where the harmful event occurred. For *The Netherlands* v *Ruffer* (Case 814/79) [1980] ECR 3807 establishes that 'tort, delict or quasi-delict' is a Convention concept not determined by the national laws. On the other hand, perhaps one needs to know the law under which the act in question is harmful before one can say where that event took place? (See the discussion of *Tessili* v *Dunlop* above.)

Related issues have arisen in three further cases decided elsewhere in Europe.

First, *Radio Monte Carlo* v *Syndicat National de l'Edition Phonographique* [1991] ILPr 264 where it was held (by the Paris Court of Appeal) that when an unlawful broadcast of copyright material was made from a studio in Monaco but the broadcast was received in France, the place where injury was caused was France, and that consequently the French courts had article 5(3) jurisdiction. This is plainly consistent with both previous cases. Secondly, *Hubert Bion* v *Schimmel Pianofortefabrik GmbH* [1991] ILPr 448, in which it was held in an economic loss case (the tort was that of 'refusing to sell') that the harm is suffered by the plaintiff at his domicile (for that is where the harm resulted) even if the refusal to sell took place elsewhere. One wonders whether this principle will apply to economic loss (suffered in the plaintiff's domicile) which is consequent upon some physical damage (which takes place elsewhere). Thirdly, in *Marinari* v *Lloyds Bank plc (Zubaidi Trading Co, Intervener)* (Case C–364/93) [1996] 2 WLR 159, the European Court of Justice held that the 'place where the harmful event occurred' did not cover the place where the victim claimed to have suffered financial loss consequential on initial damage arising and suffered by him in another Contracting State. See Chapter 10, section 10.1, for further details.

One of the alternative claimed grounds of special jurisdiction in *Tesam Distribution Ltd* v *Schuh Mode Team GmbH and Commerzbank AG* (discussed above; you should glance at the earlier discussion of the facts of that case before reading further) was based in tort. The plaintiff claimed that the bank (the second defendant) had wrongfully induced the first defendant to breach his contract with the defendant, so, quite apart from any contractual liability, the bank was liable to the plaintiff in tort. The plaintiff claimed that the loss caused by the tort had been suffered in England, thus the English courts had jurisdiction under article 5(3). The court adopted the same approach to this issue as it had in the context of the contractual claims: a mere assertion of a tort could not confer jurisdiction; the question was: was there a serious issue to be tried? In the event the court decided that the tort claim was not 'seriously arguable', and special jurisdiction was denied.

It may be noted that article 5(3) uses the past tense; thus it cannot be relied upon in seeking protective measures *before* any harm has actually occurred. This at any rate was the meaning given to article 5(3) by the Dutch courts in *De Stichting Natuur Milieu* v *Ennergiebedrijven van het Scheldeland Ebes* [1990] ILPr 246. Thus in that case an environmental group in the Netherlands was unable to sue a Belgian company (which operated a nuclear power station in Belgium) through the Dutch courts. Their case was that the power station was operated in a dangerous manner, but since they had as yet suffered no harm they could not rely upon article 5(3). They would have to sue the company in Belgium.

### Civil claims in criminal proceedings: article 5(4)

Where a court has jurisdiction to entertain a civil claim in criminal proceedings, then it is not precluded from entertaining that claim by the Convention.

## Branches and Agencies: article 5(5)

Where 'a dispute ... [arises] out of the operations of a branch or agency ... the courts for the place in which the branch [or] agency... is situated' have jurisdiction to hear the dispute. The interpretation of article 5(5) has also been before the European Court. In *De Bloos* v *Bouyer,* above, the court held that the appointment of an 'exclusive distributor' in Belgium did not amount to establishing a branch or agency in Belgium; it was necessary that the branch should be under the direction and control of the head office, and this was not the case where an independent distributor was appointed.

This was expanded upon in *Blanckaert & Williams* v *Trost* [1981] ECR 819. Here it was held that the branch must appear as 'an easily discernible extension of the parent body' (Hartley, op cit, 54), and that the requirement of direction and control would not be satisfied where the representative organises his own work and is entitled to represent other firms selling similar products as well.

*Blanckaert & Williams* v *Trost* was applied by Potter J in *New Hampshire Insurance Co* v *Strabag Bau AG* [1990] ILPr 334 where it was held that, although article 5(5) did not expressly say so, the 'branch, agency or other establishment' referred to must be a branch, agency or other establishment of the defendant, and the plaintiff's position in that respect is irrelevant. Furthermore, acting through an agent was insufficient for special jurisdiction under article 5(5) to exist.

In *Lloyd's Register of Shipping* v *Société Campenon Bernard* (Case C–439/93) [1995] All ER (EC) 531 the European Court held that it was not necessary in order for special jurisdiction under article 5(5) to exist, that the 'obligation in question' had to be performed in the Contracting State where the branch was established. If that were so, article 5(5) would be superfluous since there would always be article 5(1) jurisdiction. Thus, where the Paris branch of the LRS had agreed to certify the quality of certain steel bars in Spain, the French courts had article 5(5) jurisdiction notwithstanding that the steel was inspected in Spain. The inspection arose out of the operations of the Paris branch and that was enough.

## Trusts: article 5(6)

Disputes between the beneficiaries, settlors and trustees under a trust, whether established under statute or written instrument or orally, can be litigated in the court of the 'domicile' of the trust, in addition, of course, to the court of the 'domicile' of the defendant. Constructive trusts and resulting trusts are excluded. Moreover, trusts arising under wills are excluded under article 1 of the Convention.

## Admiralty: article 5(7)

This is a very technical matter that is not very important for your purposes, but see Hartley, op cit, 55–56.

This may, however, have important implications for Admiralty litigation. See *The Deichland* (1989) The Times 27 April.

## Co-defendants and third parties: article 6

Article 6 provides that a person 'domiciled' in a Contracting State 'may also be sued': (1) 'Where he is one of a number of defendants, in the courts for the place where any one of them is domiciled'. (2) 'As a third party in an action on a warranty or guarantee or in any other third party proceedings, in the court seised of the original proceedings, unless these were instituted solely with the object of removing him from the jurisdiction of the court which would be competent in his case.' (3) 'on a counterclaim arising from the same contract or facts on which the original claim was based, in the court where the original claim is pending.' (4) 'in matters relating to a contract, if the action may be combined with an action against the same defendant in matters relating to rights in rem in immovable property, in the court of the Contracting State in which the property is situated.' This last sub-paragraph was added by the San Sebastian Convention. The purpose of this amendment is self-explanatory: henceforth where a complex dispute arises over immovable property the contractual as well as the proprietary aspects of the case may be resolved in one action. However, this amendment should be considered in the light of the amendments – shortly to be discussed – to article 16(1).

The interpretation of article 6(1) has come before the European Court in *Kalfelis v Schroder, Munchmeyer, Hengst & Co* (above), where the court held that there must be a connection between the various claims made by the plaintiff and the different defendants such that it was desirable to rule on them together to avoid irreconcilable judgments if they were dealt with separately. Not unexpectedly the court said that this connection should be determined independently of national law.

In *Gascoine and Another v Pyrah and Another* [1994] ILPr 82 the Court of Appeal delivered a useful judgment on the text to be adopted in determining whether there is a risk of irreconcilable judgments if co-defendants are not sued together. What had happened was that Mr and Mrs Gascoine had engaged Mr Pyrah, who was domiciled in England, to find a horse for use by their daughter for show-jumping. Mr Pyrah found an apparently suitable horse, Othello, in France and was then instructed to obtain a veterinary report on the horse and arrange the sale. Mr Pyrah engaged Dr Cronau, a German-domiciled veterinarian, to inspect the horse which he did. Dr Cronau's written report revealed that Othello's right front navicular bone had a central decalcified area but, it was alleged by Mr Pyrah, Dr Cronau had told him in a subsequent telephone conversation that this was not a serious problem; and the horse was thus bought for £75,000. In fact the defect in the bone was a serious problem and rendered the horse unsuitable for show-jumping; its value was reduced to £3,000.

The Gascoines at first instituted action against Pyrah only in England (which plainly had jurisdiction under article 2). But when he raised as a defence his conversation with Cronau, they wished to institute action against Cronau as well. The English courts, of course, did not have domiciliary jurisdiction over Cronau, but was there jurisdiction under article 6(1)? At first instance the judge had concluded that there was no risk of irreconcilable judgments and had refused leave to join Dr Cronau under article 6(1).

The Court of Appeal, however, held that the risk of irreconcilable judgments applied just as much to the risk of inconsistent findings of fact as it did to inconsistent findings of law. In this case the telephone conversation was vital both to Mr Pyrah's defence to the Gascoines' cause of action; and if that factual issue was differently decided by different courts there was a risk of irreconcilable judgments. Thus under article 6(1) the English courts had jurisdiction over Dr Cronau. As Hirst LJ remarked:

'... where a potential conflict on this vital issue of fact [the telephone call] has been so clearly demonstrated ..., there must be an option, which the plaintiffs are entitled to exercise under article 6(1) to sue Dr Cronau as well as Mr Pyrah in this court.' (p95)

In *The Owners of the Cargo Lately Laden on Board the Rewia v Caribbean Liners (Caribtainer) Ltd* [1993] ILPr 507 the Court of Appeal held that to engage article 6(1) there had to be an arguable claim against the defendant domiciled in the Contracting State in which the action is brought. In other words, article 6(1) jurisdiction could not be manufactured by bringing an action that was bound to fail against a defendant domiciled within the jurisdiction simply to gain jurisdiction over a defendant not domiciled within the jurisdiction. What had happened in *The Rewia* was that the owners of a cargo of nutmeg and mace shipped from Grenada on the Rewia brought an action against the sub-charterers (domiciled in England) and the owners of the ship (who were, it was held, by the Court of Appeal but not the judge below, domiciled in Germany). The Rewia's owners contested jurisdiction but the cargo owners (the plaintiffs) relied on article 6(1) arguing that since the sub-charterers were domiciled in England, the ship owners were subject to the article 6(1) of the English courts. On a careful analysis of the bills of lading under which the plaintiffs were suing it emerged that the plaintiffs had no claim against the sub-charterers; thus article 6(1) was not complied with and the English courts did not have jurisdiction. (The position under O.11, r1(1)(c) is similar: *The Brabo* [1949] AC 326. See above section 4.2.)

A further significant case on article 6(1) is *Aiglon Ltd and L'Aiglon SA v Gau Shan Ltd* [1993] 1 Lloyd's Rep 164. An arbitration award concerning a cargo of raw cotton from Benin was made against an English company (Aiglon Ltd) and a Swiss company (L'Aiglon SA) and was now sought to be enforced against them. The English courts were held to have jurisdiction over the Swiss company in an application of article 6(1) of the Lugano Convention, since they had jurisdiction over the English company. Moreover, s49 of the Civil Jurisdiction and Judgments Act 1982 (as amended) which preserves the court's powers to stay actions 'where to do so is not inconsistent with the Convention', did not entitle the court to stay the action against the Swiss company on forum conveniens grounds since to do so would be inconsistent with the Convention: if the requirements of article 6(1) were complied with, the plaintiff had a right to proceed in England. (See below section 4.4.)

Article 6(2) was authoritatively interpreted by the European Court in *Kongress Agentur Hagen GmbH v Zeehaghe BV* [1991] ILPr 3. What had happened was that a

German firm (Hagen) had reserved certain rooms in a hotel in The Hague owned by a Dutch firm (Zeehaghe). These reservations were cancelled, and Zeehaghe sued for damages in the Dutch courts (which had jurisdiction in terms of article 5(1)). However, Hagen, although acting in its own name, had made the reservations on behalf of another German firm (Garant Shuhgilde), and thus sought to join Shuhgilde as a third party in terms of article 6(2). The European Court held, first, that it was possible for article 6(2) jurisdiction to exist even though 'the court seised of the original proceedings' was exercising a jurisdiction based upon article 5(1) rather than upon the domicile of the defendant. (Contrast article 6(1) jurisdiction which requires that at least one of the defendants is being sued in his domiciliary court.)

But, secondly, although a case might fall within article 6(2) this did not imply an obligation to exercise jurisdiction. (Note that article 6 uses the words 'may also be sued'.) The trial court should apply its own procedural rules to determine whether such jurisdiction should be exercised. However, it must not refuse such a request simply because of the foreign domicile of the third party.

In *Kinnear and Others* v *Falconfilms NV and Others* (1994) The Times 1 March it was held that where there was sufficient nexus between plaintiff's claim against a defendant and that defendant's claim against a third party to justify joinder in terms of O.16 r1(1), then there was likely to be sufficient nexus between them to bring them within article 6(2). Although this proposition has some support from the Schlosser Report (OJ 1979 No C59/71/78), it cannot be correct as a rule of law (as opposed to a useful rule of thumb) for it amounts to allowing the individual domestic laws of the Contracting States to give meaning to article 6(2) contrary to the views of the European Court in numerous cases.

Note that the article 6(2) jurisdiction may be superseded by a choice of jurisdiction under article 17 (see section 4.3 *Prorogation of jurisdiction*, below). At any rate so the Court of Appeal in Paris held in *Karl Schaeff GmbH & Co KG v Société Patrymat* [1990] ILPr 381. In this case there had been a choice of the German courts under article 17. The French plaintiff was suing the French distributor over alleged defects in certain machinery. The French distributor of the machinery sought to join the German manufacturer in the proceedings as a third party, but failed because of the valid article 17 agreement.

### Miscellaneous matters

Article 5(8) is an additional sub-section in Schedule 4; it does not exist in the parent Convention. It provides that where proceedings are brought 'concerning a debt secured on immovable property, or ... to assert, declare or determine proprietary or possessory rights, or rights of security, in or over movable property, or to obtain authority to dispose of movable property', the courts in that part of the United Kingdom in which 'the property is situated' have jurisdiction, in addition of course to the courts of the defendant's 'domicile'.

## *Exclusive jurisdiction*

Article 16 of the Convention provides that 'irrespective of domicile' certain courts shall have exclusive jurisdiction. You should understand how this differs from special jurisdiction. With special jurisdiction we were concerned with cases where a court, in addition to the court of the 'domicile', had jurisdiction. Here we are dealing with those cases where a particular court and, in principle, only that court, is given jurisdiction to the exclusion of other courts, such as the court of the 'domicile', which would otherwise have had jurisdiction. Article 16, therefore, overrides the other provisions of the Convention. Indeed so strongly did the drafters of the Convention feel about this exclusive or overriding character of article 16 that they provided in article 19 that, where 'a court of a Contracting State is seised of a claim which is principally concerned with a matter over which the courts of another Contracting State have exclusive jurisdiction by virtue of article 16, it shall declare of its own motion that it has no jurisdiction'. Moreover, the article applies 'irrespective of domicile': thus even if the defendant is not 'domiciled' in a Contracting State, article 16 applies. Note also that if the case falls within article 16 the parties cannot choose another court; they must litigate in the court of exclusive jurisdiction. This follows from article 17(3) which provides: 'Agreements ... conferring jurisdiction shall have no legal force ... if the courts whose jurisdiction they purport to exclude have exclusive jurisdiction by virtue of article 16.'

### Immovable property: article 16(1)

> '(a) In proceedings which have as their object rights in rem in immovable property or tenancies of immovable property, the courts of the Contracting State in which the property is situated [have exclusive jurisdiction];
> (b) however, in proceedings which have as their object tenancies of immovable property concluded for temporary private use for a maximum period of six consecutive months, the courts of the Contracting State in which the defendant is domiciled shall also have jurisdiction, provided that the landlord and the tenant are natural persons and are domiciled in the same Contracting State.'

Although the phrase 'rights in rem' comes from the civil law rather than English law, it is clear that most rights in property would fall within the article. Rights in contract, eg the sale of land, affect only the parties to the contract and thus would not be in rem, and would not fall within article 16.

In *Sanders* v *Van der Putte* [1977] ECR 2383 the European Court made it clear that article 16, since it deprived parties of a choice of court which would otherwise be theirs, had to be strictly construed. Thus it held that in a dispute between two Dutchmen over what in English law would be called the assignment of a lease (or possibly a sub-lease) of a flower shop in Germany, as well as payment of goodwill in respect of the flower shop, could be heard in the Dutch courts.

Article 16(1)(b) was added by the San Sebastian Convention. The reason for this amendment was that under the unamended article 16(1) as interpreted by the

European Court in *Rosler v Rottwinkel* [1986] QB 33 even short-term holiday lettings of immovable property fell within the article. This was an inconvenient rule, for it is commonplace for a person domiciled in one country to let to a person domiciled in the same country a holiday home in another country. If the landlord and tenant fell out over the property, it was most inconvenient to have to sue in the court of the country where the holiday home was situated. Although this amendment is doubtless welcome is it not still too restrictive? After all, why should the tenant and the landlord have to be domiciled in the same Contracting State? Note also that notwithstanding its position as part of article 16 we are not here dealing with an exclusive jurisdiction but with an extra type of special jurisdiction in that it provides that in addition to the defendant's domicile the courts of the place of situation of the property in question shall have jurisdiction.

Now, in a surprising development, the ECJ seems to have departed from its previous decision of *Rosler v Rottwinkel*. What had happened in *Hacker v Euro Relais GmbH* (1992) The Times 9 April; [1992] ILPr 515 (European Court of Justice) was that Hacker, was domiciled in Germany, entered into a contract (entitled *Meitvertrag* (tenancy contract)) with Euro Relais, a German firm of travel agents. In the contract the firm undertook that Hacker would have the use of a holiday home in the Netherlands and, for an additional payment, a reservation would be made for Hacker's travel to the holiday home.

The holiday home was smaller than advertised, as a result of which Hacker incurred extra expenses and returned to Germany earlier than planned. She sued in the German courts for a reduction of the price paid and damages under various heads. But did the German courts have jurisdiction in the light of (the unamended) article 16(1)? The European Court held that article 16(1) 'must be interpreted as not applying to a contract concluded in a Contracting State whereby a professional travel organiser, which has its registered office in that State, undertakes to procure for a client domiciled in the same State the use for several weeks of holiday accommodation in another Contracting State which it does not own, and to book the travel'.

This conclusion is sensible but it amounts to a departure from *Rosler v Rottwinkel*. The ECJ relied upon the more liberal strand of authority in *Sanders v Van der Putte* [1977] ECR 2383 and *Rosler v Rottwinkel* was not expressly overruled; that is not the European Court's style.

Although not dealt with in the judgment of the court, the Advocate General's opinion suggested that where article 16(1) is found to apply, then the claims for ancillary damages and the like fell within article 16(1). This was in order to prevent a multiplicity of proceedings over essentially one dispute.

The amended article 16(1), it will be recalled, already created an exception to the rigid rule in the case of holiday lettings, but only where tenant and landlord were domiciled in the same Contracting State and were natural persons. Thus, the amendment will not help the case where the letting is from an artificial person, such as a travel company, but *Hacker v Euro Relais* will, ie this exception in favour of holiday lettings goes even further than the amended article 16(1) exception! Note, too, that the exception contained for holiday lettings contained in article 16 of the Lugano Convention is also slightly different! (see section 4.3 *The difference between the Brussels and Lugano Conventions, etc*).

Of course, it may be that a dispute arises over the land which lies on both sides of an EC border (eg between Eire and Northern Ireland or between the Netherlands and Belgium); which court has jurisdiction? This question arose before the European Court in *Scherrens v Maenhout and Others* (1988) The Times 5 September. In this case the two parcels of land over which there was a dispute concerning a lease were some seven kilometres apart. The court held that:

> 'the courts of each state in whose territory a part of the property was situated had jurisdiction over that part. However, in certain circumstances (for instance, where there was one parcel of land bisected by the border) it might be appropriate to treat the property as a single unit and regard it as being exclusively situated in one of the states, so as to assign exclusive jurisdiction to the courts of that state.'

The European Court has also considered the scope of article 16(1) is *Reichert, Reichert and Kockler v Dresdner Bank* Case 115/88 [1990] 1 ILPr 105. The case is an interesting one in that it suggests a rather more restrictive attitude to the interpretation of article 16(1) than that adopted in *Rosler v Rottwinkel*. What happened was that Mr and Mrs Reichert, who lived in Germany, owned property situated in Antibes in France. They made a gift (duly executed in France) of the bare ownership of this property to their son. However, they owed a great deal of money to the Dresdner Bank, which considered that the gift to the son had been made to defraud the bank by preventing the bank from executing against the property for satisfaction of the debt. Now under French law specific provision is made for this sort of case: the 'action paulienne' which allows a debtor to contest the validity of acts performed by the creditor in fraud of the debtor's rights.

In reliance on the action paulienne the bank sued the Reicherts in France. But did the French courts have jurisdiction? Since the Reicherts were plainly domiciled in Germany, the French courts would only have jurisdiction if article 16(1) applied to grant them exclusive jurisdiction.

On a reference to the European Court the court (apart from confirming that article 16 was to be interpreted according to Community concepts) held, first, that article 16(1), since it restricted the parties' choice of court and required litigation in a court which might be the domiciliary court of neither party, should be restrictively interpreted. Secondly, the primary reason for the operation of exclusive jurisdiction under article 16 was that the courts of the Contracting State where the property was situated were in the best position to have a good knowledge of the factual situation affecting the property and to apply the rules and customs of that state. Thus, thirdly, article 16(1) should not be interpreted to cover all actions relating to rights in rem in immovable property but only those whose 'aim [is] to determine the extent, scale, ownership or possession of immovable property or the existence of other rights in rem in such property and safeguard for the holders of such rights the powers attaching to their title'.

Thus, finally, the action paulienne 'arises from the claim, viz, the creditor's right in personam against his debtor, and has the object of safeguarding the charge which the former may hold on the latter's assets. If the action is successful ... the [fraudulent] disposition ... is void as against the creditor alone. Furthermore, the court is not required to assess facts or to apply rules and customs of the place where the property is situated, which are such as to justify the jurisdiction of a court of the state where the property is situated.' Thus article 16(1) did not apply.

This conclusion by the court is doubtless correct. The dispute over the Reicherts' debt to the Dresdner Bank was plainly in personam and had nothing to do with France, save that the property happened to be in France. It was quite right that this dispute should have been litigated in Germany. Furthermore, it may be noted that the bank was, in effect, forum shopping, were it not for the availability of the action paulienne in France the bank would doubtless have sued in Germany. Thus the decision discourages forum shopping, and that is an important purpose of both the conflict of laws as a whole and the Brussels Convention in particular. (The bank tried again, alleging that the action paulienne was within article 5(3), but it failed: *Reichert v Dresdner Bank (No 2)* [1992] ILPr 404 (ECJ).)

Recently, in *Webb v Webb* (Case C294/92) [1994] ILPr 389; [1994] 3 WLR 801 the ECJ pronounced on whether an equitable interest in land was a right in rem for the purposes of article 16(1). What had happened was that the plaintiff Webb had (in 1971) provided the funds for the purchase of a flat in the south of France by his son, the defendant Webb. Father and son had now fallen out and the father sought from the English courts a declaration that his son held the property as trustee for him and that the son should execute such documents as would be required to vest legal ownership of the flat in the father's name. However, the son argued that the alleged equitable interest was a right in rem and thus the French courts had exclusive jurisdiction under article 16(1).

A straightforward illustration of the application of article 16(1) is seen in the recent case of *Re Hayward (deceased)* [1996] 3 WLR 674, in which a trustee in bankruptcy was claiming the debtor's share in a Minorcan villa. The proceedings has as their object a right in rem in immovable property (undoubtedly a claim to legal ownership), so under article 16(1) the Spanish courts had exclusive jurisdiction. See Chapter 10, section 10.1, for further details

The Schlosser Report (para 167(b), p121) and Lasok and Stone, *Conflict of Laws in the European Community* (1987), p237, and many other authorities considered equitable rights, rights in rem. After all, it is trite that equitable rights operate against the whole world with the exception of 'Equity's darling' – the bona fide purchaser for value. However, the ECJ held that for article 16(1) it was not sufficient that the action should have a link with immovable property: the action must be based on a right in rem and not on a right in personam (save for the exceptional case of tenancies). Since the father did not claim in the English proceedings that he enjoyed rights against the property that were enforceable against the whole world (ie rights in rem), but simply a declaration against his son, the action was not in rem.

Thus notwithstanding the authorities that considered equitable interests in rem, the court followed its recent general tendency of a narrow rather than a wide meaning to 'proceedings which have as their object right in rem'. For instance, in *Lieber* v *Gobel* (Case C292/93) [1994] ILPr 590 the ECJ held that a claim for compensation for the use of an immovable, since it can only be made against the person liable and not against the whole world, was not a right in rem.

(In case any reader is unfamiliar with the concept of rights in rem and rights in personam it may be pointed out that rights in rem, for example ownership, are rights that prevail against the entire world. The owner can exclude *everyone* from his property. Rights in personam, for example contractual rights, prevail against only a small number of particular individuals, the parties to the contract in question.)

### Corporations: article 16(2)

In 'proceedings which have as their object the validity of the constitution, the nullity or the dissolution of companies or other legal persons or association of natural or legal persons, or the decisions of their organs, the courts of the Contracting State in which the company, legal person or association has its seat' 'shall have exclusive jurisdiction'.

Two tricky points now arise: first, the meaning of 'seat' in the context of article 16(2) is not determined by s42 of the Civil Jurisdiction and Judgments Act 1982 (the provision we discussed above in section 4.3 *The concept of 'domicile' under the Conventions and the Civil Jurisdiction and Judgments Act 1982* in regard to the 'seat' of a company). Instead the 'seat' of a company is determined by the more restrictive provisions of s43 of the Act. Section 43 provides that a company has its 'seat' in the United Kingdom if and only if (i) 'it was incorporated or formed under the law of a part of the United Kingdom' or (ii) 'its central management and control is exercised in the United Kingdom'. And it provides that a company has its 'seat' in a part of the United Kingdom, if and only if (i) 'it was incorporated or formed under the law of that part' or (ii) 'being incorporated or formed under the law of a state other than the United Kingdom, its central management and control is exercised in that part'. (The astute may point out that some corporations may be formed under enactments that apply through the United Kingdom, so where are they 'seated'? The answer to this is provided in s43(5) which provides that such corporations are 'seated' where they have their registered offices.)

Now why did the drafters of the Civil Jurisdiction and Judgments Act 1982 make the lives of students difficult by making this change? The crucial difference between the 'seating' provisions of s42 and s43 is that s42 says that corporations may be 'seated' where they have their places of business. This means that they may have more than one seat. This means that the company or corporation could be sued in a number of courts, and that would not do under the exclusive jurisdiction of article 16!

In *Newtherapeutics Ltd* v *Katz and Another* [1990] 3 WLR 1183 the scope of article 16(2) was discussed. A dispute had arisen between a UK company (which did all of its business in France but was in terms of s43(2) still seated in England) and one of its ex-directors (who was domiciled in France). Was the matter one which fell within article 16(2) so that the English courts had exclusive jurisdiction or did the defendant have to be sued in the court of his domicile, viz, France?

The crucial allegation was that the director had breached his duty as a director in signing certain variation documents without calling a meeting of the board. On a close analysis of the actual claim against the director made by the company, Knox J concluded that the substance of the claim fell within article 16(2) and thus within the exclusive jurisdiction of the English court. The reason for this conclusion was that in Knox J's judgment the principal issue was whether, without a board resolution, the director could *validly* vary the contracts in question. It was not simply a matter that concerned the propriety of the individual director's actions which might have caused harm to the company and in respect of which the director had to compensate the company.

However, in *Grupo Torras SA* v *Sheikh Fahad Mohammed al Sabah* [1996] 1 Lloyd's Rep 7, the plaintiff (a Spanish company and its English subsidiary) brought an action for conspiracy and breach of duty against the defendant director of the company in England. The defendant contended that under article 16(2) the Spanish courts had jurisdiction and the action in England should be stayed under article 21 (see below).

The Court of Appeal held that what was at issue here was not the 'decisions' of the Spanish company, but the frauds allegedly perpetrated by the defendants. Thus, article 16 did not apply and the English court could exercise jurisdiction.

The second tricky point relates to Schedule 4. In Schedule 4, article 16(2) is truncated; it only applies to proceedings 'which have as their object the validity of the constitution, the nullity or dissolution of companies of other legal persons ...'. There is, however, in Schedule 4 an article 5A which contains the 'rest' of article 16 of the Convention. Article 5A provides that the court of the part of the United Kingdom where the company or corporation has its 'seat' shall have jurisdiction in 'proceedings which have as their object a decision of an organ of a company or other legal person of an association of natural or legal persons ...'.

Now article 5A is in the section dealing with special jurisdiction not exclusive jurisdiction; thus the effect of this change is to ensure that proceedings challenging the decisions of such bodies can be brought not only where the corporation is 'seated' but also in any other court which might have jurisdiction under another provision of the Convention. The reason for this change is the following: 'Many United Kingdom companies and associations (for example, trade unions) have their seat in London and if the courts of the seat had been given exclusive jurisdiction, Scottish and Northern Ireland courts might have been unfairly deprived of jurisdiction.' (Hartley, op cit, 57–58).

The winding up of insolvent companies or other legal persons and analogous proceedings are excluded from the Convention by article 1, so no question of jurisdiction in such proceedings arises under article 16(2).

Note finally the following point: since the 'seat' of a company is to be determined in terms of article 53 in accordance with the court's 'own rules of private international law', it may be that a particular company is 'seated' in more than one Contracting State. Prima facie each has jurisdiction, and the exclusivity of article 16 has been destroyed. Such cases should they arise will be dealt with according to the principles of lis alibi pendens under the Convention (to be discussed in section 4.3 *Lis alibi pendens* below).

### Public registers: article 16(3)
Where the validity of entries in public registers is in issue the courts of the Contracting State where the register is kept have exclusive jurisdiction.

### Trade marks and patents: article 16(4)
Where questions of the registration or validity of patents, trade marks, designs and similar rights required to be deposited or registered are in issue, the courts of the Contracting State in which the deposit or registration has been applied for or has taken place, or in terms of an international convention is deemed to have taken place, have exclusive jurisdiction.

### Judgments: article 16(5)
Proceedings concerned with the enforcement of judgments fall within the exclusive jurisdiction of the Contracting State in which the judgment has been or is to be enforced.

## Consumer contracts: articles 13–15

In order to ensure that consumers do not find that they are placed in a difficult position by the provisions of the Conventions (for example, being forced to sue the supplier of goods in the court of his 'domicile' which is in a different Contracting State from that of the consumer), the Convention provides special jurisdictional rules for consumers.

In essence, article 14 provides that the consumer can bring proceedings either in the court of the defendant's 'domicile' or in the court of his own 'domicile', and proceedings can only be brought against the consumer in the court of his 'domicile'. Of course, where a counterclaim is made then the court which has jurisdiction in respect of the original claim has jurisdiction over the counterclaim.

Special provisions apply also to choice of court clauses in consumer contracts. These are designed to ensure that a consumer (who usually has to take the terms that the other party offers) is not forced to contract out of the advantages rules just discussed. Thus article 15 provides that the provisions of article 14 cannot be varied by agreement except (i) where the agreement is made after the dispute has arisen (so if it is convenient to both parties that the matter be litigated elsewhere they can agree to that, but a choice of court clause hidden in the small print will not be valid); or (ii) which allows the consumer to bring proceedings in courts other than those specified in article 14 (thus such a clause is to the advantage of the consumer);

or (iii) 'which is entered into by the consumer and the other party ... both of whom are at the time of conclusion of the contract domiciled or habitually resident in the same Contracting State, and which confers jurisdiction on the courts of that State, provided that such an agreement is not contrary to the law of that State'.

Thus far we have not said who is a consumer for the purpose of article 14, but article 13 contains a long definition of who it is that is treated as a consumer. First, a consumer must enter into the contract 'outside his trade or profession', and, secondly, the contract must be one of the following: (i) a contract for the sale of goods on instalment credit terms; or (ii) a contract for a loan repayable by instalments, or for any other form of credit, made to finance the sale of goods; or (iii) any other contract for the supply of goods or service which was preceded by a specific invitation to the consumer or advertising in the state of the consumer's 'domicile' and in which the consumer took the necessary steps to conclude the contract in that State. The reference to specific invitation or advertising does not appear in Schedule 4 article 13. In *Société Bertrand* v *Paul Ott KG* [1978] ECR 1431 the European court held that it would use Convention concepts to determine whether a particular contract was a consumer contract or not, and not concepts from the national law of the parties. A jurisdiction clause in a credit card agreement was held ineffective to grant jurisdiction in *Weber* v *SA Eurocard* [1993] ILPr 55 because of the provisions of article 13. Since the credit card allowed the holder to make purchases without making immediate payment, its object was 'the provision of a service' and thus it fell within article 13(3). Therefore, in terms of article 14(2) the action could only be brought in the courts for place where the consumer was domiciled.

Article 13 makes it clear that where a consumer contracts with a party who is not 'domiciled' in a Contracting State, but has a branch or agency in one of the Contracting States, then in disputes arising out of the operation of that branch it shall be deemed to be 'domiciled' in that State. This part of article 13 does not appear in Schedule 4 article 13. Of course, where the defendant does not have a branch in a Contracting State different considerations apply. Thus, since article 13 applied 'without prejudice to the provisions of Article 4' (and article 4 said that if a defendant 'is not domiciled in a Contracting State' then, apart from article 16, jurisdiction over that defendant would be determined by the ordinary jurisdictional law of the Contracting State in which he was sued), it followed that article 13 did not avail plaintiffs at all where the defendant was not domiciled in a Contracting State. Thus in *Brenner and Noller* v *Dean Witter Reynolds Inc* (Case C318/93) [1994] ILPr 720, the ECJ held that two German domiciliaries who had speculated unsuccessfully in commodity futures through a US-domiciled broker (without a branch in Germany) could not rely on article 13 to establish jurisdiction in Germany.

These provisions in regard to consumers do not apply to 'contracts of transport' (article 13). Under Schedule 4 article 13 the analogues of these provisions do not apply to contracts 'of transport or insurance'.

## Insurance contracts: articles 7–12A

This is again a rather technical matter. The Convention as originally drafted sought to protect policyholders by giving them a choice of forum, but when the Accession Convention of 1978 was being negotiated the position of the London insurance market arose. The London market is the largest insurance market in the world dealing very largely with international insurance contracts, and in these circumstances it was far from clear that the policyholder (who was likely to be a large commercial enterprise or even another insurance company negotiating reinsurance on the London market) needed this protection. And too liberal a regime might have an adverse affect on the London market.

Thus the United Kingdom in the negotiations over the Accession Convention sought to reduce this choice. It was partly successful in this regard, and the Convention as it stands at present allows the parties to agree that the Convention provisions in regard to jurisdiction over insurance contracts do not apply to a wide range of risks or liability arising out of the use of sea-going ships and commercial aircraft. The parties cannot, however, contract out of the jurisdictional rule in regard to liability for personal injury to passengers and the loss or damage to their baggage. You should look at article 12A for the details in this regard. Also where the policyholder is not 'domiciled' in a Contracting State it is possible to agree that the jurisdiction rules do not apply (save where the insurance is compulsory or relates to immovable property in a Contracting State) (article 12(4)). In *J R Charman and M E Brockbank* v *WOC Offshore BV* [1993] 2 Lloyd's Rep 551 (CA) it was held that a policy that covered both marine and land risks did not fall within article 12A, so the prorogation agreement could not be relied upon.

Apart from the provisions just discussed, it is only possible to agree to vary the Convention rules in regard to insurance in circumstances analogous to those which we have just discussed for consumer contracts. (The details will be found in article 12.)

The actual provisions (contained in articles 8, 9, 10 and 11) in regard to jurisdiction in matters of insurance may be summarised as follows:

Article 8 provides that an insurer domiciled in a Contracting State may be sued in the courts of the state where he is 'domiciled', or in the courts of another Contracting State where the policy holder is 'domiciled', or, if he is a co-insurer, in the courts of the Contracting State in which proceedings are brought against the leading insurer. If an insurer is not 'domiciled' in a Contracting State, but has a branch or agency in one of the Contracting States, then in disputes arising out of the operations of that branch or agency the insurer shall be deemed to be 'domiciled' in that Contracting State.

Article 9 provides that in respect of liability insurance, or insurance of immovable property, the insurer may be sued in the place where the harmful event occurred. Moreover, article 10 provides that, if the law of the court permits, the insurer may be joined with the insured in proceedings which the injured party may bring against the insured.

Finally, article 11 provides that, irrespective of the other provisions, the insurer can always bring action in the court of the defendant's 'domicile', and that if a court has jurisdiction to hear the original claim then it also has jurisdiction to hear a counterclaim.

Before leaving insurance it ought to be pointed out that Schedule 4 contains no provision dealing with jurisdiction in insurance matters at all. Thus the general rule of article 2 of Schedule 4 applies to allocate jurisdiction to the court of that part of the United Kingdom where the defendant is 'domiciled'.

## Prorogation of jurisdiction

We have on a number of occasions discussed specific provisions whereby the parties to a contract are precluded from agreeing, or permitted to agree, that a particular court other than the court that would have jurisdiction under the Convention shall have, or not have, jurisdiction.

Article 17 in general, and article 17(1) in particular, deals with this question. As amended by the San Sebastian Convention it reads as follows:

> 'If the parties, one or more of whom is domiciled in a Contracting State, have agreed that the court or the courts of a Contracting State are to have jurisdiction to settle any disputes which have arisen or which may arise in connection with a particular legal relationship, that court or those courts shall have exclusive jurisdiction. Such an agreement conferring jurisdiction shall be either:
> a) in writing or evidenced in writing, or
> b) in a form which accords with practices which the parties have established between themselves, or
> c) in international trade or commerce, in a form which accords with a usage of which the parties are or ought to have been aware and which in such trade or commerce is widely known to, and regularly observed by, parties to contracts of the type involved in the particular trade or commerce concerned.
> Where such an agreement is concluded by the parties, none of whom is domiciled in a Contracting State, the courts of other Contracting States shall have no jurisdiction over their disputes unless the court or courts chosen have declined jurisdiction.'

The two major differences between the amended and unamended article 17 are, apart from the way the text is divided, the following: first, the formal requirements for a valid prorogation agreement are specified more precisely in the amended text. Thus the parties can (in terms of article 17(b)) now set their own form by the past practice established between those parties. So, for instance, an oral submission to the jurisdiction of a particular court would be upheld provided that was in accord with the past practice between the parties. Furthermore, there is now added to the formal requirements of article 17(c) (concerning the forms adopted in 'international trade and commerce') the requirement that the form should be 'widely known' and 'regularly observed' in that trade.

Article 17(2) provides that where such an agreement conferring jurisdiction on a Contracting State is made by parties none of whom is 'domiciled' in a Contracting

State, the courts of other Contracting States shall have no jurisdiction unless the court chosen declines jurisdiction.

Article 17(3) and (4) deal with submissions to jurisdiction contained in trust instruments. The closing words of article 17(4) are important. They provide that 'Agreements ... conferring jurisdiction shall have no legal force ... if the courts whose jurisdiction they purport to exclude have exclusive jurisdiction by virtue of Article 16.' In other words, one cannot exclude article 16 jurisdiction by an article 17 agreement.

A new article 17(6) has been added by the San Sebastian Convention. It reads as follows:

> 'In matters relating to individual contracts of employment an agreement conferring jurisdiction shall have legal force only if it is entered into after the dispute has arisen or if the employee invokes it to seise courts other than those for [sic] the defendant's domicile or those specified in article 5(1).'

The purpose of this provision is plain: it is designed to protect the employee from having an unsuitable jurisdiction imposed upon him through the greater bargaining power of the employer. Note that article 17(5) provides that where an agreement was 'concluded for the benefit of only one of the parties, that party shall retain the right to bring proceedings in any other court which has jurisdiction by virtue of this Convention'. Both these provisions are designed to prevent the exploitation of weaker parties by submission agreements.

In *Kurz v Stella Musical Veranstaltungs GmbH* [1991] 3 WLR 1046 the English court considered a 'non-exclusive' choice of jurisdiction clause, ie a clause that granted jurisdiction to the English courts but did not exclude the jurisdiction of other courts that had jurisdiction for other reasons. Did this clause comply with article 17 which, after all, dealt with 'exclusive jurisdiction'. Hoffmann J upheld the jurisdiction of the English courts and said that the word 'exclusive' in article 17

> 'does not mean "unique", [viz] that the parties are limited to choosing a single jurisdiction. It means only that their choice, whatever it is, shall ... have effect to the exclusion of the jurisdiction which would otherwise be imposed upon the parties by the earlier articles of the Convention.'

Consistently with *Kurz v Stella Musical Veranstaltungs GmbH* the Cour d'Appel in Paris has held that a 'non-exclusive' jurisdiction clause is in conformity with article 17, particularly article 17(4): *Hantarex SpA v SA Digital Research* [1993] ILPr 501 (plaintiff able to bring action in Paris court which would not otherwise have had jurisdiction, but the matter could have been heard in the other courts which were competent under the Convention). *Kurz v Stella Musical Veranstaltungs GmbH* was also approved by Waller J in *I P Metal Ltd v Route OZ SpA* [1993] 2 Lloyd's Rep 60 where it was also held that a telex following an oral agreement in these terms, ie 'law-English competent forum London', amounted to a valid article 17 agreement evidenced by the writing of the telex.

In *Powell Duffryn plc v Petereit* (1992) The Times 15 April; [1992] ILPr 300

(ECJ) it was held, unexceptionally, that an article 17 agreement could be contained in the articles of association of a company and thereby the shareholders were required to litigate their disputes with the company in a court which would not otherwise have jurisdiction – this applied irrespective of the mode of acquisition of the shares, provided the shareholders had access to the articles of association.

The wording relied on as evidence of the parties' choice of court agreement must be sufficiently specific for article 17 to apply. In *Sameon Co SA v NV Petrofina SA and Another, The World Hitachi Zosen* (1996) The Times 8 April, the defendant had applied for a declaration that the English courts did not have jurisdiction over its dispute with the plaintiff over the contribution of general average, because, as it was domiciled in Belgium, article 2 of the Brussels Convention provided that the Belgian courts had jurisdiction. The charterparty agreement provided that general average was to be adjusted in London. The plaintiff argued that adjusted meant settled or paid and, accordingly, the place of performance of this obligation was London which therefore had jurisdiction under article 5(1). Further, the agreement as to adjustment was an agreement as to jurisdiction and sufficient to bring the case within article 17.

Langley J held that the wording of the charterparty clause was not specific enough to bring it within article 17 and, therefore, the general jurisdiction rule of article 2 was not displaced. Equally, the word 'adjusted' was not sufficient to create a binding obligation as to the place of payment and the clause was not specific enough to bring the contract within the special jurisdiction of article 5(1).

Article 18 provides that 'apart from jurisdiction derived from other provisions of this Convention, a court of a Contracting State before whom a defendant enters an appearance shall have jurisdiction' except where 'appearance was entered solely to contest the jurisdiction, or where another court has exclusive jurisdiction by virtue of article 16'. It was decided by the European court in *Elefanten Schuh v Jacqmain* [1981] ECR 1671 that the provisions of article 18 prevail over those of article 17 where they are in conflict. This means simply that should there be a valid agreement conferring exclusive jurisdiction upon the courts of one Contracting State, but if the defendant none the less appears in the courts of another Contracting State, the second Contracting State has jurisdiction. And this is sensible; by appearing the defendant has in effect agreed to an alteration in the terms of the exclusive jurisdiction agreement. An otherwise valid article 17 agreement remains effective even where there is some change in the identity of the parties, eg through a company being placed into liquidation or a contractual right or obligation being lawfully transferred to another party. Thus in *Talbot and Another v Edcrest Limited* [1993] ILPr 786, a case that arose out of the Leyland-DAF insolvency, the English High Court stayed proceedings before it in the following circumstances: there had been a jurisdiction clause in favour of the Dutch courts in an outline agreement between Leyland, DAF and a Dutch haulier. This clause remained effective to give the Dutch courts exclusive jurisdiction, notwithstanding that the Leyland-DAF subsidiaries were in receivership and the receivers were suing in their own names. This conclusion is consistent with the decision of the European Court of Justice in

*Partenreederei MS Tilly Russ AG* v *Haven en Vervoerbedrijf Nova NV, The Tilly Russ* (Case 71/83) [1984] ECR 2417; [1985] QB 931, that the a valid article 17 agreement in a bill of lading bound the third party who succeeded to the shipper's rights and obligations under the bill.

Finally it may be noted that Schedule 4 article 17 omits the formal requirements of writing or evidence by writing etc required by article 17, and also provides that the jurisdiction of the court chosen by the parties is not exclusive, ie a court elsewhere in the United Kingdom that would otherwise have jurisdiction has jurisdiction in addition to the court chosen by the parties.

## Lis alibi pendens

Although, as we have seen, the basic rule of the Convention is that a defendant should be sued in the court of his 'domicile', we have also seen that it is possible for a person to be 'domiciled' in more than one Contracting State or that, in addition to the court where the defendant is 'domiciled', another court may have jurisdiction under the rules for special jurisdiction. We also saw earlier that it was theoretically possible for more than one court to have jurisdiction under the rules of exclusive jurisdiction.

Hence it may arise that more than one court is seised of the same dispute at the same time, and the Convention has to provide which proceedings should be stopped, and which should proceed. The basic rule is contained in article 21 (as amended by the San Sebastian Convention) which provides that where

> 'proceedings involving the same cause of action and between the same parties are brought in the courts of different Contracting States, any court other than the courts first seised shall of its own motion stay its proceedings until such time as the jurisdiction of the court first seised is established. Where the jurisdiction of the court first seised is established, any court other than the court first seised shall decline jurisdiction in favour of that court.'

Article 23 spells out that the same rule applies where 'actions come within the exclusive jurisdiction of several courts'. The adoption of this rule is simply an application of the maxim qui prior in tempore potior in jure (which you have probably run across in other contexts).

This is a rigid rule which contrasts sharply with the discretion that English courts usually enjoy in matters of lis alibi pendens. The idea is simply that the court can wait and see whether it is determined that the other court has jurisdiction, before declining to hear the case. And article 22 provides that where a number of actions are 'so closely connected that it is expedient to hear and determine them together to avoid the risk of irreconcilable judgments resulting from separate proceedings', then a court other than that first seised may either stay its own proceedings (ie wait until the proceedings are ended) or decline jurisdiction if the court first seised has jurisdiction over all the actions and its law permits the consolidation of related actions.

The scope of article 21 (in the unamended version) has been before the European Court in *Overseas Union Insurance Ltd and Others* v *New Hampshire Insurance Company* (Case C–351/89) [1991] ILPr 495 (European Court of Justice), and an important precedent has been laid down. What had happened here was that a complicated dispute had arisen between several insurance companies over a complicated re-insurance arrangement. OUI (and several other companies) brought an action on 6 April 1988 in England seeking a declaration that they were no longer bound by the re-insurance policy. The defendant was the New Hampshire Insurance Company, a company which was incorporated in New Hampshire (in the USA) but carried on business in the USA and in France and England. However, New Hampshire had already issued proceedings in Paris against the other insurance companies (on 4 June 1987) and OUI (on 9 February 1988). Did article 21 require the English court to decline jurisdiction? The central argument of OUI was that article 21 only applied in article 3 cases (where the defendant is domiciled in another Contracting State) but did not apply to article 4 cases (where the defendant is not domiciled in any Contracting State). However, the court held that article 21 must be interpreted as applying irrespective of the domicile of the parties to the two sets of proceedings. Thus there is no role for considerations of forum conveniens – at any rate where the two sets of proceedings are both in the courts of Contracting States.

Note this decision does not address the question of whether forum conveniens has any role to play where the clash is between proceedings in a Contracting State (eg the United Kingdom) and proceedings in a non-Contracting State. It was held in *Re Harrods (Buenos Aires) Ltd* [1991] 3 WLR 397 by the Court of Appeal that the Convention's purpose of uniformity, simplicity and certainty between the judgments of Contracting States could be achieved without excluding considerations of forum conveniens where litigation with non-Contracting States was involved. This case, however, was appealed to the House of Lords which has referred the question to the European Court of Justice. The issue is discussed more fully in section 4.4 *Forum conveniens and the Brussels Convention*.

There was a straightforward application of the principle of article 21 – that the court which was first seised should have jurisdiction – in *The Freccia del Nord* (1988) The Times 30 December. Two vessels, the Freccia del Nord and the Nord Sea, had collided in the Bay of Biscay. An English writ in rem against the Freccia del Nord was issued by the owners of the Nord Sea 20 minutes before the Nord Sea was arrested in Rotterdam by the owners of the Freccia del Nord. But the English writ was only served some two weeks later. Did the English court have priority in terms of article 21?

The court held that the English court did not have priority. The question of when a court became seised had been discussed by the European Court in *Zelger* v *Salinitri* [1984] ECR 2397. That the court first seised was the one before which the requirements for proceedings to become definitely pending were first fulfilled was the rule laid down by the European Court, but such requirements were to be determined in accordance with the national law of the courts concerned. Applying

English law applicable to an Admiralty action in rem (*The Banco* [1971] P 137 and *The Berny* [1979] QB 80), the court held that the English court was seised when the writ was served or the vessel arrested; mere issue of the writ was insufficient, thus the English court declines jurisdiction in terms of article 21.

Avoidance of forum-shopping was a consideration in the recent case of *Internationale Nederlanden Aviation Lease BV and Others* v *Civil Aviation Authority and Another* (1996) The Times 15 August. The plaintiffs sought to discontinue their action against the defendants in the English courts following a related English ruling which served to make their action academic under English law. They then commenced proceedings against one of defendants in Belgium, hoping to obtain a different result.

The discontinuance was refused. Morison J, in a very practical decision, observed that a court which was first seised of an action did not remain so seised when proceedings were discontinued and, therefore, articles 21 and 22 of the Convention which were concerned with concurrent proceedings would no longer apply. Given that, it would be unsatisfactory and unjust to discontinue proceedings simply to enable the plaintiff to start an action in another state without the obstacles of articles 21 and 22.

How is it to be determined when an English court is 'first seised' in an ordinary in personam action? This was the issue addressed by the Court of Appeal in *Dresser UK Ltd and Others* v *Falcongate Freight Management Ltd and Others* (1991) The Times 9 August. It may be recalled that in *Klockner & Co AG* v *Gatoil Overseas Ltd* [1990] ILPr 53 (QB) it was held that in personam proceedings in England (but not Admiralty proceedings or, perhaps, Order 11, rule 1(1) proceedings) were 'definitely pending' when the writ (or like document) was issued.

Whether litigants in England should have this advantage was tested in *Dresser UK Ltd*. Here there was a dispute between the owners of a consignment of electronic goods lost at sea during a voyage from Scheveningen (in the Netherlands) to Great Yarmouth (in England) and various parties associated with the carriage of those goods. Proceedings had been begun in England (writ issued 15 July 1988 and served 13 July 1989) and in the Netherlands (initiated 21 February 1989, ex parte orders published 19 May 1989, jurisdiction of the Dutch courts challenged 15 November 1989). Which was the court first seised? The court held (by Bingham LJ) that it was service of the proceedings and not issue of the writ which ordinarily activated the litigious process and imposed procedural obligation on the parties. Thus it was 'artificial, far-fetched and wrong to hold that the English court was seised of proceedings upon the mere issue of proceedings'. In straightforward cases service of proceedings would be the time when an English court was seised, but this was not the invariable rule. For instance, where there had been an actual exercise of jurisdiction (eg the issue of a Mareva injunction or the making of an Anton Piller order) before the writ was issued then the English court would be seised before the writ was served. Although this decision denies to English litigants a procedural advantage, it is plainly common sense that proceedings should generally become 'definitely pending' when the writ is served. After all, many a writ is issued but never served. (*Dresser* v *Falcongate* was followed in *Assurances Generales de France* v *Chiyoda Fire and Marine Co* [1992] 1 Lloyd's Rep 325.) Lord Justice Bingham's approach in *Dresser* was, however, made more rigid in *Neste Chemicals SA and Others* v *DK Line SA and Another* (1994) The Times 4 April, where it was held that there were no exceptions to the rule that the date of service marked the time when an English court became definitely seised of the proceedings. Thus contrary to the suggestions in *Dresser* neither the grant of leave to serve out of the jurisdiction not the exercise of the limited jurisdiction to issue Mareva injunctions or Anton Piller orders led to the English court being definitely seised.

The relationship between the exclusive jurisdiction granted by article 17 and the rigid rule of article 21 that any court other than the court first seised shall decline jurisdiction has recently been before the English courts in *Klockner & Co AG* v *Gatoil Overseas Ltd*. The problem may be simply stated: suppose one court has exclusive jurisdiction in terms of article 17, but another court has been first seised of the matter, is the article 17 court obliged to decline jurisdiction? In *Klockner* Hirst J held that the article 17 court was not obliged to decline jurisdiction in favour of the court first seised. In other words, he read article 21 as if it contained the words 'provided that another court does not have jurisdiction under article 17'. Hirst J reasoned that:

> 'A court with alleged exclusive jurisdiction under article 16 or 17 must be free itself to examine whether it has exclusive jurisdiction under one or other of those Articles, since otherwise it would be sufficient for one of the parties to claim that the contract allegedly according exclusive jurisdiction did not exist, thus depriving this part of the Convention of legal effect. This I think fits in with the pattern of the Convention as a whole, and also accords with common sense, since surely the best court to decide questions of exclusive jurisdiction is that in which such jurisdiction is alleged to reside ... I hold that I am free under article 17 to consider the validity of the English exclusive jurisdiction clause and, if that clause turns out to be valid, to allow any claims covered by it to continue here.'

It remains to be seen whether the European court will accept this reasoning. It might after all be pointed out that all that is now necessary to deprive article 21 of effect is to allege the existence of an article 17 exclusive jurisdiction clause! Moreover, it is not clear to me what would have been wrong in staying the English action under article 21(2) (which allows such staying where the jurisdiction of the other court is contested) to allow the other court (in *Klockner* the German court) to determine whether the exclusive jurisdiction clause applied. Surely, it is equally part of the scheme of the Convention that the courts of other Contracting States are to be trusted to make such decisions?

However, the Court of Appeal does not apparently share the doubts expressed above for it has held in *Continental Bank NA* v *Akakos Compania Naviera SA and Others* (1993) The Times 26 November that the structure and logic of the Brussels Convention showed that if article 17 applied, its provisions took precedence over articles 21 and 22. What had happened in this case was that the Continental Bank had granted a loan of $56 million to the Akakos Compania NA and others. This loan was guaranteed by members of the Papalios family. The loan agreement contained an exclusive jurisdiction clause in terms of which all disputes arising out of the loan were to be submitted to the English courts. In October 1991 the bank issued a writ in England seeking payment of outstanding interest from the appellants (the borrowers and the guarantors) but in May 1991 the appellant had already commenced action in Athens seeking damages against the bank and a declaration that the guarantors had been released. The Court of Appeal refused to decline jurisdiction in favour of the Greek courts on the ground that they were 'first seised'. Indeed, it said that in the right circumstances it would issue an injunction restraining the foreign proceedings.

Before too much enthusiasm develops for the English view that article 17 overrides articles 21 and 22 it should be noted that the European Court has yet to speak and it has left open whether article 17 prevails over articles 21 and 22 or not: *Overseas Union Insurance Ltd and Others* v *New Hampshire Insurance Company* (Case C–351/89) [1991] ILPr 495 (ECJ).

Articles 21, 22 and 23 do not, however, apply to proceedings for the recognition and enforcement of foreign judgments from a non-Contracting State. Thus an English court asked to enforce a foreign judgment from such a state is not obliged under article 21 to stay those proceedings because of similar proceedings are already pending before the courts of another Contracting State. This is the result of the decision of the European Court of Justice in *Owens Bank Ltd* v *Fulvio Bracco and Another* (1994) The Times 3 February. What had happened here was the following: Owens Bank had allegedly loaned a large sum of money to Fulvio Bracco and one of its companies. The loan was not repayed and the bank obtained default judgment against Bracco in St Vincent and the Grenadines (a Carribean Commonwealth state). The bank now sought to enforce this judgment against Bracco, first, in Italy (July 1989) and then in England (March 1990). Relying on articles 21 and 22 of the Brussels Convention, Bracco argued that the English court should stay its proceedings in favour of the Italian courts. (Bracco also argued that the loan documents had been forged and sought to resist enforcement on the ground of fraud as well; this issue was determined in the House of Lords in *Owens Bank Ltd* v *Bracco and Others* [1992] 2 All ER 193 discussed below in section 8.2 Defences.) The European Court (on a reference from the House of Lords) held the Convention applied only to the recognition and enforcement of the judgments of courts of Contracting States; the Convention laid down no rules for determining the forum for proceedings for the recognition and enforcement of judgments given in non-Contracting States. Thus articles 21, 22 and 23 did not apply to proceedings, or issues arising in proceedings, in Contracting States concerning the recognition and enforcement of judgments given in civil and commercial matters in non-Contracting States. The ECJ has recently delivered an important judgment on the operation of article 21. It held in *The Tatry* [1995] 1 Lloyd's Rep 302, that proceedings for a negative declaration – ie proceedings brought by a prospective defendant seeking a declaration that he is *not* liable – had the same cause of action as the substantive claim; and thus article 21 applied. This allows a person who fears that he will be sued, to commence proceedings for a negative declaration in a court convenient to him, thereby ensuring that that court is 'first seized' for the purpose of article 21. The ECJ also held that the parties had to be identical to engage article 21, but that whether the proceedings were in rem or in personam made no difference. Furthermore, where jurisdiction was regulated by a convention other than Brussels (see article 57), Brussels applied to those areas not covered by the Convention. Thus articles 21 and 22 applied to the arrest of ships, because of the Arrest Convention 1952, did not provide for lis alibi pendens.

Schedule 4 makes no provision in regard to lis alibi pendens, so within the United Kingdom the discretionary principles, that we shall shortly discuss, will continue to apply. Furthermore, it appears that the Convention has no effect on the discretionary rules where an action is pending in a non-Contracting State (see Hartley, op cit, 77).

## Mareva injunctions

Article 24 of the Convention spells out that application may be made 'to the courts of a Contracting State for such provisional, including protective, measures [eg a Mareva injunction] as may be available under the law of that state even if, under this Convention, the courts of another Contracting State have jurisdiction in the substance of the matter'. This provision is of potentially great advantage to plaintiffs for it allows a plaintiff litigating or about to litigate against a defendant 'domiciled' in, say, Germany to obtain from the English courts an order preventing the defendant from removing his assets from England. As you doubtless know a Mareva injunction is available to a plaintiff, in suitable cases, to ensure that a defendant does not remove his property from the jurisdiction, thereby evading the court's judgment. When such an injunction is issued it binds not only the defendant but also third parties who know of it, eg, a bank in which the defendant's funds are held.

The leading case is *Babanaft International Co SA* v *Bassatne* [1989] 2 WLR 232. Here the Court of Appeal held that it would be

'improper for the court to grant, after judgment, an unqualified *Mareva* injunction extending to the defendant's assets outside the jurisdiction because such an injunction would amount to an exorbitant assertion of extraterritorial jurisdiction over third parties; [thus] such post-judgment injunctions should be restricted so as to bind on the defendant personally and should contain a limiting provision to ensure that they did not purport to have an unintended extraterritorial operation and to make it clear that they did not affect third parties'.

Although the court made it clear that such orders would only issue in unusual cases, it did hold that *suitably qualified* extraterritorial Mareva injunctions could issue.

The nature of the suitable qualifications would vary from case to case, but there appear to be two broad possibilities regarding third parties: either that the injunctions were not binding on third parties at all or that third parties could be bound to the extent that the courts where the assets were situated would enforce the English injunction.

Although *Babanaft* dealt with post-judgment Mareva injunctions (ie judgment had been obtained which the defendant was seeking to evade), and what that case said about pre-judgment Mareva injunctions (in which judgment had not been obtained but it was feared that the defendant would prior to judgment remove his assets from the jurisdiction) was obiter, it has been made clear by the Court of Appeal in *Republic of Haiti* v *Duvalier* [1989] 2 WLR 261 (CA) (and in *Derby & Co Ltd* v *Weldon & Others* [1989] 2 WLR 276 (CA)) that the courts can also, in fit cases, make pre-judgment extraterritorial Mareva injunctions.

All these cases have stressed that such orders will only be made in exceptional circumstances. But, not surprisingly, plaintiffs have not been slow to exploit this possibility, and this seems likely to remain a much litigated area! Two recent cases may be mentioned: first in *Derby & Co Ltd and Others* v *Weldon and Others (Nos 3 & 4)* [1989] 2 WLR 412 (CA) the principles set out above (including the *Babanaft* proviso and availability of extra-teritorial Mareva injunctions both post- and pre-judgment) were confirmed, and it was laid down that the existence of assets belonging to the defendants within the jurisdiction was not normally a pre-condition for the operation of an extraterritorial Mareva injunction; the fact that the defendant could be debarred from defending the main action if he failed to comply with the injunction was usually sufficient sanction to ensure compliance. Furthermore, the extra-territorial Mareva injunction bound the defendant in personam; it did not bind, nor seek to bind, foreign courts, or infringe their exclusive jurisdiction. Secondly, in *Derby & Co Ltd and Others* v *Weldon and Others (No 6)* (1990) The Times 14 May the Court of Appeal held that in the exercise of its Mareva jurisdiction English courts had power to order the transfer of assets from one foreign jurisdiction to another.

For further reading on this topic see Lawrence Collings, 'The territorial reach of Mareva injunctions' (1989) 1205 *LQR* 262.

(Finally note that, notwithstanding its position in this book, the discussion above concerning extra-territorial Mareva injunctions is not only concerned with Brussels Convention cases.)

However, in *The Siskina* [1979] AC 210 the House of Lords had held that a Mareva injunction cannot be granted by the English courts unless the substantive proceedings are or are about to be instituted in England. Thus an amendment to English law was required to bring it into line with the Convention, and this is to be found in s25 of the Civil Jurisdiction and Judgments Act 1982. Section 25(1) provides that the High Court

> 'shall have the power to grant interim relief where (a) proceedings have been or are to be commenced in a Contracting State other than the United Kingdom ... and (b) they are or will be proceedings whose subject matter is within the scope of the 1928 [Brussels] Convention ...'.

Section 25(2), however, grants the court a discretion to refuse relief under s25(1) where it is 'inexpedient' to grant such relief.

Section 25(3), (4), (5) and (6) provide that the court can be given by Order in Council the power to grant interim relief in cases commenced or to be commenced otherwise than in a Contracting State and in regard to proceedings outside the 1968 Convention.

In *Republic of Haiti* v *Duvalier* [1989] WLR 261 a Mareva injunction was granted even though substantive proceedings were not contemplated in England (such proceedings were continuing in France). Furthermore, it was held that O.11 r1(1) allowed the defendant to be served with the proceedings outside the jurisdiction without the leave of the court. The relevant part of r1(2) reads as follows:

> 'Service of a writ out of the jurisdiction is permissible without the leave of the court provided that each claim made by the writ is ... a claim which by virtue of the Civil Jurisdiction and Judgments Act 1982 the court has power to hear and determine ...'

This part of the rules is designed simply to ensure that the writ can be served in cases within the Convention but in which the defendant is outside the jurisdiction. See the discussion of the other provisions of r1(2) in section 4.2 above (*Where leave is not required to serve the writ on a defendant who is not present within the jurisdiction*).

Of course, were it not for s25(1) of the Civil Jurisdiction and Judgments Act 1982, *Republic of Haiti* v *Duvalier* would have been differently decided, and the courts are still very cautious about granting extra-territorial Mareva injunctions outside the boundaries of s25. Thus in *Rosseel NV* v *Oriental Commercial Shipping (UK) Ltd and Others* [1990] 1 WLR 1387 (CA) one was refused in these circumstances: the plaintiffs were seeking to enforce in England under the relevant English legislation (s3 of the Arbitration Act 1975) an arbitration award obtained in New York. The Court of Appeal (and the trial judge) readily granted a Mareva injunction in respect of the assets of the defendants in England but refused a world-wide one. Lord Donaldson MR, with whom Parker LJ agreed, held that:

> 'There is all the difference in the world between proceedings in this country, whether by litigation or arbitration, to determine rights of parties on the one hand, and proceedings in this country to enforce rights which have been determined by some other court or arbitral tribunal outside the jurisdiction ... [Thus] apart from the very exceptional case, the proper attitude of the English courts ... is to confine themselves to their own territorial area, save in cases in which they are the court or tribunal which determines the rights of the parties. So long as they are merely being used as enforcement agencies they should stick to their last.'

## The differences between the Brussels and Lugano Conventions as well as the relationship between them

The Brussels Convention (as amended) and the Lugano Convention are very similar. Generally it can be assumed that they are the same (even the articles bear the same numbers). But there are some significant differences between them and these may be listed here: article 5(1) (Lugano vests jurisdiction in the courts of the 'place of business through which [the employee] was engaged', while Brussels says that jurisdiction vests in 'the place where the business which engaged the employee was or is now situated'); article 16(1)(b) (Lugano requires only that the tenant is a natural person and neither party is domiciled where the property is situated, but Brussels requires that both landlord and tenant are natural persons and domiciled in the same state); article 17(5) (Lugano only allows, in disputes concerning individual contracts of employment, the parties to submit to jurisdiction after the dispute arises, but Brussels is less restrictive and allows the parties to submit before the dispute arises 'if the employee invokes [the agreement] to seise courts other than those of the defendant's domicile or those specified in article 5(1)'. These slight differences are disappointing for they undermine uniformity in jurisdiction through the European Free Trade Zone. The malicious examiner may exploit these differences to set some challenging problems.

Note finally article 54B of the Lugano Convention dealing with the relationship between Brussels and Lugano: Lugano does not prejudice the application of Brussels, but where a defendant is domiciled in a Lugano State (a Contracting State that is not a member of the EC), or where a Lugano submission agreement confers jurisdiction on a Lugano State, then Lugano applies.

## 4.4 Forum conveniens

### Introduction

Once it has been determined that a particular court has jurisdiction, it does not necessarily follow that it will, or will be able to, exercise that jurisdiction. There are occasions on which it will, in its discretion, decline to do so, and there are other occasions on which it will not be able to because the plaintiff (at the behest of another court) will withdraw the action before it. In this section we will be considering these various occasions and the principles governing the exercise of the court's discretion. Given the general liberality of the English rules on jurisdiction it is necessary that the English courts should have the power in proper cases to refuse to exercise a jurisdiction which they technically enjoy. If this were not so litigants might be (indeed they sometimes have been) tempted to bring cases in the English courts which have the most remote connection with England and English law. One of the purposes of the conflict of laws is to discourage forum shopping – that process whereby a dispute is brought by the plaintiff in a forum which is not the natural or appropriate one for that dispute, in the belief that some advantage will accrue to the plaintiff before it – and declining jurisdiction in proper cases is one way in which this can be done.

An English court may decline to hear a case in two kinds of situation. First, an English court may be asked to stay the action before it because there is a more appropriate forum in which to hear the case. The court can order a stay under its inherent jurisdiction (confirmed by s49(3) of the Supreme Court Act 1981 and s49 of the Civil Jurisdiction and Judgments Act 1982 which preserves the court's power to stay 'where it is not inconsistent with the 1968 Convention'). We shall consider below the extent to which staying may be inconsistent with the Convention; for the present we assume that where there is jurisdiction under the Convention there can be no staying save as provided for in articles 21–23 (discussed above in section 4.3 *Lis alibi pendens*). *MacShannon* v *Rockware Glass Ltd* [1978] AC 795 may serve as an example of a case where the court exercised its power to stay. The case involved claims against the plaintiffs' employer for personal injury or disability which had been sustained by the plaintiffs, who were Scots, while employed in Scotland. The case had nothing to do with England save that the employer's head office was in England. The plaintiffs could equally well have sued in Scotland but in fact issued writs in England. Lord Diplock approved what Stephenson LJ had said in the Court of Appeal, viz, that 'anyone with nothing but common sense to guide him would say that [these actions] ought to be tried in Scotland', and ordered that the English proceedings should be stayed.

Secondly, an English court may refuse to exercise its discretion under RSC O.11 r1(1) to allow a writ to be served out of the jurisdiction on the ground that another court would be a more appropriate forum. *Amin Rasheed Shipping Corp* v *Kuwait Insurance Co* [1983] 2 All ER 884 may serve as an example of such a case. In brief the facts of this case were that the plaintiff, a Liberian shipowning company resident in Dubai, insured a ship with the defendant, a Kuwaiti insurance company. A dispute arose over a claim made under the insurance contract. The proper law of the contract was English law, and thus under RSC O.11 r1(1)(d)(iii) leave could be granted to serve the writ on the defendants in Kuwait. The court, however, in its discretion refused to grant leave: the courts of Kuwait were the appropriate forum to hear this dispute.

Thus far we have been considering those situations in which an English court refuses to exercise a jurisdiction which it has. There is, however, another situation in which the English court takes steps to ensure that it, and not some other court, hears the dispute. Where the English court has jurisdiction over a person who is the plaintiff in proceedings in a foreign court, it may issue an injunction against that person restraining him from proceeding in the foreign court. (Note that the English court is not seeking to tell the foreign court what to do; it is injuncting the plaintiff in those proceedings, not the court. The effect, of course, is that if the plaintiff heeds the injunction (and he can in principle, be committed for contempt if he does not), the proceedings in the foreign court come to an end). The recent case of *Société Nationale Industrielle Aerospatiale* v *Lee Kui Jak and Another* [1987] AC 871 may serve as an example. The case is a decision of the Privy Council on appeal from the Court of Appeal of Brunei Darussalam, but the decision is obviously of great weight and importance for English law. What had happened was that Yong Joon San had been killed in a helicopter accident in Brunei. The plaintiffs (presumably the dependants of the deceased) had instituted action against a variety of defendants (primarily the helicopter manufacturer and the helicopter operator) in Brunei and in Texas. (Proceedings against the manufacturer (who was French) in France were also instituted but soon discontinued.) Jurisdiction in the Texas proceedings was based upon the fact that the helicopter manufacturer (SNIAS) did business in Texas (which was sufficient under the law of Texas to give the Texas courts jurisdiction). The dispute had nothing to do with Texas, but the plaintiffs wished to sue there because of the favourable Texas law of product liability and the quantum of damages. In the event, however, an injunction was granted restraining the plaintiffs from proceeding against SNIAS in Texas: Brunei was the natural forum for the action.

We have not thus far considered the principles upon which the court should exercise its discretion to stay an action, or to grant leave under RSC O.11 r1(1), or to injunct foreign proceedings. But recently these have began to be clarified. Two points should be made: first, although there remain important differences, the principles governing the grant of a stay or the grant of a leave are similar. Put very broadly, the court exercises its discretion so that the natural or appropriate forum hears the action. But, secondly, contrary to suggestions in some cases, different principles govern the grant of an injunction to restrain foreign proceedings.

## A short history of forum conveniens in English law

### The grant of a stay

Prior to *MacShannon* v *Rockware Glass*, above, the English courts were sparing in their exercise of this jurisdiction; they took the view that it was only in exceptional circumstances that the proceedings properly begun in England by the service of a writ within the jurisdiction should be stayed. The best known dictum laying down the law was the following from Scott LJ's judgment in *St Pierre* v *South American Stores* [1936] 1 KB 382 at 398:

> '(1) A mere balance of convenience is not a sufficient ground for depriving a plaintiff of the advantages of prosecuting his action in an English court if it is otherwise properly brought. The right of access to the King's court must not be lightly refused. (2) In order to justify a stay two conditions must be satisfied, one positive and the other negative: (a) the defendant [that is the person applying for the stay] must satisfy the court that the continuance of the action would work an injustice because it would be oppressive or vexatious to him or it would be an abuse of the process of the court in some other way; and (b) the stay must not cause an injustice to the plaintiff. In both, the burden of proof is on the defendant.'

As the law stood in this case it was very difficult for a defendant to obtain a stay. A foreigner could bring an action about matters foreign against another foreigner in the English courts, and the English courts would not stay his action provided that it was not vexatious (and it was held not to be vexatious that the dispute had nothing to do with England or English law). Opening the doors of English courts was based largely (but not in my view entirely) on legal chauvinism: a belief that the inherent merits of English law and English courts should not be denied to litigants who would otherwise have to rely upon lesser foreign judges and inferior foreign courts to resolve their dispute. These rules were strongly criticised by Lord Reid in *The Atlantic Star* [1973] 2 All ER 174, and in that case a bare majority of the House of Lords held that Scott LJ's dictum should be more flexibly interpreted. The decisive step, however, came in *MacShannon* v *Rockware Glass Ltd* where Lord Diplock reformulated Scott LJ's dictum as follows:

> 'In order to justify a stay two conditions must be satisfied, one positive and one negative: (a) the defendant must satisfy the court that there is another forum to whose jurisdiction he is amenable in which justice can be done between the parties at substantially less inconvenience or expense, and (b) the stay must not deprive the plaintiff of a legitimate personal or juridical advantage which would be available to him if he invoked the jurisdiction of the English court ...'

This dictum has been widely followed, and as a result there are numerous decisions, not all consistent, laying down what is to be considered 'substantially less inconvenience or expense' and what constitutes 'a legitimate personal or juridical advantage'. (See Schuz, 'Controlling forum shopping; the impact of *MacShannon* v *Rockware Glass Ltd*' (1986) 35 *ICLQ* 374 at 381 to 399 for a discussion of all but the most recent cases.) Lord Diplock held further in *MacShannon* v *Rockware Glass Ltd* that while the onus was on the defendant to establish the first condition – that there was another convenient forum – the onus then fell upon the plaintiff, if he wished to avoid having the action stayed, to establish that he would be deprived of a 'legitimate personal or juridical advantage'.

Certainly prior to *MacShannon* v *Rockware Glass Ltd* it could not be asserted that the English courts, in deciding whether to grant a stay, adopted a doctrine of forum conveniens, ie of simply seeking out the most appropriate, convenient or natural forum and exercising their discretion accordingly. After this case considerations of convenience were crucial in dealing with condition (a), and finally Lord Diplock in *The Abidin Daver* [1984] 1 All ER 470 at 476 (a case about staying that we will look at in more detail later) said that the

> 'judicial chauvinism [of *St Pierre* v *South American Stores* and similar cases] has been replaced by judicial comity to an extent which I think the time is now ripe to acknowledge frankly is, in the field of law with which this appeal is concerned [the staying of actions], indistinguishable from the Scottish doctrine of forum non conveniens.'

And the role of forum conveniens in this area has recently been confirmed by Lord Goff of Chieveley in *Spiliada Maritime Corporation* v *Cansulex Ltd, The Spiliada* [1986] 3 All ER 843 where he said (at 853) that in

> 'cases where jurisdiction has been founded as of right, ie where in this country the defendant has been served with proceedings within the jurisdiction, the defendant may now apply to the court to exercise its discretion to stay the proceedings on the ground which is usually called forum non conveniens'.

(It does not much matter whether we refer to the principle as forum conveniens or forum non conveniens (see *Spiliada* at 853); it is the same principle).

Thus it is now clear that a stay may be refused or granted on the ground of forum conveniens. But what exactly does forum conveniens mean, you may well ask? We shall address this question in section 4.4 *Forum conveniens after* Spiliada below.

### Granting an injunction to restrain foreign proceedings

The power of the court to restrain a party subject to its jurisdiction from continuing with proceedings in a foreign court has long been recognised. Yet it too is a jurisdiction to be exercised with great caution; although the injunction is against the party, not the court, issuing such an injunction certainly has an effect on the administration of justice in a foreign country, and it is understandable that the foreign state will resent such injunctions.

Injunctions to restrain foreign proceedings have recently been reviewed by the Privy Council in *Société National Industrielle Aerospatiale v Lee Kui Jak* [1987] AC 871. (You should refresh your memory of the facts of this case: see section 4.4 *Introduction* above.) Lord Goff of Chieveley considered that the following propositions about the jurisdiction were 'uncontroversial':

1. the jurisdiction was to be exercised when the 'ends of justice' required it.
2. Where the court decided to grant such an injunction its order was directed not against the foreign court but against the parties so proceeding or threatening to proceed.
3. An injunction would only be issued restraining a party who was amenable to the jurisdiction of the court against whom an injunction would be an effective remedy.
4. Since such an order indirectly affected the foreign court, the jurisdiction was one which had to be exercised with caution.

So far, so good. But what are the principles that guide the court in deciding whether to issue an injunction? Here we approach the real significance of *Société Nationale Industrielle Aerospatiale v Lee Kui Jak*. In *Castanho v Brown and Root (UK) Ltd* [1981] AC 557 Lord Scarman, speaking for a unanimous and strong House of Lords (Lords Wilberforce, Diplock, Keith and Bridge), said:

> 'I turn now to consider what criteria should govern the exercise of the court's discretion to impose a stay or grant an injunction. It is unnecessary now to examine the earlier case law. The principle is the same whether the remedy sought is a stay of English proceedings or a restraint upon foreign proceedings. The modern statement of law is to be found in the majority of speeches in *The Atlantic Star*... [and *MacShannon v Rockware Glass*].'

Thus here, it was widely assumed, was an assimilation of the principles governing the restraint of foreign proceedings with those governing the granting of a stay. Moreover, since in *The Spiliada*, as we have seen, there was a substantial assimilation of the principles governing the grant of a stay with those governing leave to serve out of the jurisdiction, it was reasonable to believe that there had been substantial unification of the law in these areas: the principles of forum conveniens would govern whether what was sought was an injunction to restrain foreign proceedings, leave to serve out of the jurisdiction, or the stay of an action commenced in England.

This, however, is a false view of the law. We have already seen that Lord Goff of Chieveley in *The Spiliada* expressed his doubts whether the same principles governed the restraint of foreign proceedings as governed the granting of leave to serve out of the jurisdiction. (See also his doubts (as Goff LJ) in *Bank of Tokyo* v *Karoon* [1986] 3 All ER 468.) These doubts have now grown into a full and considered judgment by Lord Goff in *Société Nationale Industrielle Aerospatiale* v *Lee Kui Jak* which denies that the same principles govern the restraint of foreign proceedings.

Lord Goff reasoned as follows: if the same principles applied both to staying and to restraint of foreign proceedings, then:

'where the parties were in dispute on the point whether the action should proceed in an English or a foreign court, the English court would be prepared, not merely to decline to adjudicate by granting a stay of proceedings on the ground that the English court was *forum non conveniens*, but if it concluded that England was the natural forum, to restrain a party from proceedings in the foreign court on that ground alone.

That could not be right. It would lead to the conclusion that, in a case where there was simply a difference of view between the English court and the foreign court as to which was the natural forum, the English court could arrogate to itself, by the grant of an injunction, the power to resolve the dispute.

Such a conclusion would be inconsistent with comity and disregard the fundamental requirement that an injunction would only be granted where the ends of justice so required.'

Thus those same considerations of comity (and dislike of legal chauvinism) that led the courts to restrain their granting of leave to serve outside the jurisdiction, and to ease their discretion to grant stays, persuaded the Privy Council to exercise restraint in the matter of restraint of foreign proceedings.

The question still remains, however, when exactly will the court issue an injunction to restrain foreign proceedings? In *Société Nationale Industrielle Aerospatiale* v *Lee Kui Jak* it was made clear that, although it was not the only ground upon which an injunction might be issued:

'in a case such as the present where a remedy for a particular wrong was available both in the English (or, as here, the Brunei) court and in a foreign court, the English or Brunei court could, generally speaking, only restrain the plaintiff from pursuing proceedings in the foreign court if such pursuit would be vexatious or oppressive.

That presupposed that, as a general rule, the English or Brunei court had to conclude that it provided the natural forum for the trial of the action, and further, since the court was concerned with the ends of justice, that account had to be taken not only of injustice to the defendant if the plaintiff was allowed to pursue the foreign proceedings, but also of injustice to the plaintiff if he was not allowed to do so.

As a general rule, the court would not grant an injunction if, by doing so, it would deprive the plaintiff of advantages in the foreign forum of which it would be unjust to deprive him ...'.

Applying these principles the Privy Council concluded that (i) the natural forum for the trial of the action was Brunei; but (ii) if the Texas proceedings went on SNIAS might well be unable to proceed with its third-party claim against the helicopter operators in those proceedings, and if they were held liable to the plaintiffs in the Texas court they might have to bring a separate action in Brunei against the helicopter operators in which they might have to establish their own liability to the plaintiffs before they could be entitled to claim contribution from the operators, with all the attendant difficulties which that would involve, including the possibility of inconsistent conclusions on the issue of liability; thus (iii) in these circumstances the Texas proceedings should 'properly be regarded as oppressive'; moreover, (iv) there would be no injustice to the plaintiffs by having to sue in Brunei because SNIAS had given the plaintiffs undertakings that if the proceeding took place in Brunei they would give security for the satisfaction of any judgment, that the Texas proceedings could continue until pre-trial discovery had taken place, and that they would aid the plaintiffs in a number of ways before the Brunei courts. Thus an injunction would be granted restraining the Texas proceedings.

We may summarise the *Société Nationale Industrielle Aerospatiale* v *Lee Kui Jak* approach as follows: first it was determined whether the English court was the forum conveniens. If it were not then no injunction would be granted. Secondly, it was determined whether the foreign proceedings were vexatious or oppressive. (The mere fact that there were proceedings elsewhere did not mean that those proceedings were vexatious, nor were they vexatious simply because they were brought in an inconvenient place.) And, thirdly, in determining whether proceedings were oppressive regard had to be had both to the injustices to the defendant in the foreign court and also the advantages to the plaintiff in that forum.

*Société Nationale Industrielle Aerospatiale* v *Lee Kui Jak* was concerned with restraining foreign proceedings where there was a choice of forum: the proceedings could be brought in either Texas or Brunei. However, the problem may arise in a different context: where there is no choice of forum; the plaintiff can only bring his case before the foreign court because his claim is one which is only known to the foreign court and which would not be recognised elsewhere. The problem may be illustrated by *British Airways Board* v *Laker Airways Ltd* [1984] 3 All ER 39. The litigation arose out of the spectacular financial crash of Sir Freddie Laker's airline. Here the Laker Airways receiver started proceedings against a number of airlines (including British Airways) in the United States courts, alleging that, contrary to the United States anti-trust laws, they had conspired to drive Laker out of business and to deny him the financial support he needed. Such an action could not have been brought in England (and, indeed, the government acted under the Protection of Trading Interests Act 1980 to prevent British Airways from producing documents or information to the US courts). British Airways sought before the English courts an injunction restraining Laker from proceeding in the US. But the House of Lords refused. Lord Diplock, with whom Lords Fraser, Scarman, Roskill and Brightman agreed, held that where a foreign court was the only forum which was of competent jurisdiction to determine the claim of a plaintiff who was amenable to the jurisdiction of the English courts, an English court would intervene to issue an injunction restraining the plaintiff from bringing his claim in the foreign court, but only if it would infringe a legal or equitable right of the defendant not to be sued in the foreign court, so that it would be an injustice if the defendant was not protected from the foreign claim. Since British Airways could not show that it would be unconscionable to allow Laker to proceed in the United States, the injunction was refused. Since *Société Nationale Industrielle Aerospatiale* v *Lee Kui Jak* was plainly restricted to cases where there was a choice of forum, *British Airways Board* v *Laker Airways Ltd* remains good law.

In two other cases the principles of *Laker Airways* have been relevant. *Midland Bank plc* v *Laker Airways* [1986] 1 All ER 527 provides an example of an injunction being granted in a case where there was no choice of forum. The Laker receiver was suing the bank in the USA alleging breaches of the US anti-trust laws. But unlike British Airways in its Laker case, Midland Bank had not carried on business in the USA and the allegations of conspiracy made against it were unsupported by any evidence (save for the fact that it had loaned money to Laker and then precipitated the Laker collapse by refusing to loan more). The Court of Appeal decided that it would be 'unconscionable' to allow Laker to sue the bank in the USA and granted the injunction.

On the other hand, the House of Lords decided in *South Carolina Insurance Co* v *Assurantie Maatschappij 'de Zeven Provincien' NV* [1986] 3 All ER 487 that the court could grant an injunction (a) where a party to an action had invaded or threatened to invade a legal or equitable right of another party or (b) where one party behaved or had threatened to behave in a manner which was unconscionable. Thus the Lords did not issue an injunction to restrain the defendant from continuing a pre-trial discovery action in the United States against the plaintiff. The defendant was party to an action in England, but under the law of England such discovery was not ordinarily allowed. What the defendant was doing was not invading a legal right of the plaintiff, nor was it in the circumstances unconscionable. But note that the plaintiff here was a United States company, seeking to use the English courts to free itself from the restraint of US law!

Note that where a party sues in the foreign court in breach of a clause submitting all disputes to arbitration in England the court will readily restrain the foreign proceedings (*Tracomin SA* v *Sudan Oil Seeds Co (No 2)* [1983] 3 All ER 140). However, where the foreign proceedings were instituted (in breach of an agreement to resolve disputes in the English courts) in order to obtain security the courts are more reluctant to restrain those proceedings. Thus in *The Lisboa* [1980] 2 Lloyd's Rep 546 (CA) proceedings were brought by cargo owners against a ship in Italy apparently in breach of an agreement that proceedings would only be brought in London. The shipowners sought an injunction against the Italian proceedings but failed, since the proceedings (to seize a ship) were brought in order for the cargo owners to obtain security for the satisfaction of their claim against the shipowners.

Where the parties to the English proceedings and the foreign proceedings are different, there is even greater reluctance to restrain the foreign proceedings: *Arab Monetary Fund* v *Hashim and Others (No 6)* (1992) The Times 24 July.

The Court of Appeal in *Airbus Industrie GIE* v *Patel and Others* (1996) The Times 12 August has recently provided a review of these principles and was in no doubt that an injunction could be granted to restrain foreign proceedings where the application was not to protect proceedings in England. The Court noted that the discretion was to be exercised to prevent injustice. Three factors in particular were relevant: (1) what was the natural forum?; (2) would the plaintiff be prejudiced by continuation of the foreign proceedings?; (3) would an injunction against the defendants deprive them of a legitimate advantage? See Chapter 10, section 10.1, for further details.

## Forum conveniens after Spiliada

We have seen how forum conveniens has become the guiding principle in matters concerning the staying of actions properly begun in England and in granting leave to serve writs outside the jurisdiction. But we have yet to describe in any detail what the principle of forum conveniens is, and how it is applied in any particular case. This is the task of this section. Lord Goff of Chieveley's speech in *Spiliada* is now the leading judgment and you should read it with care. (This enthusiasm for forum conveniens does not exist throughout the common law world. The Australian High Court in *Voth* v *Manildra Flour Mills Pty Ltd and Others* [1992] ILPr 205 finally declined to adopt *The Spiliada* principles. Rather it held that question should be whether the forum chosen by the plaintiff was 'clearly inappropriate'. This required a consideration of whether the proceedings were seriously unfair, burdensome, prejudicial, damaging or producing of serious unjustified trouble and harassment [to the defendant]. The court did lay down that, questions of onus aside, the same principles governed granting a stay and granting leave to serve outside the jurisdiction.)

### Forum conveniens in general
Speaking in the context of staying of actions Lord Goff summarised the relevant principles in the following six propositions:

'a) The basic principle is that a stay will only be granted on the ground of forum non conveniens where the court is satisfied that there is some other available forum, having competent jurisdiction, which is the appropriate forum for the trial of the action, ie in which the case may be tried more suitably for the interests of all the parties and the end of justice. [Note that the search is for an appropriate rather than a convenient forum.]

b) ... In general the burden of proof rests on the defendant to persuade the court to exercise its discretion to grant a stay ... [but] if the court is satisfied that there is another available forum which is prima facie the appropriate forum for the trial of the action, the burden will then shift to the plaintiff to show that there are special circumstances by reason of which justice requires that the trial should nevertheless take place in this country ...

c) [Contrary to the position in the United States and Canada] ... I can see no reason why the English court should not refuse to grant a stay ... [where no particular forum can be described as the natural forum]. It is significant that in all the leading English cases where a stay has been granted there has been another clearly more appropriate forum ... In my opinion, the burden resting on the defendant is not just to show that England is not the natural or appropriate forum, but to establish that there is another available forum which is clearly or distinctly more appropriate ... [If] the connection of the defendant with the English forum is a fragile one (for example, if he is served with proceedings during a short visit to this country), it should be all the easier for him to prove that there is another clearly more appropriate forum for the trial overseas.

d) Since the question is whether there exists some other forum which is clearly more appropriate for the trial of the action, the court will look first to see what factors there are which point in the direction of another forum. These are the factors Lord Diplock described [in *MacShannon* v *Rockware Glass*] as indicating that justice can be done in the other forum at "substantially less inconvenience or expense". [But] ... it may be more desirable ... to adopt the expression used by Lord Keith in *The Abidin Daver* ... when he referred to the "natural forum" as being "that with which the action has the most real and substantial connection". So it is for connecting factors in this sense that the court must first look; and these will include not only factors affecting convenience or expense (such as the availability of witnesses), but also other factors such as the law governing the relevant transaction ... and the places where the parties respectively reside or carry on business.

e) If the court concludes at that stage that there is no other available forum which is clearly more appropriate for the trial of the action, it will ordinarily refuse a stay ... It is difficult to imagine circumstances when, in such a case, a stay may be granted.

f) If, however, the court concludes at that stage that there is some other available forum which prima facie is clearly more appropriate for the trial of the action, it will ordinarily grant a stay unless there are circumstances by reason of which justice requires that a stay should nevertheless not be granted. In this inquiry, the court will consider all the circumstances of the case, including circumstances which go beyond those taken into account when considering connecting factors with the other jurisdiction. One such factor can be the fact, if established objectively by cogent evidence, that the plaintiff will not obtain justice in the foreign jurisdiction ... [but here] the burden of proof shifts to the plaintiff ...'

An example of a case in which a stay was refused even though another forum was found to be more appropriate may be found in *Purcell* v *Khayat* (1987) The Times 23 November. Here, although the appropriate forum was plainly the Lebanon, the plaintiff had been convicted in his absence of a crime there and sentenced to three years' imprisonment. The Court of Appeal rejected the argument that the conviction was not relevant to forum conveniens, and the plaintiff's action was not stayed. *Jeyaretnam* v *Mahmood and Others* (1992) The Times 21 May may, however, be in conflict with this. There leave had been granted to the plaintiff (Jeyaretnam) to serve a writ for libel outside the jurisdiction (in Singapore) on several defendants. (This was probably done in terms of RSC O.11 r1(1)(f) but this is not clear from the report.) Applying the ordinary principles of forum conveniens it was clear that Singapore was clearly the more appropriate forum. The plaintiff, however, resisted the setting aside of leave on the ground of his anxiety that there would not be a fair trial of the dispute in Singapore. Although Lord Diplock had recognised in *The Abidin Daver* [1984] AC 398 at 411 that such a stay could be granted where the plaintiff established with 'positive and cogent evidence' that 'even handed justice' would not be done to him in the foreign court, the court felt that this only applied where the litigant feared that he might not receive justice in the courts of a different country from his own. Since the plaintiff was from Singapore, Lord Diplock's dictum from *The Abidin Daver* did not apply. On the contrary the judge said that the could should not embark upon an enquiry into whether the plaintiff's fears were reasonable or not. The English court had no jurisdiction over Singapore and should express no view on the quality of justice obtainable there.

When considering whether an alternative forum was available the court should have regard to the situation at the date the application was made, but also to the situation at the time of the hearing, to avoid granting a stay in patently unjust circumstances. In *Mohammed* v *Bank of Kuwait and the Middle East KSC* (1996) The Times 30 May, the defendant's preferred forum, Kuwait, was not a practical alternative for the Iraqi plaintiff, who at the time of the hearing was unable to leave his country without permission: see Chapter 10, section 10.1, for further details.

The application of these principles should in most cases give little difficulty, and the large number of cases on these questions should come to an end if trial judges simply follow what Lord Goff has laid down so clearly. As Lord Templeman said in *The Spiliada*:

> 'The solution of disputes about the relative merits of trial in England and trial abroad is pre-eminently a matter for the trial judge ... I hope that in future the [trial] judge will ... study the evidence and refresh his memory of the speech of my noble and learned friend Lord Goff in this case in the quiet of his room without expense to the parties; that he will not be referred to other decisions on other facts; and that submissions will be measured in hours and not in days. An appeal should be rare and the appellate court should be slow to interfere ...'.

If these words are heeded we will see many fewer reported cases on these subjects, although the staying of actions and the granting of leave is likely to remain an examiners' favourite!

Thus the general approach is clear. But we must look in more detail at some specific areas. However, it cannot be stressed too strongly that the *Spiliada* is a case that should be read and understood, particularly in the way in which the principles just outlined were applied to the facts of the case.

Where the parties have agreed that their dispute will be submitted to resolution before the English courts then the English courts are reluctant to find that another court is the forum conveniens. Consider, for example, *British Aerospace plc* v *Dee Howard & Co* [1993] 1 Lloyd's Rep 368. What had happened was that a contract had been made by British Aerospace (BAe), an English company, and Dee Howard Co (DHC), a Texas company, for the provision of technical assistance (by BAe). The contract provided that English law would govern and that the English courts 'shall have jurisdiction to entertain any action in respect' of the contract. A dispute arose and DHC commenced action in Texas; and a few days later BAe commenced action in England and obtained leave to serve outside the jurisdiction both on the ground that contract was made in England and that DHC had submitted to the jurisdiction of the English courts.

DHC applied to have the leave to serve abroad set aside on the ground, first, that the jurisdiction clause was not an exclusive jurisdiction clause at all (since it spoke of '*any* action' rather than *every* action); secondly, that Texas was the more appropriate forum especially since their lawyers had built up expertise in dealing with cases of this kind (this is termed the *Cambridgeshire* factor; the phrase refers to the fact that in *The Spiliada* [1987] AC 460 one of the factors that influenced the court in granting leave was that there was proceeding in England at the same time litigation over the 'Cambridgeshire' involving very similar issues, many of the same parties and the same solicitors); and, thirdly, that BAe had to show some personal or juridical advantage that was only available to them in England before they should be allowed to sue in England.

Unsurprisingly, the court held, first, that the phrase 'any action' in the jurisdiction clause was capable of meaning *all* actions, ie the clause was an exclusive jurisdiction clause. After all, since the contract was expressly governed by English law (so that leave could be granted in terms of r1(1)(d)(iii)), there was no need to agree to English jurisdiction unless it was intended to add something.

Secondly, even if the clause was non-exclusive it was a clause which the parties had freely negotiated; thus is was not open to DHC, in arguing that Texas was a more appropriate forum, to raise matters which must have been 'imminently foreseeable' when they agreed to English jurisdiction (such as their residence etc); nor could they, having commenced action themselves in Texas, raise lis alibi pendens.

Thirdly, the *Cambridgeshire* factor could not override DHC's contractual bargain not to object to English jurisdiction.

### The role of 'legitimate personal or juridical advantages'

The 'legitimate personal or juridical advantage' that featured prominently in Lord Diplock's formulation of the principle to be applied in *MacShannon* v *Rockware Glass* seems hardly to have been mentioned in this discussion of *Spiliada*. The reason for this is that the concept has been substantially downgraded by the decision in *Spiliada* as well as that in *Trendtex Trading Corporation* v *Credit Suisse* [1981] 3 All ER 520. In *Spiliada* Lord Goff of Chieveley said that 'it is necessary to strike a note of caution regarding the prominence given to "a legitimate personal or juridical advantage"'. We will look at *Trendtex* more fully in due course; suffice it to say for the moment that the House of Lords unanimously granted a stay where there existed an alternative appropriate forum, notwithstanding that they thereby deprived the plaintiff of access to the 'more generous English procedure of discovery'. The reason for downgrading this concept almost to disappearing point is simply that that which is to the defendant's disadvantage is to the plaintiff's advantage and vice versa, and these two factors balance each other out.

This move away from attaching much weight to 'legitimate personal or juridical advantages' is to be observed in *Smith Kline & French Laboratories Ltd* v *Bloch* [1983] 2 All ER 72 and *Muduroglu* v *TC Ziraat Bankasi* [1986] 3 All ER 682. Note, however, that in *Roneleigh Ltd* v *MII Exports Inc* [1989] 1 WLR 619 (CA) the Court of Appeal upheld the decision of a judge who, in an O.11 r1(1) case, had taken into account the much higher costs that would be incurred by the plaintiff in litigating in New Jersey under the contingency fee system, in deciding to grant leave to serve outside the jurisdiction.

The changing role of the 'legitimate personal or juridical advantage' was illustrated by *Du Pont* v *Agnew* [1987] 2 Lloyd's Rep 585. Put simply, this dispute was between a drug manufacturer and its insurers. The manufacturer (Du Pont) had been successfully sued in the Illinois courts for the damage caused by the negligent manufacture, distribution and selling of the anti-coagulant drug Coumadin. There were also allegations of wilful misconduct by Du Pont. After an appeal the award was for $26,172,240 and this included $13,000,000 punitive damages. The manufacturer now sought to recover these damages from its insurers (some of whom were Lloyd's underwriters and others who were foreign companies). However, Illinois public policy denied indemnification by an insurer of an insured for an award of punitive damages based upon personal liability. Thus Du Pont sued its underwriters in England seeking indemnification for the punitive damages. The Lloyd's underwriters, however, sought a stay of the English proceedings on the ground of forum non conveniens. (The underwriters also approached the Illinois courts seeking a declaration that they were not bound to indemnify Du Pont for the punitive damages.) When the matter first came before Steyn J *Spiliada* had not been decided. He, therefore, applied the old principles and held that to grant the stay would deprive Du Pont of a 'legitimate juridical advantage', viz the opportunity to pursue its claim in a forum where the insurers' public policy defence was less strong. When the matter came before the Court of Appeal, however, *The Spiliada* had been decided. Thus 'legitimate personal and juridical advantages' were less important, and the search was for the more appropriate forum. The Court of Appeal concluded after reviewing all the factors (particularly the fact that the proper law of the contract of insurance was English) that the defendants (upon whom the onus lay) had not shown that Illinois was the clearly more appropriate forum; thus the stay was refused. With the foreign insurers, however, the position was slightly different, for leave had to be sought to serve them outside the jurisdiction. And, as we know, in such cases the onus is upon the plaintiff to show that England is the clearly more appropriate forum. But the Court of Appeal (again influenced by the English proper law of the insurance policies and a desire to avoid a multiplicity of actions) concluded that England was the clearly more appropriate forum; thus the previously granted leave to serve the foreign companies outside the jurisdiction was not set aside.

In *Connelly* v *RTZ Corporation plc and Another* (1996) The Times 12 July, the Court of Appeal decided that the interests of justice weighed in favour of the forum in which the plaintiff could fund his action (by means of a conditional fee arrangement in this case) – England – which he had no prospect of doing in Namibia, the most natural forum. See Chapter 10, section 10.1, for further details.

The operation of the *Spiliada* principles can be further seen in the following cases: *Charm Maritime Inc* v *Minas Xenophon Kyriakou and Another* [1987] 1 Lloyd's Rep 433, *Islamic Arab Insurance Co* v *Saudi Egyptian American Insurance* [1987] 1 Lloyd's Rep 315, and *The Falstria* [1988] 1 Lloyd's Rep 495. However, one should not attach too much weight to later reported cases, for as Lord Templeman said in *The Spiliada* the question of forum conveniens is 'pre-eminently a matter for the trial judge'. Note that *Spiliada* principles apply in the field of family law (in particular applications for financial relief under the Matrimonial Proceedings Act 1984): *De Dampierre* v *De Dampierre* [1988] AC 92 (HL) and *Holmes* v *Holmes* [1989] 3 WLR 302 (CA).

### The remaining differences between the staying of actions and the granting of leave under RSC O.11 r1(1)

Notwithstanding the substantial unification of these two areas of law under the principle of forum conveniens, there remain differences between them. Lord Goff of Chieveley identified three. The first is obvious, and we have already mentioned it on a number of occasions. In RSC O.11 r1(1) cases the burden of proof rests on the plaintiff, whereas in staying cases the burden of proof rests on the defendant.

The second and related difference is the following: RSC O.11 r4(2) specifies that leave shall not be granted 'unless it shall be made sufficiently to appear to the Court that the case is a proper one for service out of the jurisdiction'. There is no similar provision in regard to the staying of actions; the result of this (although Lord Goff did not put it in this way) is that unless the plaintiff makes out a strong case, leave is likely to be refused.

Thirdly, as we have seen on a number of occasions, the RSC O.11 r1(1) jurisdiction is an 'exorbitant' one and should be exercised with care and caution. At any rate this used to be a difference between the grant of leave and the staying of actions. However, the grant of leave has been significantly eased by the House of Lords in *Seaconsar Far East Ltd* v *Bank Markazi Jomhouri Islami Iran* [1993] 3 WLR 756 and thus significantly reduced this difference.

Overall these three differences all suggest that, other things being equal, it will be more difficult to obtain leave to serve outside the jurisdiction than it will be to obtain a stay of proceedings begun by service of a writ in England. (It is, of course, more difficult again to obtain an injunction restraining foreign proceedings.)

### Foreign jurisdiction clauses

International commercial contracts frequently contain clauses which provide that disputes under the contract should be exclusively determined by some foreign court. In these circumstances the English courts will almost invariably stay an action that is brought in England in breach of such a clause. See, for example, *Trendtex Trading Corporation* v *Credit Suisse* [1982] AC 679 where a stay was refused because of a clause in the agreement that any dispute was to be 'judged by the Court of Geneva, exclusive of any other jurisdiction' notwithstanding that the agreement, were it governed by English law, would have been champertous and smacked of trafficking in litigation. The proper law of the contract was, however, Swiss; thus the English law was ignored and the stay was granted. In other words, the court will hold the parties to their agreement.

However, it is clear that the courts do retain a discretion to refuse a stay and hear the case in breach of the foreign jurisdiction clause. The relevant principles were laid down in *The Eleftheria* [1970] P 94 (confirmed in *The El Amria* [1981] 2 Lloyd's Rep 119 and *The Nile Rhapsody* [1992] 2 Lloyd's Rep 399.). There it was made clear that, although the court had a discretion, (i) a stay should be granted unless a strong case for not doing so is shown; (ii) the burden of showing same is on the plaintiff; and (iii) in exercising its discretion the court should take into account all the circumstances of the particular case including the following: which was the most convenient country for the evidence and which was the cheapest; was the dispute governed by foreign law and if so was that law different from English law; how close were the connections of the parties to the relevant countries; were the defendants only seeking a procedural advantage; and would the plaintiff be deprived of his security, be unable to enforce his judgment, be faced with a time-bar, or not get a fair trial if a stay were granted? (You should read *The Eleftheria* to see how finely balanced these factors were in that case.)

As an example of a case in which a stay was refused consider *The Adolfi Warski* [1976] 2 Lloyd's Rep 241. Here a cargo of onions and melons being shipped from Chile to Swansea went rotten. The defendant was Polish, and the plaintiff was essentially English. The contract contained a clause choosing Poland as the court of exclusive jurisdiction. A stay was refused because the main evidence was of English-speaking plant pathologists and it was doubted whether all the necessary witnesses would be given visas to testify in Poland. Whether this would be followed today, given the move away from legal chauvinism, may be doubted.

## Lis alibi pendens

What is the weight to be attached, in deciding whether to stay an action, to the fact that proceedings are afoot in a foreign court between the same parties in respect of the same dispute?

Two kinds of situation arise. First, where the same party is plaintiff in both proceedings: in these cases the plaintiff is usually trying to have two opportunities of succeeding against the defendant, and in these circumstances what will usually happen will be that the first action commenced will be allowed to continue and the other action stayed or restrained appropriately (*Peruvian Guano* v *Bockwoldt* (1883) 23 Ch D 225; cf Lord Denning in *Ionian Bank* v *Couvreux* [1969] 1 WLR 78, but he is almost certainly wrong).

Secondly, the plaintiff in England may be sued by the defendant in a foreign court. Here the court has to decide whether to stay the English action, or restrain the foreign one, or to do nothing at all and allow both actions to continue. For a long time, doing nothing at all was the preferred option. Brandon J, for instance, said in *The Tillie Lykes* [1977] Lloyd's Rep 124 that 'the mere existence of a multiplicity of proceedings is not to be taken into account at all as a disadvantage to the defendant [seeking a stay]'.

In *The Abidin Daver* [1984] 1 All ER 470, however, the House of Lords held that where

'a plaintiff wished to pursue his claim in the English courts despite the fact that there was already an action between the plaintiff and the defendant pending in a foreign jurisdiction which was a natural and appropriate forum for the resolution of the dispute between the parties, the court ought to exercise its discretion to stay the English action [save in special circumstances] ... although the mere balance of convenience or the mere disadvantage of a multiplicity of suits could not, of themselves, be decisive in tilting the scales, a multiplicity of suits involving serious consequences with regard to expense and other matters might easily, and most probably would, tilt the scales.'

Thus in *The Abidin Daver* a collision had occurred off the Bosphorus, in Turkish territorial waters, between a Turkish-owned ship (the Abidin Daver) and a Cuban ship. Proceedings were commenced in Turkey. However, when a sister ship of the Abidin Daver put into a Welsh port the Cuban shipowners sought to seize her and sue in England. The proceedings were stayed.

### Forum conveniens and the Brussels Convention

It appears from article 2, which states that persons 'domiciled' in a Contracting State 'shall' be sued in that state, that forum conveniens has no role to play in cases which fall within the convention. This is the orthodox view and is supported by the Schlosser Report; moreover it is consistent with the general purposes of the Convention. Note, however, that Hartley, op cit, 78–80, takes a contrary view.

This question of the continued role of forum conveniens has recently become a disputed issue amongst English judges. The orthodox view expressed in the above paragraph has received support in two recent decisions of the English courts at first instance: *S & W Berisford plc and Another v New Hampshire Insurance Co* [1990] 3 WLR 688, and *Arkwright Mutual Insurance Co v Bryanston Insurance Co Ltd and Others* [1990] 3 WLR 75. But most recently in *Re Harrods (Buenos Aires) Ltd* [1991] 3 WLR 397 the Court of Appeal disapproved of the *Berisford* and *Arkwright* decisions.

Let us make the points of dispute clearer by considering in a little more detail the facts of *Arkwright*. What had happened was that the plaintiff, an American insurance company, had paid out on a claim duly made in respect of damage to a steam turbine in Michigan. The plaintiff had, however, reinsured its risk on the London market with the defendants (who were a large number of insurance companies and syndicates operating in the London Insurance market and domiciled for the purposes of the Brussels Convention in the United Kingdom) and now sought to recover under its reinsurance policy. The defendants resisted this and commenced proceedings in New York seeking a declaration that they were not liable to the plaintiff. The plaintiff issued a writ in London, and now the defendants sought to stay this action on the grounds of forum conveniens (alleging that the New York court or some other American court was the forum conveniens) or alternatively on the ground of lis alibi pendens.

Potter J, however, held that the Convention was designed to achieve uniformity of decision within the Contracting States and to harmonise the procedural and jurisdictional rules of the various Contracting States. It followed that it would be inconsistent with the Convention to weaken this uniformity and harmony by allowing Contracting States on a discretionary basis to decline jurisdiction. Thus, in his view, as far as cases falling within the Convention were concerned (even if, as in this case, the plaintiff was not domiciled in any Contracting State), the English courts had lost their discretion to stay proceedings on the ground of forum conveniens and lis alibi pendens.

But in *Re Harrods* Dillon LJ rejected this. His lordship seemed influenced by the following consideration: s49 of the Civil Jurisdiction and Judgments Act 1982 provides that nothing in the Civil Jurisdiction and Judgments Act 1982 'shall prevent any court in the United Kingdom from staying ... striking out or dismissing any proceedings ... on the ground of forum conveniens ... where to do so is not inconsistent with the 1968 Convention'. The purpose of the Brussels Convention was that set out in article 220 of the Treaty of Rome, viz, to secure the simplification of formalities governing the reciprocal recognition and enforcement of judgments of courts in the EC. It was not necessary, to serve this purpose, to impose the common basis of international jurisdiction established by the Brussels Convention within the EC throughout the world. In particular, his lordship held that the object of the Brussels Convention was not impaired by the English courts being able to refuse jurisdiction where the defendant was domiciled in England on the ground that it was more appropriate for the courts of a non-Contracting State to decide the issue.

As far as the law of England is concerned Dillon LJ's view must now be considered correct – at least until the House of Lords or the European Court pronounces on this issue. (Although this question was referred to the European Court by the House of Lords when *Re Harrods* came before them, *Re Harrods* has now been settled so we are no closer to knowing the European Court's views on this issue.)

Finally, the question arises whether an action may be stayed where proceedings are pending in one part of the United Kingdom but another part of the United Kingdom is the forum conveniens. The position is not entirely straightforward. The allocation of jurisdiction within the United Kingdom can be seen as a purely internal matter. Moreover, there is no provision in Schedule 4 for lis alibi pendens, but if the English courts are to apply the discretionary common law rules to lis alibi pendens then surely they are to apply the discretionary rules in cases of forum conveniens. Neither the Brussels Convention nor Schedule 4 makes specific provision for this situation but as we have seen above s49 preserves the jurisdiction to stay where to do so is not inconsistent with the Convention. Other than in the awkward position where the courts in all parts of the UK stay the proceedings, thus preventing the plaintiff from suing in the UK notwithstanding that the UK has jurisdiction under the Convention, it is not self-evident that forum conveniens between different parts of the UK would be inconsistent with the Convention. Academic opinion was, however, divided (Cheshire, pp338–9 (staying possible), O'Malley and Layton, European Civil Practice, p979–80 (staying not possible)). Now, surprisingly, perhaps, Drake J has held in *Foxen v Scotsman Publications Ltd and Another* (1994) The Times 2 February that the Brussels Convention had removed the power to stay English actions where Scotland was the forum conveniens. As presently reported it is difficult to follow his Lordship's reasoning for he simply states 'it was inconsistent with at least the spirit and probably the letter of the Convention not to apply the rules [denying forum conveniens] as between different parts of the United Kingdom'.

# 5

# Choice of Law in Contract

5.1 Introduction

5.2 The common law rules governing choice of law in contract

5.3 Choice of law in contract under the EC Convention

## 5.1 Introduction

The law in this area has undergone a fundamental change with the enactment of the Contracts (Applicable Law) Act 1990. This measure, which enacts into English law, subject to some important reservations, the 1980 EC Convention on the Law Applicable to Contractual Obligations (commonly known as the Rome Convention), will henceforth dominate the law in this area, and your studies should concentrate upon it. As we shall see, the common law and the Convention contain similar principles (most prominently, they both allow the parties to make an express choice of the law to govern their contract (see section 5.2 *Ascertaining the proper law* below for the common law and article 3 of the Rome Convention); thus in many cases there will be little practical difference whether the common law or the Convention applies. None the less, this should not obscure the fact that henceforth the law will be founded upon an international convention (subject to interpretation by the European Court (see section 5.3 below) and not the common law).

Notwithstanding the fact that the law will henceforth be dominated by the Rome Convention some study of the common law is still needed. First of all, although the scope of the Convention is very wide (and it certainly is not restricted to contracts where only EC laws are involved; see section 5.3 *The scope of the Convention*) there are still some matters excluded from it (article 1(2)), and to these matters the common law will still apply. Secondly, the Convention is not retrospective (article 17), ie it does not apply to contracts made before the Convention came into force. Thus for some time to come the common law governing choice of law cases may still make an appearance in the English courts. Thus this chapter begins with a brief consideration of the common law rules.

## 5.2 The common law rules governing the choice of law in contract

### General principles

A contractual obligation cannot exist in vacuo; it must draw its existence from a legal system which specifies that in the particular circumstances a contract exists. This law, which creates and governs the contract, is usually termed the proper law of the contract. It was described by Lord Diplock in *Amin Rasheed Shipping Corp* v *Kuwait Insurance Co* [1983] 2 All ER 884 as 'the substantive law of the country which the parties have chosen as that by which their mutually legally enforceable rights are to be ascertained ...', and the major task of this chapter will be explaining how the proper law is ascertained.

Although it is sometimes easy to tell what the proper law of the contract is, it is, however, often not a straightforward matter. The reason for this is that contracts are infinitely various, and all kinds of agreement fall within the description 'contract'; it is thus impossible to have a single choice of law rule governing all kinds of contract. From time to time attempts have been made to put forward such a choice of law rule, eg, 'contracts are governed by the lex loci solutionis (the law of the place of performance)' or 'contracts are governed by the lex loci contractus (the law of the place of contracting)'.

But neither of these suggestions is satisfactory. The lex loci contractus may, after all, be entirely fortuitous. For example, when a Japanese businessman and an American businessman agree in London to the sale of goods situated in France, English law really has nothing to do with their transaction. Moreover, these days many international contracts are negotiated by telephone or telex and 'whether what turns out to be the final offer is accepted in the country where one telex is situated or in the country where the other telex is installed is often a matter of mere chance' (per Lord Diplock in *Amin Rasheed* v *Kuwait Insurance*). In these circumstances the lex loci contractus has little claim to be the proper law.

The lex loci solutionis appears more attractive at first sight, for the place of performance is unlikely to be fortuitous. However, it is unsuitable for other reasons; first, the parties' respective obligations may take place in different places, eg where the seller agrees to deliver certain goods in France in return for the buyer's promise to pay the price in London. It seems quite unreasonable that their respective obligations should be governed by different laws; after all this means that it would be theoretically possible for a defence to be available to the buyer (under his lex loci solutionis) when sued for the price, but that the seller (notwithstanding the buyer's non-payment) might be forced to deliver under his lex loci solutionis!

Secondly, the lex loci solutionis is unsuitable because it is often uncertain. The reason for this is that parties frequently enter into agreements in which the place of performance is unspecified or in which one of the parties may choose the place of performance. For example, contracts for the carriage of goods at sea (eg oil from the Gulf states) often require the precise port of destination to be specified to the carrier only after the vessel is at sea; but one might need to know what the proper law is, prior to the determination of the port of destination.

So for all these reasons it is fair to say that in modern English law, while connecting factors such as the locus solutionis and the locus contractus may be taken into consideration in determining the proper law, there is no general connecting factor that can be used to determine it. Thus determination cannot proceed along the lines of applying a standard choice of law rule in a more or less mechanical fashion.

However, the task of anyone having to ascertain the proper law of the contract is considerably facilitated by the recognition in English law of the principle of party autonomy. Put simply, this means that the parties can choose the proper law of the contract. As Lord Atkin said in *R* v *International Trustee for the Protection of Bondholders* [1937] AC 500 at 529:

> 'The legal principles which are to guide an English court on the question of the proper law of a contract are now well settled. It is the law which the parties intended to apply. Their intention will be ascertained by the intention expressed in the contract, if any, which will be conclusive. If no intention be expressed, the intention will be presumed by the court from the terms of the contract and the relevant surrounding circumstances.'

Such choices, usually contained in the agreement in a 'choice of law clause', are, as we shall see, generally recognised by the English courts. Thus if the parties have the good sense to include in their agreement the words 'this contract shall be governed by the law of X' the task of judges, counsel and students called upon to determine the proper law is straightforward.

Unfortunately, the parties do not always include such clauses in their agreement. Indeed, it is amazing how many contracts involving large sums of money and containing innumerable international elements do not contain choice of law clauses, and these are the contracts that create difficulties in determining the proper law.

Before considering the determination of the proper law in detail, it should be made clear that while the proper law is the general governing law of the contract, this does not mean that every aspect of the contract need be or is governed by the proper law. Questions of capacity, formation, performance and illegality etc may arise, and these matters, as we shall see, are not necessarily governed by the proper law.

## Ascertaining the proper law

**Where the parties have expressly chosen a law to govern their agreement**
Where the parties have expressly chosen a particular law to govern their agreement then, almost invariably, that choice will be upheld and the chosen law will be the proper law of the contract. The case which establishes this most clearly for English law is the decision of the Privy Council in *Vita Food Products Inc* v *Unus Shipping Co Ltd* [1939] AC 277. What happened here was that Unus Shipping, a Nova Scotian company, owned a cargo vessel, the Hurry On, and agreed with Vita Food

Products, a New York company, to carry a cargo of herrings from a port in Newfoundland to New York. Bills of lading containing this agreement were duly signed by the agents of the parties in Newfoundland. Through the captain's negligence the Hurry On ran aground, and the cargo of herring (although eventually delivered to New York) was damaged. Vita Foods sued in Nova Scotia for damages. The decision of the Nova Scotian courts was taken on appeal to the Privy Council.

Now the Newfoundland Carriage of Goods by Sea Act 1932 provided that the Hague Rules (these were the rules, agreed at an international conference of the major maritime nations, governing the liability of shipowners for loss or damge to cargo; their modern counterparts are the Hague-Visby Rules) should have effect 'in connection with the carriage of goods by sea in ships carrying goods from any port in this Dominion to any other port ...' and that every such bill of lading issued in Newfoundland should 'contain an express statement that it is to have effect subject to the provisions of the said Rules ...'. In fact the bills of lading (apparently through inadvertence) did not contain this statement but instead contained various other provisions (mostly exemption clauses) in regard to the shipowners' liability and, most importantly, an express choice of English law. (The Hague Rules were also part of English law but they only applied to outward shipments from English ports, so were not applicable to a shipment from Newfoundland.)

So the crucial question was: which law governed the respondent's liability for the damage to the herring? Were the bills of lading null and void because they were not issued in accordance with the law of Newfoundland (in which case, Vita Foods argued, the respondent would have been a common carrier and insurer of the safety of the cargo)? Or did the law of Newfoundland apply (notwithstanding the non-compliance with the Newfoundland Carriage of Goods By Sea Act 1932) and impose the Hague Rules? Or did English law apply, in which case liability would be determined by the various exemption clauses contained in the bills of lading?

In a striking affirmation of the parties' autonomy to select the law which governs their contract the Privy Council upheld the apparently inadvertent choice of English law. Lord Wright approved the following obiter dictum from Lord Atkin's speech in *R* v *International Trustee for the Protection of Bondholders* where he said that the intention of the parties in regard to the law governing their contract 'will be ascertained by the intention expressed in the contract, if any, which will be conclusive'. Lord Wright went on:

> 'It is objected that this is too broadly stated and that some qualifications are necessary ... But where the English rule that intention is the test applies, and where there is an express statement of the parties of their intention to select the law of the contract, it is difficult to see what qualifications are possible, provided the intention expressed is bona fide and legal, and provided there is no reason for avoiding the choice on grounds of public policy.'

The great advantage of allowing the parties to choose the law applicable to their contract is certainty. If the parties have said which law they wish to govern, that law can be applied cheaply and easily; it is not necessary to indulge in long and frequently expensive proceedings to determine the proper law.

But if it is clear that in general the parties have a free choice of law, the question arises whether there are any limitations on this principle. As we have seen, in *Vita Foods* Lord Wright laid down that the choice had to be 'bona fide and legal'; but it is difficult to know what, if anything, these words mean. Are they a substantial limitation upon the parties' freedom to choose, or are they nothing more than particular aspects of the public policy exclusionary rule (also mentioned by Lord Wright) which we know is quite unexceptional? There is no clear answer to these questions in English law. Two points may, however, be made:

First, it appears that the parties can choose a law that has no obvious connection with the contract and still make a choice that is bona fide and legal. *Vita Foods* is a clear example of such a case, for the contract had little apparent connection with England. (It had at best a hidden connection with England in that it was likely that the Hurry On was insured under a policy governed by English law.) But Lord Wright recognised that in such cases the parties none the less 'may reasonably desire that the familiar principles of English commercial law should apply'. Indeed, international commerce would be greatly inconvenienced if it was necessary for there to be a substantial connection with England before English law could be applied, for English law is frequently chosen throughout the world as a familiar, accessible and fair system of law.

Secondly, there is no reported English case in which a choice of law clause has been struck down by the courts (cf Laughton J in *The Torni* [1932] P 27). Whatever limitations there may be on the operation of the principle of party autonomy in English law, they are not very extensive; if a contract has a choice of law clause it is almost certain that that law will be the proper law of that contract (cf *Golden Acres Ltd* v *Queensland Estates Ltd* (1969) Qd R 378).

## Statutes and the express choice of law

The major reason why there is some hostility to the freedom given by English law to parties to choose the law governing their contract is the fear that this freedom enables parties to evade too easily the mandatory provisions (which are usually statutory) of the law that would otherwise be applicable to the contract. This fear is often ill-founded for three reasons.

First, there frequently exist imperative statutory rules of the lex fori which will intrude into the conflict of laws and override the provisions of the proper law. Thus, to give a well-known example, the Employment Protection (Consolidation) Act 1978 provides that where an employee ordinarily works in Great Britain then 'for the purposes of this Act it is immaterial whether the law which (apart from this Act) governs [that] person's employment is the law of the United Kingdom, or of a part of the United Kingdom or not'. Thus even if an employer and employee, who will ordinarily work in Great Britain, agree that the contract of employment will be governed by German law, the employee will continue to enjoy the protection of the Employment Protection (Consolidation) Act 1978 even although the rest of his contract will be governed by German law. The statute will override the proper law, and such statutes are known as overriding statutes. It is often difficult to tell whether particular statutes are overriding or not, ie whether Parliament intended that the statute in question should apply even where another law is the lex causae or that the statute should apply only if English law is the lex causae. For instance, in *The Hollandia* [1983] 1 AC 565 it was necessary for the House of Lords to settle a disagreement between two distinguished conflicts lawyers (Dr Mann and the late Dr Morris) as to whether the Hague-Visby rules were overriding or not. Their Lordships decided that they were overriding and applied in cases before English courts even if English law was not the lex causae.

Note that in general, in the absence of express enactment of necessary implication, English statutes are 'applicable only to English subjects or to foreigners who by coming into this country ... have made themselves subject to the English jurisdiction': *ex parte Blain; In re Sawyers* (1879) 12 Ch D 522 at 526, ie that statutes did not generally have extra-territorial effect. However, the Court of Appeal in *In re Paramount Airways Ltd (in administration)* [1992] 3 WLR 690 made it clear that this principle was simply a rule of construction that could give way in appropriate cases. Thus in s238 of the Insolvency Act 1986 (in terms of which the English had power where a company had entered into an 'undervalue transaction' with '*any person*' to 'make such order as it thinks fit for restoring the position to what it would have been if the company had not entered into that [undervalue] transaction'), the words 'any person' were given their literal meaning unrestricted as to territory and thus did apply to a Jersey bank, ie the presumption of no extra-territorial operation was overridden.

The existence of overriding statutes suggests that mandatory provisions of English law (that Parliament intends should apply irrespective of choice of law) will not be able to be too easily evaded by an express choice of the law of some other country. And if Parliament does not intend that the statute should apply irrespective of the lex causae, then why should the parties not avoid the application of that statute by choosing another law? However, where the mandatory rule evaded comes from neither the lex fori nor the chosen lex causae, but from some third legal system, then an express choice of law may ensure that the mandatory rule from that third legal system is not able to be raised before an English court. But there is no reason why an English court should pay attention to a rule from a legal system that has not been chosen through the normal choice of law process and is not part of the lex fori.

Secondly, as we shall see (below, *Illegality*), English law will not enforce a contract which requires the performance of an act which is unlawful under the laws of the place where the contract is to be performed. Thus mandatory rules of the lex loci solutionis cannot be evaded by an astute choice of law.

Thirdly, Parliament has introduced a limited doctrine of evasion into English law by means of s27(2)(a) of the Unfair Contract Terms Act 1977. The parent Act imposes severe restrictions upon the inclusion of exemption clauses in various kinds of contract, and s27(2)(a) is designed to ensure that these provisions are not evaded.

It provides that where it appears to the court that a choice of law has been 'imposed wholly or mainly for the purpose of enabling the party imposing it to evade the operation of the Act' the Act shall continue to apply.

This is in addition to a more usual provision (s27(2)(b)) that the Act shall apply notwithstanding a choice of law where one of the parties was habitually resident in the United Kingdom, dealt as a consumer, and the 'essential steps for the making of the contract were taken there'. This latter provision, you will readily appreciate, simply ensures that the Unfair Contract Terms Act 1977 overrides the normal choice of law process in the specified circumstances.

### The incorporation of foreign law in a contract

It is important to distinguish between the incorporation of particular provisions of a foreign law in the contract and the choice of a proper law. The parties may decide that they wish a particular aspect of their contract to be governed by the rules of some foreign legal system. For instance, in a contract whose proper law is German the parties may decide that they wish certain provisions of the Sale of Goods Act 1973 to apply. What such parties have done is not chosen English law but simply incorporated into their contract certain rules which they could have written out in full but for convenience have referred to as particular sections of the Sale of Goods Act. Thus their contract is still governed by German law but certain terms of it are essentially English

The significance of this distinction is that foreign legal provisions which are incorporated into the contract are applied as they were on the date that the contract was concluded; whereas, if the foreign law is the proper law of the contract, it will generally be applied as it was at the date of the action.

### Where the parties impliedly choose the proper law

As a general principle, if something may be done expressly, it may also be done impliedly. Thus if the parties impliedly choose the law that is to govern their contract, but omit to record that choice in written form, then their choice is none the less valid. These cases are usually called cases of implied or inferred choice. The difficulty lies in proving what their intentions in regard to choice of law were if they have failed to make a record of them.

*Amin Rasheed Shipping Corp* v *Kuwait Insurance Co* is the leading case at present on the subject of implied choice. You should read this case carefully as it is a good example of how the courts deal with this question. Here the plaintiff, a Liberian company resident in Dubai, insured a ship with the defendant, a Kuwaiti insurance company. The plaintiff in due course made a claim on the insurance policy; this was rejected by the defendants, so the plaintiff sought to institute action in London. Under RSC O.11 the English court would only consider granting leave to serve a writ outside the jurisdiction if the contract 'by its terms, or by implication, governed by English law' (see Chapter 4, section 4.2). There was no express choice of English law, but had the parties none the less impliedly chosen English law as the proper law, or was Kuwaiti law the proper law of the contract?

Now some factors seemed to indicate that the parties might have had Kuwaiti law in mind: the policy was issued in Kuwait, the insurers were Kuwaiti, and the payment of claims was to be made in Kuwait (although from the previous dealing between the parties it was clear that payment was frequently made elsewhere). But there were other factors suggesting that the parties might have had English law in mind. The parties had used the English language in the contract, the premiums were to be paid in sterling, and the contract was made in an English form. However, little weight was attached to these factors: the English language (and sterling) was in use throughout the world for reasons of practicality and convenience rather than as a sign of the choice of English law, and contracts made in the English form were frequently used even where the proper law was plainly not English (see Lord Wilberforce's speech in [1983] 2 All ER at 894–895). If this was where the matter had rested then it could easily have been that the House of Lords would have concluded that the proper law of this contract was Kuwaiti law.

However, Lord Diplock (with whom Lords Roskill, Brandon and Brightman agreed) felt that the surrounding circumstances as well as the terms of the contract itself 'point ineluctably to the conclusion that the intention of the parties was that their mutual rights and obligations under [the policy] should be determined in accordance with the English law of marine insurance'. The 'crucial surrounding circumstance' which led Lord Diplock to this conclusion was the fact that at the time that the policy was entered into Kuwait had no law of marine insurance! (A Code of Marine Insurance has subsequently come into force in Kuwait.) This suggested strongly and cogently that the parties did not intend their contract to be governed by the law of Kuwait. Moreover, the terms of the policy itself pointed towards English law. Lord Diplock demonstrated that sense could only be made of the terms of the policy if the English Marine Insurance Act 1906 was applicable. For these reasons he came to the conclusion that the parties had chosen English law. It is obvious from this that the modern approach to the question of implied choice is that a wide range of factors, some drawn from the terms of the contract, some drawn from the surrounding circumstances, will be considered by the judges in determining which law the parties have chosen. Plainly no one factor will be decisive, and the judges will adopt a realistic approach to the question and will have no resort to simple nostrums such as 'the parties agreed to arbitration in London, therefore they chose English law'. Given that the judges are searching for keys to the intention of the parties, the judges are doubtless correct in this attitude; but it does have the unfortunate consequence that it is frequently uncertain which law the parties have impliedly chosen and that an expensive visit to the House of Lords is necessary to answer that question.

## Where the parties do not choose, either expressly or impliedly, a law to govern their contract

We have thus far been seeking to determine what the intention of the parties actually was in regard to choice of law. Of course, it is frequently the case that the parties' minds do not meet at all on the question of choice of law, ie it is not that the parties agreed to choose a particular law but failed to record that in their contract, it is that they never gave a thought to the question of choice of law. What is the court which has to apply some law to their contract to do in these circumstances?

The short answer is that the court has to assign a proper law to the contract; but according to what principles is that assignment to take place? In *Mount Albert Borough Council* v *Australasian Assurance Society Ltd* [1938] AC 224 at 240 Lord Wright said that where there was no choice of law, either express or implied, then 'the court has to impute an intention or to determine for the parties the proper law which, as just and reasonable persons, they ought to or would have intended if they had thought about the question when they made the contract'. This approach – that of the imputed intention – does not, however, stand alone. For in *Bonython* v *Commonwealth of Australia* [1951] AC 201 at 219 Lord Simonds said that where no system of law is referred to when the contract is made then the proper law of the contract was 'that with which the transaction had its closest and most real connection'. It appears from *Amin Rasheed* v *Kuwait Insurance* (as well as numerous other cases) that the search for 'the closest and most real connection' has the upper hand, and this is the approach adopted by Dicey and Morris in Rule 145(3).

Moreover, *Amin Rasheed* v *Kuwait Insurance* suggests that the search is for the 'system of law' rather than 'the country' with which the contract is most closely connected. Generally both the system and the country will be the same, but it is possible for them to differ. For instance, in *Rossano* v *Manufacturers' Life Insurance Co* [1963] 2 QB 352, McNair J thought that the country with which the policies in dispute were most closely connected was Egypt, but Ontario law was the legal system with which they were most closely connected. Although the House of Lords was divided on this issue in *Whitworth Street Estates* v *James Miller and Partners Ltd* [1970] 1 All ER 796, Lord Diplock approved the formulation in terms of legal system in *Amin Rasheed*.

The search for the legal system with which the contract is most closely connected takes place by weighing a wide range of factors connected to the contract. Donaldson MR in the Court of Appeal in *Amin Rasheed* v *Kuwait Insurance* [1983] 1 All ER 873 described the process as involving

> 'an exercise of judgment, a weighing of a multitude of factors ... There is no limit to the number of factors, provided only they have some bearing on the "transaction". The word is important because it directs the court's attention to the contractual matrix and excludes consideration of matters which, although important to one of the parties, are extraneous to the transaction itself and may be unknown to the other party.'

(This description of the process was approved by Lord Wilberforce when the same case was on appeal in the House of Lords.)

The place of contracting, the place or places of performance, the places of residence or business of the parties, as well as the nature and subject matter of the contract, are the major matters to take into consideration (see *Re United Railways of Havana and Regla Warehouses* [1960] Ch 52 at 91). However, it must be made quite clear many factors not on this list may also be taken into consideration. Donaldson MR, for instance, lists (at 876–877) twelve factors which he was invited to take into account. But at least it now seems clear that the conduct of the parties subsequent to entering into the contract is not relevant to the question of the proper law (see Lord Wilberforce in *Amin Rasheed*).

The distinction that we have drawn in much of what has gone before between the implied choice of law and the assignment of the law with which the contract is most closely connected is in many ways an artificial one. The judges indeed frequently differ over whether a particular case is one of implied choice by the parties or of the assignment of a proper law by the judge. Thus in *Amin Rasheed* v *Kuwait Insurance* Lord Diplock and the judges who agreed with him thought that the case was one of implied choice, while Lord Wilberforce thought that it was one of assignment. The truth is, of course, that it is often quite unclear whether the parties chose, but did not record, their choice, or whether their minds never met on the matter at all. But this is just a particular aspect of the great uncertainty that bedevils this area of the law. The fact is that in most international contracts one simply does not know until a judge has finally pronounced on the question what the governing law of a contract is. This is most inconvenient and simply underlines the importance of expressing a choice of law whenever possible.

## Particular aspects

As we indicated earlier, not all contractual matters are governed by the proper law. It is now time to look at some of those areas in which the proper law is not applicable – or at least it is questionable whether it is applicable.

### Formation of the contract

The term 'formation of the contract' will be taken to include a wide range of issues including in particular issues such as consideration, offer and acceptance, mistake, misrepresentation, duress and undue influence. The reason why formation issues are not self-evidently governed by the proper law is that until the contract is validly formed there is no contract in existence, therefore the parties' choice cannot operate and it is not possible to say which legal system the contract is connected with. Thus it is widely accepted by the writers on the conflict of laws that such matters should be tested not by the proper law, for that does not yet exist, but by the putative proper law, viz, the law which would be the proper law if the contract were validly concluded. (See, for instance, Dicey and Morris Rule 146 and *The Parouth* [1982] 2 Lloyd's Rep 351). With this general proposition stated we may look at some detailed areas.

*Offer and acceptance. Albeko Schuhmaschinen* v *Kamborian Shoe Machine Co Ltd* (1961) 11 LJ 519 implicitly accepted the putative proper law approach. Here a letter had been written in England and sent to Switzerland containing an offer; the offeree alleged that he posted his acceptance in Switzerland although it was never received by the offeror. Did a contract come into existence or not? Now as you know (or should know), in English law a contract comes into existence when the acceptance is posted, whether or not the letter of acceptance is received. But by Swiss law the contract is only concluded once the letter of acceptance is received. In the event Salmon J found that the offeree had failed to prove that he did in fact post his acceptance, but he did indicate that, had the offeree proved that the letter had been posted, then Swiss law as the putative proper law would be used to determine whether there was a contract or not.

*Mistake.* Although the matter is far from clear, *Mackender* v *Feldia* [1967] 2 QB 590 can be read as supporting the putative proper law in cases of mistake.

*Consideration.* As you know consideration is required to support every English law contract not under seal. What then is the position where the English courts are faced with an agreement that is not supported by consideration? (We have already considered this question in another context: that of characterisation (see Chapter 2, section 2.3 Kahn-Freund's enlightened lex fori) This question too should be determined by the putative proper law. If the putative proper law is English law, then there is no contract; but if the putative proper law is a legal system that does not require consideration, then there may be a valid contract. Thus in *Re Bonacina* [1912] 2 Ch 394 the court tested the formation of the contract against Italian law (the putative proper law).

## Formal validity

We have already seen how the characterisation of matters such as the requirement of writing under the Statute of Frauds 1677 as procedural has led to difficulties in the English conflict of laws (see Chapter 2, section 2.4 *Evidence*). We are not here concerned with such procedural formalities, for they are clearly governed by the lex fori and there is no escaping that.

We are here concerned with non-procedural formalities. The best example of such a formality would be the requirement under some legal systems of the notarial execution of certain contracts. And the authority is sparse because modern legal systems generally impose few formalities: it is the consensus of the parties, not the compliance with formalities, that binds. However, it is accepted by most writers that compliance with either the lex loci contractus or the (putative) proper law will suffice.

## Capacity

This is another difficult topic and the judicial authority is again sparse. In principle a person's capacity to contract is a matter of personal law or status, and thus should be governed by their lex domicilii. The difficulty with this is that it is very inconvenient in a commercial contract. Is it reasonable to suppose that a person aged

20 who is domiciled in a country where 21 is the age of majority can come to England, enter into a contract here – the person with whom he is contracting assuming that he has contractual capacity as he is over 18 – and then avoid that contract on the ground that under his lex domicilii he is still an infant and lacks contractual capacity?

So the alternative view is to argue that this is a matter of the validity of contract and therefore governed by the proper law. However, we cannot allow the proper law chosen by the parties to operate because that would allow the parties to confer the necessary capacity upon themselves by a judicious choice of law. (In *Cooper* v *Cooper* (1888) 13 App Cas 88 at 108 Lord Macnaghten rejected the proposition that a party could confer capacity upon himself 'by contemplating a different country as the place where the contract was to be fulfilled'.) Hence the writers agree that in this context 'proper law' means 'the objective proper law', ie what would be the proper law had there been no choice of law by the parties.

A further alternative is to allow the lex loci contractus to determine capacity to contract. Of course, the locus contractus may be entirely fortuitous, but this rule has at least the advantage of simplicity and certainty.

The problem, however, is not simply a matter of choosing one of these three possibilities. Suppose for example that a person had capacity under his lex domicilii but lacked it under the proper law. Would it be right that he should be able to avoid the contract? Thus perhaps the ideal rule should vary depending upon which party was seeking to rely upon the incapacity, ie a party capable under his lex domicilii should not be able to set up an incapacity under the proper law. See generally Morris, *The Conflict of Laws*, 3rd ed, 1984, 285–288, for a good discussion.

As far as the English decisions are concerned it is not possible to say that there is an established view. Cases can be cited in favour of the lex domicilii (eg *Sottomayor* v *de Barros (No 1)* (1887) 3 PD 1 at 5), but these tend to be cases concerned with capacity to marry where very different considerations apply to those relevant in a commercial context. There is a decision (*Male* v *Roberts* (1800) 3 Esp 163) that supports the lex loci contractus, but it is very old. The most recent relevant English case, *Bodley Head Ltd* v *Flegon* [1972] 1 WLR 680, however, indicates a tendency towards the proper law of the contract. What was in issue here was whether the Russian author Solzhenitsyn had capacity to appoint an agent abroad. It was argued that under Russian law (which was both Solzhenitsyn's lex domicilii (at that time) and the lex loci contractus) he lacked capacity to enter into such a contract. However, his capacity was decided by the proper law of the contract, viz, Swiss law. The decision is not of particularly great weight because the issue of whether this meant the law chosen by the parties or the objective proper law was not discussed. The objective proper law was recognised as the appropriate law with which to test capacity in the Canadian case of *Charron* v *Montreal Trust Co* (1858) 15 DLR (2d) 24.

The upshot of all this is that as Morris, op cit, 288, says, the actual law that would be applied in a matter of capacity before an English court is 'anyone's guess'. My guess for what it is worth is that the objective proper law is likely to be applied.

## Essential validity of the contract

This is a matter par excellence for the proper law. Thus where pressure placed upon one of the parties amounted to duress under the lex causae, but did not amount to duress under the law of the place where the pressure was exerted, the lex causae was applied to render the contract voidable: *Dimskal Shipping Co SA* v *International Transport Workers' Federation* [1991] 4 All ER 871. Here the International Transport Workers' Federation, a trade union federation based in London that sought to prevent the employment of cheap labour on vessels flying flags of convenience, threatened to 'black' Dimskal's vessel while it was in a Swedish port unless Dimskal entered into fresh contracts with the crew (and an agreement with the ITWF) to bring the crew's conditions of employment up to ITWF standards and to pay the ITWF (for the crew) various sums in respect of past wages. In order to avoid the 'blacking' Dimskal entered into these agreements and paid these sums. However, it then sued ITWF in London for a declaration that the various contracts were void for duress and for the return of the sums paid under the void contracts. The proper law of the relevant contracts was English law; under English law a contract induced by duress was voidable by the innocent party, and one form of duress was illegitimate economic pressure (which included the 'blacking' of a ship). However, under the law of Sweden, where the duress was exercised, such pressure was lawful. Could this prevent Dimskal from recovering the sums paid under the contracts to ITWF? On analogy with tort, where, in order to recover damages in England, the act complained of had to be actionable both under the law of the place where it was performed and under the law of England (see *Boys* v *Chaplin* [1971] AC 356, and Chapter 6, section 6.3), it was argued that the fact that the duress was lawful in Sweden meant that there could be no recovery in England. However, Lord Goff of Chieveley, in the leading speech, rejected the analogy with tort since, for one thing, an act could amount to duress even if it was not tortious, and for another, the fact that the proper law of the contract was English anchored the matter in English law much more strongly than a foreign tort was anchored. It followed that English law would be used to determine whether the contracts were voidable for duress. Thus the ship owners succeeded. This must be right: under the lex causae the contract was voidable. However, would the approach be the same if the lex causae and the lex fori were not the same? Suppose the lex causae was Swedish law, would the English courts enforce the contract notwithstanding that the pressure amounted to duress under English law? In the absence of a strong public policy (for instance, if the pressure took the form of violence or threats of violence), they should do so.

Finally, note Lord Templeman's dissent: he felt that English courts should not concern themselves with acts lawful where they were committed.

## Discharge of the contract

It is generally recognised that this is a matter for the proper law, and this was the law applied in *Jacobs* v *Crédit Lyonnais* (1884) 12 QBD 589 to a question of frustration.

## Performance

The proper law of the contract governs the substance of the obligation (*Mount Albert Borough Council* v *Australasian Assurance Society Ltd* [1938] AC 224 and *Bonython* v *Commonwealth of Australia* [1951] AC 201). The latter case, however, is also authority for the view that the 'mode of performance of the obligation' is a matter for the place of performance. It may be difficult to tell in particular cases whether a matter relates to the mode of performance or the substance of the obligation.

## Interpretation

Although it is unusual, it is possible that the parties could have agreed that the law to be used to interpret the contract should be different from the proper law of the contract. Where this is the case the courts will not use the proper law to interpret the contract but will use the law which the parties intended. As Upjohn J said in *Re Helbert Wagg & Co Ltd* [1956] 1 All ER 129 at 135 'the parties may well contemplate that different parts of their contract shall be governed by different law' (see also *Hamlyn & Co* v *Talisker Distillery* [1894] AC 202 at 207).

## *Illegality*

This is a subtle, confusing but interesting topic. Let us begin by citing the words of Diplock LJ in *Mackender* v *Feldia AG* [1966] 3 All ER 847 at 851:

> '[a] English courts will not enforce an agreement, whatever be its proper law, if it is contrary to English law, whether statute law or common law;
> [b] nor will they enforce it, even though it is not contrary to English law, if it is void for illegality under the proper law of the contract.
> [c] Furthermore, subject to one exception, the English courts will not enforce performance or give damages for non-performance of an act required to be done under a contract, whatever be the proper laws of the contract, if the act would be illegal in the country in which it is required to be performed. The exception ... is where the illegality is a breach of a revenue or fiscal law of a foreign state.'

Now proposition [a] is plainly correct provided that we understand that the enforcement of a contract with a foreign proper law will only be prevented under this head if Parliament intended that the statute in question should extend to contracts with a foreign proper law, ie that the statute in question is an 'overriding statute'. An example of this principle will be found in *Boissevain* v *Weil* [1950] AC 327.

By 'common law' Diplock LJ presumably meant contrary to public policy, for it is clear that contracts that would be unenforceable if their proper law were English law may be enforceable if they have a foreign proper law. Thus money loaned for the purposes of gambling is recoverable in England if the loan were lawful under the proper law of the loan (*Saxby* v *Fulton* [1909] 2 KB 208). (Cf *Moulis* v *Owen* [1907] 1 KB 746 where the creditor failed because he sued on a cheque governed by English law rather than the original loan for the purposes of play which was valid under the French proper law.)

Proposition [b] is straightforward, and innumerable cases establish this (*Kahler v Midland Bank* [1950] AC 24 (which may have been wrongly decided for other reasons), *Zivnostenka Banka National Corporation v Frankman* [1950] AC 57 and *Dalmia Dairy Industries Ltd v National Bank of Pakistan* [1978] 2 Lloyd's Rep 223). The English choice of law process has said that the foreign law is applicable; thus it must be applied even if it means holding that the contract is invalid under the law which the parties have chosen.

We have now dealt with illegality under the lex fori (proposition [a]) and under the proper law (proposition [b]). The question arises whether illegality under any other system of law is relevant. We have already seen from our discussion of *Vita Food Products Inc v Unus Shipping Co* [1939] AC 277 (see especially at 292) that illegality under the lex loci contractus is irrelevant. But is any regard paid to the illegality under the lex loci solutionis?

Proposition [c] plainly holds that illegality under the lex loci solutionis will prevent that contract from being enforced or damages from being claimed in England. There are many decisions which approve of this principle to a greater or lesser degree, but the leading decision is *Ralli Bros v Compagnia Naviera Sota y Aznar* [1920] 2 KB 287. What had happened was that Ralli Brothers had failed to pay the agreed freight on a cargo of jute delivered to Barcelona. The charterparty, which was governed by English law, provided that half the freight was to be paid in Barcelona on delivery of the jute, but before delivery Spanish law set a maximum limit to the freight rate, and the agreed rate exceeded this. The charterparty was, however, governed by English law, and thus read in context, all that was being laid down was a rule of internal English law concerning the frustration of contracts. If the proper law of the contract was, say, German law, then *Ralli Bros* is quite consistent with the proposition that German law, not the lex fori, should determine what the effect of illegality under the locus solutionis is. Unfortunately other cases, of which *Regazzoni v KC Sethia* [1956] 2 QB 490 is the best known (see also *Foster v Driscoll* [1929] 1 KB 470 and *Dalmia Dairies Ltd v National Bank of Pakistan*, above), make the rule rest upon the public policy. Viscount Simonds, for instance, said in *Regazzoni* 'our courts ... refuse as a matter of public policy to enforce a contract which involves the violation of foreign law on foreign soil'. Although the matter cannot be considered as finally settled, it is likely that the courts will in a suitable case hold that the true basis of the rule that contracts illegal under the lex loci solutionis will not be enforced is public policy.

The principles regarding illegality were recently discussed by Staughton J in *Libyan Arab Bank v Bankers Trust Co* [1989] 3 WLR 314. This was a case that arose out of the executive order made at 4pm on 8 January 1986 by the President of the United States freezing all Libyan assets in the United States or in the possession and control of United States persons including overseas branches of US banks. The Libyan Arab Bank had accounts with the Bankers Trust (a US bank) in both New York and London, and the terms of its arrangements were that at 2pm every day funds were transferred either to or from London to ensure that the balance in the

New York account was $500,000. At 2pm on 7 January and at 2pm on 8 January there were sums of $165 million and $161 million in the New York account that ought to have been transferred to London but which were not. Such transfers would have been quite lawful at the time; it was only at 4pm that they would have become unlawful.

The plaintiffs now sought the payment of these sums in London from the defendant bank. Payment was resisted on the ground that it was impossible for the defendant to do so without committing an illegal act in the United States. Staughton J held, though, that the defendant would only be excused 'from complying with the demand for payment if the payment was illegal by the proper law of the contract or it involved the doing of an act which was unlawful in the place in which it was performed'.

Applying the general rule that the contract between a bank and its customer was governed by the law of the place where the account was kept, Staughton J concluded that in respect of the London account, English law governed. Since payment was not unlawful under the proper law and, in the circumstances, could be made at the proper time without performing any illegal act in the United States, it followed that the Libyan Arab Bank could recover the very large sums involved for the Bankers Trust's breach of contract on 7 and 8 January. A number of more technical defences based upon the details of the mode of payment sought were also rejected, as was the defence that the contract was frustrated by the US executive order.

Note, however, that it has been held that in such cases it is still 'arguable' that the relevant proper law is US law, not English law; thus O.14 applications for summary judgment are not suitable: *Libyan Arab Foreign Bank* v *Manufacturers Hanover Trust Co* [1988] 2 Lloyd's Rep 494.

An exception has been created to proposition [c] by Staughton LJ in *Howard* v *Shirlstar Container Transport Ltd* [1990] 3 All ER 366. Two aircraft had been leased from the defendant company, but the lessees had ceased to pay the hire and had taken the aircraft to Nigeria. The plaintiff was a pilot who had undertaken to recover the aircraft from Nigeria. He went to Nigeria, found one of the aircraft, and in difficult circumstances – having been warned by the Nigerian authorities that his life and that of his wireless operator were in danger – flew it to the Ivory Coast. However, the Ivory Coast government seised the aircraft and returned it to Nigeria. The defendant refused to pay the plaintiff the full amount agreed. One of the defences raised by the defendant was that the contract had been illegally performed in Nigeria since he had taken off without permission from Nigerian air-traffic control. The judge held that although the courts would not normally enforce a contract which would enable the plaintiff to benefit from his crime, the conscience of the court would not be affronted by allowing the plaintiff to succeed where the plaintiff, as here, had committed the illegal acts in order to escape the danger to his life. Thus the contract was enforced against the defendant. The judge also said that the same result would have been reached if the illegalities had been against English law. Although justice was doubtless done, this must be seen as an exceptional case limited to its own facts.

One final point on illegality: there is one situation in which English law directs that the courts should have regard to illegality under the law of another country which is neither the lex fori, nor the lex causae, nor the lex loci solutionis. In terms of the Bretton Woods Order in Council 1946 English courts are required not to enforce contracts which breach the foreign exchange control regulations of states which are members of the International Monetary Fund. This not only extends to contracts where the currency of one state is exchanged for another in breach of the relevant foreign exchange control regulations, but also includes 'disguised exchange contracts' (see *United City Merchants (Investments) Ltd* v *Royal Bank of Canada* [1982] All ER 720 and *Wilson Smithett & Cope Ltd* v *Terruzzi* [1976] 1 All ER 817). A recent example of this principle was *Mansouri* v *Singh* [1986] 2 All ER 619. Here an Iranian sought to transfer money out of Iran by buying airline tickets in Iran and then selling them to a London travel agent at a false rate of exchange. The travel agent then paid him the difference in a cheque drawn on a London bank. The cheque was not met, and the plaintiff could not sue on it because it was a disguised exchange contract contrary to the terms of the Bretton Woods Order in Council 1946.

## 5.3 Choice of law in contract under the EC Convention

### Introduction

Even before the agreement on the Brussels Convention in 1968 powerful voices within the EC favoured the unification of all the rules of private international law (or the conflict of laws) throughout the EC. This, although a noble dream – for such unification tends to enhance uniformity of decision, one of the major goals of the conflict of laws – was impossibly ambitious. And some of the other more ambitious goals (the unification of choice of law rules in the fields of property and succession as well as non-contractual obligations) have now been set aside (at least for the moment); but the uniformity of the rules applicable to contractual obligations has now been achieved by the Rome Convention. The Convention has already been incorporated into English law by the Contracts (Applicable Law) Act 1990 which came into force on 1 April 1991.

There is little point in establishing uniform rules throughout the EC if the various European legal systems remain free to interpret the Convention in different ways. The Convention itself in article 18 provides that in interpreting the Convention rules 'regard shall be had to their international character and to the desirability of achieving uniformity in their interpretation and application'. These words presumably mean that interpreters of the Convention should have regard to the decisions of other courts interpreting the Convention. We may also take it for granted that, given the European origins of the Convention, it will, like the Brussels Convention, be given a 'purposive' or 'teleological' interpretation. Moreover, as with the Brussels Convention, regard may be had to the official report on the Convention (the Giuliana-Lagarde Report) (Contracts (Applicable Law) Act 1990, s3(3)).

However, none of this will ensure that the Convention is uniformly interpreted throughout the EC. Thus the Contracting States entered into the First Protocol on the Interpretation by the Court of Justice of the European Communities of the Convention on the Law Applicable to Contractual Relations (known henceforth as the Brussels Protocol). The Brussels Protocol authorises the European Court to interpret the Rome Convention (as well as a number of other documents (the Brussels Protocol itself and the Convention on Accession to the Rome Convention)). The Brussels Protocol, like the Interpretation Protocol of the Brussels Convention, sets up a mechanism whereby preliminary rulings on the meaning of the Convention may be sought from the European court by certain English courts, where clarity on that meaning of the Convention is necessary to decide the case before the court. The UK courts which may request such a ruling are the House of Lords and other courts from which no appeal is possible, as well as any court sitting as an appeal court. The details of this procedure will not be dealt with here. Suffice it to say that they are designed to ensure that the European court has the final say on what the meaning of the Convention is; and that that meaning will be the one that will then be applied throughout the EC.

## The scope of the Convention

Article 1(1) provides that 'the rules of this Convention shall apply to contractual obligations in any situation involving a choice between the laws of different countries'. We will need to discuss a number of aspects of this article, but first it should be noted how broad the scope of the Convention is. The rules apply to '*any situation* involving a choice between the laws of different countries'. Thus they will apply not only to contracts which are connected in one way or another with EC States (for instance, if one or more of the parties are domiciled in the EC or if the contract is to be performed in the EC) but also to contracts which have no connection with any EC State, but which happened to be litigated in an English (or other EC) court. When the Contracts (Applicable Law) Act 1990 was being debated in the House of Lords Lord Wilberforce moved an amendment that would have spelt out that the Convention only applied where there was some European connection to the contract in question. But his amendment was defeated, and it must now be considered clear that the Convention has worldwide scope. The breadth of the Convention can furthermore be seen by the terms of article 2, which spells out that any law, whether of a Contracting or a non-Contracting State, 'shall be applied' if the Convention so directs.

There are, however, some difficult issues involving the interpretation of article 1(1). First of all, what legal system is to be used to determine whether a particular disputed juristic relationship amounts to a 'contractual obligation' or not? It may be, for example, that a particular matter is considered contractual under some legal systems (so that the Convention does apply) but that the same matter is non-contractual under other legal systems (so that the Convention does not apply).

Article 8(1) of the Convention has been considered of use here for it provides that the validity of a contract 'shall be determined by the law which would govern it under this Convention if the contract ... were valid' (ie the putative proper law should be applied: see section 5.2 Formation of the contract). It is tempting to suggest that one should follow this pattern in determining whether a particular matter is a 'contractual obligation' or not. But it would be illogical to yield to this temptation, for one surely cannot rely upon the Convention to determine whether the Convention is applicable at all!

Furthermore, it would be unwise to use the lex fori (the obvious other legal system that might be used) to determine whether a particular matter is contractual or not, for the answer to that question would vary depending upon where the case was brought, and a prime purpose of the Convention is to encourage uniformity of decision within the EC.

Thus it appears most likely that the European Court will follow the pattern established in the interpretation of the Brussels Convention and develop a 'Convention concept' of what will amount to a 'contractual obligation'. Doubtless the idea of legally binding voluntary agreements will be a crucial part of whatever 'community concept' the court develops.

Then, secondly, a word needs to be said about the meaning of the word 'countries' in article 1(1). Is the United Kingdom one country or three (Scotland, Northern Ireland and England)? Does the Convention apply to a situation involving a choice between Scots law and English law? Article 19(1) provides that where States consist of 'several territorial units' with different legal systems, 'each territorial unit will be considered as a country for the purposes of identifying the law applicable under this Convention'. This suggests that the Convention does apply to a choice between Scots law and English law; however, article 19(2) (inserted at the request of the UK) provides that States consisting of different territorial units are 'not bound to apply this Convention to conflicts solely between the laws of such units'. So the UK has the choice whether to apply the Convention in such cases, and s2(3) of the Contracts (Applicable Law) Act 1990 tells us how the UK has made that choice: 'notwithstanding article 19(2) ... the Conventions shall apply in the case of conflicts between the laws of different parts of the United Kingdom'. So at last we know that the Convention does apply to conflicts between Scots law and English law. (But there must have been a more straightforward way of reaching this conclusion.) There is one consequence to all this: although the Convention is applicable to the conflicts between Scots and English law, such conflicts fall outside the jurisdiction granted to the European Court in the Brussels Protocol, so they cannot be referred to the court for a preliminary ruling.

Although the breadth of the scope of the Convention has been stressed, it is important to be aware of the matters to which the Convention does not apply: these are specified in article 1(2) and (3). They include the capacity and status of natural and legal persons, contractual obligations relating to wills and succession, matrimonial property, other family law matters (including the maintenance of illegitimate children), obligations arising under most aspects of negotiable instruments, arbitration agreements, agreements on the choice of court, questions governed by company law, agency, trusts, evidence and procedure (although article 14 deals with a number of aspects of burden and proof and the like), and insurance (but not re-insurance) of risks situated in the EC. Difficult questions of interpreting the scope of some of these exceptions will, of course, arise. However, it may be noted that many of the exceptions are very similar to those contained in article 1 of the Brussels Convention, and it is to be expected that the European Court will give the same meaning to the similar words in both Conventions.

One further exception may be mentioned: article 21 provides that the Rome Convention 'shall not prejudice the application of international conventions to which a Contracting State is, or becomes, a party'.

## The basic principles of the Convention

### Party autonomy

The Rome Convention, like the common law (see section 5.2 *General principles* and *Ascertaining the proper law* above), recognises the autonomy of parties to choose the legal system governing their contract. Article 3(1) provides that:

> 'A contract shall be governed by the law chosen by the parties. The choice must be express or demonstrated with reasonable certainty by the terms of the contract or the circumstances of the case. By their choice the parties can select the law applicable to the whole or a part only of the contract.'

Naturally, just as under the common law and implied choice of law, there will sometimes be difficult cases in which it is not clear whether the parties have demonstrated their choice with 'reasonably certainty'; so it will still be prudent always to include in drafting any contract with international elements a clear and unequivocal choice of law.

The difficult question of how one determines whether the choice of law clause is valid is, however, addressed in article 3(4). This article provides that:

> 'The existence and validity of the consent of the parties as to the choice of the applicable law shall be determined in accordance with the provisions of articles 8 (material validity), 9 (formal validity) and 11 (incapacity)'.

We shall deal with these articles in detail below; for the present it suffices to mention that article 8 requires the 'law that would govern under this Convention if the contract or term were valid' (the putative proper law) to be used to determine the existence and validity of a contract or any terms thereof (including a choice of law clause). (Be sure that you understand why reliance could not be placed on article 8(1) in determining whether a particular matter amounted to a 'contractual obligation' in article 1(1): see section 5.3 *The scope of the Convention* above).

Article 3(2) makes it clear that the parties 'can at any time', ie even after the contract has been concluded and when litigation is pending, 'agree to subject the contract to a law other than that which previously governed it' whether that law was expressly chosen or not. Such variation, however, will not render an otherwise formally valid contract invalid.

## The limitations on party autonomy

We know that under the common law parties could choose a law to govern their contract that had no apparent connections with their contract (see section 5.2 Where the parties have expressly chosen a law to govern that agreement, above). If there were a restriction on the parties' freedom of choice it was ill defined and not very extensive. With the Rome Convention, however, matters stand on a rather different footing: article 5 provides that in the case of consumer contracts (defined as the supply of goods and service (or credit) to a person for a purpose outside the scope of that person's trade or profession) a choice of law by the parties 'shall not have the result of depriving the consumer of the protection afforded to him by the mandatory rules of the law of the country in which he has his habitual residence'. The reason for this limitation is obvious: the desire that the economically weak consumer does not have his legal protection rendered illusory by a choice of law foisted upon him by the economically powerful supplier.

Of course, the point may be made that often such consumer protection statutes will be held to be overriding (see section 5.2 Statutes and the express choice of law, above) and so under the common law will apply irrespective of any choice of law. However, there is a difference with article 5: it protects the consumer with the laws of the consumer's habitual residence. But under the common law doctrine of overriding statutes, only statutes from the lex fori or the lex causae (the chosen law) will be applied, and neither of these is necessarily the law of the consumer's habitual residence.

Article 6 is similar in purpose to article 5: it ensures that the rights of employees are not rendered illusory by a choice of law foisted upon the contract by an employer. Article 6(1) provides that, notwithstanding a choice of law, the employee shall not be deprived of the protection of the mandatory rules of the otherwise applicable legal system. And that which is otherwise applicable is specified in article 6(2): it is the law of the country in which the employee habitually works or, if he does not habitually work in any one country, the law of the place in which the business 'through which he was engaged is situated'. Again, as we know from section 5.2 above, as far as the United Kingdom is concerned the Employment Protection (Consolidation) Act 1978 already provides that where an employee ordinarily works in Great Britain the protection of that Act applies irrespective of choice of law. But article 6 goes further: now the protective legislation of other countries, even when not chosen by the parties, may be enforced by the United Kingdom's courts when applying the Convention.

There is, however, a further restriction on the parties' autonomy in the Rome Convention, of a more novel form than that contained in articles 5 and 6. This is to be found in articles 3(3) and 7. Article 3(3) provides that where the parties have chosen a foreign law (whether or not accompanied by the choice of a foreign court) but all the other localising elements of the contract are connected with another country, the choice of law 'shall not ... prejudice the application of the laws of that country which cannot be derogated from by contract, hereinafter called "mandatory rules"'. Let us make what this means clear with an example: suppose the parties were French, the contract was to be performed in France, and all other aspects of the contract were linked to France. Article 3(3) says that even if the parties choose English law (and submit to the jurisdiction of the English courts) the English courts will apply the mandatory rules of French law (that the parties were probably trying to evade by choosing English law). Under the common law the English courts would have applied English law to the exclusion of the French rules. (But at common law the courts would not have enforced a contract that required the parties to break the law of the place where the contract was to be performed: see section 5.2 above.)

Before article 3(3) bites, however, all elements relevant to the situation must be connected with only one other country. What is the position with mandatory rules where those elements are connected to a number of other countries? This is the question addressed in article 7, which provides that 'effect *may* be given to the mandatory rules of the law of another country with which the situation has a close connection, if and in so far as, under the law of the latter country, those rules must be applied whatever the law applicable to the contract'. But it is plain from these words that the court has a discretion whether to apply the rule in question. Indeed article 7(1) even provides what is to be considered in exercising this discretion: 'the nature and purpose' of the rules and the consequence of 'their application or non-application'. Article 7(2) makes it clear that the mandatory rules of the lex fori may still apply.

Article 7 is novel for two reasons: first, because it permits the application of rules which come neither from the lex fori nor from the lex causae. (This is not so remarkable since it shares this characteristic with articles 5 and 6.) But, secondly, it provides for a discretion in the application of such mandatory rules; it all depends upon their 'nature and purpose' and the consequences of their application. This introduces great uncertainty into the law, for it would be quite unpredictable when these mandatory rules would be applied by English courts. For this reason, the United Kingdom (as it was entitled to do under article 22(1)(a)) entered a reservation to article 7(1) and subsequently provided in s2(2) of the Contracts (Applicable Law) Act 1990 that article 7(1) 'shall not have the force of law in the United Kingdom'.

### The principle of closest connection
Thus far we have been dealing with cases where there is a choice of law (and some related matters). What is the position where there is no choice of law? What law governs? This question is tackled in article 4(1) which provides that 'the contract shall be governed by the law of the country with which it is most closely connected'.

At first sight this does not appear to be very different to the test of 'the closest and most real connection' that was emerging as the orthodox approach in the common law (section 5.2 Where the parties do not chose, either expressly or impliedly, a law to govern their contract, above, although note that article 4(1) talks of the 'country' rather than the 'legal system' with which the contract is most closely connected). However article 4(2) creates a presumption of closest connection. It provides that:

> 'It shall be presumed that the contract is most closely connected with the country where the party who is to effect the performance which is characteristic of the contract has, at the time of conclusion of the contract, his habitual residence, or, in the case of a body corporate or unincorporate, its central administration.'

We shall consider the doctrine of 'characteristic performance' shortly but must first make some additional points of detail about article 4. First, where the contract is made in the course of a party's trade or profession, the country of closest connection

> 'shall be the country in which the principal place of business is situated or, where under the terms of the contract the performance is to be effected through a place of business other than the principal place of business, the country in which that other place of business is situated'.

Secondly, the presumption is not applicable in contracts for the carriage of goods. In such contracts, the country of closest connection will be the country in which the carrier has his principal place of business provided that country is also the place either of loading or of discharge of the goods or the place where the consignor has his principal place of business (article 4(4)).

Thirdly, article 4(5) makes it clear that the rules set out in the preceding three paragraphs are only presumptions; thus they 'shall be disregarded if it appears from the circumstances as a whole that the contract is more closely connected with another country'.

Fourthly, article 4 does not exclude the possibility that reference may be made to events occurring after the contract was entered into in order to determine the country with which the contract is most closely connected. But at common law it seems that this was not possible (see section 5.2 Where the parties do not chose, either expressly or impliedly, a law to govern their contract, above).

Fifthly, article 4(3) establishes a presumption that the country of the situs of immovable property is the country with which any contract having that immovable property as its subject matter has the closest connection. This is plainly consistent with the general approach of the common law, but note that there may be difficulties similar to those in interpreting article 16 of the Brussels Convention (see Chapter 4, section 4.3 Immovable property: article 16(1)).

Now to return to the doctrine of 'characteristic performance'. This doctrine is the most innovative aspect of the Rome Convention and also one of the grounds upon which the Convention is criticised. The major grounds of criticism are that it is not straightforward to determine what the 'characteristic performance' of a particular contract may be, and that in any event the trend in the common law was away from the technique of presuming what the lex causae is (see section 5.2

Where the parties do not choose, either expressly or impliedly, a law to govern their contract, above).

However, it is perhaps possible to overemphasise the uncertainty introduced by this concept, which owes its origin to Swiss law. Reference may thus be made to Swiss jurisprudence or to the jurisprudence of other European countries that have adopted the concept to determine how it operates. Moreover, in many cases it is clear: in a contract of sale the characteristic performance is the delivery of the goods sold; in a contract of employment the characteristic performance is that of work.

### Particular aspects of the contract

*Material validity.* The material or essential validity of the contract cannot be tested by the chosen law, for, if the contract is invalid, there is no chosen law. Thus article 8(1), which we have already referred to on a number of occasions, provides that the validity of the contract (or any terms thereof) 'shall be determined by the law which would govern it under this Convention if the contract or term were valid'. This approach, usually termed that of the putative proper law, accords well with the common law (see section 5.2 Formation of the contract, above).

This principle, however, is qualified by article 8(2) which allows a party to rely upon the law of his habitual residence to establish his consent if 'it would not be reasonable to determine the effect of his conduct in accordance with the' putative proper law. The reason for this provision is this: under some legal systems (eg Danish law) silence can amount to consent. Article 8(2) ensures that a party who does not reply to an offer (which includes a choice of a governing law in which silence does amount to consent) made to him, does not find himself bound by a contract.

For a recent case that illustrates the operation of article 8(1) and (2): see *Egon Oldendorff* v *Liberia Corporation* [1995] 2 Lloyd's Rep 65. Here the plaintiffs (a German partnership) entered into an agreement with the defendants (a Japanese corporation) for a charter of bulk carriers to be built for the defendants in Japan. The agreement was subject to the defendants obtaining board approval and signing the building contracts by 15 April 1993, and contained a London arbitration clause. Agreement was reached as to the terms of the charter agreement on 23 April 1993 but the defendants failed to sign the shipbuilding contracts until 20 May 1993. The choice of law questions for decision were whether there was a valid contract between the parties, whether the arbitration clause had been validly incorporated and whether the contract was governed by English law.

The court held that under article 8(1) of the Rome Convention the validity of a contract is governed by the law which would govern it under the Convention if it were valid (the putative proper law). If the arbitration clause was validly incorporated the contract was subject to English law, as this was evidence of the parties' choice of English law. The signing subject had been lifted on 20 May, on signature of the building contracts, and therefore the previously agreed charter agreement of 23 April came into force, including the arbitration clause. As to whether the defendants could claim under article 8(2), Mance J formulated the question as 'whether it would be reasonable to determine the effect of the defendants' conduct in accordance with English law ... in considering whether any contract which may have been agreed contained a valid arbitration clause'. He held that:

> 'Clearly this question cannot be decided from the viewpoint of Japanese law. Nor ex hypothesi can it be answered from the purely domestic viewpoint of the law which would otherwise govern under article 8(1). It can only be answered by the court before which it comes adopting a dispassionate, internationally minded approach.'

Applying this approach to the course of conduct between the parties, which showed evidence that the arbitration clause would be incorporated, he rejected the claim under article 8(2).

This case illustrates the principle that the putative proper law will invariably govern issues of material validity under the Rome Convention. The reasonableness safety valve of article 8(2) will continue to be difficult to establish. While the international approach to the definition of reasonableness taken by Mance J has the virtue of not being forum-controlled, the exact ambit of article 8(2) remains unclear.

*Formal validity.* Article 9 lays down the rules that will govern the formal validity of contract governed by the Convention. Where the parties are in the same country when the contract is concluded then formal validity is tested either by the proper law (ie the governing law under the Convention) or the law of the country where the parties are (article 9(1)). Should the parties be in different countries at the time of conclusion then either the proper law or the law of either of the countries may be used (article 9(2)). With contracts concluded by agents then the country where the agent acts is the country to be used in the application of article 9(1) and (2). The putative proper law can also be used (article 9(4)). But where the subject matter of the contract is a right to immovable property or a right to use immovable property, then the formal requirements of lex situs govern.

*Incapacity.* Article 11 provides that where the parties are in the same country then a natural person can only invoke an incapacity arising out of another law if the other party knew of the incapacity or was unaware of it through his negligence. This provision is obviously not a clear choice of the law rule, and the reason for this is that the capacity of natural persons (apart from the rule in article 11) is excluded from the Rome Convention (article 2(a)). For common law rules, such as they are, see section 5.2 Capacity, above.

### The scope of the applicable law as determined under the Convention

Article 10 specifies the matters which are to be governed by the applicable law. These are interpretation, performance, the consequence of breach (including damages in so far as these are determined by rules of law), the extinguishing of obligations, limitation of actions, and the consequences of nullity of the contract.

Many problems of interpretation may arise in determining the breadth of article

10, but two points of importance should be noted: first, regarding performance as well as the steps to be taken in the event of defective performance, 'regard shall be had to the law of the country in which the performance takes place'. Compare this with the rules of the common law: see section 5.2 *Illegality*, above.

Secondly, the United Kingdom entered a reservation to article 10(1)(e) dealing with the consequences of nullity of the contract, and s2(2) of the Contracts (Applicable Law) Act 1990 provides that article 10(1)(e) 'shall not have the force of law in the United Kingdom'. The reason for this is that English law takes the view that the consequences of nullity are a matter for the law of restitution, not the proper law of the contract. Whatever the merits of this view from the point of view of principle, it will lead to disharmony of decision. For example, a contract governed by Dutch law under the Convention may be void at Dutch law. All courts in the EC will hold that the contract is void, but the consequences of that nullity will depend upon whether the issue is litigated in England or not.

### Miscellaneous matters

Note that renvoi does not apply (article 15). Where the application of a rule of the applicable law under the Convention is 'manifestly incompatible with the public policy of the forum' then the rule may then, and only then, be refused application (article 16). In addition to the various matters already discussed, other articles govern voluntary assignment (article 12), subrogation (article 13) and the burden of proof (article 14).

# 6

# Choice of Law in Tort

## 6.1 Introduction

You should at this stage be able to predict the kind of problem that we will be dealing with in this chapter. X is injured in a motor accident in France, but discovers that the driver of the other vehicle, Y, is English. If X should sue Y in England, would the English courts apply French law or English law to the case? Although it is scarcely conceivable that a legal system would not allow recovery for a person injured by the negligent driving of another, legal systems differ widely on matters such as which damages are recoverable and even the likely size of a damages award. (The quantum of damages is of course a matter for the lex fori (see Chapter 2, section 2.4 Damages); thus generous damages awarded by courts in the United States provide a considerable incentive to plaintiffs to litigate (see Chapter 4, section 4.4).)

Although for many years the question of which law to apply to tortious claims was a neglected question in many legal systems (including England's law), technological advances and modern communications have thrust the question of choice of law in tort to the forefront of conflict of laws studies. An aircraft negligently manufactured in one of the states of the United States may crash in England killing or injuring travellers from a dozen different countries. Should English law govern the resulting litigation (because that is where the damages occurred), or should the law of the appropriate state of the United States govern (because that is where the negligent manufacture took place), or should each plaintiff perhaps have his claim governed by the law of his domicile? Alternatively, a radio or television station may publish a defamatory statement that is heard in two or three different countries. Which country's law determines whether and to what extent the person defamed has a remedy? These are the sort of problems which can arise quite easily in the modern world, and with which the choice of law rules for tort should be able to deal. As we shall see, however, there are considerable deficiencies in the English choice of law rules.

## 6.2 The rule in *Phillips* v *Eyre*

*Phillips* v *Eyre* (1870) LR 6 QB 1 is the case upon which the basic English choice of law rule is based. What had happened was that the plaintiff had been imprisoned by the defendant, the Governor of Jamaica, during a rebellion on the island. After the rebellion the Jamaican legislature passed an Act of Indemnity indemnifying the Governor (and others) for wrongs done in suppressing the rebellion. None the less, the plaintiff instituted action against the Governor in the English courts on the grounds of false imprisonment. In his judgment Willes J laid down the basic English rule:

> 'As a general rule, in order to found a suit in England for a wrong alleged to have been committed abroad, two conditions must be fulfilled. First, the wrong must be of such a character that it would have been actionable if committed in England ... Secondly, the act must not have been justifiable by the law of the place where it was done.'

Since the Governor's act was justifiable under the law of Jamaica because of the Act of Indemnity, the plaintiff lost.

The dictum of Willes J establishes that a plaintiff has to mount two hurdles in order to succeed in England. The first hurdle – that the tort be 'actionable' under the lex fori – was not crucial to *Phillips* v *Eyre*, but was based upon an earlier case, *The Halley* (1868) LR 2 PC 193, which had accorded an altogether excessive role to the lex fori in choice of law in tort. Selwyn LJ said that it was

> 'alike contrary to principle and to authority to hold that an English Court of Justice will enforce a foreign municipal law, and will give a remedy in the shape of damages in respect of an act which, according to its own [ie English law] principles, imposes no liability on the person from whom damages are claimed'.

Such an attitude is both provincial and chauvinistic, and if applied in all areas would effectively destroy the conflict of laws for if the matter in dispute must be actionable in England before one can succeed, there is hardly any point in looking at any other law. The great goals of conflict of laws – uniformity of decision and the selection of the appropriate law to govern a particular dispute – would have been abandoned. The principle of *The Halley* has been subjected to unanimous academic disapproval.

None the less, the principle received unanimous approval by the House of Lords in *Boys* v *Chaplin* [1971] AC 356, the most recent pronouncement by the Lords on the question of choice of law in tort. Although Lord Wilberforce did approve the principle, he did, however, utter some apt words of criticism of it. The rule in *The*

*Halley*, he said, 'bears a parochial appearance ... rests on no secure doctrinal principle ... [and] ... outside the world of the English-speaking common law ... is hardly to be found'.

The second hurdle, although it has not been quite as unpopular as the first, is not without its own difficulties, the most important of which has been the phrase 'not ... justifiable'. Did it mean the same as 'actionable', ie would the plaintiff have an action under the lex loci, or did it mean something wider, ie that the act complained of was unlawful under the lex loci but that a remedy in the form of an action for damages was not necessarily provided? This issue came to a head in *Machado* v *Fontes* [1897] 2 QB 231.

This was an action in which the plaintiff claimed damages in respect of a libel published in Brazil. The case was in fact decided on a point of pleading, but the interesting issue from our point of view is the following: the Court of Appeal said that it was not enough for the defendant – who was arguing that the plaintiff had not surmounted the second hurdle of *Phillips* v *Eyre* – to allege that the publication of the libel was not a ground on which damages could be claimed in Brazil. He had to allege in addition that the publication of the libel was not criminal under the law of Brazil. This obviously envisaged that 'not justifiable' meant something much wider than 'actionable'. Indeed Lopes LJ said that for the defendant to succeed the act had to be 'innocent in the country where it was committed', and he equated 'not ... justifiable' with 'wrongful'. Rigby LJ agreed and said that for the defendant to succeed the act had to be 'authorised, or innocent or excusable in the country where it was committed'.

We may illustrate the effect of *Machado* v *Fontes* by consideration of the Canadian case of *McLean* v *Pettigrew* (1945) 2 DLR 65. Here the defendant had given a lift to the plaintiff in his car. Unfortunately, the defendant had driven negligently, an accident had occurred, and the plaintiff had been injured. Both plaintiff and defendant were domiciled and resident in Quebec, and so the action was commenced in the Quebec courts and went thence on appeal to the Supreme Court of Canada. However, the accident had taken place in Ontario, and there was an Ontario statute (that we shall run into again in a different context and which has since been repealed) which provided that 'the owner or driver of a motor vehicle ... is not liable for any loss or damage resulting from bodily injury to, or the death of, any person being carried in the motor vehicle'. Thus the question that faced the court in applying the rule in *Phillips* v *Eyre* was: did the statute render the defendant's negligent driving 'justifiable' and therefore prevent the plaintiff from succeeding? In reliance upon *Machado* v *Fontes* the court held that, although it was clear that the defendant was under no civil liability to the plaintiff under the law of Ontario, he was guilty of a traffic offence under that same law. The defendant's act was not therefore 'innocent' under the law of Ontario, it was 'not justifiable', and the second hurdle of *Phillips* v *Eyre* had been overcome by the plaintiff. (This is ridiculous because in fact the defendant was prosecuted for and acquitted of this offence (see Morris, *The Conflict of Laws*, 3rd ed, 1984, 310)! None the less, it was what the court said.)

Note that *McLean* v *Pettigrew* was recently overruled in *Tolofson* v *Jensen*; *Lucas* v *Gagnon* (1995) 120 DLR (4th) 289. The facts in the latter case closely resemble those in *McLean*. The plaintiffs in *Tolofson* and *Lucas* were involved in car crashes in neighbouring provinces in Canada, the defendants being local residents of these provinces. In each case proceedings were brought in the provinces in which the plaintiffs lived rather than where the tort occurred. The court held that in *interprovincial* cases there were to be no exceptions to the lex loci rule. However, it accepted that the flexible exception (actionability under the lex fori) was more defensible in international cases. The first branch of the rule in *Phillips* v *Eyre* was forcibly rejected as an anachronism, and the decision has the effect of bringing about a complete change in the choice of law in tort for Canada. See Chapter 10, section 10.3, for further details.

The effect of the *Machado* v *Fontes* interpretation of the second hurdle is to downgrade the role of the lex loci and to give preference to the lex fori. All that was necessary was that the act should be wrongful in some wide sense under the lex loci, and then the lex loci dropped out of the picture altogether. Yet the predominance of the lex fori and the first hurdle generally has been the basis of so much of the criticism of the rule in *Phillips* v *Eyre*.

You may well feel that the plaintiff in cases like *McLean* v *Pettigrew* ought to have succeeded (see now *Tolofson* v *Jensen*; *Lucas* v *Gagnon* (1995) above). But the reason why he ought to have succeeded has got nothing to do with the upgrading of the lex fori at the expense of the lex loci. It has to do with the fact that where both plaintiff and defendant come from Quebec then the fact that the accident takes place in Ontario seems irrelevant to the dispute between them. The law of Quebec is the proper law of the tort; and it ought, so one feels, to be applied to such a dispute. This concept of the proper law of the tort is one that is struggling against the orthodox rule in *Phillips* v *Eyre* to make its way into English law. We shall discuss the proper law more fully in due course (see section 6.4) for the present it is sufficient to say that it remains on the margins of English law.

The *Machado* v *Fontes* interpretation of the second hurdle has been much criticised. It was not followed or criticised in a number of important decisions (*Canadian Pacific Railway* v *Parent* [1917] AC 195 at 205 (PC), *Koop* v *Beeb* (1951) 84 CLR 629 and *M'Elroy* v *M'Allister* 1949 SC 110). Eventually, this interpretation would appear to have been overruled by the House of Lords in *Boys* v *Chaplin*. (The word 'appears' is used in the last sentence because as we shall see *Boys* v *Chaplin* is one of those decisions about which great uncertainty reigns.) Instead of requiring that the act should have been 'not justifiable' what is now required (by Lords Hodson, Wilberforce and Guest in *Boys* v *Chaplin* but not by Lords Donovan and Pearson) is actionability under the lex loci. Thus the rule in *Phillips* v *Eyre* now requires actionability under both the lex loci and the lex fori. There are doubts about exactly what is meant by actionability, but the time has now come to consider *Boys* v *Chaplin* in detail and with luck some of these doubts will be stilled by our consideration of this case.

## 6.3 The rule in *Boys* v *Chaplin*

The *Phillips* v *Eyre* rule of double actionability can work injustice. Take *M'Elroy* v *M'Allister* for example – although this is a Scottish case it illustrates the point very well. The pursuer (the Scottish term for plaintiff) was the widow of a man killed in a motor accident in England (about 20 miles south of the Scottish border). He was a passenger in a lorry owned by his employers (a Glasgow firm) and driven by a co-employee, the defender (the Scottish term for defendant). Both the defender and the deceased were residents of Glasgow. The pursuer claimed damages against the defender under a number of heads.

At Scots law the widow would have had a claim for substantial damages as a solatium (solace for the loss of her husband), but she had no such claim under English law. Thus the claim for a solatium although actionable under the lex fori (Scots law) was not actionable under the lex loci (English law). Hence it failed.

On the other hand, at English law the Law Reform (Miscellaneous Provisions) Act 1934 provided that her husband's claim for loss of expectation of life survived him, and she as executrix of her husband's estate could therefore sue to recover these damages. But Scots law was clear that rights of action based upon personal injuries caused by negligence died with the injured person. Thus although this claim was actionable under the lex loci (English law) it was not actionable under the lex fori (Scots law). Hence it failed.

There was in fact only one claim which was common to both Scots and English law: the claim for £40 in respect of funeral expenses. Thus this paltry sum was all that was awarded by the Scottish court.

This seems remarkably unjust. Once more Scots law is obviously the proper law of the tort; the fact that the accident took place in England was, if not entirely fortuitous, quite irrelevant to the resolution of the pursuer's claim. This chance occurrence, however, allowed the defender to avoid the substantial liability for damages that he would have been bound to pay had the accident occurred in Scotland. On the *Machado* v *Fontes* law the pursuer would have been better off, for the negligent driving was 'not justifiable' under English law; thus she would easily have leapt over the second hurdle and would have been entitled to damages under the lex fori (Scots law). (Although *M'Elroy* v *M'Allister* was decided before *Boys* v *Chaplin* [1971] AC 356, and thus it was open to the court to apply *Machado* v *Fontes*, it did not do so but adopted the rule of double actionability. It was after all a Scottish court, and *Machado* v *Fontes* was an English decision.)

Now *Boys* v *Chaplin* looked set fair at first to lead to as unjust a decision as that in *M'Elroy* v *M'Allister*. What had happened was that two British servicemen, normally resident in England but stationed in Malta, had been in a motor accident. The plaintiff, while a passenger on a motor scooter, had been involved in a collision with a car driven by the defendant and had been injured. Now under the law of Malta the plaintiff could only recover his expenses and loss of earnings (some £53), but under the law of England he could recover general damages for pain and suffering (some

£2303). Under the *Machado* v *Fontes* approach (adopted at first instance by Milmo J) the plaintiff could recover the £2303 since the defendant's negligence was plainly not justifiable under the law of Malta. But if a rule of double actionability was adopted, then since the claim for damages for pain and suffering was not actionable under the lex loci presumably the plaintiff could not recover them. The Court of Appeal also allowed the plaintiff £2303 damages but for different reasons. (Lord Denning would adopt the proper law of the tort as the law of England (discussed below); Lord Upjohn thought that *Machado* v *Fontes* was correctly decided and that anyway damages related to the nature of the remedy and were for the lex fori (see Chapter 2, section 2.4 Damages); and Diplock LJ dissented and would not have allowed the recovery of the £2303.) So what did the House of Lords decide?

Five speeches were delivered in the House of Lords by each of the five law lords (Lords Hodson, Guest, Wilberforce, Donovan and Pearson). All five agreed that the plaintiff should recover the damages for pain and suffering, but there the consensus evaporated, and it is a mammoth intellectual task almost certainly doomed to failure to attempt to extract the ratio decidendi of this case. What is clear, however, is that something remarkable happened in the case. As we have seen, three of the judges rejected the approach of *Machado* v *Fontes*, and thus actionability under the lex loci rather than only wrongfulness was required. But if *Machado* v *Fontes* is rejected, then one would have expected, as in *M'Elroy* v *M'Allister*, that only those damages common to both the lex fori and the lex loci would be recoverable. Two things thus seem clear: (i) that *Machado* v *Fontes* has been rejected; but (ii) that the double actionability rule of *Phillips* v *Eyre* will now be more flexibly applied.

Since *Boys* v *Chaplin* was decided, however, there has been a very convenient development: the judges too have despaired of extracting the ratio decidendi. And in *Church of Scientology of California* v *Commissioner of the Metropolitan Police* (1976) 120 SJ 690 the Court of Appeal decided that the ratio decidendi of *Boys* v *Chaplin* was to be found in the speech of Lord Wilberforce. This approach has since been adopted by Hodgson J in *Coupland* v *Arabian Gulf Petroleum Co* [1983] 2 All ER 434 (confirmed on appeal [1983] 3 All ER 226 (CA)). Thus we too may in future concentrate on Lord Wilberforce's speech, and there are three important aspects to it.

## *The rejection of* Machado *v* Fontes

Lord Wilberforce clearly held that *Machado* v *Fontes* 'ought to be overruled'. His reasons were simply that it was illogical and that it offered inducements to 'forum shopping'. What he meant by this was that if only wrongfulness under the lex loci is required then plaintiffs may be tempted to sue in England to recover greater damages than they would be entitled to under the lex loci. However, it may be fairly pointed out that the reason why this difficulty arises at all is because of the insistence on the lex fori in the first hurdle of *Phillips* v *Eyre*. If instead of *Phillips* v *Eyre* the lex loci delicti commissi was applied by the English courts, then no question of 'forum shopping' (at least between the lex loci and English law) would arise. (In one of the least persuasive parts of his speech Lord Wilberforce rejected the lex loci as the governing law in tort inter alia on the ridiculous ground that it 'would require proof of a foreign law'.)

## The meaning of actionability under the lex loci

In a long passage Lord Wilberforce set out what he understood by this concept in the second hurdle part of *Phillips* v *Eyre*. He said:

> 'The broad principle should surely be that a person should not be permitted to claim in England in respect of a matter for which civil liability does not exist, or is excluded, under the law of the place where the wrong was committed. This non-existence or exclusion may be for a variety of reasons and it would be unwise to attempt a generalisation relevant to the variety of possible wrongs. But in relation to claims for personal injuries one may say that provisions of the lex delicti, denying or limiting, or qualifying recovery of damages because of some relationship of the defendant to the plaintiff [as in *McLean* v *Pettigrew*], or in respect of some interest of the plaintiff (such as loss of consortium) [for example, the widow's solatium in *M'Elroy* v *M'Allister*] or some head of damage (such as pain and suffering) should be given effect to. I can see no case for allowing one resident of Ontario to sue another in the English court for damages sustained in Ontario as a passenger in the other's car, or one Maltese resident to sue another in the English courts for damages in respect of pain and suffering caused by an accident in Malta. I would, therefore, restate the basic rule of English law with regard to foreign torts as requiring actionability as a tort according to English law, subject to the condition that civil liability in respect of the relevant claim exists between the actual parties under the law of the foreign country where the act was done.'

This makes much clearer what was motivating the learned law lord in his speech. It is plain that 'civil liability' rather than tortious liability under the lex loci is required. Thus, presumably, it would be sufficient if the defendant's liability under the lex loci was 'contractual, quasi-contractual, quasi-delictual, proprietary or sui generis' (Morris, op cit, 315). Compensation awarded by an industrial accident board and payable by an employer is presumably not included (*McMillan* v *Canadian Northern Railway* [1923] AC 120). Mere criminal liability is not sufficient.

What still remains unclear is, how did it come about that the plaintiff recovered damages for pain and suffering in *Boys* v *Chaplin*? This is what we now explain.

## The introduction of flexibility

Those parts of Lord Wilberforce's speech which we have considered thus far represent simply a development of the orthodox approach of *Phillips* v *Eyre*; but then he went on to consider what he called 'the crux of the present case': whether some flexibility should be introduced into the orthodox double actionability rule 'in the interest of individual justice'. He came to the conclusion after the consideration of a range of American decisions (some of which we will discuss below in section 6.5) that it should. This is hardly surprising; the facts of *Boys* v *Chaplin* cry out for some way of avoiding the consequences of applying the rule of *Phillips* v *Eyre*. He said:

'I think that the necessary flexibility can be obtained from that principle which represents a common denominator of the United States decisions, namely, through segregation of the relevant issue and consideration whether, in relation to that issue, the relevant foreign rule ought, as a matter of policy or as Westlake [a leading authority on the conflict of laws] said of science, to be applied. For this purpose it is necessary to identify the policy of the rule, to inquire to what situations, with what contacts, it was intended to apply; whether or not to apply it, in the circumstances of the instant case, would serve any interest which the rule was devised to meet. This technique appears well adapted to meet cases where the lex delicti either limits or excludes damages for personal injury: it appears even necessary and inevitable. No purely mechanical rule can properly do justice to the great variety of cases where persons come together in a foreign jurisdiction for different purposes with different pre-existing relationships, from the background of different legal systems. It will not be invoked in every case or even, probably, in many cases. The general rule must apply unless clear and satisfying grounds are shown why it should be departed from ...'

The learned law lord then applied this approach to the facts. He came to the conclusion that:

'The rule limiting damages is the creation of the law of Malta ... [but nothing] ... suggests that the Maltese state has any interest in applying this rule to persons resident outside it, or denying the application of the English rule [allowing recovery for pain and suffering] to these parties. [The English] rule ought, in my opinion, to apply.'

Thus if we accept Lord Wilberforce's speech as authoritative then the English law is clear: the double actionability rule of *Phillips* v *Eyre* applies but is tempered by flexibility that allows the court to disregard limitation or exclusions contained in the lex loci. Of course, it is difficult to predict when the court will properly depart from the rule in *Phillips* v *Eyre*, although Lord Wilberforce indicated that if the defendant had been a Maltese resident he would have probably refused to be flexible. In the years since *Boys* v *Chaplin* it cannot be said that it has become any clearer when flexibility will be introduced. However, the principle of flexibility was applied in an interesting manner in *Corcoran* v *Corcoran* [1974] VR 164 (Supreme Court of Victoria), and you should look at this case to see the principle operating in practice.

More recently, *Johnson* v *Coventry Churchill International Ltd* [1992] 3 All ER 14 provides an example of the operation of the flexibility introduced by *Boys* v *Chaplin*. Here an English employee (a joiner) of an English company was able to sue the company for failing to provide a safe means of access to his place of work, notwithstanding that in Germany, the country where he actually worked, the law did not allow him to sue his employer in these circumstances. Since the plaintiff and the defendant were both English and the plaintiff could not benefit from the no fault insurance scheme set up in Germany to provide a remedy in such circumstances, the 'double actionability' rule was flexibly applied: the plaintiff was allowed to sue notwithstanding that his claim was not actionable under the law of Germany – the place where the tort took place.

*Boys* v *Chaplin*, *Corcoran* v *Corcoran*, *Johnson* v *Coventry Churchill*, and all the other cases where flexibility has been applied, have been cases where the requirement of actionability under the lex loci delicti has been dispensed with; and it is doubted in many circles whether the flexibility principle applied to actionability under the lex fori. But now, with *Red Sea Insurance Co Ltd* v *Bouygues SA and Others* [1994] 3 WLR 926 the Privy Council has changed all that. Lord Slynn, in the Privy Council's advice, said:

'In *Boys* v *Chaplin* it is not suggested that the exception [to the "double actionability" rule] can be relied on only to exclude the lex loci delicti in favour of the lex fori. Their Lordships do not consider that the element of flexibility which exists is so limited ... They consider that in principle the exception can be applied in an appropriate case to enable a plaintiff to rely exclusively on the lex loci delicti. To limit the rule so as to enable an English court only to apply English law would be in conflict with the degree of flexibility envisaged by Lord Wilberforce, though the fact that the forum is being required to apply a foreign law in a situation where its own law gives no remedy will be a factor to be taken into account when the court decides whether to apply the exception.' (at p940)

What had happened in *Red Sea Insurance* was that a dispute arose over the construction of the University of Riyadh in Saudi Arabia. The plaintiffs, who may conveniently be divided into two groups (Group 1 and Group 2), were involved in various capacities in the construction of the university and had incurred substantial losses in repairing and replacing structural damage which occurred when the buildings were constructed. They sought to recover these losses in an action in the Hong Kong courts under an insurance policy issued by the defendant insurance company (which was incorporated in Hong Kong although it had its head office in Saudi Arabia). The defendant raised various defences, but more significantly, the defendant counterclaimed against the Group 2 plaintiffs, on the ground that it was Group 2's supply of faulty precast concrete units which had caused the losses.

Now, under English law (which also applied in Hong Kong), an insurer who has paid a claim made by a policy-holder can recover from the wrongdoer who caused the policy-holder's losses, the amount he has paid. In these circumstances, the insurer brings the policy-holder's tort claim against the wrongdoer; the insurer is 'subrogated' to the policy-holder's tort claim. However, an insurer can only bring such a 'subrogated' claim if he has already paid the policy-holder; and the defendant had not done so. However, the defendant claimed that under the law of Saudi Arabia he could claim directly against the Group 2 plaintiffs in tort.

The difficulty with this was, of course, that since the Group 1 plaintiffs had not been paid, the defendant's claim was not actionable against the Group 2 plaintiffs in the courts of Hong Kong; ie the alleged wrong was not actionable under the lex fori. However, as adumbrated, the Privy Council held that, exceptionally, in an appropriate case, the plaintiff could rely exclusively on the lex loci delicti even if under the lex fori his claim would not be actionable. This is undoubtedly the most important decision on choice of law in tort since *Boys* v *Chaplin* in 1971. *Red Sea Insurance* lays down that the lex fori may, in appropriate cases, be entirely dispensed with and replaced by the legal system of the place where the wrong occurred. It is thus a much more far-reaching and radical decision than *Boys* v *Chaplin*. Indeed, the advice of the Privy Council went further and accepted that:

'... the law of England recognises that a particular issue may be governed by the law of the country which, with respect to that issue, has the most significant relationship with the occurrence and with the parties.' (Lord Slynn at p939F).

That is that to particular issues a law other than either the lex fori or the lex loci might be applied. Although the proper law of the tort is formally rejected by the Privy Council (at p939E), this case sows seeds that may in due course allow the proper law of tort to emerge as the choice of law rule for tort! (See section 6.5 'Alternatives to the present law'.)

In any event, the decision must be welcomed since it allows judges to do justice in cases which in the past would have been decided unjustly, ie according to an inappropriate lex fori. However, had the Privy Council had the courage to overrule *The Halley* (1868) LR 2 PC 193, the case that is the cause of all this difficulty, it would have been even better. For criticism of *Red Sea Insurance Co v Bouygues SA* see Briggs, 'The Halley: Holed but Still Afloat', (1995) 111 LQR 18.


## 6.4 Miscellaneous aspects of *Boys* v *Chaplin*

There are three aspects of *Boys* v *Chaplin* which we have not yet dealt with and which are sufficiently important to be considered.

First, the astute will have realised that in its standard statement in *Phillips* v *Eyre* the double actionability rule does not appear to be a choice of law rule. Precisely because it talks of actionability in certain circumstances, it appears to be laying down a jurisdictional rule, specifying when particular actions can be entertained by the courts, rather than a rule selecting the appropriate legal system to apply. However, in *Boys* v *Chaplin* Lord Wilberforce made it clear that the rule (at any rate the first hurdle thereof) was a choice of law rule, and that it specified that the lex fori governed foreign torts subject to the second hurdle and the principle of flexibility in proper cases. But this must now be considered in the light of *Red Sea Insurance* discussed above: in appropriate cases the lex loci delecti rather than the lex fori will now be the governing law.

Secondly, the astute will also have recognised that an alternative technique for approaching the *Boys* v *Chaplin* type of case would be to avoid the second hurdle of *Phillips* v *Eyre* by holding that matters of damages relate to procedure and thus are governed by the lex fori (see Chapter 2, section 2.4 Damages). This indeed was the basic approach of Lords Guest and Donovan in *Boys* v *Chaplin*. However, the approach is rather simplistic when what we are dealing with is different heads of damage – or even entirely separate causes of action – rather than questions of quantum. In any event, this approach was rejected by Lords Wilberforce, Hodson and Pearson: damages for pain and suffering were matters of substance not procedure.

Indeed, a Scottish decision has gone even further and applied the double actionability rule in the field of remedies which one might have thought was a matter clearly for the lex fori alone. Thus in *James Burrough Distillers plc and Another* v *Speymalt Whiskey Distributors Ltd* (1989) The Times 30 January it was held that an interdict (the Scottish remedy akin to injunction) could not be granted to restrain infringement of a trade mark in Italy because the double actionability rule was not satisfied.

Thirdly, *Boys* v *Chaplin* deals with foreign torts (ie torts committed outside England). The question is still open whether a foreign law could be applied if, say, two persons resident in the same foreign country were involved in a motor accident in England. This would test whether the principle of flexibility extended to the first hurdle of *Phillips* v *Eyre* or whether it was restricted to the second. The consensus, however, appears to be that an English court would apply only English law to be a tort committed in England, ie the lex loci applies provided that England is the locus! (See *Szalatnay-Stacho* v *Fink* [1947] KB 1 for authority for this proposition.)

It was confirmed in *Metall und Rohstoff AG* v *Donaldson Lufkin & Jenrette Inc* [1989] 3 WLR 563 that where a tort was in substance committed in England then only English law would be applied to the dispute, ie the double actionability rule in *Boys* v *Chaplin* would not be applied.

This case also established that where it was necessary to determine where in substance a cause of action arose English law would be applied to that question. This seems correct, since the locus of the tort here operates as a connecting factor, and such factors, as we know, are in principle governed by the lex fori.

## 6.5 Alternatives to the present law

The present law is unsatisfactory for at least two reasons. First, it accords far too much prominence to the lex fori. The English conflict of laws does not insist upon the lex fori applying in matters of contract, property, family law, succession etc, so why should it insist upon it (admittedly moderated by the second hurdle and the principle of flexibility) in tort? The source of this great reliance on the lex fori in this area (which is not shared by any other legal system – and thus the goal of uniformity of decision is undermined) – is *The Halley* (1868) LR 2 PC 193. This case arose out of a collision in Belgian waters between an English and a Belgian vessel. The collision was caused by the negligence of the pilot (whom Belgian law required to be in control of the vessel), but while Belgian law gave no defence of compulsory pilotage, this was a defence under English law. Thus insisting on the application of the lex fori gave the English shipowners a defence which was reasonable in the circumstances. Plainly this was a special case that turned on its own facts (and could just as easily have been based upon public policy); it has been, and should not have been, allowed to cast its baleful influence over the entire question of choice of law in tort. Secondly, the measure of flexibility introduced into the law in *Boys* v *Chaplin* is inherently uncertain. In these circumstances it is worth looking at some of the alternatives to the present law.

## The proper law of the tort

The existence of the concept of the proper law of the tort is very largely the work of one man, the late Dr Morris. In an article in (1949) 12 *MLR* 248 (commenting on *M'Elroy* v *M'Allister*), expanded upon in (1951) 64 *Harvard Law Review* 881, he argued that in cases where the question of choice of law in tort arose the court should search for the 'centre of gravity' of the transaction (in much the same way as it did in determining the proper law of a contract where there has been no choice of the proper law). In so doing it should consider the statute that had led to the problem arising and consider whether on its true construction it applied to the facts of the case (eg the Maltese rule denying recovery for pain and suffering was not intended to apply where both plaintiff and defendant were resident elsewhere). Also the court should consider whether its law did not have more interest in the outcome of the litigation than did the law of the state where the tort occurred.

This concept was not taken up in England, but has borne considerable fruit in the United States. In *Babcock* v *Jackson* 191 NE 2d 279 (1963) a car registered and insured in New York and with driver and passengers resident and domiciled in New York left the road during an over-the-border drive in Ontario. One of the passengers was injured and sued the driver in New York. Now under the usual rule in New York the lex loci governed matters of tort, and thus the plaintiff was met with a defence based upon the self-same Ontario statute denying recovery to passengers in these circumstances that we have already considered in *McLean* v *Pettigrew*! Fuld J, in reliance upon Dr Morris's work, applied the law of New York (and allowed the plaintiff to recover) in preference to the law of Ontario. He said:

> 'Justice, fairness and the "best practical result" may best be achieved by giving controlling effect to the law of the jurisdiction which, because of its relationship or contact with the occurrence or the parties, has the greatest concern with the specific issue raised in the litigation.'

Thus did the proper law of the tort cease to be a matter of academic speculation and become part and parcel of a judicial decision. In the litigation that has followed the proper law of the tort has been accepted in some 26 states of the United States and has been rejected in only ten. It was adopted by Lord Denning in the Court of Appeal in *Boys* v *Chaplin*.

The proper law of the tort is, of course, not without its own critics, its most prominent defect being that it is uncertain, in that judges will differ in their opinions as to which law has 'the greatest concern with the specific issue raised in the litigation'. Moreover, quite frequently the application of the proper law appears simply to mask the judges' preference for their own, as in *Babcock* v *Jackson* when its application allowed the New York judge to apply New York law. Thus when persons resident and domiciled in Ontario have been injured in motor accidents in New York, the New York courts have refused to apply the Ontario statute (see *Kell* v *Henderson* 270 NYS 2d 552 (1966)). And it is very difficult to tell what the proper law of the tort is when the driver and passenger come from different states and the accident occurs in a third. (See, generally, Morris, op cit, 325ff.)

The consensus view appears to be that the concept of the proper law of the tort was rejected by the House of Lords in *Boys* v *Chaplin* (North and Webb, 'Foreign torts and English courts' (1970) 19 *ICLQ* 24). Morris, however, attempts to argue that the concept enjoyed a partial success in that case (op cit, 313–314). The weakness in Morris's view, however, is that although some flexibility was introduced into the rule of *Phillips* v *Eyre* it was only to the second hurdle; thus even where there is flexibility, the lex fori continues to govern as the predominant law.

## The lex loci

Most of the world (outside the United States and legal systems strongly influenced by English law) applies the lex loci delicti commissi to questions of choice of law in tort. It seems the natural system to apply, for persons expect that the local law will apply. It does, however, have disadvantages: first, it is sometimes inappropriate or fortuitous (as it was in *Boys* v *Chaplin* and *Babcock* v *Jackson*). And, secondly, it is sometimes difficult to tell where a tort was committed. Is it where the harmful act was committed or is it where the damage occurred? The English rules for determining the locus of a tort are considered in Chapter 4, section 4.2.

The lex loci was rejected by Lord Wilberforce in *Boys* v *Chaplin*. None the less, it seems to me that the best rule would be to adopt the lex loci as the general rule but to allow departures from it when the parties are closely linked with another legal system and the locus of the tort is fortuitous.

## 6.6 The boundary between contract and tort: exemption clauses

Exemption clauses in contracts, purporting to exempt one or other of the parties from their tortious obligations can, and have, given rise to difficult problems on the boundary of contract and tort. It may be for example that a person who has been injured at work has agreed in his contract of employment to exempt his employer from liability for injuries caused to him by the negligence of his employer or his co-employees. Such an exemption clause may be valid under the proper law of the contract but invalid under the lex fori or the lex loci. Can the employer rely upon the clause when sued by the injured workman?

Consider, for example, *Sayers* v *International Drilling* [1971] 1 WLR 1176. Here an English-domiciled workman was employed by a Dutch company on an oil rig in Nigerian waters. He was injured through the negligence of a fellow employee, but a clause of his contract of employment exempted the employers from liability. The proper law of this contract, a majority of the Court of Appeal held, was Dutch law, (Lord Denning thought it was English); and by Dutch law such clauses were valid. On the other hand, s1(3) of the Law Reform (Personal Injuries) Act 1948 provided that clauses which exempted the employer from liability for personal injuries caused to the employee by 'the negligence of persons in common employment with him' should be void. In the event the employee was denied reliance on s1(3), and the exemption clause was held valid.

The majority of the Court of Appeal dealt with this set of facts simply as a matter of contract. Salmon and Stamp LJJ concluded that the proper law of the contract was Dutch; the clause was valid by Dutch law, hence the employer could rely upon the clause, and s1(3) was irrelevant. Lord Denning agreed with this result but for completely different reasons. He dealt with the matter as one of tort, but he ignored the rule in *Phillips* v *Eyre* and applied the proper-law approach. (He considered that Lord Wilberforce had approved that approach in *Boys* v *Chaplin.*) The proper law of the tort, he found, was Dutch law; hence the clause was valid.

Note that had the matter been treated as a tort dispute (and the rule in *Phillips* v *Eyre* applied) then the result would have been completely different. The question would have been: was the tort actionable at English law and was there civil liability under Nigerian law? In fact Nigerian law was dismissed out of hand by Salmon LJ. In many ways the most interesting question, had the rule in *Phillips* v *Eyre* been applied, was whether s1(3) could have been relied upon. Obviously, it was part of the lex fori and thus prima facie applicable, but the court might have reached the conclusion that Parliament in enacting s1(3) did not intend that it should apply outside the United Kingdom, and thus it did not apply to events that took place in Nigeria, even if English law for one reason or another was the lex causae.

A rather different approach to the question of exemption clauses was taken in the Scottish case of *Brodin* v *A/R Seljan* 1973 SLT 198. The facts were similar in their essence in that an employee was injured and later died through the negligence of his fellow employees. The proper law of his contract of employment was Norwegian law, in terms of which the exemption clause was valid. However, the accident took place in Scottish waters, and s1(3) was part of Scots law. The Court of Session approached the matter as one of delict (the Scottish term for tort) and held s1(3) applicable. Parliament in enacting s1(3) did not intend to limit its operation to contracts of employment in which the proper law was Scottish (or English). On the contrary, the locus delicti was important, and since the wrong was done in Scotland s1(3) could be relied upon. This is a far more satisfactory analysis, for it was quite artificial of the majority in *Sayers* to treat the matter simply as one of contract. The question remains open, however, whether s1(3) would apply if the locus delicti were neither England or Scotland. It may be suggested that it would not, for Lord Kissen said that the fact that the accident was in Scotland in *Brodin* was the 'vital difference' between that case and *Sayers*. (These issues were also argued in the recent case of *Coupland* v *Arabian Gulf Petroleum Co* [1983] 2 All ER 434, but the courts that heard the case did not find it necessary to decide this issue.)

The decision of the Privy Council in *Canadian Pacific Railway* v *Parent* [1917] AC 195 also dealt with this issue but did not resolve it conclusively. What happened here was that a stockman travelled with his cattle on the defendants' railway from Manitoba to Quebec. He signed a form issued by the defendants exempting them from all liability in respect of death or injury of any person travelling in charge of stock (and thus at less than full fare) caused by the negligence of the defendants or their employees. The stockman was killed in a collision in Ontario, and his widow and son brought action in Quebec. Under the Civil Code of Quebec the widow and son were entitled to succeed notwithstanding the exemption clause, but they were not entitled to recover under the law of either Ontario or Manitoba. The Privy Council denied recovery in a classical application of the rule in *Phillips* v *Eyre*; the act was justifiable under the law of Ontario, and therefore the second hurdle was not overcome.

The decided cases do not adequately deal with this question, and sooner or later the correct approach will have to be laid down by the House of Lords. For the present the unsatisfactory decision of *Sayers* must be considered the leading case in England, and the effect of *Sayers* is that if the clause is valid under the proper law of the contract it will be effective to exclude liability for tort. However, as Morris says, op cit, 320–321, the Unfair Contract Terms Act 1977 (particularly s27 discussed in Chapter 5, section 5.2 Statutes and the express choice of law) will today frequently prevent exemption clauses such as that under discussion in *Sayers* from being valid.

## 6.7 Reform

The Law Commission in Working Paper No 87 (1984) made a number of far-reaching suggestions for the reform of choice of law in tort. It has made many detailed recommendations, but its major suggestion is the abolition of the double actionability rule of *Phillips* v *Eyre* and its replacement with one of the following alternatives. Either the lex loci delicti should be the basic rule governing choice of law in tort, but there should be, in addition, a rule of displacement which would allow the lex loci to be displaced in favour of the law with which the tort has 'the closest and most real connection'. The lex loci would only be able to be displaced if there was just an 'insignificant connection' between it and the tort.

Alternatively, the proper-law approach could be adopted and the court would simply search for the law with which the tort had the 'closest and most real connection'. However, finding the proper law would be aided by a series of rebuttable presumptions. In cases of personal injury and damage to property the proper law would be presumed to be the law prevailing where the plaintiff was injured or where the propery was damaged; in cases of death, it would be presumed to be the law prevailing where the deceased was injured. And in defamation cases the proper law would be presumed to be the law prevailing where the publication of the defamatory material took place.

The Commission invited comments on these two suggestions. Subsequently, following the consideration of these comments, the Law Commission published a Report on Choice of Law in Tort and Delict (Law Commission No 193; Scottish Law Commission No 129). The government decided to implement most of the recommendations in this report and introduced into Parliament the Private International Law (Miscellaneous Provisions) Bill, Part III of which came into force on 1 May 1996. Part III of the Private International Law (Miscellaneous Provisions) Act 1995 sweeps away much of the common law concerning choice of law in tort and replaces it with statutory provisions. Various academic criticisms have been made of the drafting of Part III and, in addition, the press waged a campaign against it. Indeed, even a leader in *The Times* (19 January 1995) thundered against Part III. The press campaign seems motivated by self-interest – the press barons feared that if the 'double actionability' rule was repealed, libel plaintiffs would be able to sue them in England using foreign laws that are more helpful to plaintiffs. The press campaign was successful to the extent that an amendment to the original Bill excluding 'defamation actions' can be found in s13.

Let us now try to assess Part III of the Act on its merits. First, s10(a) abolishes the rules of common law that:

> '... require actionability under both the law of the forum and the law of another country for the purpose of determining whether a tort ... is actionable in the forum.'

ie the rule in *Phillips* v *Eyre* (1870) LR 6 QB 1 is abolished. Moreover, s10(b) abolishes the exceptions to the standard 'double actionability' rule that:

> '... allow ... for the law of a single country to be applied for that purpose.'

This wording is a little awkward since it does not cover the possibility, opened by *Red Sea Insurance*, that following the disapplication of the 'double actionability' several issues may be governed by several different laws.

Secondly, s11(1) lays down that:

> '... the general law is that the applicable law [in matters of tort] is the law of the country in which the events constituting the tort ... in question occur.'

This basic rule of the locus delicti would bring English law into line with most other legal systems with the exception of those parts of the United States that favour the proper law of the tort. Note that 'the events constituting the tort' must all occur in the same country for s11(1) to apply, because s11(2) states that 'where significant elements of those events occur in different countries' then different rules will be used to determine the applicable law. Thus in such circumstances, in cases of personal injury (including death caused by personal injury), the applicable law will be 'the law of the country where the individual was when he sustained the injury' (s11(2)(a)). (For example, if poison is put into a river in France and the water is taken from the river and drunk, causing death in Germany, the applicable law is German law.) Similarly, in cases of damage to property, the law of the country 'where the property was when it was damaged' (s11(2)(b)) is the applicable law. (For example, if sugar is put into a car's petrol tank in France, causing the engine to seize up when the car is driven off the ferry into England, the applicable law is

English law.) And, 'in any other case', the applicable law will be that 'in which the most significant element or elements of [the tort] occurred'.

Thirdly, the above rules lay down the *general rule* for choice of law in tort, but provision is also made for the displacement of the *general rule* in appropriate circumstances. Section 12 provides that the general rule is displaced where a comparison of the factors connecting the tort to the country of the applicable law (as determined by s11) and the factors connecting the tort to another country makes it appear that it is 'substantially more appropriate' that the law of that other country should be the applicable law. The factors to be taken into account include:

'... factors relating to the parties, any of the events that constitute the tort ... or ... any circumstances or consequences of those events.'

Broadly speaking, Part III follows the recommendations of the Law Commission contained in *Private International Law: Choice of Law in Tort and Delict* No 193 (1990) although Part III does not contain the Law Commission's suggestion of special rules for defamation. The Law Commission's report was not well-received in academic circles (see *Carter* 'Choice of Law in Tort and Delict' (1991) 107 LQR 405) and academic criticisms of Part III are likely to be similar (see *Briggs* 'Choice of Law in Tort and Delict' [1995] LMCLQ 519).

# 7

# Jurisdiction and Choice of Law in Property

## 7.1 The distinction between movables and immovables

We have already seen (Chapter 1, section 1.2) that in the field of the conflict of laws, English law divides property into immovables (essentially land) and movables (most other property including incorporeals such as rights of action): *Freke* v *Carbery* (1873) LR 16 Eq 461. The usual distinction in the English law of property is between realty and personalty, but the movables/immovables distinction is adopted here in recognition of the fact that most other legal systems know nothing about personalty and realty but do know about movables and immovables (see Chapter 2, section 2.3 Kahn-Freund's enlightened lex fori). Thus Farwell LJ said in *Re Hoyles, Raw* v *Jugg* [1911] 1 Ch 179 at 185:

> 'In order to arrive at a common basis on which to determine questions between the inhabitants of two countries living under different systems of jurisprudence, our courts recognise and act on a division otherwise unknown to our law into movable and immovable'.

This is a sensible attitude for English law to take, for by adopting a distinction known to the rest of the world that great goal of the conflict of laws, uniformity of decision, is advanced.

So far so good. The difficulty is that one legal system may consider a particular form of property to be movable while another legal system may consider it immovable. Let us, for example, consider the mortgagee's interest in land. The mortgagee has loaned money to the mortgagor, and the loan is secured by a mortgage over land entitling the mortgagee to possess and sell the land should the mortgagor fail to repay. Now, is the mortgagee's interest movable or immovable? In *Re Hoyles* the Court of Appeal held that mortgages on freehold land are immovables. However the New Zealand courts have held that at common law mortgages of land in New Zealand are movables (*In re O'Neill (deceased)* [1922] NZLR 468), and the Australian courts have reached the same conclusion (*Hague* v *Hague (No 2)* (1965) 114 CLR 98). Moreover, the decision in *In re O'Neill* has been fortified by statute, for the New Zealand Wills Amendments Act 1955 provides in s14(4) that '"movable property" includes a mortgage of land ...'.

You will readily appreciate that what we are concerned with now is the problem of characterisation, and what was said about characterisation in Chapter 2, section 2.3 applies equally here. But what is particularly interesting about the problem in this guise is that *Re Hoyles* lays down:

> 'No country can be expected to allow questions affecting its own land, or the extent and nature of the interests in its own land which should be regarded as immovable, to be determined otherwise than by its own courts in accordance with its own interests.'

Although this dictum could be read as simply being in favour of the lex fori, most authorities take it to mean that whether a particular interest in land is considered a movable or immovable is a matter for the lex situs of the land in question. (See *Re Berchtold, Berchtold* v *Capron* [1923] 1 Ch 192, Morris, *The Conflict of Laws*, 3rd ed, 1984, 334, and Cheshire, 780.) This means that here the court is characterising by a legal system that is not necessarily either the lex fori or the lex causae. Refer to characterisation in Chapter 2, section 2.3 to see why this is novel.

Let us illustrate this with an example. Suppose a man dies intestate domiciled in France leaving as one of his assets a mortgage over land in New Zealand. Now intestate succession to immovables is governed by the lex situs while intestate succession to movables is governed by the lex ultimi domicilii (see section 7.7 below). Thus if the mortgage is movable the intestate heirs under French law will succeed, but if it is immovable the intestate heirs under the law of New Zealand will take. Suppose this matter was litigated in England (although it is unlikely that the English courts would have jurisdiction), how would the English courts approach this problem? Well, given the usual unthinking approach to characterisation in English law, one might expect characterisation to be carried out according to the lex fori; it would be held that the mortgage was an immovable, and therefore that the intestate heirs under New Zealand law take. But, if the court interpreted *Re Hoyles* in the way that both Morris and Cheshire have, then it would apply the lex situs to determine whether the mortgage was movable or immovable; thus it would conclude that the mortgage was a movable, and that therefore the intestate heirs under French law would succeed.

In any event we can extract some rules from the decided cases about how the English courts characterise interests in land in England.

First, mortgages over land in England are characterised as immovable (*Re Hoyles*). This result aptly illustrates the extent to which the realty/personality distinction differs from the movables/immovables distinction, because mortgages are considered to be personalty for many purposes.

Secondly, leasehold interests in land in England are considered to be immovable (*Freke* v *Carbery*; *Pepin* v *Bruyere* [1900] 2 Ch 504). This again is remarkable, for land held on leasehold is considered to be personalty for many purposes.

Thirdly, the doctrine of conversion does not operate in the field of conflict of laws. (The cases do not establish this proposition in these terms, but this is believed to be the logical consequence of *Re Berchtold* [1923] 1 Ch 192.)

The doctrine of conversion, you will remember from your studies of land law, converts land held on trust for sale from real estate into personal estate; ie the beneficiaries' interests in the land are converted into interests in the notional proceeds of the sale. (This is an example of the maxim that equity regards as done that which ought to be done.) Now the doctrine of conversion has been seized upon by some United States courts 'as a means of escape from the general rule that all questions of immovables are governed by the lex situs' (Morris, op cit, 334), ie to convert an interest into an immovable (governed by the lex situs) into an interest in movables governed by some other law.

The issue arose before the English courts in *Re Berchtold*. What had happened was that Count Richard Berchtold, a domiciled Hungarian, had died domiciled in Hungary, but leaving freehold land in England. In his will he left this land (together with all his other real and personal property) to trustees to hold on trust for sale for his son Count Nicholas subject to an annual payment to his widow while she lived. Before the land was sold Count Nicholas, who was also domiciled in Hungary, died intestate.

Now the relevant conflict rules were clear: intestate succession to movables was governed by the lex domicilii, while intestate succession to immovables was governed by the lex situs. Thus Count Nicholas's heirs under Hungarian law would inherit his movables, while his heirs under English law would inherit his immovables. But was his interest in the land held on trust for sale movable or immovable? Russell J decided that it was immovable. He said:

> 'It was argued that according to English law land directed to be sold and turned into money must be considered to be money; and that on the principle that equity considers done what ought to be done, the Birmingham freeholds are, in the eye of the law, money. This argument, to be effective, must add the words "for all purposes". That the Birmingham freeholds are to be treated as money for some purposes, no one doubts. Thus

the interest of the taker is personal estate. But the equitable doctrine of conversion only arises and comes into play where the question for consideration arises as between real estate and personal estate. It has no relation to the question whether property is movable or immovable. The doctrine of conversion is that real estate is treated as personal estate, or personal estate is treated as real estate; not that immovables are turned into movables, or movables into immovables ...'.

This dictum seems to me to be entirely cogent and relegates the doctrine of conversion to its proper place; it is a doctrine that may apply once English law has been chosen as the lex causae, but it has nothing to do with the process whereby English law is chosen as the lex causae. And when the analogous situation arose in an Irish case the same result was reached (*Murray* v *Champernowne* [1901] 2 IR 232).

However, a different conclusion was reached in *Re Piercy, Whitwham* v *Piercy* [1895] 1 Ch 83 (approved, en passant, by the House of Lords in *Philipson-Stow* v *Inland Revenue Commissioners* [1961] AC 727). Here a testator who was domiciled in England devised land in Sardinia to trustees to be held on trust for sale and after sale to hold the moneys on various trusts for his children and remoter issue. The Italian law, applicable in Sardinia, which outlaws such substitutions, would in these circumstances hold that the children were entitled absolutely. Now in principle the lex situs governs the succession to immovables, and thus the children should take absolutely.

In an ingenious judgment, however, North J held that the trustees could be ordered to sell (which he did not think would be contrary to Italian law), and then the proceeds would be subject to English law and the trusts in favour of the children could attach to the proceeds. Prior to the sale the children would be entitled to the rents and profits from the land, but not thereafter. This amounts in effect to applying the doctrine of conversion to transmute the interests in the land into money and thereby evade the provisions of the Italian law. The decision has been widely criticised on this ground (see Cheshire, 509) and must be considered wrong. Note though, that Morris, op cit, 790) says that 'however suspect the reasoning the conclusion seems entirely proper'. Unfortunately, Morris does not say why he considers the conclusion proper, and it seems to me to be wrong. Succession to the land was subject to Italian law, and application of the Italian law was not contrary to public policy (although contrary to the will); there was, therefore, no good reason to avoid its application.

A difficulty arises, however, with the statutory doctrine of conversion contained in s75(5) of the Settled Land Act 1925. This provides that where there are capital moneys 'arising under this Act', ie as a result of the sale of the land by the tenant for life with the price paid to at least two trustees or a trust corporation, then those moneys 'shall, for all purposes of disposition, transmission and devolution, be considered as land'. Now, are such moneys to be considered movable or immovable?

The issue arose in *Re Cutliffe* [1940] Ch 565. An intestate died domiciled in Ontario; at the time of his death he was entitled to an interest in certain English investments which were the proceeds of a sale of land subject to the predecessor of the Settled Land Act 1925. Did s75(5) apply to transmute the interest in the investments into immovables, so that the intestate heirs under English law should take, or did s75(5) not apply, in which case the heirs under the law of Ontario were entitled? The court held that the interest in the investments was an immovable.

There are two ways of justifying this decision. Since the statute said that the money was to be considered land 'for all purposes', this suggests that s75(5) was an overriding statute that applied irrespective of the choice of law process. (See Chapter 5, section 5.2 Statutes and the express choice of law, if you have forgotten what an overriding statute is.) Alternatively, the decision could be justified on the ground that the lex situs determines how a particular asset is to be characterised. Since the investments (as well as the land which they represented) were in England, English law was used to determine whether the interest was movable or immovable. Note further that, while the equitable doctrine of conversion transmutes realty into personalty, s75(5) transmutes moneys or investments into land; and whether an interest is land or not is far more relevant to the question of whether it is a movable or an immovable than is the question of whether it is personalty or realty.

## 7.2 Jurisdiction in property cases

*English courts have no jurisdiction to try title to foreign land but do have jurisdiction to try title to English land*

There is a fundamental rule of the common law (now subject to a number of exceptions) based on the case of *British South Africa Company* v *Companhia de Mocambique* [1893] AC 602 which holds that an English court

'has no jurisdiction to entertain an action for (1) the determination of title to, or the right to possession of, any immovable situated out of England: or (2) the recovery of damages for trespass to such immovable'.

(Dicey and Morris, rule 79, in *Dicey and Morris's The Conflict of Laws*, 11th ed, 1987, edited by L Collins.)

The first head of the rule is justified by the consideration that in matters in rem (such as title or possession of land) the court of the situs is the proper court. And in the ultimate analysis it is only that court that can determine title or possession to the property. Moreover the two heads of the rule are related, for the court in the *Mocambique* case was plainly influenced by the fact that actions for damages for trespass although in personam (and the court may have jurisdiction under some basis discussed in Chapter 4), and although not involving possession of the land, can easily involve questions of title. The origins of the *Mocambique* rule are technical and historical (Morris, op cit, 337–338, gives a good account of them), and the rules has been criticised – especially where no question of title to the foreign land arises – but the House of Lords, in *Hesperides Hotels Ltd* v *Muftizade* [1978] 3 WLR 378, refused to depart from it.

New life has recently been breathed into the technical reasoning that justified the rule. In *Tyburn Productions Ltd* v *Conan Doyle* [1990] 3 WLR 167 Vinelott J refused to adjudicate upon the American copyright of the last fourteen works of Sir Arthur Conan Doyle. His surviving daughter was in dispute with American film companies and distributors who wished to make and distribute films depicting the adventures of Sherlock Holmes. The reasoning was essentially the same as that which justified the *Mocambique* rule, that matters of copyright – like title to immovables – was a matter for the local sovereign to order. Similar principles governed patent rights.

Where no substantial question of title arises, then the case for excluding the English courts is weak, and Parliament has dealt with this issue in s30(1) of the Civil Jurisdiction and Judgments Act 1982. It provides that:

'The jurisdiction of any court in England and Wales or Northern Ireland to entertain proceedings for trespass to, or any other tort affecting, immovable property shall extend to cases in which the property in question is situated outside that part of the United Kingdom unless the proceedings are principally concerned with a question of the title to, or the right to possession of, that property.'

You should note that under article 16(1) of the Brussels Convention, as far as the Contracting States are concerned, the courts of the lex situs have exclusive jurisdiction 'in proceedings which have as their object rights in rem in, or tenancies of, immovable property' (see Chapter 4, section 4.3 Immovable property: article 16(1), for a fuller account of this jurisdiction).

The relationship between s30 of the Civil Jurisdiction and Judgments Act 1982 and article 16(1) raises an interesting question: does s30(1) give the English courts jurisdiction to entertain proceedings for trespass to land situated elsewhere in the EC? Although s30(2) specifically provides that s30(1) 'has effect subject to the 1968 Convention', article 16(1), which gives exclusive jurisdiction to the lex situs, only applies to 'proceedings which have as their object rights in rem in, or tenancies of, immovable property' and does not include claims for trespass or other torts concerning the land. But the other provisions of the Convention provide an answer: the action can be brought either in the court of the defendant's 'domicile' under article 2 (see Chapter 4, section 4.3 *The central jurisdictional rules under the Convention*) or in the court 'where the harmful event occurred' under the special jurisdiction of article 5(3) (see Chapter 4, section 4.3 Tort: article 5(3)). These provisions of the Convention, presumably, abrogate the *Mocambique* rule when they apply, and there is no need to have recourse to s30(1).

## *Exceptions to the* Mocambique *rule*

First, where the court has jurisdiction in personam over a defendant, then the court 'has jurisdiction to entertain an action against him in respect of a contract or equity affecting foreign land' (Morris, op cit, 339). This exception rests upon the case of *Penn* v *Baltimore* (1750) 1 Ves Sen 444. What had happened was that Penn (who owned Pennsylvania) and Baltimore (who owned Maryland) had contracted to settle the boundaries between the two provinces. The court ordered the specific performance of the contract notwithstanding the defendant's objection that the court had no jurisdiction because the case involved title to foreign land. Since *Penn* v *Baltimore* there have been numerous cases where contracts in regard to foreign land have been enforced.

The crux of this exception is that there is some personal obligation between the plaintiff and the defendant and from which the plaintiff's rights derive, and it is that obligation or right in personam that the court enforces, not a right in rem to the land. Making the same point more technically, there must be privity of obligation between the parties. It follows that where the personal obligation derives from a fiduciary relationship or fraud between the parties, then the principle is equally applicable (*Deschamps* v *Miller* [1908] 1 Ch 856 at 863).

Note, however, that the jurisdiction will not be exercised if it is not possible for the decree of the English court to be effective under the lex situs. As Lord Cottenham said in *Re Courtney* (1840) Mont & Ch 239:

> 'If ... the law of the country where the land is situated should not permit or not enable the defendant to do what the court might otherwise think it right to decree, it would be useless and unjust to direct him to do the act.'

(Cf Morris, op cit, 340.)

This is a principle that the English courts have not always observed (see *Cood* v *Cood* (1863) 33 LJ Ch 273).

Moreover, the jurisdiction will not be exercised against third parties ('strangers to the equity'). Consider *Norris* v *Chambres* (1861) 29 Beav 246 (followed in *Deschamps* v *Miller*). Certain land in Prussia was sold by Simons to Sadlier, but Simons refused to transfer ownership and instead sold and transferred the land to Chambres (who knew of the contract with Sadlier). Norris (representing Sadleir) sued Chambres in England. Sir John Romilly MR dismissed his claim and said:

> 'In all [the previous cases] ... a privity existed between the Plaintiff and the Defendant; they had entered into some contract or personal obligation had been incurred moving directly from one to the other. In this case I cannot find anything of the sort exists ... Simons having received this money [a deposit] repudiates the contract and sells the estate to a stranger. That constitutes no personal demand which Sadleir could enforce in this country against the stranger. There is no contract between them, there are no mutual rights, and there is no obligation moving directly from one to the other.'

Where, however, the land is transferred to the third party subject to existing burdens on the land, then the third party can be sued (*Mercantile Investment and General Trust Co* v *River Plate Trust, Loan and Agency Co* [1892] 2 Ch 303).

Secondly, the *Mocambique* rule does not apply where the English court has jurisdiction to administer an estate of a trust and some of the assets in that estate or trust consists of foreign land. The authority in support of this exception is not strong but it 'undoubtedly exists in practice' (Cheshire, 261). See, however, *Nelson* v *Bridport* (1846) 8 Beav 547, *Re Hoyles* [1911] 1 Ch 179 and *Re Duke of Wellington* [1948] Ch 118.

Thirdly, where the court exercises its admiralty jurisdiction in rem it appears that the Mocambique rule does not apply. Thus in *The Tolten* [1946] 1 All ER 74; [1946] 2 All ER 372, an admiralty action in rem was brought (against shipowners) to recover damages in respect of damage caused by their ship when it collided, through negligent navigation, with a pier in Lagos. The court held that under admiralty law a maritime lien arose in favour of the person injured in such circumstances, and that lien could be enforced anywhere in the world. That principle could not be frustrated by the *Mocambique* rule.

There are several other exceptions to the *Mocambique* rule. For the details see Cheshire, 255–263.

## 7.3 Choice of law and immovables

Although criticised as being too broad (see Morris, op cit, 343–345), the well-established general rule is that questions concerning immovables are governed by the lex situs. It is furthermore relatively clear that by this is meant the entire lex situs, including its rules of choice of law. Thus if the court of the lex situs would apply another law to the dispute, then the English court should too. In other words, the foreign-court approach to renvoi is applied (see Chapter 2, section 2.3). The reason for this is that 'uniformity with the lex situs is important because in the last resort land can only be dealt with in a manner permitted by that law. Consequently, any decision by a non situs court which ignored what the courts of the situs had decided or would decide might well be brutum fulmen' (Morris, op cit, 345). Cases such as *Re Ross* [1930] 1 Ch 377 and *Re Duke of Wellington* [1947] Ch 506 established that the foreign-court approach to renvoi will be applied in this area.

The breadth of the principle that immovables are governed by the lex situs may be illustrated by mentioning some of the matters where it has been held to govern.

First, the formal validity of a transfer of immovables is governed by the lex situs. Thus in *Adams v Clutterbuck* (1883) 10 QBD 403 one domiciled Englishman transferred by writing certain shooting rights in Scotland to another domiciled Englishman. At English law such a conveyance had to be under seal, but by Scots law writing was sufficient. The transfer was upheld since it complied with the formalities of the lex situs.

Secondly, the essential validity of a transfer of immovables is governed by the lex situs. Various cases hold that it governs what estates can be created in foreign land (*Nelson v Bridport*), whether gifts of land to charities are hit by statutes of mortmain (*Curtis v Hutton* (1808) 14 Ves 537 and *Duncan v Lawson* (1889) 41 Ch D 394 (land in England) and *Re Hoyles* (foreign land)), and whether the rule against perpetuities and accumulations is infringed (*Freke v Carbery*).

Thirdly, the capacity to transfer land is governed by the lex situs. This at any rate is the result of *Bank of Africa v Cohen* [1909] 2 Ch 129. What happened here was that a married woman domiciled in England agreed with an English bank to mortgage her land in South Africa as security for loans made and to be made to her husband. She then refused to do so, and when the bank sued for specific performance raised the defence that under South African law married women, save in certain special circumstances, did not have the capacity to give security for their husbands' debts. The court applied South African law as lex situs and upheld the defence. (It is interesting to compare this decision with the New Hampshire case of *Procter* v *Frost* (1938) 89 NH 304 where the facts were rather similar, in that a married woman domiciled in Massachusetts mortgaged her land in New Hampshire to secure her husband's debts. A New Hampshire statute prevents a married woman from standing surety for her husband, but the New Hampshire court rejected this defence and held that the purpose of the statute was to protect New Hampshire married women, not Massachusetts married woman. See Morris, op cit, 347.)

The result of *Bank of Africa* v *Cohen* seems unjust and harsh on the bank. It is in this area that the breadth of the lex situs principle is most open to criticism, for matters of capacity are in principle governed by the lex domicilii. On the other hand, if the lex situs applies the lex domicilii to the question of capacity then, in accordance with the foreign court approach to renvoi, the lex domicilii can be applied, ie if the South African courts would have applied the lex domicilii to the question of Cohen's capacity, then the English courts should also apply it. Or if the South African courts would apply the lex situs to Cohen's capacity, then the English courts would do so too. In this way uniformity of decision is preserved. After all, supposing the English court managed to force Cohen to execute the mortgage in South Africa but the South African courts applied the lex situs to capacity, then the bank's security would be worthless, for the South African courts would not allow the bank to foreclose on the property!

A more profound criticism of the reasoning in *Bank of Africa* v *Cohen* is this one: Cohen had only contracted to execute a mortgage, she had not in fact done so (see Cheshire, 787–788). So the question was not one of capacity to execute a mortgage (as in *Procter* v *Frost*) but the capacity to make such a contract. And it is not necessary that the same rules govern capacity to contract as govern capacity to execute a mortgage. And it is not necessary that a contract to transfer land (or execute a mortgage over land) should be governed by the lex situs of the land; it could be governed by the proper law of the contract.

This is borne out by *British South Africa Co* v *De Beers Consolidated Mines Ltd* [1910] 2 Ch 502 where Cozens-Hardy MR said:

'... an English contract to give a mortgage on foreign land, although the mortgage has to be effected according to the lex situs, is a contract to give a mortgage which – inter partes – is to be treated as an English mortgage, and subject to such rights of redemption and such equities as the law of England regards as necessarily incident to a mortgage.'

It follows from this that the formal validity as well as the essential validity of a contract to transfer an immovable may be determined by the proper law of the contract or some other law chosen by the application of the rules for the choice of law in contract (see Chapter 5, section 5.2 Formal validity, Capacity, Essential validity of the contract ).

## 7.4 Choice of law and movables

### *The general rule*

We are here concerned with particular transfers of movables. This means that we are not concerned with a general transfer of movables such as takes place on bankruptcy or succession on death, but with the transfer of a particular movable pursuant to a contract of sale or a gift or some similar transaction. Also keep clearly in mind that we are concerned with property, not with contract, ie we are not concerned with whether, say, the plaintiff has a right in contract that the defendant should transfer the movable to him; we are concerned with whether the plaintiff has a proprietary right in the movable which the defendant is denying.

As with immovables, the basic rule is that the validity of a particular transfer of movables is governed by the lex situs. What makes movables slightly more complicated than immovables is that movables may change their situs; but even here, as we shall see, the basic rule remains that the lex situs governs.

That basic rule was well stated by Diplock LJ in *Hardwick Game Farm* v *Suffolk Agricultural Poultry Producers' Association* [1966] 1 WLR 287 at 330 (affirmed by the Lords [1969] 2 AC 31):

'The proper law governing the transfer of corporeal movable property is the lex situs. A contract made in England and governed by English law for the sale of specific goods situated in Germany, although it would be effective to pass the property in the goods at the moment the contract was made if the goods were situate in England, would not have that effect if under German law ... delivery of the goods was required in order to transfer the property in them.'

So far so good. Now what happens when the situs changes? Consider *Winkworth* v *Christie Manson and Woods Ltd* [1980] 2 WLR 937. Here works of art were stolen from the plaintiff in England and taken to Italy, where they were sold and delivered to the second defendant in circumstances in which he may have acquired good title under Italian law. The second defendant then handed the works of art to the first defendants, a firm of auctioneers, for sale in England. The plaintiff sought a declaration that they were his property.

Slade J said this:

'Security of title is as important to an innocent purchaser as it is to an innocent owner whose goods have been stolen from him. Commercial convenience may be said imperatively to demand that proprietary rights to movables shall be generally determined by the lex situs under the rules of private international law. Were the position otherwise, it would not suffice for the protection of a purchaser of any valuable movables to ascertain that he was acquiring title to them under the law of the country where the goods were situated at the time of the purchase; he would have to try to effect further investigations as to the past title, with a view to ensuring, so far as possible, that there was no person who might successfully claim a title to the movables by reference to some other system of law ...'.

Thus the plaintiff was refused a declaration and the sale went ahead.

From this we may derive the rule that if movable property is validly transferred according to its lex situs at that time, then that transfer will be recognised in England. *Winkworth v Christie Manson and Woods Ltd* is not the only authority in support of this proposition, and we must at least mention the leading case of *Cammell v Sewell* (1860) 5 H & N 728. Here a cargo of timber was shipped from Russia to England on a Prussian vessel, the Augusta Bertha. The vessel was wrecked in Norway and the damaged cargo was sold by the master (without the consent of the timber owners) in Norway. Such a sale validly transferred title under Norwegian law (and in fact a challenge to the sale in the Norwegian courts failed). The timber was then brought to England in another vessel and sold to the defendants, but the original timber owners (in fact their insurers) challenged the defendants' title. They failed; there had been a valid transfer of title under the lex situs at the time of the transfer, and that would be recognised in England.

The law can thus be simply stated: when the validity of a transfer of a movable is in issue before an English court, all that needs to be determined is whether the disputed transfer was valid under its lex situs. If the answer to that question is yes, then the transfer will be recognised in England (unless, of course, there has been a later transfer valid under its lex situs). The lex situs is the whole lex situs, ie the doctrine of renvoi applies; thus if the courts of the lex situs would refer the question of title to some other legal system, then the validity of the transfer would be determined by that legal system (see Slade J in *Winkworth v Christie* at 953).

## *Reservation of title*

Some tricky points arise in regard to clauses in instalment sale contracts that reserve title to the seller until the final instalment is paid. The English authority is sparse, but we can illustrate the point with the leading American case, *Goetschius v Brightman* (1927) 245 NY 186; 156 NE 660. A car was sold in California on terms that reserved title with the seller until it had been fully paid for, and until it was fully paid for it was not to be removed from California. Before it was paid for, however, the car was taken to New York without the seller's consent. There it was sold to a bona fide purchaser. By the law of New York, the bona fide purchaser acquired good title because such reservation of title clauses were void against subsequent purchasers in good faith, unless the contract was registered in a New York register (and the original Californian sale was not so registered). But by the law of California the original seller's title was good against even innocent subsequent purchasers.

However, the New York court held that the New York statute that required registration was limited to domestic, ie New York, transactions. Thus the New York law did not prevent the recognition of the reservation of title in a Californian sale.

Since the Californian purchaser did not acquire title under the law of California, the Californian seller's title would be recognised in New York.

Note that the reason why the Californian title was recognised in New York was not because of any deviation from the lex situs rule: the New York requirement of registration was ignored because, properly interpreted, it did not apply to the Californian reservation of title. If the New York law, properly interpreted, did apply to the Californian case, then the New York purchaser would acquire good title in accordance with the lex situs rule. Take, for example, the Canadian case of *Century Credit Corp* v *Richard* (1962) 34 DLR (2d) 291. The facts, slightly simplified, were that M had sold a car to F under a contract that reserved title to M until the price was fully paid. All this took place in Quebec. The car was then taken by F to Ontario and sold to R. Under the law of Quebec a reservation of title clause was valid without registration, but under the law of Ontario it had to be registered to be effective. The case appears to be on all fours with *Goetschius* v *Brightman*, but R's title was upheld by the Ontario courts.

The difference lies in s25(2) of the Ontario Sale of Goods Act which provides that where

> 'a person having bought or agreed to buy goods obtains, with the consent of the seller, possession of the goods ... in good faith and without notice of any lien or other right of the original seller ... [it] has the same effect as if the person making the delivery ... were a mercantile agent in possession of the goods ... with the consent of the owner'.

In other words, in the circumstances of the case, F was treated as the agent of the owner and R acquired good title. Thus under the law of Ontario R acquired good title, and since Ontario was the lex situs, that title was recognised. Thus even if the registration provisions of Ontario law, properly interpreted, did not apply to sales in Quebec, that was irrelevant, because other provisions of Ontario law overrode M's prior title.

Thus, although the position is sometimes subtle and difficult to perceive, the lex situs rule is applied. There are two other American cases which Morris, op cit, discusses (at 356–357) that we should mention, but they do not affect the principle we have discussed at all. In *Marvin Safe Co* v *Norton* (1886) 48 NJL 410 a safe had been sold in Pennsylvania and title had been reserved until the full price had been paid. The safe was then taken to New Jersey and sold to a purchaser without notice of the original seller's rights. The reservation was void against subsequent purchasers under the law of Pennsylvania, but good against third parties under the law of New Jersey. The law of New Jersey was applied (ie the lex situs was applied), and the Pennsylvania seller's title was upheld. Consider, on the other hand, *Dougherty & Co* v *Krimke* (1929) 105 NJL 470. Here a diamond was handed over to a broker for sale in New York but no title passed to the broker. The broker took the diamond to New Jersey and pledged it to a third party. Under New York law a broker in these circumstances was deemed to be the owner of the chattel, but under the law of New Jersey the reservation of title was good against third parties. But in this case the third party's title was upheld by the New Jersey courts.

Apparently *Marvin Safe* and *Dougherty & Co* are in conflict, but Morris reconciles them by arguing (at 357) that:

'In the *Marvin* case the court must have held that the Pennsylvania law only applied to subsequent creditors or purchasers in Pennysylvania, while in the *Dougherty* case the court must have held that the New York Factors Act was wide enough to cover subsequent purchasers anywhere.'

This is so, but only on condition (which Morris does not make clear) that in *Dougherty* the law of New Jersey did not override all subsequent titles.

### Goods in transit

Where goods are in transit through a number of countries it is often difficult to know exactly what their situs is at any particular time and, moreover, it may be quite fortuitous. Thus, although there is no English authority, it appears that there is an exception to the rule of the lex situs. In Dicey and Morris's words (at 560) 'if a tangible movable is in transit, and its situs is casual or not known, a transfer which is valid and effective by its proper law will (semble) be valid and effective in England'. See Cheshire, 534–536.

### Other possible exceptions

Slade J in *Winkworth* v *Christie* mentioned (at 941) five exceptions to the lex situs. Most of these are trite. They include the public policy exclusionary rule, the overriding effect of statutes of the lex fori and the special rules about general transfers of movables, eg succession on death. However, one is novel: where a purchaser claiming title has not acted bona fide. This suggestion, it is submitted, should not be supported; bona fides is properly a matter for the lex situs, and there is no reason why the English rule should override the normal choice of law rule. In extreme cases public policy can be used to prevent fraud.

## 7.5 Assignment of intangible movables (choses in action)

For matters falling within the Rome Convention this issue is now governed by article 12. Article 12(1) provides that the Convention determines the law governing 'the contract between assignor and assignee'. On the other hand, the law governing the right assigned (article 12(2)) determines the

'assignability [of that right], the relationship between assignee and debtor, the conditions under which the assignment can be invoked against the debtor and any question whether the debtor's obligations have been discharged'.

The common law rules follow.

The first point to realise is that in any case concerning the assignment of a debt, there are two possible legal systems that may be relevant. There is the law that governs the debt itself. We shall call it the proper law of the debt (and in the case of an ordinary contractual debt it is the proper law of the contract). There is also the law governing the assignment. We shall call it the proper law of the assignment, and deciding what is the proper law of the assignment is the major problem facing us in this section.

Now, as Morris (op cit, 359) points out, there are four issues that may arise in this context that should be carefully distinguished.

First there is the question of whether the debt is assignable, and this is governed by the proper law of the debt. The point here is that some debts cannot be assigned (eg future wages, pensions, insurance policies under some systems of law), and it is reasonable that the proper law of the debt should determine whether that debt is assignable. Two English cases, *Re Fry* [1946] Ch 312 and *Campbell Connelly & Co Ltd* v *Noble* [1963] 1 WLR 252, support this view.

Secondly, the issue may be that of the validity of the assignment, and this is governed by the proper law of the assignment. Here the position is frankly confused. Different aspects of validity may be governed by different laws, and in any event the cases are far from coherent. There are two relevant cases that we may begin by describing.

In *Republica de Guatemala* v *Nunez* [1927] 1 KB 669 what had happened was that the President of Guatemala had deposited £20,000 in a London bank. Shortly before being deposed by his political opponents he assigned this sum to his illegitimate son Nunez; shortly after being deposed, however, while he was in prison in Guatemala, his political opponents forced him to assign the sum to the Republic of Guatemala. Thus it was that Nunez and Guatemala became involved in litigation over who was entitled to the £20,000. Now under English law the assignment to Nunez was valid, but it was formally invalid under Guatemalan law because such assignments had to be made on stamped paper before a notary and also because Nunez lacked capacity to accept the assignment since assignments to minors (such as Nunez) could not be accepted without the appointment of a tutor by the court.

Both the judge at first instance and the Court of Appeal held that both assignments failed; thus the money went to the ex-president's creditors! The assignment to the Republic of Guatemala failed for duress (and this would have been so on grounds of public policy), while the assignment to Nunez was held to be subject to Guatemalan law and therefore void for failure to comply with the various provisions of Guatemalan law mentioned above. The difficulty is that the judges were not at one over why the assignment to Nunez was governed by Guatemalan law.

The other case, *Lee* v *Abdy* (1886) 17 QBD 309, concerned the following point: a husband domiciled in the Cape Colony assigned there an insurance policy (issued by an English company) on his life to his wife. Such an assignment was void under the law of the Cape Colony as a gift between husband and wife; it was valid under English law. The court held that the law of the Cape Colony governed, and the assignment was void.

Now what is to be made of this? Well, the capacity to take under an assignment was obviously a crucial issue in both cases, but in both cases the lex loci of the assignment and the lex domicilii of the assignee coincided, so there was no need to choose between them, and the judges in both cases did not do so. Morris, op cit, 362, suggests that the proper law of the assignment should govern the capacity to assign and to accept an assignment. The lex domicilii is clearly unsuitable, especially in the case of commercial assignment where an enquiry into the lex domicilii in every case would be impractical. (Many of the matters we discussed in Chapter 5, section 5.3 *The basic principles of the convention*, are relevant here.)

In *Nunez* it was said that the lex loci of the assignment would govern the formal validity of the assignment. But as Morris argues (at 361), on analogy with the contractual rules (see Chapter 5, section 5.3 *Introduction*), compliance with the formalities prescribed by the proper law would suffice. And essential validity, although not crucial to either of the cases, should in principle be governed by the proper law of the assignment.

Thus if we accept Morris's arguments, it follows that the proper law of the assignment should govern all aspects of the intrinsic validity of the assignment. But what is the proper law of the assignment? There is no consensus on this point. One could, on analogy with contract, hold that the proper law is the law with which the assignment is most closely connected. On the other hand, a number of more certain (although unsatisfactory) alternatives have been put forward. There are some suggestions from old writers and from *Nunez* that the creditor's domicile should be used. But this seems awkward and impractical; modern commerce would be very difficult, if not impossible, if every assignment had to be preceded by an investigation into the assignor's domicile.

So the suggestion is sometimes made that the lex situs of the debt should be used. Debts are generally situated where they are recoverable, and this usually means the debtor's residence. *Kwok Chi Leung Karl* v *Commissioner of Estate Duty* [1988] 1 WLR 1035 (PC) confirmed that a debt, whether immediately payable or only payable in the future, was situated where it was recoverable (this is generally at the debtor's residence). However, since a person may be resident in a number of places the debt may be situated in a number of places; thus the rule will fail to select a single proper law! Moreover, it seems to have been rejected in *Nunez* (since the debt was situated in London). Finally, the suggestion is made that the proper law of the debt should be identical with the proper law of the assignment. This might be convenient in some cases, but usually the proper law of the debt coincides with the lex situs of the debt, so this solution too is impliedly rejected by *Nunez*.

The position, therefore, is far from clear or satisfactory. See Morris, op cit, 358–362, and Cheshire, 809–818, for fuller accounts.

For a recent case discussing lex situs and the recovery of choses in action: see *Macmillan Inc* v *Bishopsgate Investment Trust plc and Others (No 3)* (1995) The Times 7 November. In this case the plaintiff (a Delaware company controlled by Robert Maxwell) owned shares in Berlitz, a company incorporated in New York. Maxwell agreed in London with certain investment banks to pledge these shares as security for loans. The shares were transferred in New York. The plaintiff claimed against the banks for the return of the shares. The Court of Appeal held that the issue of law as to ownership of the shares should be decided by the lex situs, which would usually be the place of incorporation. Staughton LJ stressed that situs and incorporation had the advantage of pointing to one system of law which was unlikely to be transient and which could not be manipulated by a purchaser of shares in order to get priority.

Thirdly, questions of priorities are governed by the proper law of the debt. It is quite possible for there to be two assignments of the same debt, each intrinsically valid according to each proper law of the assignment. Which assignment is to be valid? It would be widely agreed that the proper law of either assignment could not be relied upon in these circumstances. Nor could one rely upon the lex loci of the assignment since the loci of the assignments might be different.

The lex fori is a possibility (see Chapter 2, section 2.4 *Priorities*), but it was implicitly rejected in *Le Feuvre* v *Sullivan* (1855) 10 Moo PC 1 where in an appeal from the Jersey Courts the Privy Council applied not Jersey law but English law (which was the proper law of the insurance policy (the debt)). *Kelly* v *Selwyn* [1905] 2 Ch 117 is indecisive but not inconsistent with the proper law of the debt. On balance the proper law of the debt appears to be most suitable; there is only one debt, thus the suggested rule will work, and it will frequently be clear what its proper law is.

Fourthly, questions of garnishment are governed by the lex situs of the debt. Garnishment is a form of involuntary assignment, and it is assumed that you are familiar with the basic principles. The problem from the point of view of the conflict of laws is that unless the garnishee orders are recognised by foreign courts, the garnishee, having paid the creditor in England, may find that he is forced to pay again by a foreign court. The rule adopted in *Swiss Bank Corporation* v *Boehmische Bank* [1923] 1 KB 673 was that an English court would make a garnishee order if England was the situs of the debt.

The House of Lords has now made it clear in *Deutsche Schachtbau und Tiefbohrgessellschaft mbH and Others* v *R'As al-Khaimah National Oil Co, Shell International Petroleum Co Ltd intervening* (1988) The Times 25 June (HL) (Court of Appeal judgments in [1987] 3 WLR 1023; [1987] 2 All ER 769) that where there was a serious risk that a debtor might be forced to pay the same debt twice, the English courts would not make a garnishee order absolute.

What had happened was that DST and RAK had entered into an oil exploration agreement which provided for disputes to be settled by arbitration in Geneva. A dispute was referred to arbitration, and an award was made in favour of DST. DST now sought to enforce this award in England (as it was entitled to in terms of the Arbitration Act 1975). However, RAK now sued DST in the courts of R'As al-Khaimah (in breach of the agreement to submit to arbitration in Geneva) and succeeded in obtaining rescission of the contract and damages. (Neither party took any part in the other's proceedings.) RAK's judgment, however, was of little value outside R'As al-Khaimah (and RAK's attempt to enforce its judgment in England failed (see s32(1)(a) of the Civil Jurisdiction and Judgments Act 1982). DST, on the other hand, sought to garnish a debt, situated in England (a debt is situated generally where it is recoverable, and a garnishee order given by the courts where the debt is situated is usually recognised everywhere (see at 782b–d of the All ER report)), owed by Shell International to RAK and to satisfy its award therefrom. A Mareva injunction was granted to prevent Shell from paying the debt. RAK now sued Shell in R'As al-Khaimah and obtained judgment, and when the New London, a ship chartered by an associated company of Shell, put into R'As al-Khaimah port it was seized, and the court announced that it would be held until Shell paid the debt due to RAK. Meanwhile, DST sought to have its garnishment of the debt made absolute. The House of Lords, however, refused to make the garnishee order absolute; Lord Oliver held that there was a real and substantial risk that if forced to pay in England, Shell might also be forced to pay in R'As al-Khaimah. This risk was the result of the failure of the courts of R'As al-Khaimah to recognise the arbitration award and the garnishment of Shell's debt. But that made no difference to the principle that Shell should not be made to run the risk of paying the same debt twice. Although Lords Goff, Keith and Brandon agreed, Lord Templeman dissented; although there was a real risk that Shell would have to pay twice, the courts should not be influenced by the threats of R'As al-Khaimah or the coercive detention of the New London.

## 7.6 Governmental seizure of property

During the 20th century many governments of various political complexions have seized, sometimes with compensation and sometimes without compensation, the property of their citizens (and non-citizens). When such property is subsequently brought to England the original owners have, in numerous cases, sought to recover their property or otherwise frustrate the confiscatory or expropriatory decree through litigation in the English courts. Although there are many decided cases, they are all (with the exception of two that will be separately discussed) reconcilable with the simple proposition that, if the lex situs considers that the property has been validly expropriated, then its expropriation will be recognised by the English courts; but if the lex situs does not consider the expropriation as valid then it will not be recognised in the English courts (*Luther* v *Sagor* [1921] 3 KB 532 and *Princess Paley Olga* v *Weiss* [1929] All ER Rep 513). This is the same as saying that English courts will not allow expropriatory decrees to have extraterritorial effect.

Although the issues arising out of government seizure of property are often considered an aspect of public policy, in fact, if the simple proposition given above is correct, no question of public policy arises; it is simply a question of applying the standard rule (discussed in section 7.4 above) for testing whether particular movables have been validly transferred or not. Of course, particular expropriatory decrees may be penal or infringe public policy in some other way, in which case they will not be enforced before an English court on public policy grounds (*Banco de Vizcaya* v *Don Alfonso de Borbon y Austria* [1935] 1 KB 140). Penal in this context means either that the property is expropriated as a punishment to the owner or that it is discriminatory in that it is directed against a particular person, family, race or nationality (*Frankfurther* v *W L Exner Ltd* [1947] Ch 629). It does not appear that a decree will be considered penal simply because it makes no, or inadequate, provision for compensation (see *Bank voor Handel en Scheepvaart NV* v *Slatford* [1953] 1 QB 248 at 260–263).

We may test these propositions by looking at the latest decision of the House of Lords on this point: *Williams & Humbert Ltd* v *W & H Trade Marks (Jersey) Ltd* [1986] 1 All ER 129. What had happened was that the Spanish government had expropriated all the shares in Rumasa SA, a Spanish company which owned the entire share capital of the holding company of Williams and Humbert Ltd, an English firm of port and sherry shippers. One of the latter's assets used to be the 'Dry Sack' sherry trade mark, but this had been earlier assigned to a Jersey company, W & H Trade Marks (which was controlled, through nominees, by the major shareholders in Rumasa). This did not disrupt the firm's business: W & H granted a licence to them to continue to use the trade mark. The licence, however, was liable to be cancelled should the shares of Rumasa be expropriated. After the expropriation Williams and Humbert, now under the control of the Spanish government, sought a declaration that the assignment of the trade mark was null and void.

W & H's defence was that Williams and Humbert's action sought indirectly to enforce the foreign expropriatory legislation. Now it was beyond dispute that expropriatory legislation would be recognised as having transferred ownership in property, provided it was situated within the expropriating state at the time of expropriation. It was equally clear that had the property been outside the expropriating state at the time of expropriation then the foreign state's title would not be able to be enforced in England. But was what Williams and Humbert were trying to do an attempted extraterritorial enforcement of the expropriatory decree? Both the Court of Appeal and the House of Lords rejected this on the persuasive ground that all that the Spanish legislation had done was to operate on the shares of Rumasa which were situated in Spain. Once the Rumasa shares belonged to the Spanish government, the operation of the decrees was complete, and there was nothing left to enforce in England. In reaching this conclusion the court rejected the view of Dr Mann (expressed in (1962) 11 *ICLQ* 471 and elsewhere) that an expropriated company cannot claim its English property, in so far as in substance that amounted to a step in the completion of the confiscatory measures, and that instead a receiver should be appointed to collect the assets in England of the foreign company, pay the company's debts, and then distribute the surplus to the erstwhile shareholders. Dr Mann is not happy with the decision in *Williams & Humbert* and has written a critical note in (1986) 102 *LQR* 191.

It remains to consider the exceptional cases. These are *Anglo-Iranian Oil Co* v *Jaffrate, The Rose Mary* [1953] 1 WLR 246 and *Lorentzen* v *Lydden & Co* [1943] 2 KB 202. Both these cases are much criticised and must be considered wrong. In *Lorentzen* v *Lydden & Co* the extra-territorial expropriatory legislation of a friendly state was recognised during wartime. (The decree was one issued by the Norwegian state (shortly before the Norwegian government fled to England) expropriating all Norwegian ships in the United Kingdom.) But the public policy considerations involved in that case hardly apply generally or in less extreme circumstances. *The Rose Mary* arose out of the expropriation of the Persian oil fields by the Persian Government in 1951. A vessel containing oil from the Persian fields (which oil would, the expropriatory decree aside, have belonged to the expropriated companies) put into the port of Aden. The plaintiffs sued the master, charterers and ship-owners claiming either delivery of the oil or a declaration that it was their property. In finding for the plaintiffs Campbell J was obviously influenced by the fact that it was the property of non-nationals that was expropriated. It might, therefore, have been possible to support this decision on the ground that the decree was discriminatory. However, *The Rose Mary* has been disapproved of in *Re Helbert Wagg & Co Ltd* [1956] Ch 323 and *Bank voor Handel en Scheepvaart NV* v *Slatford* (where a Dutch decree analogous to that in *Lorentzen* v *Lydden & Co* was refused enforcement).

You should note that if the foreign decree is not intended, when properly interpreted, to have extra-territorial effect the question does not arise at all (*Lecouturier* v *Rey* [1910] AC 262). Similarly, if the foreign decree in the circumstances of the case has not been complied with (eg because the property has not been seized as required by the statute) the point also does not arise (*Attorney-General for New Zealand* v *Ortiz* [1983] 2 WLR 809 (HL)).

## 7.7 Intestate succession

Where a person dies without leaving a valid will the law can be very simply summarised: once his debts have been paid, his remaining movable property will be distributed according to the law of his last domicile, while his immovable property will be distributed according to its lex situs. Although the law is simple, Morris has been very critical of it ((1969) 85 *LQR* 839) and would like to make it still simpler and have succession to both movables and immovables governed by the lex domicilii.

The essential reason for his criticism is that since practically all countries, in their internal law of intestate succession, do not distinguish between different kinds of property (in the past legal systems based upon the common law used to distinguish between personalty and realty for the purposes of intestate succession), no distinction should be drawn between different kinds of property at the private international level either. Indeed, drawing such distinctions leads to anomalies. Suppose a man dies intestate leaving movables in one country and immovables in another, and both countries make provision for a statutory legacy to his widow. The widow will take one statutory legacy from his movables and another from his immovables, whereas the intent of the law in both countries was that she should take only one such legacy.

The traditional view, however, has been confirmed in *Re Collens (decd), Royal Bank of Canada (London) Ltd* v *Krogh and Others* [1986] 1 All ER 611. The deceased had died intestate domiciled in Trinidad and Tobago, leaving property in Trinidad and Tobago, Barbados and the United Kingdom. Some of the property in the United Kingdom was immovable property. The widow had, in a compromise settlement, accepted a large sum in full settlement of all her rights to the property situate in Trinidad and Tobago. Now the widow, in reliance on s46 of the Administration of Estates Act 1925, claimed that she was entitled to a statutory legacy of £5000 from the immovable property situated in England.

Although Browne-Wilkinson V-C recognised the force of Morris's arguments, he none the less concluded that s46 applied to those of the deceased's assets which were subject to English law, and thus created a charge 'on the proceeds of the English immovable property which was unsatisfied'. This judgment follows the orthodox view (it relied upon two cases which were previously the leading authorities: *Re Rea, Rea* v *Rea* [1902] IR 451 and *Re Ralston* [1906] VLR 689) and goes no way towards meeting Morris's criticisms; the judge said simply that 'my job is to administer the law as it is now'.

The final point to make about the law of intestate succession is one that we have already mentioned in our discussion of characterisation in Chapter 2, section 2.2 Characterisation by the lex causa. Where an intestate domiciled abroad dies without next of kin and leaving movables in England, the state of his domicile is entitled (to the exclusion of the Crown's right to bona vacantia) if that state's claim under the foreign law is a claim as an heir, but not if it is a ius regale (a right of the Crown) (*Re Maldonado* [1954] P 223).

## 7.8 Testate succession

A prerequisite for the operation of the rules of testate succession is the existence of a valid will; thus we may begin with the rules for determining the formal validity of wills.

### The formal validity of wills

As we have seen during our discussion of renvoi in Chapter 2, section 2.3 *Renvoi*, the choice of law rules for determining the formal validity of wills were rigid. Wills of movables had to comply with the law of the testator's last domicile (lex ultimi domicilii) (this was a senseless rule since a testator might change his domicile between executing his will and dying), while wills of immovables had to comply with the lex situs. Some flexibility was introduced by the doctrine of renvoi, and

Lord Kingsdowne's Act of 1861, although very badly drafted, did introduce some further alternatives. However, the Wills Act 1963, giving effect to the Hague Convention on the Formal Validity of Wills of 1961, has changed the law entirely. English law is now very similar to the law in a large number of other countries that have also implemented the Hague Convention but equally important is the fact that a very great degree of flexibility was introduced into the law by providing a wide range of legal systems that could be used to test the formal validity of a will; and if the will was formally valid under any of those systems it would be recognised as formally valid in England.

Section 1 of the Wills Act 1963 provides that a will

'shall be treated as properly executed if its execution conformed to the internal law in force in the territory [a] where it was executed, or in the territory where, at the time of execution of the testator's death, [b] he was domiciled or [c] had his habitual residence, or in a state of which, at either of those times, [d] he was a national'.

There are eight potential legal systems here that can be used to test formal validity: the lex loci actus (the law of the place of execution), the lex domicilii, the law of habitual residence, and the lex patriae (the national law), each of which can be either at the time of execution or at the time of death. Note that the internal law of the relevant legal system must be used, ie renvoi is excluded (see s6(1)).

However, if the will is not valid under any of these eight systems, s2 goes on to provide some more:

1. where a will is made on board an aircraft or ship the internal law of the place of registration of that ship or aircraft or the law with which that ship or aircraft is most closely connected;
2. where a will disposes of immovable property, the internal law of the territory where the property is situated;
3. where a will revokes another will (or portion of another will) then any law which under the Act would uphold the validity of the revoked will (prior to revocation) can be used to test whether the revoking will effectively revokes the earlier will; and
4. the formal validity of the exercise of a power of appointment can be tested by the law governing the essential validity of the power.

To this wide range of legal systems that can be used to test formal validity a new 'international' testing law has been recently added. Section 27 of the Administration of Justice Act 1982 provides that the Washington Convention on International Wills of 1973 should have the force of law. The convention provides that a will shall be formally valid provided that it is in writing and signed by the testator in the presence of two witnesses and an 'authorised person' (viz a solicitor or notary) who then attest the will, and the 'authorised person' then attaches a certificate to the will. Such a will can be deposited for safe custody with the Principal Registry of the Family Division, but this is not obligatory.

So it is difficult to see a will failing if it complies with the formnal requirements of any relevant legal system. There are, however, a number of technical points about the Wills Act 1963 that need to be made clear.

First, s6(2) attempts to deal with the problem that arises where there is more than one system of law in force in a particular territory or state. Suppose, for instance, that we are attempting to use the lex patriae of a national of the United States to test the validity of his will. Which of the fifty states' legal systems should be used? The rule of s6(2) is that, if there is a rule in force 'throughout the state or territory [in our example, the United States] indicating which of those systems can properly be applied in the case in question, that rule shall be followed', but, if there is no such rule (and usually there will be no such rule, certainly there is none in the United Kingdom or the United States), the system 'with which the testator was most closely connected at the relevant time' shall be used; and the relevant time is the time of execution, except where 'the matter is to be determined by reference to circumstances prevailing at his death' when the time of death is to be used.

Secondly, s6(3) deals with changes in the relevant law after execution; such changes will be effective if they render an invalid will valid, but not if they invalidate the will. Apparently, even changes after death can be relied upon!

Thirdly, we have already noted that the phrase 'internal law' is used throughout the Act and that it is defined in terms that effectively exclude renvoi. Morris, op cit, 395, however, makes the astute point that the Act does not in fact abolish the common law; so reliance can still be placed on the common law, and when this is done renvoi can be relied upon!

Fourthly, some legal systems provide that certain classes of testators can only make wills in a particular form. For instance, Dutch law provides that Dutch nationals cannot make wills outside the Netherlands, except in the form prescribed by Dutch law. Now it was controversial amongst the writers on the conflict of laws whether such provisions related to capacity to make a will (discussed below) or to form. Section 3, however, now imposes a classification upon such provisions as formal. This seems to be an appropriate point at which to turn to consider the capacity to make a will.

## Capacity to make a will and capacity to take under a will

The basic rule appears clear: capacity to make a will of movables is governed by the law of the testator's domicile (*In the Estate of Fuld (No 3)* [1968] P 675 at 696), and the capacity to make a will of immovables is probably governed by the lex situs (Dicey and Morris, 615).

Two points of difficulty seem worthy of note. First, is the reference to domicile a reference to the domicile of the testator at the time of execution of the will or at the time of death? The favoured opinion of the writers (see Morris, op cit, 392) is that domicile at the time of execution is meant, and, this, it is submitted, is quite correct in principle. For if the domicile at the time of death was used, this would mean that a will might be invalid (through the testator's lack of capacity under his then lex domicilii) at the time of execution, but could become valid when the testator changed his domicile. But surely a will should either be valid or invalid, once and for all, when it is executed, and this principle should only be departed from in exceptional cases.

Secondly, it is not always clear whether particular rules are to be characterised as relating to capacity or as formalities. Matters such as whether a minor or a married woman or a very ill person can make a will clearly relate to capacity. As we have seen, s3 of the Wills Act 1963 provides that rules providing for special classes of testator to observe special formalities relate to formalities. Given the liberality of the reformed law relating to formalities and the modern tendency to uphold wills, there will probably be a tendency to characterise difficult provisions as relating to formalities.

Finally, in regard to capacity to take under a will, it was suggested by *Re Hellman's Will* (1886) LR 2 EQ 363 that capacity to take a legacy may be tested by either the recipient's domicile or the testator's domicile. There is little other English authority on the point, but in principle, since the matters relates to the capacity of the recipient, the recipient's lex domicilii alone should be used.

## Essential validity of a will

The general rule is easily predicted: the essential validity of a will of movables is governed by the law of the testator's domicile (*Re Levick's Will Trusts* [1963] 1 All ER 311 inter alia), while the essential validity of a will of immovables is governed by the lex situs (*Nelson v Bridport*; *Re Hoyles* and *Re Ross*). It appears that the connecting factor is the testator's domicile at the time of death (*Re Goss, Goss v Goss* [1915] 1 Ch 572). This means regrettably, it is submitted, that a will may be invalid at the time that it is executed, but when the testator changes his or her domicile it becomes valid.

The following issues have been held to be matters of essential validity or have been dealt with as matters of essential validity: whether relatives are entitled to a legitimate portion of the deceased's estate (*Re Goss*), whether beneficiaries can witness a will (*Re Priest* [1944] Ch 58), and whether gifts to charities are valid (ie do not fall foul of Mortmain Acts) and whether a gift breaches the rule against perpetuities or accumulations (*Freke v Carbery*). In addition, with regard to bequests of land, the lex situs determines what estates can be created in that land and what the incidents of those estates are (*Nelson v Bridport* and *Re Miller* [1914] 1 Ch 511). The doctrine of election is considered part of essential validity (*Re Ogilvie* [1918] 1 Ch 492 at 498), although difficult questions sometimes arise in applying it.

## Interpretation of the will

The construction of the will is governed by the law which the testator intended, and in the absence of contrary indications this will be taken to be the law of the testator's domicile (*Re Cunnington* [1924] 1 Ch 68). Where the testator changes his domicile between execution and death, his lex domicilii at the time of execution prevails (*Philipson-Stow* v *IRC* [1961] AC 727 at 761 per Lord Denning MR). Section 4 underlines this by providing that the 'construction of a will shall not be altered by reason of any change in the testator's domicile after the execution of the will'.

It is sometimes difficult to tell whether a matter relates to construction or essential validity. But it seems clear that construction has a wide meaning rather than a narrow one; obviously it includes the meaning and effect of words, but it goes further to include other matters such as a failure of the testator to make provision for foreseeable events, such as the predecease of one of the beneficiaries named in the will.

It appears that the same principles apply to the interpretation of the will whether it relates to movables or immovables. Of course, in interpreting a will of land the court will attempt not to conflict with the lex situs, but in the final analysis the lex situs will, as it must in land cases, triumph.

## Revocation

A will may be revoked in a number of ways. First, it may be revoked by a later will or codicil. Where there is an express revocation then its effectiveness depends upon the validity of the will in which it is contained, and the usual rules for determining formal validity, essential validity and capacity apply. On the other hand, where there is only an implicit revocation of the earlier will (eg where the testator disposes of property in the later will that he has already disposed of in the earlier will) then this is a question of interpretation, and it is governed by the law of his domicile at the time of execution. Note also the provisions of s2(1)(c) of the Wills Act 1963 discussed above.

Secondly, the will may be revoked by destruction (including burning and tearing); then the view seems to be that the lex domicilii governs in the case of wills of movables and that the lex situs governs in the case of wills of immovables (Morris, op cit, 401). The question, of course, arises whether this means the domicile at the time of revocation or the date of death. In principle, it must be the testator's domicile at the time of revocation, but there is no authority on this point.

Thirdly, the will may be revoked by operation of law (eg when marriage, even a voidable marriage, revokes (at English law) previous wills of the spouses). This is governed by the testator's domicile at the time of marriage (*Re Martin* [1900] P 211). In the days when the wife took her husband's domicile on marriage, she frequently changed her domicile on her wedding day; it was the changed domicile that was applied for the purpose of this rule (*Re Martin* and *Re Groos, Groos* v *Groos* [1904] P 269). The modern writers and a number of Commonwealth decisions suggest that this rule extends to wills of immovables as well as movables, but there is some authority in England contrary to this (*Re Caithness* (1890) 7 TLR 354).

## 7.9 Trusts

Conflicts of law problems can readily arise in the context of trusts. A trust established in England may control property situated in a number of foreign countries: will English law govern the administration of the trust and the powers of the trustee? When will the trustee under a foreign trust be recognised as such in England? Given this range of problems it is perhaps surprising that there is so little authority on these problems in the common law. But as Morris, op cit, says, there is 'a dearth of English and Commonwealth authority on what law governs the validity and administration of trusts in the conflict of laws' (at 419). The interested reader is referred to Morris for an account of the common law, such as it is.

Recently, however, Parliament has enacted the Recognition of Trusts Act 1987 which implements in English law the Hague Convention on the Law Applicable to Trusts. This Act will henceforth dominate the law in this area.

The Convention (set out in Schedule 1 of the Act) is a relatively short but wide-ranging document. A trust is widely defined in article 2 as including

'the legal relationship created – inter vivos or on death – by a person, the settlor, when assets have been placed under the control of a trustee for the benefit of a beneficiary or for a specified purpose',

but the convention only applies to trusts 'created voluntarily and evidenced in writing' (article 3). Furthermore, it does not apply to preliminary issues relating 'to the validity of wills or other acts by virtue of which assets are transferred to the trustee'.

The heart of the convention is to be found in articles 6 and 7 which provide that the settlor may, either expressly or impliedly, choose the law that governs the trust, but if no law is chosen the trust will 'be governed by the law with which it is most closely connected.' In addition the second paragraph of article 7 specifies how it is to be determined with which law the trust is most closely connected: the place of administration indicated by the settlor, the situs of the trust assets, the residence and place of business of the trustee and the objects of the trust are all to be taken into account. Article 8 specifies the wide range of matters that shall be governed by what we may call the proper law of the trust.

Article 11 of the Convention then provides that should a trust be validly created under the proper law specified in articles 6 and 7, then such a trust shall be recognised; and this would then be so in every country that was party to the Convention.

Subsidiary provisions (articles 17, 18 and 22) provide that renvoi is excluded, that recognition may be refused on the ground of 'manifest incompatibility' with public policy, and that the convention is retrospective.

## 7.10 The administration of estates

Upon the death of a testator or an intestate the question arises who is to pay the deceased's debts and distribute his assets in accordance with his will or the applicable rules of intestate succession. This task is usually undertaken by a personal representative of the deceased. In England, unlike many civil law countries, the personal representative, even if appointed in a will, must obtain the authority of the court before he can act.

From the point of view of the conflict of laws two kinds of issue can arise. First, under what circumstances can an English court appoint a representative? The English courts have a wide jurisdiction to make a grant of representation. They may now make a grant of representation even where the deceased leaves no property in England (s2(1) of the Administration of Justice Act 1932 and s25(1) of the Supreme Court Act 1981) (this used not to be the case: *In bonis Tucker* (1864) 3 Sw & Tr 585), and a grant will normally extend to all the deceased's property, wherever situated. Note, however, that whether the English representative will be able to deal with the property situated in foreign countries will depend upon whether his English grant is recognised there. Where the deceased died domiciled in a foreign country, the English court will make the grant in the first instance to the person entrusted with the administration of his estate under the law of his domicile (Non-Contentious Probate Rules 1954, rule 29(a) as amended).

Secondly the question arises, when will the English court recognise a grant of a foreign representative? It will generally be necessary for the representative to apply for recognition by the English court before he will be able to deal with property situated in England. We have already seen that usually the representative under the law of the deceased's domicile will be recognised, but the courts are not bound to recognise such a grant and will not make a grant to someone who is disqualified under English law from being given such a grant.

# 8

# The Recognition and Enforcement of Foreign Judgments

8.1 Introduction

8.2 Judgments rendered outside the EC

8.3 Judgments rendered within the EC

## 8.1 Introduction

We now come to the third topic which forms part of the conflict of laws: the recognition and enforcement of foreign judgments (see Chapter 1, section 1.1 *The scope of the conflict of laws*). A plaintiff may sue a defendant in a foreign court, hear with pleasure judgment given in his favour, and then discover that he cannot enforce that judgment against the defendant in that country because the defendant and his assets have absconded to England. Thus the plaintiff has to follow the defendant to England and attempt to enforce his judgment against him in England, and the central task of this chapter is to consider the circumstances in which an English court will come to the aid of such a plaintiff.

The Civil Jurisdiction and Judgments Act 1982 plays a crucial part in this part of the law. Article 31 of the Brussels Convention provides:

> 'A judgment given in a Contracting State and enforceable in that State shall be enforced in another Contracting State when, on the application of any interested party, the order for its enforcement has been issued there.'

This provision (which we shall consider more fully in section 8.3 below) is the basis of the liberal and easy regime for the enforcement in the United Kingdom of the judgments of courts elsewhere in the EC. The reasoning of the Convention is essentially that, because of the detailed rules of jurisdiction (including provisions for the protection of defendants) that now apply throughout the EC because of the Convention, the enforcement of a judgment rendered by an EC court should be very easy in all other EC countries. If a plaintiff is to be forced to sue the defendant in a particular court in the EC because that is where the defendant is 'domiciled', then he should be able to rely upon that judgment being enforced anywhere in the EC without difficulty.

The judgments of courts outside the EC continue to be governed by the traditional common law rules fortified by statute. However, the Civil Jurisdiction and Judgments Act 1982 is very important here too because it corrects many of the flaws and illogicalities that had grown up in the common law over the years.

We should also mention here the distinction between recognition and enforcement. We have used these two terms freely, almost interchangeably, above, but there is a distinction between them. When a foreign judgment is recognised this simply means that the English court takes note of the result of the judgment. Thus if English law recognises a foreign divorce decree, this simply means that the English court in dealing with the case before it (which may be any kind of case) will treat the erstwhile husband and wife as unmarried. On the other hand, what the plaintiff may be seeking is enforcement, ie he wishes the English court to make an order ordering the defendant to pay him a certain sum. Obviously, a judgment needs to be recognised before it will be able to be enforced. In the context of this chapter, we will be dealing mostly with the enforcement of foreign judgments, but some judgments, typically where the foreign court gives judgment for the defendant, only call for recognition by the English court (should the plaintiff attempt to sue again in England).

One final point that should be made before we turn to the detailed provisions of the law. Over the years there has been much theorising about how it is that judgments of foreign courts, loyal to a foreign sovereign, should be given effect in England. We, fortunately, need not concern ourselves over much with these matters. (Those interested may begin by reading Morris, *The Conflict of Laws*, 3rd ed, 1984, 106–107, and *Schibsby* v *Westenholz* (1870) LR 6 QB 155.) For us a foreign judgment, just like foreign law in general, is enforced in England because the law of England so directs (see Chapter 1, section 1.1 *The nature of the conflict of laws*). And the Civil Jurisdiction and Judgments Act 1982 has simply rendered clearer some of the relevant rules of English law directing when foreign judgments are to be enforced.

## 8.2 Judgments rendered outside the EC

### The central rule

The central rule that has to be understood is that an English court will generally enforce a judgment of a foreign court, provided that the foreign court had jurisdiction to render that judgment. But two important points need to be understood about the concept of jurisdiction in this context. First, the inquiry is into whether the foreign court had jurisdiction in the eyes of the English law; it is not generally relevant whether the foreign court had jurisdiction under its own rules of jurisdiction (*Buchanan* v *Rucker* (1809) 9 East 192; see, however, section 8.2 *Defences and non-defences to an action on a foreign judgment*, below). In other words, the English court is concerned to see whether there is sufficient of a link between the foreign court and the defendant to justify it in enforcing the foreign court's judgment.

Secondly, however, it does not follow that, because an English court in similar circumstances would have held that it had jurisdiction over the defendant, the foreign court had jurisdiction 'in the eyes of English law'. Suppose, for instance, that the foreign court either did or could have exercised jurisdiction over the defendant on a ground analogous to service of a writ out of the jurisdiction under RSC O.11 r.1(1); would the English court recognise and enforce such a judgment? The answer would appear to be no (*Schibsby* v *Westenholz*, above, *Turnball* v *Walker* (1892) 67 LT 767; cf *Re Dulles' Settlement (No 2)* [1951] Ch 842 at 851 (per Lord Denning)). Thus the English courts do not hold that foreign courts have competence or jurisdiction to hear a case simply because an English court would have jurisdiction in like circumstances. In order to avoid confusion between the domestic English law of jurisdiction and the principles upon which English courts will consider that foreign courts will have jurisdiction or competence, we will refer to the latter principles as being those of international jurisdiction or international competence. (But note that all the time we are dealing with different aspects of English law, not international law.)

In the field of recognition of foreign divorce decrees a principle of reciprocity applied at one time (*Travers* v *Holley* [1953] P 246), ie the English courts would recognise the exercise of jurisdiction by a foreign court if an English court would have exercised jurisdiction in like circumstances. However, in the general liberalisation of the grounds of recognition of divorce decrees (a topic that falls outside the scope of this book) the *Travers* v *Holley* principle was swamped by later more liberal cases (such as *Indyka* v *Indyka* [1969] 1 AC 33) and reforming statutes (presently Part II of the Family Law Act 1986). It has not been followed outside the field of family law.

We shall shortly deal in detail with the rules specifying when a court will be internationally competent or have international jurisdiction. For the present it is sufficient to say that courts will generally be internationally competent if the defendant is resident there or has submitted to the foreign court's jurisdiction.

## The non-merger rule

There is first a rather technical matter that we should deal with; it will be best to get it out of the way at the beginning. In the past a plaintiff who was successful in the foreign court had the choice of either bringing an action in England against the defendant based on the foreign judgment or commencing litigation afresh before the English court on the same cause of action. The reason for this was a technical one: the foreign court was not 'a court of record', and thus its judgment did not extinguish the original cause of action, so the plaintiff could institute action afresh and not be met by the plea of res judicata. This inconvenient rule has now been replaced by s34 of the Civil Jurisdiction and Judgments Act 1982 which provides:

'No proceedings may be brought by a person in England and Wales or Northern Ireland on a cause of action in respect of which a judgment has been given in his favour in proceedings between the same parties, or their privies, in a court in another part of the United Kingdom or in a court of an overseas country, unless that judgment is not enforceable or entitled to recognition in England and Wales or, as the case may be, in Northern Ireland.'

This is obviously a sensible rule, and must be welcomed. This provision came into force on 24 August 1982 and is not retrospective; it does not apply to earlier judgments (see Schedule 13, Part II, paragraph 10 of the Civil Jurisdiction and Judgments Act 1982).

Section 34 was before the courts for the first time in *Black* v *Yates* [1991] 3 WLR 90. What had happened was that the plaintiff's husband had been killed in a motorcycle accident in Spain. He was a pillion passenger on the defendant's motorcycle, and it was not contested that the defendant's negligence had caused the plaintiff's husband's death. Criminal proceedings were taken against the defendant in Spain, and under Spanish law compensation claims can be dealt with in the criminal proceedings unless the right to bring a civil action is expressly reserved in the criminal proceedings. This was not done, although the plaintiff (and her children on whose behalf she was also suing) was represented by a Spanish lawyer in those proceedings. In the event the Spanish court awarded compensation of about £18,000, but the plaintiff and her children would probably have been awarded about £75,000 by an English court. The plaintiff now, on her own behalf, on behalf of her children, and on behalf of the deceased's estate, brought an action in England against the defendant. She was met, however, with a defence based upon s34.

Mr Justice Potter held (1) that as far as the plaintiff's claims on her own behalf were concerned the English proceedings were brought on the same cause of action as that in respect of which the Spanish judgment had been given. Since the Spanish judgment was enforceable in England the requirements of s34 were complied with, and thus the defence succeeded.

But (2) the claims brought by the plaintiff on the part of the children (under the Fatal Accidents Act 1976) and on behalf of the deceased's estate (under the Law Reform (Miscellaneous Provisions) Act 1934) stood on a different footing. Since the plaintiff had not purported to act on behalf of the estate in the Spanish proceedings, the estate was not bound by the Spanish proceedings. And, as far as the children were concerned, the Spanish proceedings were contrary to their interests and there was no evidence that they were able to give an informed consent to the power of attorney that led to their representation in the Spanish proceedings. Section 34 was not intended to defeat the English law of infancy. Thus the court could repudiate the power of attorney; the children were therefore in law not represented in the Spanish court, and the actions brought on their behalf could proceed in England.

Although one's sympathies lie with the plaintiff, this decision is plainly right. The plaintiff's remedy, if any, must lie in negligence against her legal representatives (both in Spain and in England). So lawyers ignorant of the conflict of laws be warned!

Section 34 was applied in *The Indian Grace* [1993] AC 410, although *Black v Yates* was not mentioned. The House of Lords made clear though that the parties could waive s34 and in the right circumstances could be estopped from relying upon the section.

## International competence under the common law

Discussions of this topic in the standard textbooks usually begin with consideration of *Emanuel v Symon* [1908] KB 302 where Buckley LJ specified five grounds of international jurisdiction in actions in personam. But the dictum is less useful than it appears. In reality one of his five grounds (nationality) was not a ground of international jurisdiction at all, three are variations on the theme of submission to the foreign court's jurisdiction (submission is a ground of international jurisdiction), and only one (residence) is clearly correct without qualification. Thus there are in effect two grounds of international jurisdiction in judgments in personam at common law, residence and submission, and we can consider each in turn.

### Residence

Where a defendant is sued successfully in the court of his residence he has little ground for complaint if an English court subsequently accepts the judgment of that court as valid, and it is widely recognised that where the foreign court is the court of the defendant's residence the foreign court has international jurisdiction (*Schibsby v Westenholz* (1870) LR 6 QB 155 at 161 and *Sirdar Gurdyal Singh v Rajah of Faridkote* [1894] AC 670 (enforcement refused because defendant not resident)).

Two points arise and are worthy of note. First, will the 'mere presence' of the defendant be sufficient? We know that mere presence, if a writ is served, will be sufficient to give an English court jurisdiction under internal English law, but is it sufficient to give a foreign court international competence? Although *Carrick v Hancock* (1895) 12 TLR 59 supports mere presence (an Englishman was served with a writ (and appeared) while he was in Sweden on a short visit; the judgment of the Swedish court was enforced against him in England), the better view of all the academic writers (see Cheshire, 349–350, and Morris, op cit, 111) is that mere presence is not enough. This view is here supported, but note how the English law of international jurisdiction diverges from the English law of internal jurisdiction.

A recent, and unwelcome, development has been dicta in the Court of Appeal in *Adams and Others v Cape Industries plc and Another* [1990] 2 WLR 657 (CA) that suggest that 'mere presence' would suffice for international competence. Slade LJ said (at 736G) that:

'[We] regard the source of the territorial jurisdiction of the court of a foreign country to summon a defendant to appear before it as being his obligation for the time being to abide by its laws and accept the jurisdiction of its courts while present in its territory. So long as he remains physically present in that country, he has the benefit of its laws, and must take the rough with the smooth, by accepting his amenability to the process of its courts. In the absence of authority compelling a contrary conclusion, we would conclude that the voluntary presence of an individual in a foreign country, whether permanent or temporary and whether or not accompanied by residence, is sufficient to give the courts of that country territorial jurisdiction over him under our rules of private international law.'

It remains to be seen whether the courts will take this reasoning to its logical conclusion. For instance, suppose a writ is served on a defendant when he is in transit at JFK Airport in New York on his way from London to the Cayman Islands. Suppose further that the dispute has nothing to do with New York and that neither the plaintiff nor the defendant has anything to do with New York or the United States. Will the English courts enforce the default judgment of the New York court against the defendant in England? I very much doubt it, but that is the implication of this dictum. Fortunately, it is likely that the Court of Appeal did not mean what it said, as we shall see when we consider what was said in *Adams* v *Cape Industries* about the meaning of the 'presence' of a company, which we now discuss.

The second point that arises concerns the residence or 'presence' of corporations. A corporation is, of course, not resident in the same way that an individual may be resident. However, where a corporation carries on 'substantial business ... at some definite and more or less permanent place in the country of trial' it is considered to be resident there (Cheshire, 350–353). The point may be illustrated by *Littauer Glove Corporation* v *F W Millington Ltd* (1928) 44 TLR 746. Here the director of the defendants (an English company with no place of business in New York) was served with a writ while staying in a New York hotel (and making occasional use of an office in New York belonging to one of the company's customers). The director did nothing more, and in due course default judgment was taken against the company in the courts of New York. However, the enforcement of the judgment in England was refused; the company was not resident everywhere that the director happened to be or even everywhere the company happened to do business. It was held necessary for enforcement that 'the company must to some extent carry on business in that state at a definite and reasonably permanent place'.

The same sort of point has arisen in a number of cases about whether the appointment of an agent subjects a company to the jurisdiction of that state where the agent is. Consider, for instance, *Vogel* v *R and A Kohnstamm Ltd* [1971] 2 All ER 1428. Here the defendants, an English company trading in leather, had appointed an agent in Israel to elicit orders from customers but not to contract with them on their behalf. The plaintiff was a dissatisfied customer who sued them successfully in Israel and then sought to enforce the Israeli judgment in England. Ashworth J (in reliance on *Sfeir & Co* v *National Insurance Co of New Zealand* [1964] 1 Lloyd's Rep 330 – a similar case where the appointment by the insurance company of an agent in Ghana with authority only to settle claims of less than £5 was held insufficient to subject the company to Ghanaian jurisdiction – and *Okura & Co Ltd* v *Forsbacka Jernwerks Aktiebolag* [1914] 1 KB 715 – a case on the residence of a company in internal law) said:

'I have asked myself anxiously in this case whether in any real sense of the word the defendants can be said to have been there in Israel; and all that emerges from this case is that there was a man called Kornbluth [the agent] who sought customers for them, transmitted correspondence to them and received it from them, [but] had no authority whatever to bind the defendants in any shape or form. I have come to the conclusion really without any hesitation that the defendants were not resident in Israel at any material time.'

The requirements that had to be fulfilled before a company was subject to the jurisdiction of a foreign court sufficiently to justify the enforcement of that foreign court's order were much discussed in the very long judgment of Slade LJ in *Adams v Cape Industries*. The Court of Appeal tended to equate the concepts of 'presence' and 'residence' in the context of companies provided that it was understood that, in that context, these were artificial concepts. The general principles applicable to determining whether a particular company was resident or present were set out in detail at 747A–748E.

These principles were, first:

'The English courts will be likely to treat a trading corporation incorporated under the law of one country ("an overseas corporation") as present within the jurisdiction of the courts of another country only if either (i) it has established and maintained ... a fixed place of business of its own in the other country and for more than a minimal period of time has carried on its own business at or from such premises by its servants or agents, ... or (ii) a representative of the overseas corporation has for more than a minimal period of time been carrying on *the overseas corporation's* business in the other country at or from some fixed place of business ...'

Secondly, where the overseas corporation has had a representative in the foreign country it will have to be investigated

'whether or not the fixed place of business from which the representative operates was originally acquired for the purpose of enabling him to act for the overseas corporation ... whether the overseas corporation directly reimbursed him ... for the cost of his accommodation ... [and] staff ... what other contributions, if any, the overseas corporation makes to the financing of the business of the representative ... whether the representative is remunerated ... by commission, or by regular fixed payments ... what degree of control the overseas corporation exercises over the running of the business conducted by the representative ... whether the representative reserves part of his accommodation or part of his staff for conducting business relating to the overseas corporation ... whether the representative displays the overseas corporation's name at his premises or on his stationery, and if so, whether he does so in a way as to indicate that he is the representative over the overseas corporation ... what business, if any, the representative transacts as principal exclusively on his own behalf ... whether the representative makes contracts with customers ... in the name of the overseas corporation ... and whether the representative requires specific authority in advance before binding the overseas corporation.'

The judge then make it clear that this list of questions was 'not exhaustive ... [or] necessarily conclusive'! Thus even if the representative did not have authority to contract on behalf of the overseas company, it did not necessarily follow that the company was not present in the foreign country. The absence of such authority was, however, 'a powerful factor pointing against the presence of the overseas corporation'.

These principles were then applied to the complex facts of *Adams* v *Cape Industries*. In brief Cape Industries, an English company, was concerned with the mining and marketing of asbestos. Asbestos was marketed in the USA through its subsidiary, an Illinois company, NAAC. Worldwide marketing was in the hands of another subsidiary, Capasco. Various plaintiffs instituted product liability suits against Cape Industries in a court in the Texan town of Tyler (these were the Tyler I actions). These actions were settled and damages were paid. Other plaintiffs then flocked to Tyler and instituted further actions (these were the Tyler II actions), but Cape and Capasco refused to have anything to do with these actions. Default judgment was given against them (in rather peculiar circumstances, see section 8.2 Defences, below, but since Cape and Capasco had no assets in the USA (and had even liquidated NAAC) these judgments had to be enforced against them in England. But could they be? Only if it could be established that Cape and Capasco were present in Texas (or perhaps the USA (although Slade LJ discussed at great length the question of whether presence in Illinois implied presence elsewhere in the USA, eg Texas, in the end he left this point open)).

Slade LJ held not; there was a difference between parent and subsidiary companies, thus the presence of NAAC in Illinois did not establish the presence of Cape or Capasco in the USA. Neither did that of its successor CPC (another Illinois corporation). A substantial part of NAAC business was its own business in the USA (buying asbestos directly from suppliers, etc), and it had no general authority to contract on behalf of Cape or Capasco. The transactions concerning the liquidation of NAAC and the establishment of CPC were lawful and there was no reason to pierce the corporate veil and hold that NAAC was simply the alter ego of Cape. The onus was on the plaintiff to establish that the defendant was present in the foreign jurisdiction, and it had failed to do so.

### Submission

If the defendant has submitted to the jurisdiction of the foreign court then that court will be recognised as internationally competent, and its judgments will be recognised and enforced in England (*Emanuel* v *Symon*, above). There are, however, a number of ways in which a defendant may be taken to have submitted to the foreign jurisdiction.

First of all, where the defendant counterclaimed in the foreign court, ie he invoked that court's jurisdiction as a plaintiff, then he cannot be heard to say that he is not subject to that tribunal's jurisdiction (*Schibsby* v *Westenholz*, above, at 161).

Secondly, where the defendant has entered into an express agreement to submit to the foreign court's jurisdiction, then once more that court will be held to be internationally competent (*Feyerick* v *Hubbard* (1902) 71 LJ KB 509 and *Copin* v *Adamson* (1874) LR 9 Ex 345).

It is useful to note here that s32 of the Civil Jurisdiction and Judgments Act 1982 provides:

'A judgment given by the court of an overseas country in any proceedings shall not be recognised or enforced in the United Kingdom if (a) the bringing of those proceedings in that court was contrary to an agreement under which the dispute in question was to be settled otherwise than by proceedings in the courts of that country; and (b) those proceedings were not brought in that court, or with the agreement of, the person against whom the judgment was given; and (c) that person did not counterclaim in the proceedings or otherwise submit to the jurisdiction of that court.'

The submission agreement must not have been 'illegal, void or unenforceable or ... incapable of being performed for reasons not attributable to the fault of the party bringing the proceedings' (s32(2)). (Section 32 came into force on 24 August 1982; it is retrospective save for some exceptional cases specified in Schedule 13, Part II, para 8 (see *Tracomin SA* v *Sudan Oil Seeds (No 1)* [1983] 1 WLR 1026).) The point about s32 is that if judgments emanating from courts other than those to which the parties have submitted are to be denied enforcement, then a valid submission agreement must grant to the court submitted to international competence.

The interesting question that now arises is whether it is possible for a party to submit to the jurisdiction of the foreign court implicitly. In *Blohn* v *Desser* [1962] 2 QB 116 Diplock J said:

'Where a person becomes a partner in a foreign firm with a place of business within the jurisdiction of a foreign court, and appoints an agent resident in that jurisdiction to conduct business on behalf of the partnership at that place of business ... these matters to be notified to persons dealing with that firm by registration in a public register, he does impliedly agree with all persons to whom such notification is made ... to submit to the jurisdiction of the court of the country in which the business is carried on in respect of transactions conducted at that place of business by that agent.'

And in *Sfeir & Co* v *National Insurance Company of New Zealand Ltd* it was also held that there could be an implied agreement to submit. But the older authorities, *Sirdar Gurdyal Singh* v *Rajah of Faridkote* and *Emanuel* v *Symon*, clearly support the proposition that an undertaking to submit must be express, and in the most recent case, *Vogel* v *R and A Kohnstamm Ltd*, Ashworth J refused to follow the later cases and held that there could be no implied agreement to submit. This conclusion has wide academic approval. It may be noted, however, that s32(1)(a) of the Civil Jurisdiction and Judgments Act 1982, discussed above, refers only to 'an agreement' that a court of another country would have jurisdiction, and that presumably includes implied as well as express agreements. So the position may still be open to argument (see Cheshire, 637).

Finally, where the defendant has voluntarily appeared before the foreign court and pleads to the merits of the plaintiff's case, he will be taken to have submitted to the jurisdiction of the foreign court (*Guiard* v *De Clermont* [1914] 3 KB 145). If he contests the jurisdiction of the court but none the less pleads to the merits, he will still be taken to have submitted to the foreign court's jurisdiction (*Boissiere & Co* v *Brockner* (1889) 6 TLR 85).

The interesting question that used to arise in this context was, what was the position if the defendant appeared solely to contest the jurisdiction of the foreign court? A number of cases suggest that in these circumstances the defendant in appearing and contesting the jurisdiction of the foreign court will be taken to have submitted to that jurisdiction and, consequently, the foreign court's judgment will be able to be enforced against him in England! These cases were *Harris* v *Taylor* [1951] 2 KB 580 (appearance essentially to protest jurisdiction, judgment enforced in England against defendant) and *Henry* v *Geoprosco International Ltd* [1976] QB 726 (appearance to request court not to exercise jurisdiction, judgment enforced in England against defendant, although question left open whether appearance merely to protest jurisdiction would be sufficient). There were a number of cases that might have suggested that appearance to protest the jurisdiction did not amount to submission. These were *Re Dulles's Settlement (No 2)* [1951] Ch 842 (but this was a case on submission in internal law and the dictum was in any event obiter) and *NV Daarnhouwer & Co Handelmaatschappij* v *Boulos* [1968] 2 Lloyd's Rep 259 (but this was only a single judge decision at first instance), and the dicta from these cases were disapproved of in *Henry* v *Geoprosco*.

Allied to this question is the problem that arises where the defendant appears before the foreign court solely in an attempt to protect property of his which is subject to the jurisdiction of that court (and which may be seized if the judgment goes against him there). The cases hold that appearance to protect property that has not yet been seized will be taken as submission (*Guiard* v *De Clermont* (note that Morris's account of this case at 113 is entertaining rather than accurate) and *Voinet* v *Barrett* (1885) 55 LJ QB 39).

Both these problems (and the unsatisfactory state of the law on these points) have been tackled by s33 of the Civil Jurisdiction and Judgments Act 1982 which provides:

> 'The person against whom the judgment was given shall not be regarded as having submitted to the jurisdiction of the court by reason only of the fact that he appeared (conditionally or otherwise) in the proceedings for all or any one or more of the following purposes, namely (a) to contest the jurisdiction of the court [overruling *Harris* v *Taylor*]; (b) to ask the court to dismiss or stay the proceedings on the ground that the dispute in question should be submitted to arbitration or to the determination of the courts of another country [overruling *Henry* v *Geoprosco*]; (c) to protect, or obtain the release of, property seized or threatened with seizure in the proceedings [overruling *Guiard* v *De Clermont*].'

Section 33 came into force on 24 August 1982 and is retrospective, save for exceptional cases (see Schedule 13, Part II, paragraph 9 of the Act and *Tracomin SA* v *Sudan Oil Seeds (No 1)*).

In *Adams* v *Cape Industries plc and Another* (1988) The Times 23 June Scott J held that submission in one action could not be taken to imply submission in a later action with similar plaintiffs. Moreover, his lordship said that he doubted whether an agreement to submit could be made impliedly. A representation to submit, moreover, was only binding if it was relied upon by the plaintiffs. When *Adams* v *Cape Industries* was before the Court of Appeal this point does not appear to have been discussed at any length; presumably it was abandoned by the defendants.

## Other requirements to be satisfied before enforcement

### The foreign judgment must be final and conclusive

Before a foreign judgment can be enforced in England not only must the foreign court have international jurisdiction but the judgment must be 'final and conclusive', ie it must have determined all the relevant points of dispute between the parties and should not be able to be altered by the court which delivered the judgment (*Nouvion v Freeman* (1889) 15 App Cas 1 and *Blohn v Desser*). The judgment must be 'final and conclusive' in the court which pronounced it; thus if the foreign judgment is subject to appeal to a higher court, that does not mean that it is not 'final and conclusive' (*Colt Industries Inc v Sarlie (No 2)* [1966] 1 WLR 1287). However, if an appeal is pending before a higher court the English court will usually stay execution until such time as the appellate court's verdict is known (*Scott v Pilkington* (1862) 2 B & S 11; cf *Colt Industries*), and it seems that if the effect of an appeal under the foreign law is to suspend execution of the judgment, then an English court will not allow an action for enforcement until the appellate court has delivered its judgment (*Patrick v Shedden* (1853) 2 E & B 14; cf *Berliner Industriebank AG v Jost* [1971] 2 QB 463 at 470).

Different considerations apply with regard to maintenance orders, for these may usually be varied from time to time as circumstances change. The position seems to be that where the payer has fallen into arrears, then those arrears can be recovered provided that the original court has no power to alter the arrears (*Beatty v Beatty* [1924] 1 KB 807).

### The foreign judgment must be for a fixed sum of money

At common law a foreign judgment for an injunction, specific performance or delivery of goods (or the equivalent of these remedies under the foreign law) could not be enforced in England. All that could be enforced was a judgment for a specific sum of money (*Sadler v Robins* (1808) 1 Camp 253 at 256). This rule is not breached if the precise sum can be determined by a simple calculation (*Beatty v Beatty*).

## Defences and non-defences to an action on a foreign judgment

Notwithstanding that it is proved that a foreign court with international jurisdiction has rendered a final and conclusive judgment for a specific sum of money, there are a number of limited occasions upon which the defendant can successfully argue that the judgment should not be enforced against him in England. But these occasions are relatively limited, and it is more useful to begin by dealing with those matters which are not defences and which cannot be successfully raised by a defendant sued on a foreign judgment.

### Non-defences

The merits of the foreign judgment cannot be re-opened before the English court even if the foreign court is in error in reaching its conclusion (*Castrique v Imrie*

(1870) LR 4 HL 414). Thus if the foreign court makes an error in applying English law (as, say, the proper law of a contract) the judgment can still be enforced in England (*Godard* v *Gray* (1870) LR 6 QB 139; *Simpson* v *Forgo* (1863) 1 H & M 195 is universally regarded as wrong). An error in regard to its own law by the foreign court does not prevent the enforcement of the foreign judgment (*Henderson* v *Henderson* (1844) 6 QB 288). An error of fact will likewise be disregarded.

What is the position if, although the foreign court had international jurisdiction in the eyes of English law, it lacked jurisdiction under its own internal law? In *Pemberton* v *Hughes* [1899] 1 Ch 781 Lindley LJ said (at 791) that apart from international competence the 'competence [of the foreign court] in any other sense is not regarded as material by the courts of this country'. And this is borne out by *Vanquelin* v *Bouard* (1863) 15 CB(NS) 341 where the plea that, although the French court had international jurisdiction, it had no jurisdiction under its internal rules over the defendant (because he was a trader) was rejected.

On the other hand, *Castrique* v *Imrie* (at 429 and 448), *Papadopoulos* v *Papadopoulos* [1930] P 55 and *Adams* v *Adams* [1971] P 188 all contain dicta that suggest that the internal competence of the foreign court is relevant. Morris, op cit, at 123, submits that the key to the problem is to be found in a distinction drawn in *MacAlpine* v *MacAlpine* [1958] P 35 (at 41 and 45) between voidable and void judgments. If the foreign judgment is a complete nullity under the foreign law, then it should be treated as a complete nullity in England and not enforced. But if the foreign judgment is merely voidable, ie it stands until it is set aside in the foreign country, then it should be treated as valid in England until set aside. As Morris points out (at 124), most jurisdictional errors under most systems of law render the judgment voidable not void; thus 'the practical result is that lack of internal competence is hardly ever a good defence'.

Although *De Cosse Brissac* v *Rathbone* (1861) 6 H & N 301 at 304 suggests that the discovery of fresh evidence that was not before the foreign court (eg a receipt showing that the sum due had been paid) cannot be raised when the judgment is sought to be enforced in England, Morris, op cit, 124, points out that fresh evidence can sometimes be used to set aside an English judgment and 'there seems to be no reason why a foreign judgment should be in a better position'.

### Defences
First, fraud, either by the plaintiff on the foreign court or by the court itself, may be raised as a defence when sued on a foreign judgment (*Ochsebein* v *Papelier* (1873) LR 8 Ch App 695 and *Price* v *Dewhurst* (1837) 8 Sim 279). The argument that proving the fraud may involve a re-examination of the merits, and that this would be contrary to the principles just discussed, has not prevailed in the courts (*Abouloff* v *Oppenheimer* (1882) 10 QBD 295 and *Vadala* v *Lawes* (1890) 25 QBD 310). Indeed, even if the defendants do not raise the plaintiff's fraud before the foreign court, they are not precluded from raising it before the English court (*Syal* v *Heyward* [1948] 2 KB 443). This means that foreign judgments are more easily set

aside on the ground of fraud than are English judgments which can only be set aside on the ground of fraud not raised at the trial if the evidence thereof has been discovered since the trial.

Staughton LJ confirmed in *Jet Holdings Inc and Others v Patel* [1990] QB 335 that just as a foreign court's view of whether it had jurisdiction was not conclusive, so too its view of whether the proceedings were tainted by fraud was not conclusive. Thus the defendant was able to raise allegations of fraud that had been rejected in the foreign court.

Note, however, that issue estoppel does apply in this area. Thus if the issue of whether the proceedings had been tainted by fraud had been tried in a separate action between the parties in the foreign court, the defendant would be estopped from raising that issue against when enforcement proceedings were brought in England: *House of Spring Gardens v Waite* [1990] 3 WLR 347 (CA). This case concerned complicated litigation originally commenced in Ireland in which the plaintiffs claimed very large damages (about £3 million) against the defendants for misuse of confidential information and breach of copyright. The plaintiffs were largely successful before the Irish courts; very briefly, they succeeded in establishing before Costello J that the defendants had tricked the plaintiffs into parting with valuable information about the design of certain bullet-proof vests, and consequently very large damages were awarded to them.

Two of the defendants, however, sought to have Costello J's judgment set aside by the Irish courts on the ground that one of the plaintiffs 'had deceived Costello J regarding the role which he played in developing the armoured vest'. This allegation of fraud by the plaintiff was rejected by Egan J after a 21-day hearing. The plaintiffs now sought to enforce the original Irish judgment in England. (Note that this was enforcement under the common law, not under the Civil Jurisdiction and Judgments Act 1982.) However, the plaintiffs were met with the defence based upon the same alleged fraud as had been tried at such great length by Egan J.

The Court of Appeal denied the plaintiffs the opportunity to raise the alleged fraud as a defence to the enforcement of the Irish judgment on the ground set out above: that the defendants were estopped from raising an issue that had been finally determined between them in the proceedings before Egan J. (As an alternative to issue estoppel the court said that it would be an abuse of the process of the court to allow the same issue that was determined in the Egan proceedings in Ireland to be re-litigated in England.)

Note that *Jet Holdings Inc and Others v Patel* [1990] QB 335 was distinguished on the ground that there the issue of fraud had been raised before the foreign court in the substantive proceedings and not in a separate action. Whether this is an entirely logical ground of distinction may be doubted. After all, the foreign court may have looked with great care at the issue of fraud in the substantive proceedings before rejecting the allegation. However, it was clear that the Court of Appeal wished to restrict the scope of the defence of fraud. Stuart-Smith LJ, for instance, said of *Jet Holdings* and the other earlier cases: 'The scope of these decisions should not be extended. In none of these cases was the question, whether the judgment sued upon was obtained by fraud, litigated in a separate and second action in the foreign jurisdiction.'

Two final points about this case may be made: first, that if the defence had been that Egan J's judgment on the fraud issue had itself been obtained by fraud the result might have been different, for the issue of that second fraud would not have been tried before the Irish courts! (See at 355E–F.)

Also, note that one of the defendants (McLeod) had been sued in Ireland in the Costello action but had played no part in the Egan decision. Could this defendant raise fraud as a defence when sued in England to enforce the Costello judgment?

The Court of Appeal, in reliance upon *Carl Zeiss Stiftung* v *Rayner & Keeler Ltd (No 2)* [1967] 1 AC 853 (HL), held not; even though McLeod did not join in the Irish proceedings to set aside the Costello judgment he was well aware of those proceedings and was privy to them and thus, in the absence of any new evidence, was also estopped from raising the fraud in the English enforcement proceedings.

*Owens Bank Ltd* v *Bracco and Others* [1991] 4 All ER 833 is the latest case on fraud as a defence to enforcement of a foreign judgment. This was an action to register (for enforcement) a judgment granted by a St Vincent court under the Administration of Justice Act 1920 (see section 8.2 *Statutory enforcement* ..., below). The plaintiff bank alleged that it had lent a very large sum in Swiss francs to the defendants (an Italian company and its managing director). It successfully established this before the St Vincent court at first instance and before the St Vincent Court of Appeal. The defendants' defence was that the documents that they had signed had been altered after they had signed them, but this was not considered by the St Vincent courts for it was raised at too late a stage. By this time the parties were also suing each other in Italy. Amongst several other defences the defendants sought to resist the registration of the judgment on the ground of fraud.

Parker LJ held inter alia that the rules in regard to raising fraud as a defence to an action brought on a foreign judgment are wider than the rules in regard to fraud preventing the enforcement of English judgments. Fresh evidence was not required, nor did it matter if the fraud had been raised before the foreign court. However, issue estoppel operated in this area (*House of Spring Gardens* v *Waite*); thus if the Italian courts held that the fraud in the St Vincent court was not established, then fraud would not be able to be raised as a defence in England. Where such proceedings were pending the English proceedings could be stayed, but this was not a proper case for the exercise of that discretion for it was not clear that the Italian courts would decide the fraud issue, nor was a decision from them expected shortly. The House of Lords' decision in this case has been reported ([1992] 2 All ER 193). The Lords (per Lord Bridge) confirmed that the rules in regard to raising fraud as a defence to enforcement were wider than in a purely common law context. However, the Lords referred to the ECJ the question of whether articles 21 and 22 (or other parts of the Brussels Convention) applied to enforce a judgment from a non-Contracting State.

The second defence which may be raised is where the enforcement of the foreign judgment would be contrary to public policy. This is not remarkable, and the principles applicable are those that we have already discussed in Chapter 2, section 2.2. Although the courts will not enforce a foreign judgment for a penalty, where the penalty is coupled with a compensation award the compensation portion of the judgment can be enforced (*Raulin* v *Fischer* [1911] 2 KB 93).

Thirdly, a foreign judgment may be set aside if the defendant was denied natural justice before the foreign court. The outlines of this defence are very vague. A judgment is not obtained contrary to natural justice if it appears to be wrong, for that would simply be to re-open the merits (*Robinson* v *Fenner* [1913] 3 KB 835). However, if the foreign court denies to the defendant an opportunity to present his case that will amount to a breach of natural justice (*Jacobson* v *Frachon* (1928) 138 LT 386). Where the defendant is not given adequate notice of the proceedings, that will also be a breach of natural justice. However, if the defendant has agreed to submit the dispute to the foreign court, then he is bound by the provisions of the foreign law in regard to notice and like matters (*Vallee* v *Dumergue* (1849) 4 Exch 290).

These principles were applied by the Court of Appeal in *Adams* v *Cape Industries*. There after default judgment had been given against the defendants in a Texas court the judge left it to the plaintiffs' counsel to determine, within limits, the quantum of damages to be paid! Such judgments could not be enforced against the defendants since they were contrary to established English law views of substantive justice. The fact that the defendants did not appear before the Tyler court and contest this method of assessing damages, or apply to have the default judgments set aside on this ground, did not prevent raising the issue of natural justice when the judgment was sought to be enforced.

Fourthly, where there are two conflicting foreign judgments both pronounced by courts of competent jurisdiction entitled to recognition and enforcement, the earlier judgment was to be recognised (and, if necessary, enforced) to the exclusion of the later judgment. This was what was held by the Privy Council in determining an appeal from the Jersey courts in *Showlag* v *Mansour* [1994] 2 WLR 615. What had happened was that the personal representatives of the late Sheikh Showlag alleged that Mansour (who had been employed by the sheikh) had stolen £17.5 million from his employer and they sought to recover that sum from him. They had obtained a judgment in England in their favour on the 5 December 1990 but Mansour also faced a criminal trial in Egypt which the personal representatives had joined as parties civile seeking recovery of the money stolen. Although the representatives were successful in Egypt at first instance (on 31 December 1990), this judgment was overturned on appeal (23 May 1991) and although it had been appealed further in Egypt that appeal had not yet been determined. Would the Egyptian judgment provide a defence to an action to enforce the English judgment in Jersey? Although the Privy Council recognised that there might be special circumstances in which the plaintiff might be estopped from relying on the earlier judgment or it might be unfair to allow him to do so, it held that where both courts were of competent jurisdiction the general rule was that the earlier judgment prevailed. Thus, the English judgment was enforced. The Brussels Convention, disappointingly, leaves the analogous issue (competing judgments from EC states) unaddressed. See article 27 of the Brussels Convention (Chapter 8.3 Grounds on which recognition and enforcement may be refused).

Finally, s5 of the Protection of Trading Interests Act 1980 provides that judgment for multiple damages (ie 'a judgment for an amount arrived at by doubling, trebling or otherwise multiplying a sum assessed as compensation') cannot be enforced. And where such an award has been made against a United Kingdom citizen, a company incorporated in the United Kingdom, or a person carrying on business in the United Kingdom, s6 provides that such portion of the damages as exceeds the amount of compensation can be recovered in England. These remarkable provisions are designed to protect businesses in the United Kingdom from the anti-trust laws of the United States.

## Procedure for enforcement at common law

A foreign judgment is not an English judgment, so direct execution of it is not possible. The proper course is to bring an action against the defendant based upon the foreign judgment. The plaintiff can speed matters up, however, by applying for summary judgment under RSC O.14.

There are two statutes that provide, in broad terms, for enforcement of foreign judgments by applying to register them in the English courts and, once registered, the foreign judgment can be treated for most purposes as a local judgment for the purposes of execution. Thus let us now consider these statutes.

## Statutory enforcement apart from enforcement under the Civil Jurisdiction and Judgments Act 1982

First, there is the not very important Part II of the Administration of Justice Act 1920. This provides for the 'Reciprocal Enforcement of Judgments in the United Kingdom and in other Parts of His Majesty's Dominions'. The provisions of Part II are intended to be reciprocal, ie they only apply to any one of His Majesty's dominions where:

> 'His Majesty is satisfied that reciprocal provisions have been made by the legislature of any part of His Majesty's dominions for the enforcement within that part of His dominions of judgments obtained in the High Court in England, the Court of Session in Scotland, and the High Court in Ireland, His Majesty may by Order in Council declare that this Part of this Act shall extend to that part of His Dominions ...'.

Part II has been extended by Order in Council to a large number of Commonwealth countries. The list is too extensive to repeat here; it includes most territories that were colonies at that time, most of the Australian states and New Zealand. It does not include Canada or South Africa (which used to be part of Her Majesty's Dominions).

Provided that the judgment which the plaintiff wishes to enforce emanates from a court of a country to which Part II has been extended, the plaintiff can within 12 months after the date of the judgment (or longer if the court allows) apply to the High Court to 'register' the judgment in the High Court; and the court 'may, if in all the circumstances of the case they think it is just and convenient that the judgment should be enforced in the United Kingdom ... order the judgment to be registered'. Where a judgment is so registered, then s9(3)(a) (as amended (see also s9(3)(b))) provides that that 'judgment shall, as from the date of registration, be of the same force and effect, and proceedings may be taken thereon, as if it had been a judgment originally obtained ... on the date of registration in the registering court'.

Note, however, that registration is within the discretion of the court, although s9(2) restricts this discretion by providing six grounds upon which registration would be refused. Speaking very broadly, these are similar to the defences which would be available under the common law. There is not much point in teasing apart the differences between the common law and the provisions of s9(2) because the importance of Part II of the Administration of Justice Act 1920 is very largely overshadowed by the Foreign Judgments (Reciprocal Enforcement) Act 1933.

This Act is far more detailed, but it tends to follow the substance of the common law so the differences are not great. We shall point them out when we come to them. The Act can be extended by Order in Council to both Commonwealth and politically foreign countries. In the Order in Council Her Majesty specifies not only the country involved but also which courts in that country are 'recognised courts', ie whose judgments would be enforced. The 1933 Act was intended to take the place of the Administration of Justice Act 1920 (and therefore Commonwealth countries were included within its ambit). However, in practice it has only been extended to five politically foreign countries (Austria, Israel, Norway, Surinam and Pakistan) and six Commonwealth countries (Australian Capital Territory, Guernsey, Isle of Man, Jersey, India (parts of) and Tonga).

As before, an application is made for registration of the foreign judgment (within six years of the date of judgment), and once registration is granted then 'a registered judgment shall, for the purposes of execution, be of the same force and effect ... as if the judgment had been a judgment originally given in the registering court and entered on the date of registration' (s2(2)). The major difference between Part II of the Administration of Justice Act 1920 and the Foreign Judgments (Reciprocal Enforcement) Act 1933 lies in the fact that under the latter Act, if the provisions of the Act are satisfied, 'the court shall ... order the judgment to be registered' (s2(1)), ie registration is not in the discretion of the court. As we shall see, though, the defendant can apply to have the registration set aside.

Well, what are the provisions of the Act that must be satisfied before a judgment is registered? These are, broadly speaking, specified in s1(2) which requires that the judgment is 'final and conclusive as between the judgment debtor and the judgment creditor or requires the former to make an interim payment to the latter', that there is 'payable under it a sum of money, not being a sum payable in respect of taxes or other charges of a like nature or in respect of a fine or other penalty'. Section 1(3) provides that a judgment 'shall be deemed to be final and conclusive notwithstanding that an appeal may be pending against it, or that it may still be subject to appeal, in the courts of the country of the original court'. However, s5 provides that 'the court, if it thinks fit, may, on such terms as it may think just, either set aside the registration [of the judgment] or adjourn the application to set aside the registration [until the applicant has taken the necessary steps to have the appeal disposed of by the foreign court]'.

The exclusion of taxes and penalties is simply a statutory enactment of the exclusionary rule we have already discussed (see Chapter 2, section 2.2 *Penal laws* and *Revenue laws*). It is worth pointing out that in *SA General Textiles* v *Sun & Sand Ltd* [1978] 1 QB 279 (CA) it was held that an award of damages for 'resistance abusive' or unjustified opposition to the plaintiff's claim under French law was not hit by this provision, the reason being that it was payable to a private person and not exigible by the state as a punishment. (This reasoning is fully consistent with *Huntington* v *Atrill* [1893] AC 150 (see Chapter 2, section 2.2 *Penal laws*).) The same reasoning would doubtless be followed if it was sought to enforce a judgment for a contractual penalty under the common law.

Once a judgment is registered, however, that is not the end of the matter, for the defendant can make application to have the registration set aside. Section 4(1), (2) and (3) specify the circumstances in which the court either must or may set aside the registration.

The court 'shall' set aside the registration of the judgment in the following circumstances:

1. the judgment was registered in contravention of the Act (ie the judgment does not fall within the scope of the Act, for instance, if it was rendered by a court that is not a 'recognised court');
2. the foreign court had no jurisdiction; although residence and submission are the basic grounds of jurisdiction, 'jurisdiction' here means something slightly different from the meaning of international jurisdiction under the common law. Section 4(1)(a)(i) specifically provides that appearing 'for the purpose of protecting, or obtaining the release of, property seized, or threatened with seizure, ... or of contesting the jurisdiction of that [foreign] court' does not amount to submission. Thus here 'jurisdiction' in terms of the Act, has a narrower meaning than international jurisdiction (at least prior to the coming into force of s33 of the Civil Jurisdiction and Judgments Act 1982). On the other hand, s4(2)(a)(v) provides that 'if the judgment debtor, being a defendant in the original court, had an office or place of business in the country of that [foreign] court and the proceedings in that court were in respect of a transaction effected through or at that office or place' the foreign court will be deemed to have jurisdiction. This is wider than the common law, for the mere doing of business by an individual (without residence or submission) would not be enough to give

the foreign court jurisdiction under the common law (see section 8.2 *International competence under the common law*, above). With regard to corporations, however, the statute (s4(2)(a)(iv)) requires that a corporation is resident where it has 'its principal place of business'. The common law requires only a reasonably permanent place of business.

3. where the judgment is obtained by fraud, or its enforcement would be contrary to public policy. There appears to be no significant difference from the common law here.

4. where the rights under the judgment are not vested in the person by whom the application for registration is made.

It may be noted that neither the Administration of Justice Act 1920 nor the Foreign Judgments (Reciprocal Enforcement) Act 1933 deals with an absence of natural justice before the foreign court. However, both statutes provide that the registration either may or (in the case of the Foreign Judgments (Reciprocal Enforcement) Act 1933) must be set aside if the defendant did not receive proper notice of the proceedings (s4(1)(a)(iii)).

Registration may be set aside in the circumstances specified in s4(b). This provides that where the registering court is satisfied that 'the matter in dispute in the proceedings in the original court had previously to the date of the judgment in the original court been the subject of the final and conclusive judgment by a court having jurisdiction in the matter'. The situation contemplated here is that the plaintiff may have secured the judgment in the foreign court (that he is now seeking to enforce in England) only after the matter had been settled in another court; in these circumstances the court may set aside the registration.

Finally, on the Foreign Judgments (Reciprocal Enforcement) Act 1933 it may be pointed out that the registration procedure is the exclusive means of enforcing the foreign judgment, ie where a case falls within the Act, then the provisions of the Act must be used. Section 6 provides that: 'No proceedings for the recovery of a sum payable under a foreign judgment, being a judgment to which this Part of this Act applies, other than proceedings by way of registration of this judgment, shall be entertained by any court in the United Kingdom.' This, however, still left open to the plaintiff the option of commencing action afresh, but s34 of the Civil Jurisdiction and Judgments Act 1982 now precludes this possibility (see above).

Before leaving statutory enforcement it may be mentioned that under the State Immunity Act 1978 effect is given to the European Convention on State Immunity of 1972. Section 18 provides that a judgment given in the courts of Convention States against the United Kingdom may be recognised in the courts of the United Kingdom. This principle is subject (in terms of s19) to the usual public policy exclusionary rule. Section 31 of the Civil Jurisdiction and Judgments Act 1982 provides that judgments against other states may in like circumstances be recognised in the United Kingdom.

## 8.3 Judgments rendered within the EC

### *Introduction: the basic principle*

We have seen in Chapter 4.3 that a range of new and restrictive rules in regard to jurisdiction were introduced into the law by the Civil Jurisdiction and Judgments Act 1982. (If you have not yet read Chapter 4.3 you should do so now, for otherwise this section is likely to be incomprehensible.) In broad terms, where a defendant is 'domiciled' in a EC country then, special and exclusive jurisdiction aside, he can only be sued in the court of his 'domicile'. Since the English jurisdictional rules were (and where the Convention does not apply, are still) relatively liberal, the effect of these changes has been to make it much more difficult to sue defendants who are not 'domiciled' in England, but are 'domiciled' elsewhere in the EC, in English courts. Moreover, various other provisions of the Convention protect the position of defendants. For instance, article 20 provides that where 'a defendant [is] domiciled in one Contracting State and does not enter an appearance, the court [of another Contracting State] shall of its own motion declare that it has no jurisdiction unless its jurisdiction is derived from the provisions of this Convention'. And, further, that the 'court shall stay the proceedings so long as it is not shown that the defendant has been able to receive the document initiating the proceedings ... in sufficient time to enable him to arrange for his defence ...'. These provisions are designed to ensure, and very largely do ensure, that a defendant 'domiciled' in the EC will only be sued in a court with which he has a substantial link. And if this is so, then there is no reason why, once that court has given judgment, that judgment should not be readily enforced against the defendant anywhere in the EC. As Morris, op cit, at 130, puts it: 'The strictness of these provisions [in regard to jurisdiction) has its counterpart in the extreme liberality of the provisions on recognition and enforcement, which are designed to allow judgment given in one Contracting State to run freely throughout the Community.'

Thus one finds that article 26 provides that a 'judgment given in a Contracting State shall be recognised in the other Contracting States without any special procedure being required'. Furthermore, in regard to enforcement, article 31 provides that a 'judgment given in a Contracting State and enforceable in that State shall be enforced in another Contracting State when, on the application of any interested party, it has been declared enforceable there' (amended by the San Sebastian Convention), and article 34 provides that the 'application [for enforcement] may be refused only for one of the reasons specified in articles 27 and 28 [we shall consider these in due course]'. And article 25 gives a very wide meaning to 'judgment'; it means 'any judgment given by a court or tribunal of a Contracting State, whatever the judgment may be called, including a decree, order, decision or writ of execution, as well as the determination of costs or expenses by an officer of the courts'.

## The breadth of the basic principle

You will have already realised that the basic principle that judgments rendered by EC courts should be recognised and enforced is very broad. However, there are three aspects of its breadth that deserve to be dealt with separately.

First, in our consideration of the recognition and enforcement of foreign judgment at common law we saw that the basic rule was that the foreign court had to have jurisdiction in the eyes of English law. Under the Convention, however, the English court is generally precluded from inquiring into the jurisdiction (in the eyes of English law or its own law) of the foreign court, the principle being that the judgment-granting court will have applied the strict jurisdictional rules of the Convention carefully, and therefore it is not necessary to go into the question again. Thus article 28(3) provides that (subject to an exception that we do not need to consider presently): 'The jurisdiction of the court of the State in which the judgment was given may not be reviewed; [and] the test of public policy referred to in Article 27(1) [which allows the refusal of recognition on public policy grounds] may not be applied to the rules relating to jurisdiction.'

However, and this is the second aspect of the breadth of the basic principle, if the judgment-recognising court is precluded from reviewing the jurisdiction of the judgment-granting court, what prevents the judgment-granting court from exercising jurisdiction on an 'exorbitant' ground such as the service of the writ outside the jurisdiction under RSC O.11 or taking jurisdiction on the ground of the plaintiff's nationality under article 14 of the French Code Civil? Article 3, as we have seen (in Chapter 4), provides that the various 'exorbitant' jurisdictions of the Contracting States cannot be used where the defendant is 'domiciled' in one of the Contracting States. Nothing, however, prevents a Contracting State from exercising an 'exorbitant' jurisdiction against a defendant who is not 'domiciled' anywhere in the EC (article 4). And the judgment so obtained will then be recognised throughout the EC because of the provisions of the Convention!

Let us make this clear with an example. D may be domiciled in New York and not 'domiciled' anywhere in the EC. He is sued by P in the French courts which exercise jurisdiction on the grounds of P's French nationality. The judgment of the French court obtained in this way will be recognised throughout the EC. Following much criticism from non-Contracting States, article 59 partially addresses this problem by providing that Contracting States may enter into bilateral conventions with non-Contracting States, not to recognise

> 'judgments given in other Contracting States against defendants domiciled or habitually resident in the [non-Contracting State] ... where ... the judgment could only be founded on a ground of a jurisdiction specified in the second paragraph of Article 3 [this is the article that lists the various forms of 'exorbitant' jurisdiction in the EC]'.

At the time of writing, however, although negotiations are proceeding with a number of countries the United Kingdom has not entered into any such conventions. (There is, however, such a convention in force between Norway, Sweden, Denmark, Finland and Iceland.)

Thirdly, as we have seen, 'judgment' is very widely defined. The significance of this is that proceedings for enforcement under the Convention are not limited to money judgments (as is the position under the common law and the Foreign Judgments (Reciprocal Enforcement) Act 1933).

Note, however, the following limitation. In *Owens Bank Ltd* v *Fulvio Bracco and Another* (1994) The Times 3 February the European Court of Justice held (on a reference from the House of Lords ([1992] 2 All ER 193)) that provisions of the Convention applied only to the recognition and enforcement of the judgments of courts of Contracting States; the Brussels Convention laid down no rules for determining the forum for proceedings for the recognition and enforcement of judgments given in non-Contracting States. Thus articles 21, 22 and 23 did not apply to proceedings, or issues arising in proceedings, in Contracting States concerning the recognition and enforcement of judgments given in civil and commercial matters in non-Contracting States. See the discussion above in section 4.2 *Lis alibi pendens* for the facts and the detail of this case.

## Procedure for enforcement

Just as is the case under the Foreign Judgments (Reciprocal Enforcement) Act 1933, the basic procedure is to apply to the specified court for registration of the judgment (in the case of England this is the High Court of Justice (article 37)). Although the procedure for making the application for enforcement is governed by the 'law of the State in which enforcement is sought' (article 33), article 34 provides: 'The court applied to shall give its decision without delay; [and] the party against whom enforcement is sought shall not at this stage of the proceedings be entitled to make any submissions on the application.' In other words, in order to ensure that the defendant does not remove his assets from the state where the judgment is sought to be enforced, he need not be informed of the impending registration and is not heard until the judgment is registered. However, articles 27 and 28 specify certain circumstances in which the judgment 'shall not be recognised'. We shall consider these in detail later. Should the application for enforcement be refused, then the applicant has a right of appeal to the High Court under article 40.

Once the judgment is registered, then s4(3) of the Civil Jurisdiction and Judgments Act 1982 provides that 'for the purposes of its enforcement, [it shall] be of the same force and effect, ... as if the judgment had been originally given by the registering court'. However, this does not mean that the defendant is without remedy.

First, if 'enforcement is authorised, the party against whom enforcement is sought may appeal against the decision within one month of service thereof' [and] two months if 'that party is domiciled in a Contracting State other than that in which the decision authorising enforcement was given'. This appeal is to the court specified in article 37, and in the case of England and Wales this is the High Court of Justice. A further appeal by either party is allowed to the Court of Appeal (or by the 'leap frog' procedure to the House of Lords) but only on a point of law (articles 37 and 41, and s6 of the Civil Jurisdiction and Judgments Act 1982). Where there is an appeal against an enforcement order, then article 39 provides: 'No measures of enforcement may be taken other than protective measures taken against the property of the party against whom enforcement is sought.'

Secondly, the court that is asked to recognise or enforce a judgment may stay the proceedings 'if an ordinary appeal against the judgment has been lodged' (articles 30 and 38). Obviously an appeal against the judgment in the judgment-granting state is envisaged here, but the concept of an 'ordinary appeal' is a Community concept not drawn from the laws of the national States (*International Diamond Supplies* v *Riva* [1977] ECR 2175). It is clear that the concept has a wide meaning and, provided that the process could result in the annulment of the original judgment, it will be considered an 'ordinary appeal'. Although the concept of the 'ordinary appeal' could have been applied in the United Kingdom, both article 30 and article 38 make special provision for judgments given in the United Kingdom (and Ireland). Article 30 (which applies to recognition) provides that the proceedings may be stayed in such cases 'if enforcement is suspended in the State in which the judgment was given by reason of an appeal', and article 38 provides that 'any form of appeal available in the State in which it was given [ie Ireland or the United Kingdom] shall be treated as an ordinary appeal'.

A decision not to stay proceedings under article 38 is not appealable under article 37: *Van Dalfsen* v *Van Loon* (C–183/190) [1992] ILPr 5 (ECJ).

In *Petereit* v *Babcock International Holdings Ltd* [1990] 1 WLR 350 Anthony Diamond QC sitting as a deputy High Court Judge delivered a thoughtful judgment about the principles that should guide a court asked to enforce a judgment and considering a stay under article 38. What had happened was that the plaintiff (the receiver of a bankrupt German firm) had obtained a judgment against the defendant in Germany for DM40m and sought to enforce that judgment against the defendant (an English company). The defendant had appealed against the judgment in Germany.

However, the plaintiff sought to enforce the judgment against the defendant in England. The judgment was registered in terms of article 4, and the defendant appealed to the High Court of Justice (articles 36 and 37) seeking a stay of the enforcement on the ground that an appeal had been lodged in Germany. But what principles should guide the court in deciding whether to grant a stay in terms of article 38?

Anthony Diamond QC drew three conclusions from his perusal of the Conventions and the other relevant materials (see at 358I and 359F):

'(i) that the enforcing court has a general and unfettered discretion under the Convention to stay the enforcement proceedings if an appeal is pending in the state in which judgment was obtained; (ii) that a judgment obtained in a contracting state is to be regarded as prima facie enforceable, and accordingly the enforcing court should not adopt a general practice of depriving a successful plaintiff of the fruits of the judgment by an imposition of a more or less automatic stay, merely on the ground that there is a pending appeal; (iii) that the purpose of articles 30 and 38 is to protect the position of a defendant in an appropriate case and to ensure that, if the appeal succeeds, then the defendant will be able to enforce the order of the appeal court and will not be deprived of the fruits of enforcement of the judgment. It seems to me that the court's discretion to grant a stay should be exercised with this purpose in mind.'

The learned deputy High Court Judge went on to point out that there were two courses of action open to the enforcing court in terms of article 38: either the actions could be stayed (either unconditionally or subject to conditions to protect the plaintiff) or the defendant's position could be protected by making enforcement subject to appropriate conditions.

The crucial difference between a stay subject to conditions and enforcement subject to conditions is whether the plaintiff or the defendant has the use of the disputed sum of money during the period between the enforcement proceedings and the giving of final judgment in the appeal court. Now suitable conditions could ensure that appropriate interest on the sum was paid, but this did not take account of differences in the positions of the parties. In the instant case the defendant was a company actively involved in business, and removing DM40m from that business would, even if it was repaid if the German appeal succeeded, have a deleterious affect. On the other hand the plaintiff as liquidator of the company did not have a vital need for these funds and would suffer no hardship if payment of them was delayed until the appeal was dismissed. A further factor was that the defendant might suffer an exchange loss if forced to pay now and then recover in due course, while the plaintiff would not. (This does not strike me as a persuasive consideration: surely it could have been guarded against by suitable conditions.) Taking all these considerations into account, enforcement was stayed subject to conditions to protect the position of the plaintiff. The prime condition was the provision of a guarantee by the defendant to pay, if the appeal went against him, the full principal sum as well as interest and legal costs. The costs of the enforcement proceedings, however, were made to depend upon the outcome of the German appeal.

In *Van Dalfsen* v *Van Loon (C–183/90)* [1992] ILPr 5 the European Court of Justice had to consider the principles governing the exercise of the article 38 discretion to stay. In this case a Belgian court ordered Van Dalfsen (domiciled in the Netherlands) to pay certain rent arrears to Van Loon (domiciled in Belgium). This judgment was provisionally enforceable even though the court recognised Van Dalfsen's right to reimbursement for certain moneys expended on the leased property. Van Loon now sought to enforce this judgment in the Netherlands.

Van Dalfsen, however, asked the Zwolle court (in the Netherlands) to stay enforcement of the judgment in accordance with article 38(1) on the ground, inter alia, that an appeal had been lodged in Belgium. The Zwolle court, however, refused the application to stay the proceedings but made enforcement conditional upon the provision by Van Loon of a bank guarantee to secure Van Dalfsen's alternative claim. Van Dalfsen appealed further to the Hoge Raad which referred several questions to the ECJ, of which only one need concern us. Could the Zwolle court in exercising its article 38(1) powers take into account circumstances which the foreign court had already taken into account in its judgment? And in particular could it base those decisions on the chances of success in the appeal that had been lodged in the foreign court?

The ECJ held that article 38(1) must be interpreted strictly to ensure that the effectiveness of the article 31 procedure was not impaired. If the court in making its decision whether to stay or not could take into account arguments already considered by the foreign court, there was a real risk that it would embark upon a review of the substance of the foreign court's judgment, and that, of course, was prohibited by the Convention (article 29). Hence only such submissions as the party lodging the appeal was unable to make before the court of the State in which the judgment was given may be made.

This approach of the ECJ is probably not inconsistent with the approach outlined by Anthony Diamond QC in *Petereit v Babcock International Holdings Ltd* (above), provided that the considerations that weighed with the learned judge in that case (essentially to ensure that the defendant, if successful before the foreign court on appeal, will not be deprived of the fruits of that success by being forced to pay the judgment before that appeal was decided) were not before the foreign court. But where these self-same matters were before the foreign court, then they cannot influence the decision whether to stay under article 38.

One final point on enforcement. If a matter falls within the Convention, then the only way in which it can be enforced in the United Kingdom is by way of the procedure just outlined. It is no longer possible to commence an action on the judgment at common law. This is the result of the decision of the European Court in *De Wolf v Cox* [1976] ECR 1759. And s34 of the Civil Jurisdiction and Judgments Act 1982 prevents reliance upon the original cause of action.

## Grounds on which recognition or enforcement may be refused

The Convention spells out at a number of points that 'under no circumstances may a foreign judgment be reviewed as to its substance' (article 29, and see article 34). Thus the foreign judgment cannot be reviewed on its merits. However, articles 27 and 28 contain a number of grounds on which recognition and enforcement shall be refused.

These are (under article 27) the following:

1. where 'such recognition is contrary to public policy in the state in which recognition is sought'. This is relatively straightforward, but note that the consensus is that since the Convention makes no specific reference to refusal of recognition or enforcement on the ground of fraud, fraud is taken to be included in 'public policy' (see Morris, op cit, 132 and *Kendall v Kendall* [1977] Fam 208).

   In *Interdesco SA v Nullifire Ltd* [1992] ILPr 97; [1992] 1 Lloyd's Rep 180 Phillips J had to consider the circumstances in which fraud was a defence under article 27.

   This was an application to enforce in England a judgment obtained in the French courts. The English defendant (Nullifire) sought to resist enforcement on several grounds, including fraud.

Nullifire believed, and had evidence that suggested, that Interdesco had misled the French court in regard to whether it had had dealings with Nullifire's competitors. Would the generous common law approach to fraud as a defence to a foreign judgment be applied? In the context of the Brussels Convention Phillips J held that different considerations applied. Generally, 'it accords with the spirit of the Convention that all issues [including fraud] should, so far as possible, be dealt with by the State enjoying the original jurisdiction. [Moreover,] the courts of that State are likely to be better able to assess whether the original judgment was procured by fraud.' In reliance upon the Schlosser Report the judge held that it would not be contrary to English public policy to enforce the judgment allegedly tainted by fraud. It should be noted, though, that Nullifire had further remedies before the French courts to set aside the judgment; and, of course, articles 29 and 34 require that 'under no circumstances' should a foreign judgment be reviewed as to substance, and allowing fraud as a defence would often require precisely that review as to substance. (*Interdesco* v *Nullifire* was followed by the Court of Appeal in *Société d'Informatique Service Realisation Organisation* v *Ampersand Software BV* [1994] ILPr 55 which dealt with alleged fraud by the expert appointed by the French courts in an action about breaches of copyright in computer programmes; the defendant had to pursue his remedies for the fraud before the French courts. However, the enforcement proceedings were stayed in England while the French appeal was pursued.)

But it plainly follows that the defence of fraud under the public policy head of article 27(1) is much narrower than the defence available under the common law.

Note, however, that the European Court has generally interpreted the concept of public policy narrowly (*Van Duyn* v *Home Office* [1974] ECR 1337), and that article 28(3) provides that public policy is not to be applied to the question of jurisdiction.

2. where the foreign judgment was given in default of appearance, if the defendant was 'not duly served' with the document instituting the proceedings in the foreign court 'in sufficient time to enable him to arrange for his defence'. The concept of 'due service' must comply with the law of the judgment-granting court, but that of 'sufficient time' is for the judgment-recognising court (see *Klomps* v *Michel* [1981] ECR 1593 and *Pendy Plastic Products* v *Pluspunkt* [1982] ECR 2723). In *Thierry Noirhomme* v *David Walklate* [1992] 1 Lloyd's Rep 427 a defendant who sought to resist enforcement on the ground that he was 'not duly served' received short shrift when it was shown that he had received the documents (by post), but had ignored them. The applicable rules (the Hague Convention of 1965) allowed service by post.

The European Court interpreted article 27(2) in *Minalmet GmbH* v *Brandeis Ltd* [1993] ILPr 132 and held that where the proceedings did not come to the notice of the defendant in time to defend himself at trial, there is no compliance with article 27(2), even if the defendant learnt of the judgment in time to apply to have it set aside. Thus an English default judgment which had been obtained by Brandeis against Minalmet in the following circumstances was not enforceable in Germany: a notice informing the recipient that the documents commencing litigation were available at the local post office had been pushed through the door of the company's premises, however, the company claimed to have been unaware of this. Did this constitute proper service of the writ instituting proceedings in Germany? Article 5(a) of the Hague Convention on the Service of Judicial and Extrajudicial Documents Abroad provided that German Civil Law governed service of the documents; and under that law substituted service was only possible when the notice of the documents' presence at the post office was left at the private address of a director of the company rather than its business address. Nor did it make a difference that Minalmet had subsequently learnt of the judgment and it was still open to it to apply to the English court to set aside the default judgment. There had not been 'due service' for the purposes of article 27(2).

This result is plainly correct: if the company was right that it had not learnt of the impending proceedings before they took place through a failure of proper service, then they had been deprived of the opportunity to defend themselves which article 27(2) protected. The ability to apply to set aside the judgment is no substitute for that.

Note, further, that the French Cour de Cassation in *Polypetrol* v *Société Generale Routiere* [1993] ILPr 107 held that the document which commenced proceedings, was required to contain particulars of the subject matter of the claim or there was no compliance with article 27(2). In addition, in that case the judgment (from the German courts) that was sought to be enforced in France did not state the reasoning on which it was based, and enforcing such a judgment was contrary to French public policy and so would be denied enforcement under article 27(1).

3. if the judgment is irreconcilable with a judgment given in a dispute between the same parties in the State in which the recognition is sought, ie the recognising court does not need to give preference to the foreign judgment over one of its own. In *Hoffmann* v *Krieg* Case 145/86 [1988] ECR 645 the European Court applied article 27(3) in the following circumstances: a wife had obtained a maintenance order from the courts in Germany and sought to enforce that order against her husband in the Netherlands in terms of article 31. However, the courts of the Netherlands had, shortly after the original maintenance order had been made, dissolved the marriage between the parties. (This dissolution of the marriage fell outside the terms of the Brussels Convention and was not recognised in Germany.) The court held that a foreign decision ordering a husband to pay maintenance to his wife, pursuant to his obligations of maintenance flowing from the marriage, was irreconcilable, for the purposes of article 27(3) of the Convention, with a national decision decreeing a divorce between the spouses concerned.

There was a straightforward application of *Hoffmann* v *Krieg* by the English courts in *Macaulay* v *Macaulay* (1990) The Times 29 November where an Irish maintenance order against the husband was held to be irreconcilable with an English divorce decree. Two points may be noted: first, in addition to enforcement under the Brussels Convention, Irish maintenance orders are also enforceable in England under the Maintenance Orders (Reciprocal Enforcement) Act 1972 (see Chapter 9.5). However, one of the grounds on which the enforcement of the Irish order could be resisted under the relevant Order in Council (Reciprocal Enforcement of Maintenance Orders (Republic of Ireland) Order (SI 1974 No 2140), made under the Maintenance Orders (Reciprocal Enforcement) Act 1972, was that the order was 'irreconcilable with a judgment given in the United Kingdom in proceedings between the same parties' (article 6). The court gave a uniform interpretation to these words and to article 27(3) of the Brussels Convention, for to hold otherwise 'would destroy the consistency of the approach' of the Convention and the Order in Council. Secondly, the court pointed out that the erstwhile wife was not without a remedy; she could apply to the English courts for a maintenance order against her husband under the Matrimonial Causes Act 1973.

4. similarly, where there is a judgment of a non-Contracting State that has earlier given an irreconcilable judgment that has to be recognised in the judgment-recognising state.

5. where the judgment-granting state has decided a preliminary question 'concerning the status or legal capacity of natural persons, rights in property arising out of a matrimonial relationship, wills of succession in a way that conflicts with a rule of the private international law' of the judgment-recognising state 'unless the same result would have been reached by the application of the rules of private international law of that State'.

It may be noted that article 27, subject to certain qualifications in regard to parties and cause of action, provides for the situation where there is a conflict between a judgment given in a non-Contracting State and a judgment given in a Contracting State (article 27(5)), as well as for the situation where there is a conflict between a judgment of the lex fori and a Contracting State. Article 27 does not, however, provide for the situation where there is a conflict between two judgments emanating from different Contracting States (other than that of the forum). The Jenard Report suggests that this difficulty can be dealt with by givng an extensive interpretation to article 27(3) so that the words 'judgment *given* in a dispute between the same parties in the State in which recognition is sought' include a judgment given in another Contracting State but which is entitled to recognition in the State in which recognition is sought. There is a little warrant in the words of article 27(3) for such an interpretation, but at least such an interpretation would avoid difficulty and absurdity. The question is discussed by Cheshire, at 431. Note that at common law where there are two competing judgments from courts of competent jurisdiction, the earlier judgment generally prevails: *Showlag v Mansour* (1994) The Times 29 March (discussed above), ie a rule analogous to that of article 27(5) is adopted.

## Recognition and enforcement of English judgments in other parts of the United Kingdom

This subject is now covered by s18 and Schedules 6 (money judgments) and 7 (non-money judgments) of the Civil Jurisdiction and Judgments Act 1982 (replacing the Judgments Extension Act 1868 and the Inferior Courts Judgments Extension Act 1882). The extension of non-money judgments is the principal innovation. In broad terms a certificate of the judgment from the judgment-granting court is registered with the judgment-recognising court. The registration can be carried out by a court official; it does not have to be done by the judge. Thus this is an easier procedure than that required of judgments from other EC states.

## Maintenance orders

Special provisions apply to the enforcement of maintenance orders; these are to be found in s5 of the Civil Jurisdiction and Judgments Act 1982. The major difference is that enforcement takes place through the magistrate's court, not the High Court.

## Provisional and protective measures

Article 24 provides that application 'may be made to the courts of a Contracting State for such provision, including protective measures [such as *Mareva* injunctions], as may be available under the law of that State, even if, under this Convention, the courts of another Contracting State have jurisdiction as to the substance of the mattter'. In addition, such provisional or protective measures if made in one Contracting State are enforceable in another Contracting State. However, they are not enforceable unless the defendant has been given an opportunity to be heard (*Denilauler v SNC Couchet Frères* [1980] ECR 1553).

# 9

# Family Law

9.1 Introduction

9.2 The validity of marriage

9.3 Polygamy

9.4 Divorce and the nullity of marriage

9.5 Maintenance: the recognition and enforcement of foreign orders

9.6 Legitimacy, adoption, custody and guardianship

9.7 The effect of marriage on property

## 9.1 Introduction

This is one of the most important but also one of the more difficult areas of private international law. It is important because, as is obvious, men and women of different domiciles and different nationalities may fall in love and marry in the country in which they then happen to be. Years later the validity of their marriage may be called in question before the courts of yet a further country (which may be, but need not be, the court of their present residence or domicile or nationality). It is far from obvious what law should determine such issues. Or perhaps the parties have been divorced by a court in another country; will that divorce decree be recognised by the lex fori?

The issues raised will concern not only the husband and wife but also their children and their property. It is self-evident that the lex fori is not necessarily the appropriate law to apply, but it is far from self-evident what law should be applied. The need for a sophisticated set of choice of law rules is obvious. As Mr Justice Jackson said in the American case of *Estin* v *Estin* 334 US 541 (1948) at 553: 'If there is one thing that people are entitled to expect of their lawmakers, it is rules of law that will entitle individuals to tell whether they are married and, if so, to whom.'

However, it must be said that the law is not as clear and satisfactory as it should be. There are two related reasons for this. The first is that there is no clear concept of marriage: the different legal systems of the world mean very different things by 'marriage'. Under some legal systems monogamy is the heart of marriage; under other legal systems marriage is polygamous or polyandrous. Under some legal systems death is the only event that can end marriage, but in others it may be simply by the one party expressing the view (with the required formality) that he wishes the marriage to be at an end. In others again a web of complex rules surrounds the possibility of divorce. So it is difficult to develop a set of choice of law rules appropriate for dealing with such diverse juristic concepts.

But, secondly, the nature of marriage and family relationship generally are in many contexts core concepts that define the structure and nature of that society; thus not surprisingly public policy raises its head with some considerable force. To what extent should English courts recognise polygamous marriages? Should English courts recognise divorces granted in non-judicial proceedings or even where there are no proceedings at all? Thus even clear simple choice of law rules would find themselves being overturned by considerations of public policy. Unfortunately, English judges have often been coy about the public policy considerations that have influenced their decisions in this area. Instead, in order to achieve their public policy objectives, they have warped and bent and twisted the law away from sound principle and rational development. It would be far better if the judges were more straightforward and stated frankly in their judgments the extent to which public policy had influenced their judgments. Anyway, putting it simply, the law in this area is a mess!

## 9.2 The validity of marriage

### *Formal validity: governed by the lex loci celebrationis*

**How the distinction between formal and essential validity arose**
Let us take a straightforward example: H and W, who are both domiciled in France, meet and fall in love while both have temporary jobs in Italy. A very attractive offer of a job in England is made to H, so he and W decide to marry in Italy and to move to England. They do this and in due course acquire a domicile in England. Many years later they seek a divorce from the English courts, but before they can be divorced they have to show that they are married. But what law should be used to determine the validity of their marriage, and are all aspects of that question to be governed by the same law?

For many years the answer to this question was straightforward: the law of the place of celebration of the marriage (the lex loci celebrationis – in our example, Italian law) determined whether the marriage was valid: *Scrimshire* v *Scrimshire* (1792) 2 Hagg Con 395. (For more modern authority in favour of the lex loci celebrationis – but restricting it to matters of form – see *Berthiaume* v *Dastous* [1930] AC 79 (especially at 83).) This simple rule – easy to apply and clear – still applies in some countries but no longer in England. Here it has been complicated by the addition of an extra rule to deal with matters of essential validity (including capacity to marry).

The problem with the simple rule was that the lex domicilii was too easily evaded. Consider the facts of *Brook* v *Brook* (1861) 9 HLC 193, 4 LT 93 (HL). During the 19th century (and in some respects still today) the English rules on consanguinity and affinity were rather stricter than they were in continental countries, especially in Scandinavia. In particular, in England it was not possible for a man to marry his deceased wife's sister. This was, however, exactly what William Charles Brook had done in 1850 three years after the death of his first wife. He and Emily Armitage (who were both domiciled in England) had married in Denmark (during a short visit to that country) where such marriages were lawful; after the marriage the couple returned (as they had intended) to England where they lived (and where the three children of the marriage were born) until both died in an outbreak of cholera in 1855. After the death as an infant of one of the children of the second marriage the surviving children began to fight over the division of the estate; a crucial issue was whether the children of the second marriage were legitimate or illegitimate, and that depended upon whether their parents' marriage was valid.

But was the marriage valid? If one applied the lex loci celebrationis then there was little doubt that the marriage would be valid; there was no impediment to the marriage under the law of Denmark. In today's tolerant atmosphere in England it may seem surprising that the question of 'marriage with deceased wife's sister' should have raised great passions, but it did in the 19th century. After *Brook* v *Brook* almost annual attempts were made in Parliament to allow such marriages, but it was not until 1907 that they became lawful (and it was 1921 before a woman could marry her deceased husband's brother). (See Morris, *The Conflict of Laws*, 3rd ed, 1984, at 162; he also points out that the problem was mentioned in Gilbert and Sullivan's *Iolanthe*!) Anyway the House of Lords felt strongly in *Brook* v *Brook* that the marriage should be held void and the children of the second marriage were consequently illegitimate.

Now one way in which the House of Lords might have achieved this end would have been to rely upon public policy as such: upholding such a marriage was repugnant to fundamental English ideas of public policy and could not be tolerated for that reason (see Chapter 2, section 2.2). Today such an approach would probably be adopted to the marriage of a brother and a sister. But this was not, I believe, the crux of their complaint: the House of Lords, although partly concerned about public policy, was primarily concerned that the ordinary English rules were being evaded. After all, the court made it plain that it would not have nullified the marriage in Denmark of a widower with his deceased wife's sister if they had been domiciled in Denmark at the time, even if they had subsequently come to reside in England. Furthermore, Lord Campbell said: 'No civilised state can allow its domiciled subjects or citizens, by making a temporary visit to a foreign country, to enter into a contract [eg marriage] to be performed in the place of domicile, if the contract is forbidden by the place of domicile ...'.

The trouble was that, as we have seen (see Chapter 2, section 2.2), English law does not have a doctrine of the evasion of the law, so the House of Lords could not proceed in that way. Instead, it proceeded to restrict the basic rule of the lex loci celebrationis to matters of form and stated that 'the essentials of the contract depend upon the lex domicilii ... and [the law of the place] in which the matrimonial residence is contemplated'. This led to the main challenge to the orthodox rules: the suggestion that the lex domicilii or the law of the intended matrimonial home determined matters of essential validity. We shall consider essential validity in full below.

### The application of renvoi in this area

One further point on the application of the lex loci celebrationis to test formal validity: the consensus seems to be that renvoi (see Chapter 2.3) should apply in this area. Thus even if the marriage is formally invalid by the domestic law of the place of celebration, but that law would consider it valid (in an application of its rules of private international law), then that marriage should be held formally valid by the English courts: *Taczanowska* v *Taczanowski* [1957] P 301 at 305 and 318. Of course, this question may arise in the converse form: suppose that the domestic requirements of the lex loci are complied with, but the lex loci would refer the matter to another law under which the marriage would be void; is the marriage void or valid? In principle if renvoi is applied in the one case, then it should be applied in the other; thus the marriage should be held void. This is, it is believed, consistent with *Hooper* v *Hooper* [1959] 2 All ER 575, although the case is poorly reported.

To sum up: we have seen that in the mid-19th century, for reasons associated with a dislike of evasion of the law, the lex loci celebrationis was restricted to matters of formal validity. Essential validity was determined by the lex domicilii of the parties at the time of marriage or possibly by the law of the intended matrimonial home. However, there are a number of exceptions to the lex loci celebrationis rule, viz, occasions on which the marriage is upheld by English courts even though it does not comply with the lex loci celebrationis.

### *Exceptions to the lex loci celebrationis rule*

### 'Consular marriages'

The Foreign Marriage Act 1892 provides that where one of the intending parties is a British subject, their marriage may be solemnised outside the United Kingdom by British Ambassadors and High Commissioners, and by consuls who have been duly authorised by a warrant issued by the Secretary of State. The Secretary has issued appropriate warrants to consular officers in many countries (mostly but not exclusively in the Middle East). Although it is technically possible, consular officers have not been authorised in Commonwealth countries.

The Foreign Marriage Act itself lays down the necessary formalities to be observed, and these naturally will be different from those prevailing in the place where the marriage is celebrated. Consular marriages will, however, be upheld in English courts so this implies a deviation from the lex loci rule in regard to these marriages.

Note, however, that under the Foreign Marriages Order 1972 (SI 1970 No 1539 made under the authority of s21 of the 1892 Act) the consular officer has to be satisfied not only that at least one of the parties is a British subject, and that the parties will be regarded as validly married 'by the law of the country to which each party belongs', but also that the authorities in the foreign country 'will not object to the solemnisation of the marriage and that insufficient facilities exist for the marriage of the parties under the law of that country'. Furthermore, a consular marriage officer may refuse to solemnise a marriage if he considers that it 'would be inconsistent with international law or the comity of nations'. Thus, although many of these provisions are vague and uncertain, it is clear that regard can be had to the provisions of lex loci when deciding whether to celebrate a consular marriage.

### Marriages of British servicemen and women serving abroad

The Foreign Marriage Act 1892 provides that when a marriage is celebrated in foreign territory (excluding the Commonwealth) by a chaplain in the British forces (or a person authorised by the commanding officer of the relevant forces) and at least one of the parties is in the British forces or is employed in a related capacity (which has to be specified in an Order in Council), then the marriage shall be valid as if celebrated in the United Kingdom. It is not necessary that either of the parties should be a British subject. Once more it is plain that a marriage celebrated contrary to the provisions of the lex loci may be upheld in English courts.

### Marriages celebrated in conditions in which compliance with the local form is impossible

Rather benevolently, the courts have been prepared to hold that where there is no local form of marriage (or the local form presents some insuperable difficulty, eg, only permitting polygamy or marriage according to a particular religious rite) then it will be sufficient if the marriage complies with the formal requirement of the common law. These, it turns out, once the statutory encrustations of the last two hundred years are stripped away, are few in number: essentially all that is required is that the parties should agree in each other's presence to take each other as man and wife (per verba et de praesenti). In *R* v *Millis* (1843–4) 10 Cl & F 534 the House of Lords held that the common law required that the marriage should take place before an episcopally ordained clergyman. However, it is now universally agreed that this decision was erroneous, and it is now clear that an episcopally ordained clergyman is not essential where one is not available, or his presence would be inappropriate because, for instance, of the religion of the parties: *Isaac Penhas* v *Tan Soo Eng* [1953] AC 304 (PC). Consistently with these principles the courts have upheld marriages celebrated between two Canadian nationals (one domiciled in Canada and the other domiciled in England) in the province of Hupeh in China performed by a clergyman (not episcopally ordained) from the Church of Scotland (*Wolfenden* v *Wolfenden* [1946] P 61) and between a Chinese woman (who was not a Christian) and a Jew in which the ceremony was a mixture of traditional Jewish and Chinese ritual (*Isaac Penhas* v *Tan Soo Eng*, above). (These were both cases, however, in which it was clear that the common law applied (because of the provisions of various treaties and charters) and the question was simply, what did the common law require in the circumstances?)

Similar principles have also been relied upon by the courts in considering various cases that arose out of the chaos in Europe following the Second World War. Many thousands of marriages invalid under whatever local form survived were entered into informally by persons of diverse nationality swept far from their homes by the misfortunes of war. The courts created an exception where one of the parties (in essence the husband) was a member of the belligerent occupying forces or forces associated with the occupying forces (or perhaps even escaped prisoners of war). In these circumstances, since the husband is present under orders he is taken not to have submitted to the lex loci and so it does not apply to him; thus he can marry if he complies with the common law formalities alone. The leading case is *Taczanowska* v *Taczanowski*, above, where the Court of Appeal upheld a marriage celebrated in 1946 in Italy by a Roman Catholic priest (serving as a Polish Army chaplain) between a Polish officer serving with the British Army and a Polish civilian. The marriage did not comply with the lex loci (and there would have been no insuperable difficulty in complying with it), but it was none the less upheld. (The marriage was also not valid by Polish law.)

This is a remarkable principle, and it has been much criticised. As Morris, op cit at 156, remarks:

> 'It is indeed a remarkable proposition that a marriage celebrated in a foreign country between persons domiciled in another foreign country who have never visited England in their lives, and may never do so, can derive formal validity from the compliance with English domestic law as it existed 200 years before the marriage. It cannot be supposed that such parties ever intended to submit to English common law. If the lex loci is inapplicable for any reason, it would seem more sensible to refer the formal validity of the marriage to the law of the parties' domicile; but this ... the courts decline to do.'

Consequently, the principle of *Taczanowska*, although followed in a number of cases – *Kochanski* v *Kochanska* [1958] P 147 (upholding a marriage in a Polish displaced persons' camp in Germany; this seems to be more of an extension of *Taczanowska*, for neither party was a member of the army of occupation) and *Preston* v *Preston* [1963] P 411 (a marriage in a Polish military camp, in fact a different part of the same camp as that which featured in *Kochanski*) – has been restricted in other cases. For instance, in *Lazarewicz* v *Lazarewicz* [1962] P 171 the *Taczanowska* principle was held not to apply where one of the parties was actually a national of the country whose local form was being disregarded. Furthermore, in that case the husband, although a soldier, was not 'within the lines of the army of occupation, but [just] a sojourner'.

Although special rules are perhaps justified on policy grounds both where there is no suitable local form and in the circumstances of Europe after the Second World War, it must be frankly admitted that the juristic basis of these exceptions to the rule of the lex loci celebrationis is far from plausible or persuasive.

## Essential validity: probably governed by the antenuptial domicile of the parties

### General

Let us leave formal validity now and consider essential validity (or capacity to marry). We shall take it for granted for the time being that the distinction between matters which relate to form and matters which relate to substance is clear and presents little difficulty. (In fact, it does present difficulties but we will discuss them later.)

Although the matter cannot be taken to be settled, the balance of authority in the decided cases (as well as much of the academic writing) is in favour of the 'dual domicile' text as being the orthodox test of the validity of marriage. The matter is not entirely beyond doubt because, although there are many cases which can be cited in support of the 'dual domicile' test, it is rare for couples to marry and not to intend to make their matrimonial home where either the husband or the wife is domiciled. Thus many of the cases, although they may purport with a greater or lesser degree of clarity to apply the 'dual domicile' test, would have had the same result if the 'intended matrimonial home' test had been applied. For instance, in *Brook* v *Brook*, *Mette* v *Mette* (1859) 1 Sw & Tr 416, *Re Paine* [1940] Ch 46 and *Pugh* v *Pugh* [1951] P 482 the results would have been the same whatever test was applied. And only in *Re Paine* and *Pugh* v *Pugh* was the 'dual domicile' test unequivocally adopted in the judgments.

On the other hand *Padolecchia* v *Padolecchia* [1968] P 314 appears only compatible with the 'dual domicile' test. Here the husband's domicile (in Italy, and under Italian law he was incapable of marrying) differed from the intended matrimonial home (in Denmark). Since the court found that it could decide the case without proper proof of whether the husband had capacity under the law of Denmark, and relied solely on the domiciliary law, this decision must be taken as strong support for the 'dual domicile' test.

Furthermore, *Sottomayor* v *de Barros (No 1)* (1877) 3 PD 1 (CA) is inconsistent with the intended matrimonial home test. What had happened here was that two cousins with strong Portuguese connections had married in England and lived together there for six years (although without consummating their marriage). Under Portuguese law a marriage between cousins was not valid unless Papal consent (which had not been obtained) was granted. In these preliminary proceedings the parties were assumed to be domiciled in Portugal (although their intended matrimonial home was presumably England), and their incapacity under Portuguese law was held applicable. Had the 'intended matrimonial home' test been followed then the Portuguese incapacity would have been irrelevant. (Note that this is *Sottomayor* v *de Barros (No 1)*; we shall discuss *Sottomayor* v *de Barros (No 2)* below.)

Finally, *Shaw* v *Gould* (1868) LR 3 HL 55 is a decision of the House of Lords which appears inconsistent with the intended matrimonial home approach. There the woman's incapacity under her domiciliary law (English law, under which she was already married) prevented her from being able to marry validly in Scotland even though the intended matrimonial home was in Scotland.

It is on the basis of these cases that the orthodox view that the 'dual domicile' test is the correct one rests. However, there are a number of modern cases in which reliance has been placed, expressly or impliedly, upon the 'intended matrimonial home' test. These may be briefly mentioned, but none upsets the balance of authority in the cases discussed above. The test was preferred by the judges who heard both *Perrini* v *Perrini* [1979] Fam 84 (Sir George Baker P) and *Lawrence* v *Lawrence* [1985] Fam 106 and [1985] 3 WLR 125 (CA) (Lincoln J in the court below and Sir David Cairns in the Court of Appeal), but both these cases are explicable on other grounds (they are discussed below in section 9.4). The 'intended matrimonial home' test was also adopted in *Radwan* v *Radwan (No 2)* [1973] Fam 35 but was expressed to be limited to the question of capacity to contract a polygamous marriage (discussed below in section 9.3).

There have also been dicta from cases (and from academic writing: see, for instance, Fentiman (1985) 44 *CLJ* 256) which have suggested that 'a proper law of the marriage' – the law with which the marriage is most closely connected – should be sought and used to test the essential validity of the marriage. The dictum which most clearly supports this comes from *Vervaeke* v *Smith* [1983] 1 AC 145 where Lord Simon of Glaisdale spoke of the 'quintessential validity' of a marriage depending upon the law of the country 'with which the marriage has the most real and substantial connection'. However, the issues in that case were public policy and res judicata, not capacity to marry as such. The major difficulty with adopting such a proper law approach is its inherent uncertainty; how is one to know which law is the law to be used to test essential validity unless there is a clear and relatively mechanical rule that can be adopted to determine the issue? This is not a practical approach for a world in which men and women want and need to know quickly and cheaply whether their marriage is valid; they do not wish to have to pay a visit to the House of Lords, with all the expense that that entails, to discover with which law their relationship is most closely connected!

There is a range of difficulties associated with the 'intended matrimonial home' test too. The most obvious one is that it allows the parties to invest their marriage with a validity that it might not otherwise have simply by intending to live in a country where it would be valid. Moreover, what is the position if, although they intended to settle in a particular country after marriage, they never in fact do so, or perhaps only do so for a short time before deciding that that country is not for them? Furthermore, Collier makes the point (*The Conflict of Laws*, 1987, at 263) that the question of capacity does not always arrive after the event; it may arise before when the parties are in search of a clergyman or registrar to marry them. What if he does not believe them when they say that they are planning to live in a country where their marriage is valid even though it would be invalid under their domiciliary laws? Whatever the flaws in the law of domicile, at least everyone has a domicile at all times (see Chapter 3, section 3.2) so the 'dual domicile' test will work under all circumstances and in all places. It may not always give the answer that the parties desire, but that is a different matter.

### Characterisation as formal or essential validity

It will be recalled that we had earlier assumed that it was self-evident whether a matter related to formal validity or essential validity. However, although some matters are straightforward (the number of witnesses etc is plainly a matter of form, while whether the parties are too closely related to marry, or whether they are old enough to marry, is, public policy aside, a matter of essential validity), it is sometimes far from clear whether a matter relates to form or substance.

What we are concerned with here is actually a question of characterisation (see Chapter 2.3). Let us give an example from the decided cases: *Ogden* v *Ogden* [1908] P 46. What had happened was that a domiciled Frenchman had married a domiciled Englishwoman in England. He did not, however, obtain the consent of his surviving parent as required by the French Civil Code. Was this marriage valid? Now if the rule of French law requiring parental consent related to the essential validity of marriage, then, in principle, it should have applied to render the marriage void or at least voidable. On the other hand, if it related to formal validity, which was governed by English law, then the state of French law was irrelevant and the marriage was valid.

In the event the English court upheld the marriage, thus, in effect, characterising the French rule as relating to formalities rather than to capacity or essential validity. This seems artificial, but again note the influence of the external factors on the English judges: they would have had to have held invalid a marriage celebrated in England which was not contrary to English law. This, however, is consistent with the court's view of parental consent as shown in *Compton* v *Bearcroft* (1769) 2 Hagg Con 83; (1767) 2 Hagg Con 444. See also *Simonin* v *Mallac* (1860) 2 Sw & Tr 67.

Another possibly controversial classification is that adopted in *Apt* v *Apt* [1948] P 83: whether a marriage could be celebrated by proxy is a matter of formal, not essential, validity. Thus in this case a marriage celebrated in Argentina, in which the woman was not present but indicated her assent by proxy, was upheld even although proxy marriages were not allowed by English law. Note, of course, that if we were concerned with whether in fact the woman had consented (and not with the question of how she showed that consent), public policy questions would be raised.

### The precise meaning of the 'dual domicile' test

Two points should be noted under this head: first, where the husband and the wife have different antenuptial domiciles it is not enough that the one party should be free to marry; he or she must be free to marry the other party. This point may be illustrated by *Pugh* v *Pugh* (above). Here a British Army officer, domiciled in England, had married in Austria a girl of only fifteen years of age. She was domiciled in Hungary. Under Hungarian law the marriage had become valid (since it had not been set aside before she reached the age of 17), and it was valid under Austrian law. None the less the marriage was held void, since the Age of Marriage Act 1929 prohibited marriage 'between persons either of whom is under the age of sixteen'. Thus while the husband had capacity to marry under his lex domicilii, and the wife had capacity to marry under her lex domicilii, the marriage was still void because the husband did not have, under his lex domicilii, capacity to marry that particular wife.

Secondly, in principle and in practice it appears that renvoi (see Chapter 2.3) applies in this area. Thus even if one of the parties lacks capacity under his or her lex domicilii the marriage will be upheld if that lex domicilii would, in an application of its rules for choice of law, uphold the marriage. Thus in *R* v *Brentwood Superintendent Registrar of Marriages, ex parte Arias* [1968] 2 QB 956 a man was refused permission to marry in England in these circumstances: he was an Italian national but domiciled in Switzerland; he had previously been married but had been divorced in Switzerland. The difficulty was that Swiss law tested capacity to marry by the lex patriae (or national law), and at that time Italian law did not recognise divorce. Had the English court excluded renvoi, it would have looked no further than his lex domicilii and held that he was free to marry under Swiss law. But the court applied renvoi and considered what law the Swiss courts would apply to the issue, and then applied that law, viz Italian law. Note, however, that the result of this case has been overturned by legislation (see below in section 9.4).

**An exception to the rule of the 'dual domicile':** *Sottomayor* v *de Barros (No 2)*
The case of *Sottomayor* v *de Barros (No 1)* has already been mentioned above. *Sottomayor* v *de Barros (No 2)* concerned a later stage of the same proceedings. The facts were the same as set out above except that it had now been determined (contrary to the assumption in the first proceedings that both parties were domiciled in Portugal) that the husband was in fact domiciled in England although the wife was domiciled in Portugal. If the 'dual domicile' rule had been applied in the normal way the conclusion would have been readily reached that the marriage was void: although the husband had capacity to marry under his lex domicilii, the wife lacked that capacity under her lex domicilii. However, Sir James Hannan P upheld the marriage saying that 'injustice might be caused to our own subjects if a marriage [celebrated in England] were declared invalid on the ground that it was forbidden by the law of the domicil of one of the parties'. Although the precise reasoning of the court could be clearer, the result of the case is generally taken to mean that where a marriage is celebrated (i) in England between persons (ii) one of whom is domiciled in England then, in effect, capacity is simply tested by English law. (Strictly speaking the case directs that the validity of the marriage is not affected by any incapacity that exists under the foreign law, but which does not exist under English law.)

This rule has been much criticised: it shows an unjustified preference for English law over and above the laws of other nations. Moreover, as a consequence of this failure to pay due regard to the laws of other countries, it leads to 'limping marriages', ie marriages which are valid in one country (in *Sottomayor* v *de Barros (No 2)*, England) but which are invalid in another (in *Sottomayor (No 2)*, Portugal). The case thus dismisses one of the great goals of the conflict of laws: the achievement of international uniformity (or harmony) of decision. The Law Commission has recommended the abolition of this rule in its Working Paper No 89 on Choice of Law Rules in Marriage.

## Essential validity and the lex loci celebrationis

What is the position if a marriage is formally valid under the lex loci celebrationis and essentially valid under the parties' domiciles, but is essentially invalid under the lex loci celebrationis? Is the lex loci strictly restricted to formal validity or does it have a role to play in essential capacity too? The answer to this question appears to depend upon where the marriage is celebrated.

Where the marriage takes place in England (ie the lex loci and the lex fori coincide) it seems that for public policy reasons such marriages will be held void. For example, even if an uncle and his niece could marry validly under the law of their domicile, they would not be allowed to marry validly in England. (See Collier, op cit, 264). What this means is that, in addition to the requirement that the marriage should be valid under the parties' domiciliary laws, the marriage must also be valid under the lex loci celebrationis where the marriage is celebrated in England.

But suppose that the marriage takes place outside England; would the same rule be followed? Suppose the parties managed to marry (in accordance with the local form) in a country that held their marriage invalid (because of some incapacity) although the marriage was valid under the law of their domicile; is the marriage valid or invalid?

A number of Commonwealth decisions (for example, *Reed* v *Reed* (1969) 6 DLR (3d) 617) suggest that validity, other than formal validity, under the lex loci is irrelevant. Thus in *Reed* v *Reed* the court of British Columbia upheld the validity of a marriage in the following circumstances: the parties, although domiciled in British Columbia, had managed to marry (according to the local form) in Washington in the United States. They were first cousins, and such marriages were not valid under the lex loci but were valid under the parties' lex domicilii. Here then the lack of capacity under the lex loci did not prevent the validity of the marriage.

However, the only relevant English decision, *Breen* v *Breen* [1964] P 144, suggests otherwise. In that case Karminski J suggested obiter that the lex loci was relevant to matters of essential validity even where the lex loci did not coincide with the lex fori. In this case the husband had previously been married but had divorced his first wife in England. Although both he and his second wife were domiciled in England, he married his second wife in Ireland. However, the Irish Constitution outlawed divorce. Did this mean that their marriage in Ireland (which complied with the local form) was none the less invalid (even though they both had capacity to marry under the law of their domicile)? In the event Karminski J decided that notwithstanding the Irish constitution the English divorce would be recognised in Ireland; thus their marriage in Ireland was valid under Irish law. Implied in this result, however, is the suggestion that should the English divorce not be recognised in Ireland, then the marriage would be invalid notwithstanding its compliance with Irish law in regard to form and English law (the parties' domiciliary law) in regard to capacity.

## The 'dual domicile' test and s50 of the Family Law Act 1986

This important topic will be discussed below in section 9.4.

## 9.3 Polygamy

### Introduction: the extent of recognition

There are strong (and obvious) public policy reasons why English courts should dislike the concept of polygamy. Thus the traditional approach to polygamous marriages, whether actually polygamous or only potentially polygamous, has been to deny those marriages any effect (even if under the ordinary rules the marriage is both formally and essentially valid). So in *Hyde* v *Hyde* (1866) LR 1 P & D 130, Lord Penzance refused to recognise (and, therefore, refused to dissolve) a Mormon marriage celebrated in Utah (where the court believed that such polygamous marriages were lawful) between an Englishman and a Utah woman. (The Englishman had previously been a Mormon but had foresaken that faith during a missionary visit to the Sandwich Islands.) Parties to a polygamous marriage or potentially polygamous marriage, he said, 'are not entitled to the remedies, the adjudication, or the relief of the matrimonial law of England'.

On the other hand, a very large part of the world's population live according to regimes which permit polygamy; are all their marriages of no effect under English law? Moreover, there has been significant immigration into the United Kingdom in recent years by persons who have contracted polygamous or potentially polygamous marriages outside England, so the English courts are increasingly faced with problems arising out of the break-up of polygamous marriages and the like. The parties to these marriages might not be domiciled in England, but they are certainly resident here. Could the courts ignore these problems entirely on the ground that the relationships involved were polygamous?

For these reasons English law has in recent years been moving away from its traditional refusal to recognise the existence of polygamous unions. Cheshire, indeed, states that 'the wheel has almost come full circle since [*Hyde* v *Hyde*]' (in *Private*

*International Law* at 616). Certainly the position has developed so far today that a polygamous marriage celebrated outside the United Kingdom and valid according to the rules to be discussed below, will generally be recognised. It must be made quite plain, however, although it is not established by the decided cases, that no marriage celebrated in due form in England can be a polygamous marriage.

It is, perhaps, worth mentioning, though, that even before the recent more liberal attitude towards polygamy in English law the courts were seldom as absolute in their refusal to recognise polygamous marriages as *Hyde* v *Hyde* might be read as suggesting. Thus, for instance, the children of a valid polygamous marriage (whether actual or potential) are legitimate (*Bamgbose* v *Daniel* [1955] AC 107). Indeed, in *Hashimi* v *Hashimi* [1972] Fam 36 even the children of an invalid marriage (in casu a monogamous marriage that was void because of the existence of an earlier valid polygamous one) were held legitimate; but this decision probably goes too far. Moreover, a valid polygamous marriage prevents a valid second marriage (even a monogamous one); but, oddly, this will not found a prosecution for bigamy: *R* v *Sagoo* [1975] QB 885.

## Matrimonial relief and polygamy

This move away from the traditional approach is perhaps most sharply seen in the area of matrimonial relief. Following the *Hyde* v *Hyde* approach the parties to a polygamous marriage could not approach the courts for a divorce or a decree of nullity or, perhaps most importantly, a maintenance order in favour of a party to such a marriage. Thus a couple married under a law that permitted polygamy (although their marriage was de facto monogamous) might immigrate to England. Should their marriage break up there would be no obligation, enforceable through the courts, for the one party to maintain the other. This is now dealt with by s47(1) of the Matrimonial Causes Act 1973 which provides that the court 'is not precluded from granting matrimonial relief or making a declaration concerning the validity of a marriage by reason only that the marriage was entered into under a law that permits polygamy'. Matrimonial relief includes (s47(2)) making divorce and nullity decrees and maintenance orders. This provision has gone a long way towards overturning the general rule laid down in *Hyde* v *Hyde*. (But this is not wholesale recognition of polygamous marriages; as we shall see, however, persons domiciled in England cannot contract actually or potentially polygamous marriages.)

Regarding social security, the broad position is that in regard to many benefits the relevant regulations allow a valid polygamous marriage to be treated as a monogamous one, provided that it has always been monogamous (or where it has not been, it may be treated as monogamous for every day that it actually was monogamous) (see s162(b), Social Security Act 1975, s9(2)(a) Child Benefit Act 1976 and regulations made thereunder). For tax and many other purposes tax relief may be claimed for the support of a wife in a potentially polygamous marriage; and, although it is not established in the cases, it seems that a polygamous wife or wives will be able to claim under the Fatal Accidents Act 1976 in respect of the death of her/their husband.

## The nature of polygamous marriages

From the above it is clear that it will sometimes (although much less frequently than in the past) be necessary to determine whether a particular marriage is polygamous or not. Although in principle one might have thought that this was a matter of capacity and thus for the law of the antenuptial domicile, in fact this is not so. The position seems to be that the lex loci celebrationis determines the nature of the marriage, and then, given the public policy aspects of the subject, English law determines whether a relationship with that nature amounts to a polygamous marriage. Thus in *Lee* v *Lau* [1967] P 14 a customary Chinese union (which recognised concubinage) celebrated in Hong Kong was held to be polygamous even although under that law there was only one wife and the other partners of the husband were simply recognised concubines.

In principle one might have though that it was for the personal law of the parties to determine the nature of the relationship, but this is clearly not so; the lex loci celebrationis predominates, save in the one exceptional circumstance to be discussed below under the capacity to enter a polygamous marriage.

Finally, it should be noted that a potentially polygamous marriage may become a monogamous marriage if the appropriate circumstances change. Typically the parties may undergo religious conversion to a faith that only permits monogamy (*The Sinha Peerage Claim* [1946] All ER 348), or the law governing their marriage may be changed to prohibit polygamy (*Parkasho* v *Singh* [1968] P 233), or a change of domicile to a country which does not permit polygamy may have this effect (*Ali* v *Ali* [1968] P 564).

## The validity of polygamous marriages (in practice, capacity to enter a polygamous marriage)

Under what circumstances will a marriage which has the nature of a polygamous marriage under the lex loci celebrationis be considered valid? Since presumably the marriage will be formally valid under the lex loci, the question reduces itself into the question of whether the parties have the capacity to enter a polygamous marriage. Now, in accordance with the general principle discussed above, that is a matter for the parties' antenuptial domicile.

However, in *Radwan* v *Radwan (No 2)* (above) Cumming-Bruce J rejected this and held (at least as far as the capacity to contract a polygamous marriage was concerned) capacity was governed by the law of the intended matrimonial home! Thus he upheld the validity of an actually polygamous marriage celebrated in Paris between an English-domiciled woman and an Egyptian-domiciled man where the parties' intended matrimonial home was Egypt! This decision was vehemently criticised, and Parliament intervened and enacted s11(d) of the Matrimonial Causes Act 1973 which provides that 'in the case of a polygamous [including a potentially polygamous] marriage entered into outside England and Wales [the marriage shall be void if] either party was at the time of the marriage domiciled in England and Wales'.

One might have thought that this meant (at least where the antenuptial domicile was English) that there was no capacity to contract a polygamous marriage. Suppose, therefore, a man domiciled in England contracted a marriage which was polygamous under the lex loci celebrationis, surely that marriage would be void; he lacked capacity under his antenuptial domiciliary law. But this is not the way that s11(d) was interpreted in *Hussain* v *Hussain* [1983] Fam 26 (CA). Here a man domiciled in England went through a ceremony, polygamous in form, in Pakistan with a woman domiciled in Pakistan. This, held the Court of Appeal (to everyone's surprise), was a valid monogamous marriage: the man being domiciled in England could not, because of s11(d), contract a polygamous marriage, while the woman could not under the law of Pakistan enter a marriage to more than one husband; thus the marriage was monogamous from her point of view! Note that had the genders been the other way round the marriage would have been void! And also that this amounts to a rejection of the role of the lex loci celebrationis in determining the nature of the marriage (as discussed above).

In these circumstances it is not surprising that the Law Commission recommended that the law should be changed to restrict the incapacity to actually polygamous marriages.

Part II of the Private International Law (Miscellaneous Provisions) Act 1995, which is now in force, sets out to achieve this. Part II of the Act is designed to ensure that English domiciliaries, irrespective of sex, are only prevented from entering into *actually* polygamous marriages abroad. Section 5(1) of the Act provides that a marriage contracted abroad:

'... between parties neither of whom is already married is not void under the law of England and Wales on the ground that it is entered into under a law which permits polygamy and that either party is domiciled in England and Wales.'

This means that English domiciliaries who are not already married can marry abroad under legal systems that allow polygamy; such marriages will be valid but they will be monogamous and will always remain so under English law. The Act provides a consequential amendment to s11(d) to make it clear that it only applies to actually polygamous marriages (Schedule, para 2(2)).

Although s5 is retrospective (s6(1)), provision is made to protect the position of persons who, for instance, have remarried in the belief that their first marriage was void under s11(d) (s6(2)), marriages which have been annulled (or in respect of which annulment proceedings have been commenced; s6(3) and (4)), as well as rights under a will or settlement (s6(6)(a)) or entitlement to benefits, allowances or pensions (s6(6)(b)).

Finally, a recent case of interest is *R* v *Immigration Appeal Tribunal, ex parte*

*Asfar Jan* [1995] Imm 440. The applicant, a Pakistani citizen, was refused entry into the United Kingdom as the wife of a British citizen (her putative third husband and sponsor) on the grounds that the marriage was void and she would therefore be dependent on public funding for her maintenance. In accordance with Islamic law, the applicant's second husband already had one wife when he married her. He then divorced the applicant under Islamic law by talaq (see section 9.4) which was pronounced in the United Kingdom. The applicant sought judicial review of the refusal of entry on the grounds that the marriage was valid.

It was held that the talaq was an overseas divorce 'obtained otherwise than by way of proceedings' within the scope of the Family Law Act 1986 and was therefore not recognised under English law as the husband had been habitually resident in the United Kingdom prior to the divorce. Despite the polygamous nature of the marriage to the second husband, this second marriage was valid under s11(d) Matrimonial Causes Act 1973 as the marriage had taken place outside England and Wales. Further, as required by s11(d), neither party to the polygamous marriage was domiciled in England or Wales at the time of the marriage. The polygamous marriage was therefore valid and the applicant therefore did not have capacity to marry her third husband under English law.

The revisions contained in Part II of the Private International Law (Miscellaneous Provisions) Act 1995 will not affect cases such as this. The issue here arose from the non-recognition of the initial divorce by talaq and the subsequent incapacity of the applicant to marry again under English law as any such marriage would be de facto polygamous. Part II only provides relief for potentially polygamous marriages – those where neither party is already married, and does not provide a safe harbour for those who are already married either de facto or because the requirements for the recognition of a divorce have not been complied with under the Family Law Act.

## 9.4 Divorce and the nullity of marriage

### Introduction and history

The sort of problems that we are dealing with in this section are straightforward. H1 and W may be married to each other, but the marriage fails and they wish to be divorced. They obtain a divorce from the courts in one country, say Utopia, but now W moves to England, and wishes to marry H2 there. Whether she can do so will depend upon whether the Utopian court's decree of divorce will be recognised in England; if it is not, then she is still married to H1 and cannot remarry. Naturally, the law is mostly concerned with the nature of the link between W and H1 and the Utopian courts; is it strong enough to justify that court exercising jurisdiction, or is it a merely transitory connection (eg mere presence or temporary residence)?

The original common law in this area is simple and easy to understand – but very unjust. For this reason amongst others the law today is entirely statutory, and the most important relevant statute is Part II of the Family Law Act 1986. However, a word or two about the common law should be said to serve as an introduction.

The central rule of the original common law was that the court of the matrimonial domicile (in other words the husband's domicile, see Chapter 3, section 3.3 *Married women*) and only that court had jurisdiction to grant a divorce. And it followed from this that only a divorce decree granted by the court of the matrimonial domicile would be recognised in England. (This was the rule established in *Le Mesurier* v *Le Mesurier* [1895] AC 517 PC, in fact a case before the Privy Council dealing with the Roman-Dutch law of Ceylon (now Sri Lanka), but the English courts have followed this case ever since.) The great merit of this rule was that if a divorce was granted by the court of the domicile, then it would be recognised in most other parts of the world (certainly all parts of the Commonwealth). Persons were either married or unmarried everywhere, and there were relatively few 'limping marriages', ie marriages in which the parties were unmarried in one country and married in another (because their divorce was not recognised there).

The strictness of this rule was slightly ameliorated by the rule in *Armitage* v *Attorney-General* [1906] P 135 which provided that if the divorce decree of a non-domiciliary court was recognised by the domiciliary court, then it would be recognised in England.

Now this state of the law was very unjust. Consider the position of the wife deserted in England by her husband who was previously domiciled in England. Her husband has left, swearing never to return to England or his wife. He has gone to another part of the world and decided to settle there permanently; he has acquired a domicile there. (The wife might not even know where he has acquired a domicile although that is where she is domiciled!)

If she wishes to obtain a divorce (this seems reasonable enough in the circumstances), she must sue for divorce in the courts of that foreign country. This is very inconvenient. Obviously it is very expensive to sue in a foreign court. But finance aside there are many other difficulties. Even where it is known where the husband is, and even where the other country involved is one with which the United Kingdom has good diplomatic and political links, it is difficult. But suppose the husband is now domiciled in a very distant country with which the United Kingdom has no such links (eg Patagonia or Persia). Effectively, the deserted wife has no remedy.

For these reasons, during the first half of this century legislatures all over the Commonwealth liberalised their rules relating to jurisdiction for divorce; it was laid down that the courts would have jurisdiction to grant divorces to deserted wives (and others), even where the parties were not domiciled within the court's jurisdiction, provided that certain other conditions were fulfilled. Typically, the plaintiff would have had to have been resident in the jurisdiction for a number of years and possibly to have been deserted in the jurisdiction or domiciled there prior to desertion.

However, no provision was made for the recognition of such divorces elsewhere in the world. Thus a court in, say, New South Wales, Australia, might, basing its jurisdiction upon residence in New South Wales and the fact that desertion took place there, grant a divorce to a couple who were not domiciled in New South Wales. Would this divorce be recognised in England should one of the couple come to England and wish to remarry here? In principle, the answer to this question had to be no, for the couple had not been domiciled in New South Wales at the time that the New South Wales court granted the divorce. Yet the position was ludicrous because had exactly the same facts arisen before an English court, then the English court would have exercised jurisdiction to grant a divorce on the English rules (which were very similar to the New South Wales rules) extending jurisdiction to non-domiciliary cases!

Fortunately, in *Travers* v *Holley* [1953] P 246 the Court of Appeal, in a constructive and creative piece of law-making, recognised a divorce granted by the non-domiciliary court. Hodgson LJ said that: 'Where ... there is in substance reciprocity, it would be contrary to principle and inconsistent with comity if the courts of this country were to refuse to recognise a jurisdiction which mutatis mutandis they claim for themselves.' *Travers* v *Holley* formed the basis of a complete re-examination and extension of the grounds on which foreign divorces would be recognised in English law. The law in fact became very liberal. The effect of *Indyka* v *Indyka* [1969] 1 AC 33 HL was that if either party had 'a real and substantial connection' with the jurisdiction that granted the divorce, then that divorce would be granted. This was a rather vague test and was much criticised as leaving people uncertain whether their divorce would be recognised and thus whether they were married and, if so, to whom!

A reaction has now set in, and the law on the recognition of foreign divorce is now statutory, and although much more liberal than it used to be is also, generally speaking, clearer. The first step was the enactment of the Recognition of Divorces and Legal Separations Act 1971 (which was enacted to give effect in the law of the United Kingdom to the Hague Convention on the Recognition of Divorces and Legal Separations). This was an awkward statute with many distinctions seemingly without purpose drawn between divorces granted in different ways in different parts of the world (see Morris, op cit, 192–206, for an account of the details of these rules). However, this legislation has now been repealed and its place taken by Part II of the Family Law Act 1986, which contains the present law. We shall turn to the detailed discussion of Part II in a moment but, before we do that, there are a number of miscellaneous matters that we should clear out of the way.

First, the history outlined above related to the recognition of divorces. At common law decrees of nullity stood on a different footing to divorce decrees, and an entirely different (and very technical) body of law governed when an English court had jurisdiction to grant a decree of nullity and when an English court would recognise a decree of nullity granted elsewhere. Fortunately, the Law Commission recommended in 1984 (Report No 137: Recognition of Foreign Nullity Decrees) that the rules with regard to the recognition of nullity should be dealt with on the same basis as divorce. This was achieved with Part II of the Family Law Act 1986, so we need not treat this nullity separately. Indeed, the relevant rules are now so similar that in what follows, unless it is specifically stated to the contrary, you should assume that a reference to 'divorce' includes annulments and legal separations.

Secondly, one of the problems that bedevilled the 1971 legislation was the treatment of extra-judicial divorces. In earlier days it had been presumed that a divorce could only be granted by a court and by no other body. But under many legal systems it is possible to divorce far more informally. Typically, under the Islamic law it is possible for a husband to divorce his wife simply by pronouncing the word *talaq* to her three times. Many Islamic countries have now grafted onto this very informal divorce a range of formalities (proper notice to the wife, formal conciliation proceedings only after the failure of which does the divorce become effective, and the like). In the interim large numbers of immigrants had come from Islamic countries and settled in the United Kingdom, so the question had to arise whether such divorces would be recognised and, if so, under what circumstances. So this is another topic that Part II of the Family Law Act 1986 addresses and which we will have to discuss below.

Thirdly, the applicable law prior to Part II was a complex mixture of statute and common law. Section 45 makes it clear that, the exceptional cases aside, 'a divorce, annulment or legal separation obtained in a country outside the British Islands ... shall be recognised in the United Kingdom *if, and only if,* it is entitled to recognition by virtue of [the relevant parts of the Act or some other enactment]'. In practice this means that we can restrict ourselves to the Family Law Act 1986 alone in this area.

## Part II of the Family Law Act 1986

### Divorces and annulments granted within the British Isles

Naturally divorces granted by courts of civil jurisdiction in the British Isles (the territories included are the United Kingdom (England, Scotland, Wales and Northern Ireland), the Channel Islands (Jersey, Guernsey, Alderney and Sark) and the Isle of Man) are entitled to special recognition by other courts in the United Kingdom. Thus s44(2) of the Family Law Act 1986 provides that 'the validity of any divorce, annulment or judicial separation granted by a court of civil jurisdiction in any part of the British Islands shall be recognised throughout the United Kingdom'. This is subject to only two exceptions which are discussed below (see Refusal of recognition, below).

Section 44(1) clarifies another point: 'No divorce or annulment obtained in any part of the British Islands shall be regarded as effective in any part of the United Kingdom unless granted by a court of civil jurisdiction.' This makes it clear that only judicial divorces can be obtained in the British Isles. This shuts the door firmly on the proposition that an extra-judicial divorce obtained in Britain but not obtained by proceedings could be recognised in England if it was recognised under the law of the parties' domicile. However, this door was in any event only just open (see Morris, op cit, 205).

## The distinction in s46 between overseas divorces 'obtained by means of proceedings' and 'obtained otherwise than by means of proceedings'

Let us begin with a technical point. Section 46(1) deals with the recognition of divorces (including, of course, annulments and legal separations) 'obtained by means of proceedings', while s46(2) deals with such recognition of divorces, etc, 'obtained otherwise than by means of proceedings'. What is the meaning and significance of this distinction?

The distinction relates to different kinds of extra-judicial divorce. As adumbrated above, in some Islamic countries a man may divorce his wife simply by addressing the *talaq* statement to her three times. This is the so-called 'bare *talaq*', and the cases under the old legislation made it clear that such were not divorces obtained by 'proceedings' (*Chaudhary* v *Chaudhary* [1985] Fam 19). On the other hand, in other Islamic countries, eg, Pakistan, a more formal procedure, as laid down in the Muslim Family Law Ordinance 1961, was required. Under this procedure the pronouncement of *talaq* did not take effect for 90 days (during which time the parties might be reconciled), written notice had to be given to the wife, and notice had also to be given to the relevant state body (the Union Council) in Pakistan. But the Council had no power to prevent the divorce from becoming effective if the parties were not reconciled at the end of the period. Such a procedure was held to constitute 'proceedings' under the old legislation (*Quazi* v *Quazi* [1980] AC 744).

Now what is clear is that the distinction between a 'bare *talaq*' and a 'full *talaq*' is preserved in the new legislation. 'Full *talaqs*' fall to be dealt with under the less onerous s46(1), while 'bare *talaqs*' fall under the more onerous s46(2). Note, however, that in both forms of *talaq* the man may by unilateral act end his marriage; the only real difference being that the ending of the marriage is delayed in the 'full *talaq*'. Thus from the public policy point of view the two institutions place the wife in a similarly weak and unenviable position, and it seems artificial to distinguish between them. Yet this is what the law does.

Many, indeed, most divorces for which recognition is sought are granted by the judicial authorities, and thus these cases (along with extra-judicial divorces obtained by 'proceedings') are governed by s46(1) (see s54(1)), and to a description of this provision we now turn.

## Overseas divorces obtained by 'proceedings'
Section 46(1) provides as follows:

> 'The validity of an overseas divorce, annulment or legal separation obtained by means of proceedings shall be recognised if (a) the divorce, annulment or legal separation is effective under the law of the country in which it was obtained; and (b) at the relevant date *either party* to the marriage (i) was *habitually resident* in the country in which the divorce,

annulment or legal separation was obtained; or (ii) was *domiciled* in that country; or (iii) was a *national* of that country.'

A number of technical points should be noted about this section.

First and most importantly, s46(5) provides:

'For the purposes of this section a party to a marriage shall be treated as domiciled in a country if he was domiciled in that country either according to the law of that country in family matters or according to the law of the part of the United Kingdom in which the question of recognition arises.'

What this means is that if the foreign court exercises its jurisdiction on a ground called 'domicile', then that will be sufficient for recognition in the relevant part of the United Kingdom. The significance of this is that the 'quickie' divorces obtained in some American states (eg Nevada), in which the courts consider someone to be domiciled there after a relatively short period of residence, even if the intention is to leave as soon as the divorce has been obtained, will be recognised in England.

Secondly, note also that this is an example of determining the meaning of a connecting factor in an English statute by the law of another country. Usually such matters are determined by the lex fori (see Chapter 1, section 1.3 Determination of the connecting factor).

Thirdly, note that s46(5) applies to divorces sought to be recognised under s46(1) ('obtained by proceedings') and s46(2) ('obtained otherwise than by proceedings').

Fourthly, the concept of 'relevant date' for s46(1) divorces is defined in s46(3)(a) as 'the date of the commencement of the proceedings'. For s46(2) divorces the 'relevant date' is the date on which the divorce 'was obtained'.

Once these points are understood, it is clear that s46(1) is a wide-ranging reform. The useful rule in *Armitage* v *Attorney-General*, discussed above, is however abolished; where a divorce is obtained in a non-domiciliary court it is no longer sufficient for recognition of that divorce in England that that divorce should be recognised by the domiciliary courts (of either party).

The requirement specified in s46(1)(a), that the divorce decree should be 'effective under the law of the country in which it was obtained', is worth a word or two. Clear examples of such decrees would be decrees that are not absolute, or are suspended pending appeal, or which do not dissolve the marriage until a certain period of time has elapsed. This is straightforward. The interesting point arises over extra-judicial divorces obtained by proceedings.

For instance, a *talaq* (with proceedings) may be obtained in a country where the parties are domiciled or habitually resident, or which they are nationals, but is not effective under the law of that country; the divorce cannot be recognised under s46(1). Bear in mind, however, the role of renvoi here: if the country where the extra-judicial divorce was obtained would recognise it, not because it complied with the internal law of that country, but because of the application of its choice of law rules, it would still be effective under the law of that country.

A question that has arisen before the courts on a number of occasions (see, for instance, *R* v *Registrar-General of Births, Deaths and Marriages, ex parte Minhas* [1977] QB 1 and *R* v *Secretary of State, ex parte Ghulam Fatima* [1986] AC 527 (HL)) is: what is the position where part of the 'proceedings' takes place in one country and another part takes place in a further country? Suppose a man, a national of Pakistan resident in England, pronounces the *talaq* in England but gives the requisite notice to the Union Council in Pakistan. Is this a divorce obtained in Pakistan or obtained in England, or is it obtained in both? *Ex parte Ghulam Fatima* makes it clear that such a divorce is obtained in England (because that is where the proceedings were instituted). Although this case was decided under the old legislation, the position would be the same under Part II of the Family Law Act 1986. And *Berkovits* v *Grinberg, Attorney-General intervening* (1995) The Times 13 January confirms this. Thus, a Jewish get written in London before the Beth Din under Jewish ecclesiastical law and delivered to the wife at a Rabbinical Court in Israel was not recognised under s46(1) of the Family Law Act 1986. A divorce by means of a get was obtained by means of 'proceedings' and s46(1) envisaged that the 'proceedings' should take place in one country. A transnational divorce could not be recognised under the Act. This result is doubtless correct where the *talaq* is pronounced in England (or another country that does not permit extra-judicial divorces in its internal law), but suppose the *talaq* is pronounced in Dubai (which does allow *talaq* divorces) and notice is given in Pakistan. There is no reason in principle or policy why that divorce should not be recognised. But this is not the law; such transnational divorces will not be recognised in England.

## Overseas divorces obtained otherwise than by proceedings
Section 46(2) provides as follows:

> 'The validity of an overseas divorce, annulment or legal separation obtained otherwise than by means of proceedings shall be recognised if (a) the divorce, annulment or legal separation is effective under the law of the country in which it was obtained; (b) at the relevant date (i) *each* party to the marriage was *domiciled* in that country; or (ii) *either* party was domiciled in that country and the other party was *domiciled* in a country under whose law the divorce, annulment or legal separation is recognised *as valid*; and (c) *neither* party to the marriage was *habitually resident in the United Kingdom* throughout the period of one year immediately preceding that date.'

First a general comment on this section seems appropriate. We have already seen that English law adopts a relatively strong policy against extra-judicial divorces: a divorce obtained in any part of the British Islands must be granted 'by a court of civil jurisdiction' (s44(1)). The reasons for this are obvious and need not be rehearsed here. However, English law cannot adopt so strong a policy as to deny recognition to all extra-judicial divorces wheresoever obtained. Much of the population of the world lives under such systems of law, and when persons who have married and divorced under such systems of law (and who might have no prior connection with England) come before English courts, chaos (and much injustice) would result if these extra-judicial divorces were ignored. Second marriages would be void (and wives and children unable to stay with their husband or father), family finances in chaos and the like. So a balance has to be struck between the dislike of extra-judicial divorces as a matter of policy and the fulfilment of the expectations of persons who have, reasonably, relied upon the validity of such divorces. Part of the balance is struck by s46(1) which, in effect, treats overseas extra-judicial divorces obtained by proceedings on the same footing as overseas judicial divorces.

Now in s46(2) the balance is struck in a different place for overseas divorces (such as the 'bare *talaq*') obtained without proceedings. Predictably, the conditions to be satisfied before a 'bare *talaq*' will be recognised are more onerous. The effect of the provision is that the extra-judicial divorce must be recognised by the domiciliary law (this is the extended meaning of domicile, already discussed above, set out in s46(5)) of *both parties* (under s46(1) recognition by *either* party's law would suffice). Note also that this has to be domicile; the other connecting factors used in s46(1) (habitual residence and nationality) have no role to play here.

More importantly, if either party was habitually resident in the United Kingdom for the preceding year the divorce will not be recognised (s46(2)(c)). This clear section replaces a similar but poorly drafted provision attempting to achieve the same end in the earlier legislation.

Finally, note that 'the relevant date' means something different in s46(2) from what it means in s46(1) (as discussed above). Section 46(3)(b) provides that this shall be 'the date on which [the divorce] was obtained'. It is obvious that a different rule has to be applied in s46(2), for there are no proceedings so there cannot be 'a date of the commencement of the proceedings' as required by s46(3)(a). Also, where 'the relevant date' (under either s46(1) or s46(2)) falls after the death of either party (this is possible with annulments) then the relevant date is the date of death (s46(4)).

### Proof of facts relevant to recognition of divorces obtained by means of proceedings

Section 48 of the Family Law Act 1986 contains a number of provisions designed to facilitate the proof of facts upon which the recognition of a divorce 'obtained by means of proceedings' may depend. It provides that 'any finding of fact' (which includes a finding [whether express or implied] that either party was habitually resident, or domiciled or a national of the country in which the divorce was obtained) 'on the basis of which jurisdiction was assumed in the proceedings' shall be 'conclusive evidence of the fact found' provided that both parties took part in the proceedings (appearing in judicial proceedings being sufficient). If both parties did not take part in the proceedings, then that finding is simply 'sufficient proof of that fact unless the contrary is shown'.

### Refusal of recognition

Sections 51 and 52 deal with the occasions on which a divorce which otherwise qualifies may, none the less, be refused recognition. Section 52 can be dealt with simply: it covers divorces obtained before the commencement of Part II of the

Family Law Act 1986. The section itself should be referred to should such a case arise. Section 51, on the other hand, must be dealt with more fully.

First, it provides that the recognition of a divorce (whether granted by a court within the British Isles or obtained overseas)

> 'may be refused in any part of the United Kingdom if the divorce (etc) ... was granted or obtained at a time when it was irreconcilable with a decision determining the question of the subsistence or validity of the marriage of the parties previously given ... by a court of civil jurisdiction in that part of the United Kingdom or by a court elsewhere and recognised or entitled to be recognised in that part of the United Kingdom' (s51(1)).
>
> Secondly, a divorce (whether an overseas divorce or one obtained in the British Islands) may be refused recognition in any part of the UK 'if the divorce or separation was granted or obtained at a time when, according to the law of that part of the United Kingdom (including its rules of private international law and the provisions of this Part), there is no subsisting marriage between the parties'.

The purpose and operation of this provision is obvious: the English court should not have to recognise a divorce if in English law the parties were never married to each other (or at any rate were not married to each other at the time the divorce was obtained).

Thirdly, s51(3) deals with the more traditional public policy grounds for refusing recognition. It provides that where the divorce is 'obtained by proceedings' recognition may be refused if either party was not given reasonable notice of the proceedings and a reasonable opportunity to take part in them (s51(3)(a)(i) and (ii)).

And where the divorce is not 'obtained by proceedings' recognition may be refused unless there is an 'official document' certifying that the divorce is effective under the law of the country where it was obtained and, where either party is domiciled elsewhere, there is an 'official document' setting out that the divorce is recognised in that country. This provision simply facilitates compliance with the provisions of s46(2).

Finally, s51(c) provides that with any overseas divorce recognition may be refused where such recognition would be 'manifestly contrary to public policy'.

### Non-recognition of a divorce in another jurisdiction: a bar to remarriage?

We saw in our discussion of 'the incidental question' in Chapter 2.3 that problems could arise where a divorce was bound to be recognised under the relevant rules of English law but that divorce might not be recognised under the law of the antenuptial domicile that would usually be used to test capacity to marry (and to remarry). *Lawrence* v *Lawrence* (above) is a good example of this. There a woman domiciled in Brazil had divorced her first husband in Nevada (and married her second husband there). The law of Brazil did not recognise divorce, but under the rules of English law the divorce had to be recognised (now s46(1): judicial divorce in the country of domicile of one of the parties (although not domiciled in Nevada under English law, she was under the law of Nevada).) An English court had to decide whether she was validly married to her second husband, and that depended upon whether the divorce had rid her of her first husband. The English courts held that she had capacity to marry her second husband. But the various judges who heard the case gave some odd reasons for this result. The couple intended to live in England, so there was some reliance upon the intended matrimonial home to test validity, and there was also reliance upon the legal system with which the marriage was most closely connected.

The position is now settled by s50 which provides that the fact that a divorce (whether granted in the UK or required to be recognised under Part II) would not be recognised elsewhere shall not preclude either party to the marriage from re-marrying in that part of the United Kingdom or cause the remarriage of either party (wherever the remarriage takes place) to be treated as invalid in that part'. Of course, if the decision in *Lawrence* v *Lawrence* were correct this provision would be unnecessary.

## Miscellaneous provisions of Part II
We have thus far assumed, when talking of a divorce obtained in a particular country and effective under the law of that country, that all states had a single legal system operative within them. But in fact, as we know, this is not so. Many states, eg, the United States, have a number of legal systems operative within them. (In the USA every one of the 50 states has a different legal system.) Section 49 addresses this problem.

Broadly speaking s49(2) provides that where the ground of jurisdiction on which recognition is sought is either habitual residence or domicile then each territory in which a different system of law applies shall be treated as if it were a separate country. On the other hand, where the jurisdictional ground is nationality then the divorce has to be effective throughout that country. Thus, if a divorce obtained in Nevada is sought to be recognised on the ground of US nationality, then it must be effective throughout the USA; it is not enough that it is effective under the law of Nevada.

## Jurisdiction of the English court to grant a divorce, and choice of law in divorce actions before the English courts
Thus far we have been discussing the grounds on which a divorce granted elsewhere will be recognised in the United Kingdom. Now we touch briefly on the question of the grounds upon which the English courts will exercise jurisdiction to grant a divorce. Although under the common law only the court of the domicile had jurisdiction to grant a divorce, the present provision under statute (s5(2) of the Domicile and Matrimonial Proceedings Act 1973) is that if either party is domiciled in England at the time of commencement of proceedings, or if either party had been habitually resident in England for a year before the commencement of proceedings, the English courts will have jurisdiction. Similar rules govern the jurisdiction of the English courts to grant nullity decrees (s5(3) of the same Act). The only difference derives from the fact that a declaration of nullity may be made after the death of one

or both parties; then domicile or habitual residence for the requisite period before death is required.

There are various circumstances in which a stay of a divorce petition will be granted. Those interested should consult Cheshire, at 635–639. Although the issue can be very technical, in broad terms principles similar to *The Spiliada* will apply where matrimonial relief is sought: *De Dampierre* v *De Dampierre* [1988] AC 92 (HL) and *Holmes* v *Holmes* [1989] 3 WLR 302 CA. In choice of law matters the invariable rule is that the lex fori applies.

## 9.5 Maintenance: the recognition and enforcement of foreign orders

We have already touched upon this issue with regard to maintenance orders made in other EC states (Chapter 8, section 8.3 *Maintenance orders*) which are enforceable in England by virtue of the Civil Jurisdiction and Judgments Act 1982. Further special provision is made under the Maintenance Orders (Facilities for Enforcement) Act 1920 (for the enforcement of orders made by those Commonwealth countries to which the Act has been extended by Order in Council) and the Maintenance Orders (Reciprocal Enforcement) Act 1972 (for the enforcement of the orders of other countries for which arrangements for reciprocal enforcement have been made). See Cheshire, 703–708 for a fuller account of these statutes, and see the discussion in Chapter 8, section 8.3 *Grounds on which recognition or enforcement may be refused*, paragraph (iii), over the interrelationship between these provisions and the Brussels Convention.

The reason why special arrangements have to be made for the enforcement of maintenance orders is a simple one: maintenance orders are orders for the payment of various sums *periodically* and for an indefinite period of time. They are not, therefore, final and conclusive, and thus, in the absence of special provisions, are not enforceable. See Chapter 8, sections 8.2 and 8.3.

## 9.6 Legitimacy, adoption, custody and guardianship

### *Legitimacy and legitimation*

The history of the English law applicable to this area is, as it so often is, a chapter of accidents. As Morris, op cit, 239–240 points out, there are three conflicting theories of which law to use to determine whether a particular person is legitimate or not.

First, one can hold that a child is legitimate if and only if he or she is born or conceived in a marriage recognised as valid in accordance with the English choice of law rules already discussed. This view is favoured by *Shaw* v *Gould* (above). As Morris says, according to 'this theory English law has no conflict rule for legitimacy, only a conflict rule for the validity of marriage' (at 239). This is a harsh approach, for under many legal systems (including now English domestic law) the children of a void marriage that was believed by the parties to be valid are legitimate.

Secondly, one can hold that a child is legitimate if it is legitimate under its domicile of origin. The snag with this theory is that the child's domicile of origin depends upon whether it is legitimate or illegitimate (see Chapter 3, sections 3.3 and 3.5)!

Thirdly, it can be argued that this is not an issue for the conflict of laws at all; it is simply a question of the interpretation of words such as 'child' or 'issue' appearing in documents such as wills. But as Morris points out, this approach is of no use should the issue of legitimacy arise as an abstract issue (say, in regard to a declaration of legitimacy sought under s45(1) of the Matrimonial Causes Act 1973).

It is difficult to be dogmatic about what the English law on this point actually is. Probably *Shaw* v *Gould* (which is, after all, a decision of the House of Lords) indicates the orthodox view. However, in *Re Bischoffsheim* [1948] Ch 79 and in *Bamgbose* v *Daniel* (above) attempts have been made to move in favour of the child's domicile of origin. These cases have not, however, distinguished *Shaw* v *Gould* persuasively.

The tide is now definitely running against *Shaw* v *Gould*. This is seen in the most recent case of *Motala and Others* v *Attorney-General and Others* [1990] 2 FLR 261. Although this case was decided in the Family Division, it was a nationality case concerned with whether the children of Mr and Mrs Ismail Motala were citizens of the United Kingdom and Colonies or not. However, it is not necessary for us to enter the maze of nationality law. Suffice it to say that the nationality status of some of the children depended upon whether they were legitimate or not.

The circumstances surrounding the marriage of the parents were the following: the marriage took pace according to Sunni Muslim rites in 1950 in what is now Zambia but was then Northern Rhodesia. Apparently this would have been an invalid marriage under the lex loci celebrationis, but under the law of India the marriage would have been valid and the children legitimate. Throughout the parents retained their domicile of origin in India. The crucial question was whether two children, Safiya and Faruq, born in Northern Rhodesia before independence were legitimate (in which case they were citizens of the United Kingdom and Colonies) or illegitimate (in which case they had no such entitlement)?

The Attorney-General relied strongly on *Shaw* v *Gould* for the proposition that in the absence of a valid marriage the child cannot be legitimate in England even if regarded as legitimate under its domicile of origin. However, Sir Stephen Brown stressed that *Shaw* v *Gould* must be considered as limited to its own facts; he followed instead dicta from *Re Bischoffsheim*, above, and *Re Goodman's Trusts* (1881) 17 Ch D 266 and held that a person's status was determined by the law of his domicile, and since the domicile of origin of the children was plainly Indian, and Indian law considered them legitimate, they were legitimate under English law and entitled to British nationality. (An appeal against Brown J's judgment on grounds other than the legitimacy point was dismissed by the Court of Appeal on 30 January 1991.)

Note that in this case both the mother and the father were domiciled in India so there was no doubt that the children's domicile of origin was in India. But if the parents had been domiciled in different countries then a difficult logical problem would have arisen: the children's legitimacy would have depended upon their domicile of origin, but their domicile of origin would have depended upon their legitimacy! (See Chapter 3, sections 3.3 and 3.5.)

With legitimation (ie a child born illegitimate but becoming legitimate, typically through the subsequent marriage of its parents) the position is also difficult. English law did not know of the concept of legitimation – a child was either legitimate or illegitimate for all time – until the Legitimation Act 1926. However, the English courts had to consider their attitude to foreign legitimations. Thus the common law rule was developed that if the child's father was domiciled at the time of birth, and at the time of the subsequent marriage with the child's mother, in a country whose law recognised legitimation, then the legitimation would be recognised in English law: *Re Goodman's Trusts*.

The Legitimacy Act 1976, however, now provides (in s3) for the recognition of foreign legitimations in English law, provided that at the time of the subsequent marriage the father was domiciled in a country by whose law the child is legitimated by subsequent marriage.

In *Motala* v *Attorney-General* the court made the obvious point that where the law of the father's domicile did not recognize legitimation per subsequens matrimonio then there could be no reliance on the predecessor of s3 of the Legitimacy Act 1976.

## Adoption

Statutory provision is made for the recognition of foreign adoption orders (s4(3) of the Adoption Act 1968). The procedure requires that the Secretary of State specify the countries whose adoption orders will be recognised. Most Commonwealth countries (but not India or Pakistan or Bangladesh) and most Western European countries are included.

At common law an order made under the law of the adopter's domicile will be recognised, subject, of course, to English public policy. See Collier, *The Conflict of Laws*, 314 and *Re Valentine's Settlement* [1965] Ch 831 CA.

## Custody and guardianship

Statutory rules contained in Part I of the Family Law Act 1986 now govern the jurisdiction of English courts to make such orders.

The recognition and enforcement of foreign orders are governed by different principles. The common law is uncertain on the jurisdictional grounds that will justify the recognition of foreign orders. However, ultimately at common law the court is guided by an overriding principle of upholding the best interests of the child, so a custody order may not be enforced if it appears contrary to the enforcing court's view of the best interests of the child. See *McKee* v *McKee* [1951] AC 352 (PC).

Such a rule can appear to reward the parent who 'kidnaps' the child in breach of a custody order and takes the child to another country. If that country then reassesses the interests of the child it may well conclude that further disruption is not in the best interests of the child and refuse to enforce the otherwise entirely proper foreign award!

The Child Abduction and Custody Act 1985 is designed to reduce the chances of being able successfully to 'kidnap' a child in breach of a custody order. It implements the Hague Convention of 1980 on the Civil Aspects of International Child Abduction and a Council of Europe Convention on Recognition and Enforcement of Decisions Concerning Custody of Children and Restoration of Custody of Children of 1980. The Act sets up machinery, operating through the Lord Chancellor's department, that is designed to facilitate the return of abducted children.

The provisions of the Act have been before the courts recently in *Re G (A Minor)* [1990] 2 FLR 325. The case arose out of a complicated custody dispute between the Belgian parents of G, a minor child. In brief, the parties divorced and the divorce decree incorporated an agreement between them that they should have joint custody of the child but that if one parent left Belgium the child should live with the remaining parent. The mother left Belgium and made her home in Birmingham but, apart from holidays, the child remained with his father in Belgium.

The mother decided that she would like to have the child living with her and applied to the Belgian courts for an order of sole custody. She then discovered that such an order had already been made in favour of sole custody for the father, restricting her access to the child, and prohibiting her from taking the child outside Belgium without the father's consent. She had not been given proper notice of this because the Belgian courts had made a mistake with her address.

Anyway with the father's consent she took the child on holiday to Italy, but after the holiday returned to England not Belgium. The father then applied, through the Lord Chancellor, under Part II of the Child Abduction and Custody Act 1985 (which implements the European Convention of Recognition and Enforcement of Decisions Concerning the Custody of Children and on the Restoration of Custody of Children 1980) for the registration and enforcement of the Belgian court's orders. (The Council of Europe Convention rather than the Hague Convention was relied upon because that was the convention to which Belgium was party.)

There was little doubt that the order had been made by a court of competent jurisdiction, viz, the habitual residence of the defendant or the child or the last common habitual residence of both parents which is still the habitual residence of one of them (article 9(a)(b)). So, in principle, under the Convention the order should have been enforced. But the defendant raised a number of defences.

First, she argued that the fact that she had not had proper notice of the original Belgian order meant that enforcement should be refused under article 9(1)(a) which provided that enforcement 'may be refused ... if in the case of a decision given in the absence of the defendant or his legal representative, the defendant was not duly served with the document which instituted the proceedings ... in sufficient time to enable him to arrange his defence'. Booth J, however, rejected this defence: the judge had a discretion in such circumstances to refuse enforcement, and the mother, once she became aware of the Belgian order, had had every opportunity to inform the Belgian court of the true position and had not availed herself of these opportunities. In addition, it was plain from the evidence that she was determined to remove the child in breach of the order. So the judge decided to refuse to exercise his discretion not to enforce the Belgian order.

Secondly, the defendant relied upon article 10(1)(a) and (b) which provided that enforcement may be refused

> 'if it is found that the effects of the decision are manifestly incompatible with the fundamental principles of [family] law ... in the State addressed' or 'if it is found that by reason of a change in the circumstances including the passage of time but not including a mere change of residence of the child after an improper removal, the effects of the original decision are manifestly no longer in accordance with the welfare of the child'.

But both these defences were rejected; enforcing the Belgian order amounted simply to enforcing the parties' agreement that had been embodied in the divorce decree, and that could not be said to be 'manifestly incompatible with the fundamental principles of [family] law ...'. Moreover, it could not be said that the passage of the ten months since the child came to England was such a change of circumstances to render the original decision 'no longer in accordance with the welfare of the child'. This conclusion was reached not withstanding that the views of the child (obtained as required by article 15) were that he wished to stay with his mother.

Thus, in the end, Booth J held that the order should be enforced. In some ways this seems harsh: the child was unwilling to be returned, and the mother had not had proper notice of the Belgian proceedings. But there are wider considerations of public interest here: almost automatic enforcement of the custody orders of courts of competent jurisdiction is necessary in order to reduce the number of abductions of children and 'tug-of-love' battles in the courts.

On the other hand a Belgian order suffered a different fate in *In re H (A Minor)* [1994] 2 WLR 269. After the divorce of the parents the Belgian juvenile court made a contact order entitling the father to contact with his daughter in Belgium during her school holidays. In breach of this order the child was brought to England; and the father sought registration here of the order in accordance with s16 of the Child Abduction and Custody Act 1985 and the wife opposed this. The Court of Appeal held, however, that while the Belgian order would be recognised, enforcement did not automatically follow. The child was determined not to have any contact with her father and the expert reports said she would suffer damaging trauma if forced back to her father. In these circumstances, although a heavy burden rests on the party resisting enforcement (*In re L (Child Abuduction: European Convention)* [1992] 2 FLR 178 at 182) the court exercised it powers under article 10(1)(b) of the European Convention and refused to enforce the order.

*In re S (Minors) (Abduction: Wrongful Retention)* [1994] 2 WLR 228 is an example of the enforcement of custody rights under the Hague Convention. Article 3 of this Convention provides that the removal or retention of a child is wrongful where 'it is in breach of rights of custody attributed to a person ... under the law of the state in which the child was habitually resident immediately before the removal or retention'; and article 12 provides that where a child was wrongfully removed or retained in breach of article 3 then, provided less than one year had elapsed since the child was removed or retained, the judicial authority concerned 'shall order the return of the child forthwith'. In this case the mother and father, Israeli citizens resident in Israel, who had equal rights and responsibilities over their two children under Israeli law, brought the children to England to reside here with their parents for one year. During the year in England the marriage broke down and the father returned to Israel but the mother said that she did not intend to return the children to Israel either before or after the elapse of the agreed one year in England. The father applied to the English court for their immediate return to Israel on the ground that the wife was retaining the children in England contrary to article 3. The Family Division held that, if the mother wished to retain the children in England for the remainder of the agreed year, they would not be wrongfully retained for the father could not unilaterally terminate that agreement. However, since she intended to retain the children beyond that period she was retaining them in breach of article 3 and their immediate return to Israel was ordered.

*In re F* [1995] 3 All ER 641, the court strived to balance the need for international comity with the rights of the child by exercising the discretion to refuse the return of the child under Schedule 1, article 13(b) of the Act. In this case the father had equal and separate rights under Colorado law and the removal by the mother of the child was a clear breach of those rights contrary to article 3 of the Hague Convention. The court found that the return of the child would expose him to 'physical and psychological harm' and the court would therefore exercise its discretion under article 13(b).

In a case where abduction is alleged, the onus of proof with respect to consent under article 13 is on the person opposing the return of the child. Consent in writing is not required, but evidence of consent needs to be clear and cogent: *Re C (Abduction: Consent)* [1996] 1 FLR 414; see Chapter 10, section 10.2, for further details. Evidence of acquiescence to the non-return of a child could objectively be drawn from the absence of any statement requiring the return of the child where the party alleged to be acquiescing had commenced matrimonial proceedings in a religious court: *H v H* (1996) The Times 14 August. Unless there was a clear indication that the religious court proceedings were ancillary to Hague Convention summary proceedings for the return of a child, acquiescence could be inferred. See Chapter 10, section 10.2, for further details.

Where a child is habitually resident in a non-Convention country then the powers of the courts fall outside of article 4 of the Hague Convention which provides that for the Convention to apply any child must be habitually resident in a contracting state immediately before the breach of custody rights. Habitual residence requires a voluntary, settled physical presence in the place or country in question and is therefore a matter of fact. The habitual residence of the children of servicemen who had been posted overseas was the country of posting and where the family lived voluntarily with a degree of continuity. Residence in a military base overseas is not a continuation of residence in the country which the serviceman served: see *Re A and Others* [1996] 1 All ER 24.

## 9.7 The effect of marriage on property

The choice of law rules applicable to matrimonial property are not yet particularly clear. However, where there is an antenuptial contract (or marriage settlement) the terms of that contract will be decisive provided that that contract is valid. The proper law of such a marriage contract is, if the parties have not expressly chosen another law, the law of the matrimonial domicile, ie the law of the husband's domicile at marriage: *Duke of Marlborough* v *Attorney-General* [1945] Ch 78. Of course, before the contract can be valid the parties must have capacity to enter into such a contract. In principle, one expects that capacity to enter into such a contract will be governed by the lex domicilii of the party whose capacity to contract is in question. Although Morris (op cit, 417–418) suggests that the proper law of the contract should be used to test capacity in these circumstances, the general current of authority, although not devoid of doubt, suggests that the lex domicilii should be used: *Cooper* v *Cooper* (1888) 13 App Cas 88 and *Re Cooke's Trusts* (1887) 56 LJ Ch 637.

In the absence of a marriage settlement the law of the matrimonial domicile continues to apply until such time as that domicile is changed; thereafter, at least as far as movables are concerned, the law of the new domicile applies (both to inter vivos transactions and in respect of succession), although vested rights acquired under the law of the earlier domicile are protected (Dicey & Morris, rule 156). Immovables will probably still be governed by the matrimonial domicile; that seems implicit in *Chiwell* v *Carlyon* (1897) 14 SC 61 where a husband and wife domiciled in the Cape of Good Hope, where in the absence of an antenuptial agreement community of property applied, acquired a domicile in England. The English court held that the land which the husband had bought in Cornwall was still subject to the South African community of property.

# 10

# Recent Cases

10.1 Jurisdiction in personam

10.2 Family law

## 10.1 Jurisdiction in personam

*Airbus Industrie GIE* v *Patel and Others* (1996) The Times 12 August
Court of Appeal (Nourse, Hobhouse and Aldous LJJ)

Forum non conveniens – granting an injunction to restrain foreign proceedings

### Facts
Following proceedings in Texas against the plaintiffs arising from a airline crash
which decided that the plaintiffs were immune from suit, the defendants sought to
appeal. The plaintiffs, however, obtained a judgment from a Bangalore court that
the defendants could not proceed against the plaintiffs except in Bangalore and
applied for an injunction to restrain the defendants from pursuing the appeal in
Texas.

### Held
Appeal allowed. It was clear from recognised principles that an injunction could be
sought to restrain foreign proceedings even where the application was not to protect
proceedings in England. However, the discretion to grant such an injunction was to
be exercised to prevent an injustice. Here, to allow the defendants to continue their
action in an inappropriate forum would be unconscionable and oppressive and unjust
to the plaintiffs. Hobhouse J highlighted three factors which were relevant to the
determination of whether there would be an injustice if the injunction was not
granted. What was the natural forum for the action? Would the plaintiffs be
prejudiced by the continuing of proceedings in Texas? Would granting an injunction
against the defendants deprive them of a legitimate advantage?

### Commentary
This clarification by Hobhouse J of when an 'injustice' will arise such that an
injunction will be granted to restrain foreign proceedings is to be welcomed.

## *Connelly* v *RTZ Corporation plc and Another* (1996) The Times 12 July Court of Appeal (Sir Thomas Bingham MR, Evans and Ward LJJ)

Forum non conveniens – whether alternative forum available – conditional fee arrangement

### Facts

The plaintiff brought an action against his employer in negligence for personal injuries sustained while working in Namibia. He then appealed against the stay imposed on the grounds that the action should have been commenced in Namibia, arguing that although Namibia was the most natural forum for the claim, he could not afford to prosecute the claim there, whereas legal aid was available in England. The court rejected his claim, finding that it was precluded from taking legal aid into account by virtue of the Legal Aid Act 1988. On further appeal against the stay, the plaintiff claimed that his circumstances had changed and he now proposed to enter into a conditional fee arrangement with his solicitor.

### Held

Appeal allowed. The Court found that where the plaintiff had no prospect of ever funding the action in a foreign jurisdiction, which was nevertheless the most natural forum for the action, but could do so in England, which was not an inappropriate forum, by means of a conditional fee arrangement, the interests of justice weighed in favour of the English forum.

### Commentary

The Master of the Rolls was clearly aware of the possible abuses which could arise and he stressed that the court must be satisfied that the fee arrangement is not a device or subterfuge. Interestingly, in deciding that the interests of justice would tend to weigh in favour of the forum where the plaintiff could assert his rights, he alluded to the international obligations undertaken by the United Kingdom in the European Convention for the Protection of Human Rights and Fundamental Freedoms (s6(1)) and the International Covenant on Civil and Political Rights (article 14(1)).

## *Re Hayward (deceased)* [1996] 3 WLR 674 Chancery Division (Rattee J)

Convention on Jurisdiction and Judgments in Civil and Commercial Matters 1968 – arts 16(1) and (3) – interest of a trustee in bankruptcy – object of proceedings – whether a right in rem

### Facts

The widow of a debtor who died intestate subsequent to the purchase by him jointly with H of a villa in Minorca, his interest in which vested in his trustee in bankruptcy when he became bankrupt, declared that she was entitled to his interest under his intestacy and purported to transfer it to H. H then became the sole registered owner on the Minorcan property register. The trustee then sought an order entitling him to the debtor's share and a declaration that this interest had been part of the debtor's bankruptcy estate. At first instance the action was struck out for want of jurisdiction as, under article 16(1), the Spanish courts had exclusive jurisdiction to deal with the ownership of land situated in Spain.

## Held

The trustee's claim was in proceedings which had as their object a right in rem in immovable property and, accordingly, under article 16(1), the Spanish courts had exclusive jurisdiction. Further, to the extent that the trustee required rectification of the Minorcan property register as it showed void proceedings, the proceedings also had as their object the validity of entries in a public register and therefore exclusive jurisdiction also rested with Spain under article 16(3).

## Commentary

In this case, Rattee J felt that it was difficult to contemplate any right more clearly a right in rem than a right to legal ownership such as the one-half interest claimed here by the trustee which was the basis of the action. Article 16(1) was, therefore, easy to apply. Indeed, the Schlosser Report (ppl20–121, para 166) refers to ownership as being the most comprehensive right in rem. The difficulties arise where it is difficult to classify the right on which the action is based, although *Webb v Webb* [1994] QB 696 at least provides that an action which has as its object rights in personam will not found jurisdiction under article 16(1).

## *Marinari* v *Lloyds Bank plc (Zubaidi Trading Co, Intervener)* Case C–364/93 [1996] 2 WLR 159 European Court of Justice (Iglesias CJ, Schockweiler, Kapteyn and Jann PPC; Mancini, Kakouris, de Almeida, Puissochet, Hirsch, Ragnemalm and Sevon JJ; Darmon and Leger, Advocates-General)

Convention on Jurisdiction and Judgments in Civil and Commercial Matters 1968 – article 5(3) – place where harmful event occurred – consequential financial loss

## Facts

The plaintiff, of Italian domicile, lodged promissory notes with an English bank which, suspecting that the notes were of dubious origin, contacted the police, who then arrested the plaintiff and sequestered the notes. The plaintiff subsequently brought an action in Italy seeking compensation representing the exchange value of the notes and compensation for the damage he claimed to have suffered from his arrest, including the damage to his reputation. The loss in exchange value occurred in Italy, as did the losses arising from the damage to his reputation. A reference was made to the European Court as to whether the reference to the place where the harmful event occurred in article 5(3) referred only to the place where physical harm was caused to the person or things or also to the place where the financial loss suffered by the plaintiff occurred.

## Held

The 'place where the harmful event occurred' under article 5(3) did not cover the place where the victim claimed to have suffered financial loss consequential on initial damage arising and suffered by him in another Contracting State. Neither did the place where the harmful event occurred cover any place where the adverse consequences of an event that had already caused actual damage elsewhere could be felt.

## Commentary

The Court in this judgment stresses the fact that article 5(3) is a rule of special jurisdiction and cannot be extended beyond the particular circumstances which justify its application. In an echo of *Shevill and Others* v *Presse Alliance SA* [1995] All ER (EC) 2899, the Court also points out that the Convention does not seek to link the rules on jurisdiction with national substantive laws on non-contractual civil liability. Thus, a determination that the relevant national law does not require an actual adverse effect on goods or rights is irrelevant to the question of jurisdiction, which is founded on other considerations. Thus, it would appear that although it may appear obvious from a tort law perspective that jurisdiction be extended to cover this type of financial consequential loss, the problem must be approached from the perspective of jurisdiction, which explains the narrow interpretation given by the Court.

## *Mohammed* v *Bank of Kuwait and the Middle East KSC* (1996) The Times 30 May Court of Appeal (Evans, Saville and Morritt LJJ)

Forum non conveniens – whether alternative forum available – timing of determination

## Facts

The plaintiff, an employee of the Bank of Kuwait and an Iraqi citizen, returned to Iraq on leave during his employment and was unable to return as Kuwait had banned Iraqi nationals and the Iraqi government forbade its nationals to leave Iraq without permission. In the subsequent action by the plaintiff for payment under his contract of employment, the defendant objected to jurisdiction in England and was granted a stay. The plaintiff appealed on the grounds that the judge erred by deciding the application with reference to the situation at the time of the hearing. The defendant, in turn, contended that the issue as to whether justice could be achieved was only for consideration once it had been determined that an alternative jurisdiction was available.

**Held**

The Court of Appeal held that, in deciding whether an alternative forum was 'available' to the plaintiff, the question as to whether substantial justice was likely to be achieved was relevant. If the defendant could prove that there was such an alternative foreign forum available, it was then up to the plaintiff to assert an additional reason why, in the interests of justice, the action should proceed in England. However, the evidence on which the application to stay was based should reflect the situation at the date the application was made. If a defendant challenged the jurisdiction and applied to set aside a writ or an order, then the time when the determination was to be made was the date when such an order was made. However, the court should also have regard to the situation at the time of the hearing to avoid granting a stay in patently unjust circumstances. Here, Kuwait had not been shown to be available to the plaintiff in a practical sense as an alternative forum.

## 10.2 Family law

### *Re C (Abduction: Consent)* [1996] 1 FLR 414 Family Division (Holman J)

Child Abduction and Custody Act 1985, Sch 1, article 13 – consent to removal of child – evidence re consent

**Facts**

A British mother removed two children from Alaska to Britain and the American father sought their summary return as he claimed he had only agreed that they spend a short holiday in Britain. The mother raised the defence of consent as the father had stood by while she arranged the trip to Britain and agreed to her taking the children.

**Held**

The onus of proof with respect to consent was, under article 13, on the person opposing the return of the children. Consent was an important issue in abduction cases and was proved on the balance of probabilities, but evidence of consent needed to be clear and cogent. However, consent in writing was not required and neither was it necessary that it be in a positive form. In this case, it was clear that up to the time of the departure the father agreed that the mother would bring the children up in Britain permanently. The court therefore would exercise its discretion under article 13(a) to refuse the summary return of the children.

## Commentary

This case usefully discusses the idea of consent as a defence to international child abduction. Consent is a central concept of the Hague Convention and a lax approach to evidence of consent would drive a coach and four through the Convention. In this case, Holman J emphasises the importance of establishing consent clearly.

## *H v H* (1996) The Times 14 August Court of Appeal (Stuart-Smith, Waite and Otton LJJ)

Child Abduction and Custody Act 1985, Sch 1, article 13 – acquiesence to removal

## Facts

A British born mother removed her two children from Israel to England in breach of the father's custody rights under the law of Israel. Each parent (both orthodox Jews) then invoked the jurisdiction of the local rabbinical court, the Bet Din, and the mother also obtained a civil order in England. In the subsequent action for return of the children, the mother appealed against a return order on the grounds of acquiesence by the father in that he was pursuing remedies through religious proceedings unaccompanied by any request for the summary return of the children, and that he requested that the children spend Passover with him.

## Held

Article 13 provides that the courts of the requested state are not bound to order the return of the child where there is acquiesence in the removal of the child. The Court of Appeal allowed the appeal of the mother, holding that where a person had recourse to a religious court in connection with the wrongful removal of a child abroad, it was necessary for that person to make it clear that such proceedings were ancillary to the civil action for the summary return of the child. Waite LJ found that an objective inference of acquiesence could be drawn from the fact that, although the father had initiated matrimonial proceedings in the religious court, he had not made any overt statement insisting on the summary return of the children.

## Commentary

In this judgment Waite LJ stresses that recourse to religious authorities does not carry the automatic inference of acquiesence, and that such authorities can be invaluable in conciliation, but that it must be made clear that recourse to religious authorities is ancillary to or parallel with Hague Convention summary proceedings and not in substitution of such summary remedies. Given the international and cross-cultural context in which abductions may happen, this decision is of particular practical significance.

# Index

# Old Bailey Press

The Old Bailey Press integrated student library is planned and written to help you at every stage of your studies. Each of our range of Textbooks, Casebooks, Revision WorkBooks and Statutes are all designed to work together and are regularly revised and updated.

We are also able to offer you Suggested Solutions which provide you with past examination questions and solutions for most of the subject areas listed below.

You can buy Old Bailey Press books from your University Bookshop or your local Bookshop, or in case of difficulty, order direct using this form.

Here is the selection of modules covered by our series:

Administrative Law; Commercial Law; Company Law (no Single Paper 1997); Conflict of Laws (no Suggested Solutions Pack); Constitutional Law: The Machinery of Government; Obligations: Contract Law; Conveyancing (no Revision Workbook); Criminology (Sourcebook in place of a Casebook or Revision WorkBook); Criminal Law; English Legal System; Equity and Trusts; Law of The European Union; Evidence; Family Law; Jurisprudence: The Philosophy of Law (Sourcebook in place of a Casebook); Land: The Law of Real Property; Law of International Trade; Legal Skills and System (Textbook only); Public International Law; Revenue Law (no Casebook); Succession: The Law of Wills and Estates; Obligations: The Law of Tort.

Mail order prices:

Textbook £11.95

Casebook £9.95

Revision WorkBook £7.95

Statutes £9.95

Suggested Solutions Pack (1991–1995) £6.95

Single Paper 1996 £3.00

Single Paper 1997 £3.00

# To complete your order, please fill in the form below:

| Module | Books required | Quantity | Price | Cost |
|---|---|---|---|---|
|  |  |  |  |  |
|  |  |  |  |  |
|  |  |  |  |  |
|  |  |  |  |  |
|  |  |  |  |  |
|  |  | Postage |  |  |
|  |  | TOTAL |  |  |

For Europe, add 15% postage and packing (£20 maximum).
For the rest of the world, add 40% for airmail.

## ORDERING

**By telephone to Mail Order at 020 7385 3377**, with your credit card to hand.

**By fax to 020 7381 3377** (giving your credit card details).

**By post to:**

**Old Bailey Press, 200 Greyhound Road, London W14 9RY.**

When ordering by post, please enclose full payment by cheque or banker's draft, or complete the credit card details below.

We aim to despatch your books within 3 working days of receiving your order.

Name

Address


Postcode                              Telephone

Total value of order, including postage: £

**I enclose a cheque/banker's draft for the above sum, or**

charge my          ☐ Access/Mastercard          ☐ Visa          ☐ American Express
Card number

☐☐☐☐ ☐☐☐☐ ☐☐☐☐ ☐☐☐☐

Expiry date          ☐☐☐☐

Signature: ..................................................Date: .........................................